A to Z
OF AFRICAN AMERICANS

AFRICAN-AMERICAN
SOCIAL LEADERS
AND ACTIVISTS

Revised Edition

Jack Rummel
Revised by G. S. Prentzas

Note on Photos

Many of the illustrations and photographs used in this book are old, historical images. The quality of the prints is not always up to current standards, as in some cases the originals are from old or poor quality negatives or are damaged. The content of the illustrations, however, made their inclusion important despite problems in reproduction.

African-American Social Leaders and Activists, Revised Edition

Facts On File, Inc.
An imprint of Infobase Publishing
132 West 31st Street
New York NY 10001

Library of Congress Cataloging-in-Publication Data

Rummel, Jack.
African-American social leaders and activists / Jack Rummel ; revised by G.S. Prentzas.—Rev. ed.
     p. cm.—(A to Z of African Americans)
Includes bibliographical references and index.
ISBN 978-0-8160-8092-2 (acid-free paper) 1. African Americans—Biography—Dictionaries. 2. African American social reformers—Biography—Dictionaries. 3. African American political activists—Biography—Dictionaries. 4. African American leadership—Dictionaries. I. Prentzas, G. S. II. Title.
E185.96.R88 2011
920'.009296073—dc22   2010042295

Facts On File books are available at special discounts when purchased in bulk quantities for businesses, associations, institutions, or sales promotions. Please call our Special Sales Department in New York at (212) 967-8800 or (800) 322-8755.

You can find Facts On File on the World Wide Web at http://www.factsonfile.com

Excerpts included herewith have been reprinted by permission of the copyright holders; the authors have made every effort to contact copyright holders. The publishers will be glad to rectify, in future editions, any errors or omissions brought to their notice.

Text design by Joan M. Toro
Composition by Hermitage Publishing Services
Cover printed by Sheridan Books, Ann Arbor, Mich.
Book printed and bound by Sheridan Books, Ann Arbor, Mich.
Date printed: January 2011
Printed in the United States of America

10 9 8 7 6 5 4 3 2 1

This book is printed on acid-free paper.

CONTENTS

LIST OF ENTRIES

Allen, Richard
Allensworth, Allen
Barber, Jesse Max
Bates, Daisy Lee Gatson
Benjamin, Robert Charles
    O'Hara
Bethune, Mary McLeod
Bibb, Henry Walton
Bolin, Jane Matilda
Bowles, Eva Del Vakia
Boykin, Keith O.
Brock, Rosyln McCallister
Brown, Hallie Quinn
Brown, William Wells
Burroughs, Nannie Helen
Butts, Calvin Otis, III
Carmichael, Stokely
Carson, Benjamin S.
Carver, George Washington
Chambers, Julius Levonne
Chase, William Calvin
Chester, Thomas Morris
Cinque, Joseph
Cleaver, Eldridge
Cobb, James Adlai
Connerly, Ward
Copeland, John Anthony
Corbin, Joseph Carter
Cornish, Samuel Eli
Crosswaith, Frank Rudolph

Cuffe, Paul
Dancy, John Campbell, Jr.
Davis, Angela
Davis, Benjamin Jefferson, Jr.
Day, William Howard
De Baptiste, George
Delany, Martin Robison
Derricotte, Juliette Aline
Desdunes, Rodolphe Lucien
Douglass, Frederick
DuBois, W. E. B.
Dunjee, Roscoe
Eagleson, William Lewis
Edelman, Marian Wright
Evers, Medgar Wiley
Fard, Wallace D.
Farmer, James Leonard, Jr.
Farrakhan, Louis
Forbes, George Washington
Ford, Barney Launcelot
Forman, James
Forten, James
Fortune, Timothy Thomas
Freeman, Elizabeth
Garnet, Henry Highland
Garnet, Sarah
Garvey, Marcus
Gates, Henry Louis, Jr.
Green, Shields
Greener, Richard Theodore

Guinier, Lani
Hall, Prince
Hamer, Fannie Lou
Hart, William Henry
Hastie, William Henry, Jr.
Haynes, George Edmund
Height, Dorothy
Henry, Aaron
Higginbotham, Aloysius
    Leon, Jr.
Hill, Thomas Arnold
Hilyer, Amanda Victoria Gray
Hilyer, Andrew Franklin
Houston, Charles Hamilton
Hrabowski, Freeman A., III
Hunton, Addie D. Waites
Hunton, William Alphaeus
Jackson, Jesse
Jealous, Benjamin Todd
Johnson, Charles Spurgeon
Johnson, James Weldon
Jones, Eugene Kinckle
Jones, Nathaniel R., Jr.
Jones, Scipio Africanus
Jordan, Vernon Eulion, Jr.
Karenga, Ron
King, Martin Luther, Jr.
Leary, Lewis Sheridan
Lemus, Rienzi Brock
Malcolm X

INTRODUCTION

Whether abolitionists or slave revolt leaders, civil rights activists or educators, newspaper publishers or foundation executives, African-American activists and social leaders have been at the forefront of the struggle for civil rights, racial equality, and social justice for more than 200 years. From the fight to end slavery to the push for a place in the world of business, the professions, universities, and the factory floor, African-American leaders have defined the key issues of their day and galvanized the energies of their community. Through mutual-aid societies, fraternal and professional organizations, labor unions, newspapers, women's clubs, and civil rights organizations, these men and women have been crucially important in holding the African-American community together and expressing its opinions and goals.

From the beginning of the republic, blacks were active in setting their own agenda. In 1783, Elizabeth Mumbet Freeman, a 41-year-old slave, successfully sued her master for cruel treatment and won her freedom, effectively ending the institution of slavery in the state of Massachusetts. Three years later, Moses Sash, a free African American living in western Massachusetts, became embroiled in Shays's Rebellion, an armed protest by white and black farmers against Massachusetts's ruling coastal elite. Acting as one of Shays's principal lieutenants, Sash with his soldiers held the state militia at bay for many months before the rebellion was crushed. Sash was eventually pardoned for his part in the insurrection. The revolt had the desired political effect. Taxes were lowered so that farmers would not be bankrupted by paying an unfair share of the leftover costs of the Revolutionary War.

In the beginning of the American republic, the abolition of slavery was the issue that trumped all others in the black community. African Americans north and south of the Mason-Dixon line fought against slavery in a variety of ways. In 1800, Richard Allen, a former slave from Delaware who bought his own freedom and moved to Philadelphia, petitioned the Pennsylvania legislature to abolish slavery in that state. Allen, a minister and later a bishop in the African Methodist Episcopal (AME) Church, believed it his religious as well as civic duty to work peacefully to rid the nation of slavery.

Other African-American leaders followed Allen's path. In 1827, John Brown Russwurm, then age 28 and a recent graduate of Bowdoin College in Maine, founded *Freedom's Journal*, the first black-owned and -edited newspaper in the United States. The voice of the free black community in New York City, *Freedom's Journal* was distributed throughout the Northeast. The paper soon attracted some of the most militant writers of its day. In 1829, *Freedom's Journal* published *David Walker's Appeal*, a call to arms to all blacks in the United States to rise up and violently overthrow the slave system. David Walker, the author of this tract, was a Boston used-clothes merchant who took advantage of his proximity to Boston's wharves to smuggle his "Appeal" into ports in the South. Walker's work infuriated the southern planter class, some of whose members placed a $10,000 bounty on his head.

In the South, some enslaved African Americans were determined to confront slavery directly, not with the pen but the sword. At least three major slave revolts and conspiracies occurred between 1800 and 1831, the first a revolt in the Richmond, Virginia, area led by Gabriel Prosser in 1800. Prosser, who was literate and well read in the Bible and the U.S. Declaration of Independence, had as his goal the creation of a free black state for freed slaves in Virginia. Denmark Vesey organized another major revolt in Charleston, South Carolina, in 1822. A former slave who had won his freedom in a lottery, Vesey had become free and wealthy, not the most likely candidate to lead a rebellion in which he could lose everything he had acquired. Yet, burning with indignation at the treatment of his enslaved people, Vesey generated what would have been a very large rebellion, had it not also been betrayed by some of the participants. Both Prosser's and Vesey's rebellions were nipped in the bud when word of their plans leaked to white authorities. The last major slave revolt in the South was organized by another literate slave, Nat Turner, who lived in Southampton County, Virginia. Inspired, as Prosser had been, by the biblical story of the Jews' exodus from slavery in Egypt, Turner began his revolt successfully, his plan undetected by white authorities. It was a bloody affair that ended in the death of some 60 whites and perhaps 100 enslaved African Americans. In all three revolts, the leaders were hanged along with key lieutenants, and scores of slaves were given terrible physical punishments for their roles, however slight, in these rebellions.

As armed rebellion fed white anxiety in the South, free blacks in the North pressed ahead with an organized protest and political campaign to end slavery once and for all. James Forten, Wil-liam Whipper, and William Still of Philadelphia contributed money and time to aid such groups as the American Anti-Slavery Society, one of the key abolitionist organizations that had sprung up in the North in the 1830s. They also contributed their money and skills to the Underground Railroad, the clandestine arm of the abolitionist movement that helped escaped slaves find a new life in the North and Canada. Later abolitionists such as Frederick Douglass, Sojourner Truth, and Henry Highland Garnet carried on this tradition until slavery was destroyed during the Civil War.

The goal of most abolitionists, as well as most African Americans, was to attain the same legal rights under law as white citizens and to find a place for themselves in an integrated, multiracial American society. However, some African-American leaders presented an alternate vision to the black community. From as early as the 1780s, some blacks voiced a concern that African Americans would never be fully accepted in U.S. society and therefore would be unlikely to free themselves of the crushing social and legal discrimination visited on them by whites. Prince Hall in 1787 and Paul Cuffe, a wealthy New England shipping magnate, in 1810 called on free blacks to migrate back to the motherland of Africa. Cuffe made a visit to Sierra Leone on Africa's west coast in 1810 to scout a venue for a colony for immigrating blacks. By the 1830s, such a colony had been established farther south on the coast at a place that was named Liberia. From the 1830s until the end of the 19th century, a steady trickle of African Americans immigrated to Liberia. However, the total number of immigrants was small, probably no more than 15,000. As late as the 1920s, Marcus Garvey was calling for a return to Africa, and in 1969 Stokely Carmichael, a former civil rights activist, quit the United States for Guinea. Most African Americans stayed at home, courageously and doggedly working for full inclusion in American society.

After the end of the Civil War in 1865, the efforts of the African-American community turned from trying to end slavery to working for full civil and legal rights and helping former slaves integrate themselves into U.S. society as free men and women. This was a time of great hope and effort as African Americans, encouraged by the federal government's commitment to help former slaves in the South during the Reconstruction era, flocked south to participate in a bold new social experiment. Educators such as Richard Greener, a Harvard-educated college professor, went south to teach college. David Straker, born in the West Indies, immigrated to the United States to teach former slaves in Kentucky and later became a Republican Party activist in South Carolina. Southern-born blacks such as John Rayner of Texas also participated in the political process. Most of these efforts were snuffed out with the end of Reconstruction in the late 1870s. Greener and Straker moved back to the North; Rayner would stick it out against heavy odds in the South.

Black leaders always recognized that education was central to the human as well as the social and economic development of the African-American community. In the 19th century, Booker T. Washington and George Washington Carver became national heroes through their efforts to educate black students and common people at the Tuskegee Institute. Mary McLeod Bethune, founder of Bethune-Cookman College, carried on this tradition in the 1920s through the 1940s, as did Frederick Patterson, president of Tuskegee Institute and founder of the United Negro College Fund (UNCF), one of the main fund-raising arms of African-American higher education. Dr. Freeman A. Hrabowski III and Dr. Benjamin S. Carson continue that legacy today.

The militant tradition of African-American newspapers pioneered by *Freedom's Journal* in the early 1800s did not wane after emancipation. Indeed, African-American publishing flourished in a golden age from the 1890s until the late 1940s. Although frequently at odds with each other, T. Thomas Fortune and William Monroe

Trotter kept blacks informed about themselves and the larger society in their respective newspapers, the *New York Age* and the *Guardian* of Boston. Later papers, such as Robert Vann's *Pittsburgh Courier* and P. B. Young's *Norfolk Journal and Guide,* kept up a drumbeat for full civil rights for blacks and covered black athletic and social life. Twentieth-century journalists Daisy Bates, Wallace Terry, and Nancy Hicks Maynard ensured that African-American perspectives appeared in print.

African Americans had always sought to be fully included in every trade and profession in the United States. As in other areas of life in the United States, blacks had to overcome great odds to get fair wages at the same level as whites and even to be hired for certain jobs. One of the first great black labor leaders was Isaac Myers, a former ship's hull caulker, who organized a cooperative shipyard for unemployed black shipyard workers in Baltimore in the 1860s. Myers also pushed the leading labor federation of his day, the National Labor Union, for full integration in the national union. Even though the cooperative shipyard was a success, the goal of integration of labor unions was not achieved at that time. A. Philip Randolph was probably the greatest black labor leader of the 20th century. Randolph guided the formation of the Brotherhood of Sleeping Car Porters (BSCP), the first large-scale African-American union to achieve full recognition by a major American corporation. Randolph also pushed relentlessly for integration of unions and eventually lived to see the complete integration of the American union movement through the American Federation of Labor and Congress of Industrial Organizations (AFL-CIO).

In spite of the best efforts of black labor leaders, for most of U.S. history, blacks were the last hired and the first fired during the booms and busts of the American economy. Black social welfare and mutual-aid-society leaders have filled a need by helping African Americans who were caught by poverty and hard times. Prince Hall, founder of the black Masons, began a trend of self-help through voluntary benevolent organizations in Boston in 1775. Many other black leaders contributed to this trend; one of the best known was James Finley Wilson, president of the Order of the Elks from 1922 to 1952. In the arena of social welfare, Nannie Burroughs founded the National Training School for Women and Girls, a trade school for poor black women in 1909. Addie Hunton and her husband, William Hunton, helped African Americans who had immigrated from the South to the North through the Young Women's Christian Association (YWCA) and Young Men's Christian Association (YMCA) during the early years of the 20th century.

The African-American quest for full rights under law would not be successful until the middle part of the 20th century. Arguably the most important organization that pressed for full African-American civil rights was the National Association for the Advancement of Colored People (NAACP), founded by the great thinker and activist W. E. B. DuBois in 1909. Through the efforts of its brilliant legal team of Charles Hamilton Houston and Thurgood Marshall, the NAACP would eventually batter down state laws that segregated blacks from whites in separate and unequal institutions in the United States.

The effort for full civil rights would also need its militant peace warriors to press demands on the street. Martin Luther King, Jr.; Robert Moses; and Fred Shuttlesworth, to name but a few, supplied the leadership that would eventually culminate in the landmark federal legislation of the Civil Rights Act and Voting Rights Act of the mid-1960s. Today's young African-American leaders, such as Marc Haydel Morial, Benjamin Todd Jealous, and Roslyn M. Brock, are developing news ways to organize a new generation to end discrimination, achieve economic parity, and improve the African-American experience

The leaders mentioned in this introduction, and dozens of others profiled in this book, have contributed to a rich and complex web of human associations that is the African-American community in the United States. Through their lives and work, these social leaders and activists have left a legacy of accomplishment and success to succeeding generations of African Americans and have defined what it means to be a black citizen of the United States.

Allen, Richard

(1760–1831) *abolitionist, minister, community organizer*

In a long and full life, Richard Allen rose from slavery to become arguably one of the most influential African-American leaders of his time. Among his many accomplishments, he founded the Free African Society, an important mutual-aid network; the Bethel Church, the first black church in Philadelphia; and the African Methodist Episcopal Church, the first independent, black religious organization in the United States. He also was a partner in an insurance company, an organizer of schools for African-American students, and a political activist who worked to have slavery abolished.

Allen was born on February 14, 1760, in Philadelphia. His parents were slaves who worked for the Pennsylvania colonial attorney general, Benjamin Chew, who was also chief justice of the commonwealth from 1774 to 1777. In 1767, Chew seems to have suffered a business setback and consolidated his finances by selling the entire Allen family (at that time, Allen's mother, father, and three siblings) to Stokeley Sturgis, a planter in Dover, Delaware.

Even though they suffered under the cruel system of slavery, the Allens were relatively fortunate to be sold to Sturgis. In his letters, Allen recalled that Sturgis was "tenderhearted. [He was] unconverted . . . but . . . what the world called a good master." With Sturgis's approval Allen taught himself to read and write. Nonetheless, the family was still vulnerable to the whim of their master and his fortunes. When Sturgis ran up against hard times, he sold Allen's mother and three of his five siblings.

Methodism, a new denomination of Protestantism, espoused by John Wesley and his brother, Charles, had made its way from England to British North America in the early 1760s through the work of itinerant preachers such as Robert Strawbridge and Philip Embury, two Irish Methodists, who had settled in Maryland and New York City, respectively. Soon these two had inspired others, who began to travel on circuits preaching the Methodist beliefs that each individual had the ability to know God within himself or herself and that the Holy Spirit could affect and change the consciousness of the believer. Although most Methodist ministers and congregations were white, there does not seem to have been much racial discrimination in their acceptance of converts into the fold during their early days in North America.

Several Methodist preachers must have frequently passed near Stokeley Sturgis's estate in Dover because by the early to mid-1870s Richard Allen had converted to Methodism. After his conversion, Allen sought to learn as much as he could about the Methodist faith. Every week, he and his brothers attended Methodist meetings on Thursday evenings and Bible classes on other days. This religious fervor frightened Sturgis's white neighbors, who complained that his slaves were not working hard enough and would cause him financial ruin. In response to this criticism, Allen and his brothers decided that they "would attend more faithfully to our master's business, so that it should not be said that religion made us worse servants."

Allen's tactic dispelled the neighbors' gossip. It also convinced Sturgis to accede to Allen's wish that Methodist ministers preach at Sturgis's house.

A sketch of Richard Allen from the early 1800s. Allen was an important community leader in Philadelphia and one of the founders of the African Methodist Episcopal Church. *(Moorland-Spingarn Research Center, Howard University)*

One of those who dropped by to spread the word was Freeborn Garretson, a white preacher. Garretson declared that the souls of slaveholders were "weighed in the balance [for the sin of holding slaves] and . . . found wanting."

Garretson's message affected Stokeley Sturgis. According to Allen, Sturgis believed "himself to be one of that number [slave owners whose souls were doomed]." He converted to Methodism, "and after that he could not be satisfied to hold slaves, believing it wrong." After his conversion, Sturgis suggested that Allen and his brother begin to work in whatever capacity paid them the most money and that they use their wages to purchase their freedom.

After a year or so of working as a laborer and a teamster for the army during the American Revolutionary War, Allen had accumulated enough currency to pay for his freedom. He then embarked on a career as an itinerant preacher in Delaware, New Jersey, and Pennsylvania.

Throughout the 1780s, Allen continued to preach on the Methodist gospel circuit. Allen's commitment to his new faith did not diminish his desire to help fellow African Americans, especially those who were still held in bondage. He refused to accompany Bishop Francis Asbury through the South because Asbury would not allow him to associate with slaves.

In 1786, Allen returned to Philadelphia, and after a dispute with white Methodist Church officials over the subservient position of black congregants in the Methodist Church, Allen and Absalom Jones led the black congregants out of the St. George's Methodist Church to form a new congregation, which in 1794 became the Bethel Church.

During his first years in Philadelphia, Allen met a woman named Sara who had moved to the city from Virginia. The two fell in love and were married sometime in the late 1780s. They seem to have enjoyed a long and happy marriage and had four sons and a daughter.

From the beginning, Allen was very active in the African-American community of Philadelphia. In 1787, he organized the Free African Society, one of the first all-black mutual-aid groups for free blacks in the United States. This group served as a kind of informal insurance provider for its members, who pooled their resources to help each other weather periods of unemployment, illness in their families, and other hardships. The Free African Society also saw itself as a vehicle for moral regeneration and forbade its members to indulge in drunkenness, improper behavior, and sexual indiscretions. Urged on by Allen, free blacks in Newport, Rhode Island; Boston; and New York City formed their own branches of the Free African Society.

During Philadelphia's yellow fever epidemic of 1793, Allen and other members of the Free African Society distinguished themselves when they organized the African-American community to serve as nurses and undertakers for all of the people of the city. Soon after this epidemic, Allen affiliated the newly built Bethel Church with the first multistate organization of black churches. Allen called this new organization the African Methodist Episcopal (AME) Church, and in 1816, Allen was consecrated as the AME's first bishop, a post he held until his death. Between 1799 and 1816, new AME congregations were established in a number of cities along the northeastern Atlantic seaboard.

From 1795 to 1800, Allen was active in politics and community organizing in Philadelphia. He opened a school for African-American students in Philadelphia in 1795 and attracted 60 students. He later organized a society whose purpose was to teach reading and writing to young and old free blacks in the city. In 1799 and 1800, Allen was one of the main organizers of a drive among Philadelphia's free black community to petition the Pennsylvania legislature and the Congress to abolish slavery.

In 1816 and 1817, Allen became embroiled in a controversy about whether freeborn American blacks should be encouraged to return permanently to Africa. Ideas about returning to Africa had been floated as early as the 1780s, most notably by PAUL CUFFE, a wealthy African-American sea captain who lived in Massachusetts. Cuffe and other freeborn American blacks felt that African Americans would never be completely accepted in the United States and could realize their full potential only by returning to Africa. There was also a missionary element to this scheme. Deeply religious African-American Christians believed that they had a duty to return to Africa to spread the Christian gospel.

In 1816, yet another scheme for returning free American blacks to Africa was hatched, this time by the Reverend Robert Finley, a white Presbyterian minister from Basking Ridge, New Jersey. Finley, with the support of numerous powerful men in Washington, D.C., most notably Henry Clay, a slave owner and senator from Kentucky, formed the American Colonization Society, whose purpose was to induce freeborn African Americans to return to Africa. Allen organized protests among the African Americans of Philadelphia against this project, arguing in a sermon, "This land which we have watered with our tears our blood, is now our mother country; & we are well satisfied to stay where wisdom abounds & the gospel is free."

In the 1820s, Allen lent his support to abolitionist groups that favored the immediate end of slavery in the United States and sought the integration of African Americans into the mainstream of American life. He helped found *Freedom's Journal*, the first African-American newspaper in the United States, an ardently abolitionist newspaper.

Near the end of his life, possibly in despair that so little progress had been made to abolish slavery and end racism, Allen embraced the idea of forming communities of refugee American blacks in Canada. With WILLIAM WHIPPER, he formed the American Society of Free Persons of Color, the group that was to oversee this project. Before he could do much work to advance this latest cause, in 1831, Allen died at the age of 61 in Philadelphia.

Further Reading

Allen, Richard. *The Life, Experience, and Gospel Labors of the Rt. Rev. Richard Allen.* Available online. URL: http://docsouth.unc.edu/neh/allen/allen.html. Downloaded July 16, 2009.

Newman, Richard S. *Freedom's Prophet: Bishop Richard Allen, the AME Church, and the Black Founding Fathers.* New York: New York University Press, 2008.

PBS. Africans in America, Resource Bank. "Richard Allen." Downloaded July 16, 2009. URL: http://www.pbs.org/wgbh/aia/part3/3p97.html. Available online.

Allensworth, Allen

(1842–1914) *chaplain, soldier, town founder*

A fugitive slave, soldier, and minister, Allen Allensworth led a full life that culminated in the founding of a town in California that took his name. Allensworth was born into slavery in Louisville, Kentucky, on April 7, 1842, the son of Levi and Phyllis Allensworth, who were slaves.

When he was 20, Allensworth managed on his third attempt to run away from his owner. He ended up in Illinois, where he enlisted as a nurse in the 44th Illinois Infantry Division of the Union army, a unit that saw service around Nashville and other parts of the South during the Civil War. In 1863, Allensworth transferred to the navy, and served on the gunships *Queen City, Tawah,* and *Pittsburgh.*

After the war, Allensworth moved to Saint Louis, where he was successful in the restaurant business. After selling his restaurants, he moved back to Louisville and attended the Eli Normal School, run by the Freedmen's Bureau. After a brief stint as a teacher at Freedmen's Bureau schools, Allensworth in 1868 was ordained a minister in the Baptist Church. He served as a minister at congregations in Kentucky and worked as a business agent for the Kentucky General Association of Colored Baptists. Allensworth was also active in politics as a Republican Party stalwart. He attended the

Allen Allensworth ca. 1890 in Fort Bayard, New Mexico. An escaped slave, Allensworth served as an army chaplain for 20 years and later founded the town of Allensworth, California. *(© California State Parks, 2003)*

Republican National Conventions as a delegate from Kentucky in 1880 and 1884.

After serving two years as a minister in a Baptist church in Cincinnati, in 1886, Allensworth won from President Grover Cleveland an officer's commission as a chaplain for the 24th Infantry Regiment, an all-black outfit. Allensworth would remain in the army for the next 20 years. His first tours of duty were in the West in places such as Fort Supply in Indian Territory (now Oklahoma) and Fort Bayard, New Mexico.

Allensworth began innovative programs with the troops he counseled, helping them and especially their children obtain an education while they were in the army. He established special schools for enlisted men and their children in which reading and arithmetic were emphasized.

Allensworth's education programs were so successful that other army units copied them, and in 1891, he was asked to give a talk to the National Educational Association about his work.

Allensworth retired from the army in 1906 as a lieutenant colonel, the highest-ranking African-American officer. In 1908, Allensworth moved to California and founded the town of Allensworth in Tulare County, which is midway between Los Angeles and San Francisco. Allensworth's vision was that Allensworth, California, would be a sanctuary for African Americans, and to attract black citizens he placed advertisements in leading African-American newspapers. At the height of its development the town had nearly 200 families, a hotel, a rail station, and a post office.

Allensworth's death on September 14, 1914, slowed the town's development. During the next 20 years, it faded as Allensworth had trouble obtaining water and as larger urban areas such as Oakland attracted blacks, who moved there to work in industrial jobs.

Further Reading

Alexander, Charles. *Battles and Victories of Allen Allensworth.* Boston: Sherman, French, 1914. Available online. URL: http://docsouth.unc.edu/neh/alexander/alexander.html. Downloaded July 16, 2009.

California State Parks. *Colonel Allensworth State Historical Park.* Available online. URL: http://www.parks.ca.gov/pages/583/files/ColonelAllensworth.pdf. Downloaded July 16, 2009.

Barber, Jesse Max
(ca. 1878–1949) *journalist, civil rights leader*

A pioneering journalist and militant advocate of civil rights for African Americans, Jesse Max Barber was born in the late 1870s in Blackstock, South Carolina, to Jesse Max and Susan Crawford Barber.

Young Max earned a teaching degree at Benedict College in South Carolina, then enrolled in Virginia Union University, an all-black school located in Richmond. Barber edited the school newspaper, the *University Journal*, and was elected president of the Literary Society.

After graduating from Virginia Union in 1903, Max Barber returned briefly to South Carolina to teach. In 1904, he was offered a job in Atlanta as editor of a new publication, *Voice of the Negro.*

Austin Jenkins, a liberal white publisher who was a partner in the J. L. Nichols Company, financed *Voice of the Negro.* Jenkins felt that there was a market for a lively journal that addressed the issues and concerns of educated African Americans, especially southerners. John Wesley Edward Bowen, a professor at Gammon Theological Seminary, was hired as coeditor, but he left most of the paper's management decisions to Barber.

Barber stepped into a lively and thriving African-American community when he moved to Atlanta. Black businesses such as Atlanta Life Insurance and Citizens Trust Bank supported a solid middle class. The city boasted several middle-class black neighborhoods such as the Sweet Auburn and Summer Hill districts. Furthermore, the city's five primarily African-American colleges—Morehouse, Atlanta, Clark, Spelman, and Morris Brown—had made Atlanta a black intellectual mecca.

Barber and his staff were adept at soliciting ads that partially funded the monthly magazine, but he knew he also would need interesting and outspoken writers. Each issue featured articles on visual art, literature, or science, and there were always poems and several book reviews. Barber also had an eye for the visual design of the magazine, and he solicited political cartoons and illustrations from a number of young black artists.

The heart of *Voice of the Negro* was its nonfiction writing. Barber worked hard to attract the best nonfiction writers he could find. This group included W. E. B. DuBois, MARY ELIZA CHURCH TERRELL, and William Pickens.

Barber set the tone of *Voice of the Negro* in his editorial in the first issue, published in January 1904. "It shall be our object to keep the magazine abreast with the progress of the times," he wrote. "We want to make it a force of race elevation. . . . We expect to make of it current and sociological history so accurately given and so vividly portrayed that it will become a kind of documentation for the coming generations."

In his editorials and his activities outside the magazine, Barber urged African Americans to become more politically engaged and militant in demanding full rights under the Constitution. He was especially insistent that blacks should have full voting rights, as he saw enfranchisement as the key to obtaining equality in the American system.

Increasingly Barber gravitated toward the thinking of one of his most important writers, W. E. B. DuBois. In 1905, his second year as editor of *Voice of the Negro*, Barber joined with DuBois and 27 other participants in Buffalo, New York, to form a new, nationwide African-American organization, the Niagara Movement. Composed of local branches in 30 U.S. cities, the Niagara Movement lasted from 1905 until 1910, when it disbanded to make way for the National Association for the Advancement of Colored People (NAACP). In many ways, *Voice of the Negro* served as an outlet for the ideas of the Niagara Movement.

Barber remained in Atlanta until 1906, when a race riot drove the paper out of the South. The Atlanta riot of September 1906 was fueled by false rumors that black men were raping white women. Assisted by policemen, white mobs burned down several black neighborhoods. The riot lasted five days, during which 25 African Americans were killed and 1,000 homes and many black businesses were destroyed.

By October 1906, Barber and *Voice of the Negro* had moved to Chicago. The paper was sold to TIMOTHY THOMAS FORTUNE and its name was changed to *The Voice*, but the vitality it had achieved in Atlanta was gone. By October 1907, *Voice of the Negro* had gone out of business.

For a while, Barber worked for the *Chicago Conservator*; then he became involved in civil rights work, attending the Negro Political League conference in Philadelphia in 1908 and the National Negro Conference in New York City in 1909. Without a regular job, however, by 1909 he

began looking for another way to support himself. That year he enrolled in the school of dentistry at Temple University in Philadelphia. He graduated from Temple in 1912 and set up a dental practice in Philadelphia.

Gradually, Barber left the world of journalism and politics. He married Hattie B. Taylor in 1912, and when she died a few years later, he remarried. He worked for the local branch of the NAACP through the early 1920s. Toward the end of his life, he devoted his energies to having a statue erected in the memory of the white abolitionist John Brown at Brown's gravesite in North Elba, New York. This he accomplished in 1935.

Having retired from public life for more than a decade, Max Barber died, in his early 70s, in Philadelphia in 1949.

Further Reading

Bullock, Penelope. *The Afro-American Periodical Press: 1837–1909*. Baton Rouge: Louisiana State University Press, 1981.

Godshalk, David Fort. *Veiled Visions: The 1906 Atlanta Race Riot and the Reshaping of American Race Relations*. Chapel Hill: University of North Carolina Press, 2005.

Johnson, Abby Arthur, and Ronald M. Johnson. "Away from Accommodation: Radical Editors and Protest Journalism, 1900–1910." *Journal of Negro History* 62 (October 1977): 325–338.

Bates, Daisy Lee Gatson

(1913?–1999) *newspaper publisher, civil rights activist*

As the president of the state chapter of the National Association for the Advancement of Colored People (NAACP), Daisy Lee Gatson Bates was a key leader in the effort to integrate public schools in Little Rock, Arkansas. Born in Huttig, Arkansas, she never knew her parents. Daisy's mother was murdered by a group of white men when Daisy was still an infant. Fearing for his life, her father left town, leaving Daisy in the care of his friends, Susan and Orlee Smith. The Smiths eventually adopted Daisy. At age 15, she started dating L. C. Bates, a 28-year-old insurance salesman. They would marry in 1942.

L. C. Bates had worked as a journalist, and he dreamed of starting his own newspaper aimed at African Americans. The couple moved to Little Rock in 1941 and started publishing a weekly newspaper, the *Arkansas State Press*. The paper examined issues important to the state's black community, including news articles detailing local racial incidents. For example, a 1942 article reported the murder of a black soldier by a white Little Rock policeman.

The *Arkansas State Press* also ran editorials demanding equal rights for African Americans. Daisy Bates became increasingly involved in local civil rights activities. In 1952, she was elected president of the Arkansas chapter of the NAACP. In this role, she would be thrust into the center of the nation's civil rights movement. In 1954, the U.S. Supreme Court ruled in *Brown v. Board of Education* that segregated public schools were unconstitutional. It overturned the longstanding separate but equal doctrine, which provided the legal basis for segregated public facilities. In a later case, the Court directed local school boards to integrate their schools "with all deliberate speed." Many school boards around the nation used this vague language to delay desegregating their schools. The delays gave whites opposed to integration time to organize protests. In a 1956 *Arkansas State Press* editorial, Bates implored Little Rock's black community to support a lawsuit initiated by the NAACP's Legal Defense and Education Fund. The black plaintiffs in *Cooper v. Aaron* sought to have the federal district court hasten the integration of public schools in Little Rock.

During summer 1957, three school districts in other parts of Arkansas voted to desegregate their classrooms. Two of the districts integrated without any protests. They were the first school districts in any of the former Confederate states to integrate. The board of the third school district, however,

reversed its vote. They changed their minds when menaced by a group of angry white citizens. In September, the Little Rock school board announced that nine black students would enroll at Central High School. The announcement created an uproar in Little Rock's white community.

On the first day of the school year, September 4, the black students—six girls and three boys—tried to attend Central High. Warning that "blood would run in the streets," Arkansas governor Orval Faubus had sent state National Guard soldiers to surround Central High. They prevented the black students from reaching the school. A federal court, however, ordered Faubus to allow the students to enter the school. During this time, Bates provided advice and support to the black students, who had become known as the Little Rock Nine, and to their families. She hired bodyguards for the students and served as a media spokesperson.

On September 23, the Little Rock Nine successfully entered the school. A hostile mob of about a thousand white students and adults gathered outside the school. City police removed the black students from the school to prevent a full-scale riot. Television viewers throughout the country watched the events unfold. Little Rock suddenly became the bitter new face of segregation.

President Eisenhower stepped in. He sent U.S. Army troops to escort the black students to school. On September 25, the students again entered the school. For the rest of the school year, U.S. Army and Arkansas National Guard troops walked the black students to school and monitored the hallways. Despite the presence of the soldiers, white students harassed and threatened the nine black students. In May 1958, Ernest Green would become the first black graduate of Little Rock Central High School.

Bates continued to provide advice and support to the Little Rock Nine as they faced taunts and physical intimidation. As the African-American community's most visible representative during the crisis, Bates became the target of threats. Her

In her capacity as the president of the Arkansas State Conference of the NAACP, Daisy Gatson Bates served as an adviser to the Little Rock Nine and their families. *(University of Arkansas Libraries, Special Collections, Daisy Bates Papers)*

home's windows were broken by rocks. Crosses were burned on her lawn. White businesses stopped buying ads in the *Arkansas State Press.* Bates and her husband eventually had to stop publishing the paper.

In 1957, Bates was convicted of violating a city ordinance that required organizations to provide the city their financial records and a list of the names of their officers and staff. Bates refused to supply the information for the state NAACP chapter. These disclosure lists has been used to identify and threaten NAACP leaders in other cities with similar laws. Three years later, the U.S. Supreme Court would unanimously overturn her conviction. In *Bates v. Little Rock* (1960), it would rule that the ordinance violated Bates's and other

members' First Amendment right to freedom of association.

For her efforts in the integration of Little Rock Central High School, Bates was named as the Associated Press's 1957 Woman of the Year in Education. Through the years, Bates remained active in the civil rights movement. The University of Arkansas awarded her an honorary degree in 1984, and Little Rock named an elementary school after her. In 1999, Congress voted to award Bates and the Little Rock Nine the congressional gold medal. Bates died before the awards ceremony. The State of Arkansas honored her by allowing her casket to lie in state on the second-floor rotunda of the Arkansas capitol. While mourners paid their respects, President Bill Clinton presented congressional gold medals to the nine students whom she had mentored. In 2001, the Arkansas general assembly designated the third Monday in February as Daisy Gatson Bates Day in the state.

Further Reading

Documenting the South. "Interview with Daisy Bates." Available online. URL: http://docsouth.unc.edu/sohp/G-0009/G-0009.html. Downloaded July 10, 2009.

Encyclopedia of Arkansas. "Daisy Lee Gatson Bates." Available online. URL: http://www.encyclopedia ofarkansas.net/encyclopedia/entry-detail.aspx? entryID=591. Downloaded July 22, 2009.

New York Times. "Daisy Bates, Civil Rights Leader, Dies at 84." Available online. URL: http://www. nytimes.com/1999/11/05/us/daisy-bates-civil-rights-leader-dies-at-84.html?scp=3&sq=daisy% 20bates&st=cse. Downloaded July 10, 2009.

Benjamin, Robert Charles O'Hara

(R. C. O. Benjamin)
(1855–1900) *reporter, journalist*

An itinerant journalist and occasional author, R. C. O. Benjamin wrote about the condition of African Americans during Reconstruction and its aftermath, a time of hope that was transformed into a period of oppression for American blacks.

Born in 1855 on the Caribbean island of St. Kitts, which at the time was a British colony, Benjamin may have lived and studied in England for several years of his childhood. In autobiographical writings, he claims to have worked as a hand on board ships from his early teens. He first entered the United States in 1869 when he was 14. He remained in New York City for only a few months and soon thereafter shipped out again. In all, he traveled throughout the Caribbean, to Venezuela, and as far away as the Indonesian islands.

Benjamin finally returned to New York to stay in late 1869. He befriended the noted former abolitionist HENRY HIGHLAND GARNET and possibly through Garnet landed a job as a sales representative at the *New York Star*. Benjamin then jumped to the *Progressive American*, another New York–based periodical, where he worked as a reporter and editor until about 1876.

During the 1876 election, Benjamin worked for the campaign of the Republican Party's candidate for president, Rutherford B. Hayes. When Hayes was elected as a result of a deal with southern Democrats in a vote of the U.S. Congress, Benjamin was rewarded with the post of letter carrier in New York City. Detesting the boredom of the job, Benjamin quit after only a few months. Ironically, Hayes, who was Benjamin's hope for the presidency, agreed to end Reconstruction in exchange for the votes that made him president. This deal inaugurated a period of intense racial conflict in the South.

After resigning from his post office appointment, Benjamin moved to the South. For a number of years he taught in black schools in Alabama, Arkansas, and Kentucky. He is also believed to have practiced law and to have continued working as a journalist.

Benjamin suffered under the new political realities of the South after the end of Reconstruction. He is reported to have been beaten several times by whites as a result of his political reporting. He eventually moved back to the North, where he worked for the *Chronicle* in Evanston, Indiana, and the *Colored Citizen* in Pittsburgh.

Around 1888, Benjamin moved to California, where he worked as an editor for the *Los Angeles Observer* and the *San Francisco Sentinel*. He was the author of frequent editorials denouncing the wave of violence against blacks in the South. He also authored several books about race relations. These include *The Negro Problem and Its Solution* (1891) and *Southern Outrages, A Statistical Record of Lawless Doings* (1894).

Sometime before 1900, he seems to have moved to Kentucky to work as editor of the *Lexington Democrat*. While working at this job and helping to register blacks to vote in Lexington, R. C. O. Benjamin was murdered in October 1900.

Further Reading

Drape, Joe. *Black Maestro: The Epic Life of an American Legend*. New York: Morrow, 2006.

Logan, Rayford, and Michael Winston. *Dictionary of American Negro Biography*. New York: W. W. Norton, 1982.

Mitchell, Michelle. *Righteous Propagation: African Americans and the Politics of Racial Destiny after Reconstruction*. Chapel Hill: University of North Carolina Press, 2004.

Bethune, Mary McLeod

(1875–1955) *educator, social reformer, community leader*

Born into a poor family, Mary McLeod Bethune passionately believed that education offered a path to social and political advancement for African Americans. She devoted her life to this belief. The 15th of 17 children, Mary McLeod was born on July 10, 1875, in Mayesville, South Carolina, to parents who had been slaves. She was a bright child and was fortunate that the Presbyterian Church opened an elementary school for African-

American children near her house. She did so well at her elementary school that she won a scholarship to Scotia Seminary, a high school in North Carolina. After graduating from Scotia Seminary in the early 1890s, McLeod continued her education at the Moody Bible Institute in Chicago. The only African-American student, she excelled in her studies.

On graduating from the Moody Bible Institute, Mary McLeod had hoped to go to Africa as a missionary and teacher. Discovering that there were no openings at the time she applied for these positions, she instead remained in Chicago for a year. Realizing that "Africans in America needed Christ and school just as much as Negroes in Africa . . . [and that her] work lay not in Africa but in my own country," she visited prisoners in jail and worked at the Pacific Garden Mission, where she served lunches to the homeless and helped residents of Chicago's slums.

In 1895, she returned to Mayesville to teach in the Presbyterian Mission School, in which she had received her education. She remained in South Carolina for a year before moving to Augusta, Georgia, to teach at the Haines Institute.

The following year, 1897, McLeod moved again, this time to Sumter, South Carolina, where she taught at the Kendall Institute. She married Albertus Bethune in Sumter in 1898 and gave birth to a son, Albert, in 1899 after she had moved yet again. She then lived in Savannah, Georgia, a town in which her husband had found a new job. Mary McLeod Bethune spent the first part of 1899 caring for her newborn, but later in the year, restless because she was not teaching, she moved to Palatka, Florida, where she had been offered a teaching job at another mission school. Her husband soon followed, but the couple was not getting along. Although they remained on good terms, they separated in 1907.

Bethune stayed in Palatka for five years teaching at the mission school. This was a difficult time for her. Living on a meager salary, she also had to sell life insurance to make ends meet. Still feeling

Mary McLeod Bethune ca. 1940. Bethune, a leader in African-American education in the early 20th century, founded Bethune-Cookman College in Florida and served as an informal adviser to Eleanor Roosevelt. *(Library of Congress, Prints and Photographs Division, LC-USZ62-42476)*

restless and believing that she could do more, in 1904 she moved to Daytona, Florida, with the idea of founding a school for African-American girls.

Living at first with her son in a single room of a boardinghouse, Bethune scouted Daytona for a house she could rent for her school. Finally she found a place, a bare and worn house without furniture. She went from shop to shop in Daytona, acquiring cast-off furniture and carpets for the school. By October, she had enough makeshift desks to open the school, which she called the Daytona Industrial and Educational School. Her beginning class consisted of five girls, each of whom paid 50 cents a week for instruction.

In line with the ideas of her time, Bethune included practical domestic skills in the curriculum that she offered her students. As a result, classes in cooking and cleaning were given along-side the basics of reading, writing, and arithmetic. Because of her strong religious background and beliefs, Bethune also made Bible studies an important part of the school activities. The idea was that when a young woman graduated from the Daytona Industrial and Educational School she would be ready to confront all of the challenges of living in the world.

By 1907, Bethune had managed through intense door-to-door fund-raising to acquire enough money to move the school to a newer and permanent building. Throughout the 1910s and 1920s, she continued raising money to add new buildings to the school and eventually a farm so that the students could grow crops and make themselves self-sufficient. As news of her determination and dedication spread, the amount of money she was able to collect for her school increased. Gradually the school grew to include a campus of 32 acres, 14 buildings, and 400 students. In 1923, the school opened itself to young men when it merged with Cookman Institute of Jacksonville, Florida, and became Bethune-Cookman College.

An activist in the larger society outside her school, Bethune always fought for a wider role for African-American women in the civil life of the United States. To push for the right of African-American women to vote, she joined the Equal Suffrage League, an offshoot of the National Association of Colored Women, in 1912.

After women acquired the right to vote in 1919 with the passage of the Nineteenth Amendment, Bethune organized a campaign to raise money for women in Daytona to pay the poll tax, a fee that had been levied by many southern states in an effort to discourage poor blacks from voting. Bethune acquired enough money to pay for 100 women to vote. She also organized classes that taught the women to pass the literacy test, another obstacle devised by white southern politicians to prevent blacks from voting. Bethune's organizing was so effective that it aroused a Ku Klux Klan mob, who tried to intimidate her. She ignored the

mob, and she and her 100 followers voted for the first time in an election.

By the early 1920s, Bethune had earned a national reputation as a result of her work. She began to serve on a number of national boards of black organizations, including the National Urban League and National Association of Colored Women. She was elected president of the Interracial Council of America, and in 1935 she founded and was elected the first president of the National Council of Negro Women.

With the election of Franklin D. Roosevelt as president in 1932, Bethune moved to Washington to work on the national stage. In 1936, she was appointed director of the National Youth Administration's Division of Negro Affairs, a position she held until 1944. After the end of World War II, she worked with Eleanor Roosevelt, the widow of the late president, on drafting the United Nations (UN) Charter.

For her accomplishments, Bethune was awarded the Spingarn Medal (given by the National Association for the Advancement of Colored People [NAACP]) in 1935, the Frances Drexel Award for Distinguished Service in 1937, and the Thomas Jefferson Award for leadership in 1942. She became the first African American to receive an honorary degree from a white southern college, the doctor of humanities degree from Rollins College, in 1949. Mary Bethune died on May 18, 1955. Almost 20 years after her death, she was the first African American to have a statue created in her image in a public park. It stands in Lincoln Park in Washington, D.C.

Further Reading

Bethune, Mary McLeod, Audrey Thomas McCluskey, and Elaine M. Smith. *Building a Better World, Essays and Selected Documents.* Bloomington: Indiana University Press, 2002.

Botsch, Carol Sears. "Mary McLeod Bethune." University of South Carolina Aiken Website. Available online. URL: http://www.usca.sc.edu/aasc/bethune.htm. Downloaded July 15, 2009.

Coleman, Penny. *Adventurous Women: Eight True Stories about Women Who Made a Difference.* New York: Macmillan, 2006.

Holt, Rackham. *Mary McLeod Bethune: A Biography.* Garden City, N.Y.: Doubleday, 1964.

Bibb, Henry Walton
(1815–1854) *abolitionist, lecturer, publisher*

Born into slavery, Henry Bibb escaped from servitude and made his way to the North and later to Canada, where he worked tirelessly to end the slave system of the South.

Henry Walton Bibb was born in 1815 on a plantation in Shelby County, near Louisville in central Kentucky. His mother was a slave named Mildred Jackson and his father was a white politician, James Bibb, who served in Kentucky's legislature. Henry Bibb's mother later married a free black man who worked on riverboats and wanted to buy her freedom. Willard Gatewood, the owner of the plantation where the Bibbs were held, refused this offer. During the years of Bibb's youth, most of his brothers and sisters were sold to other slaveholders.

Bibb proved to be a difficult slave. He was confrontational and rebellious, and as a result he was frequently sold by one owner to the next. He married but had to watch as one slave owner forced his wife into prostitution. He escaped numerous times, each time trying to free some member of his family. He was always recaptured. In 1842, he finally gave up his effort to free his large and extended family, and he made one last escape, this one successful. He ended up a free man in Detroit, Michigan.

In Detroit, Bibb was taught to read and write by the Reverend William C. Monroe. Quickly mastering the basics of his education, Bibb began to work for the newly established Liberty Party in Michigan. The Liberty Party had been founded in 1840, two years before Bibb had made his successful escape from slavery; its main goal was the elimination of slavery.

Befriending another former slave, FREDERICK DOUGLASS, Bibb embarked on a career as a lecturer for abolitionist groups such as the American Anti-Slavery Society (AAS). He was described as a captivating lecturer, a man who could by turns make an audience cheer, laugh, and weep.

Touring the abolitionist lecture circuit, Bibb spoke from Michigan to Boston and at many places in between. While attending to this business, in 1848 he met and married Mary Miles, a Bostonian. The following year he published his memoirs, *Narrative of the Life and Adventures of Henry Bibb, an American Slave.* It was greeted with fanfare and curiosity, making Bibb an even better known figure in American life.

In 1850, the year after the publication of Bibb's book, the U.S. Congress took up the issue of the admission of California into the union, which rekindled questions about whether slavery should be limited to the states of the old South plus Texas. To gain California's admission as a free state, Senators Henry Clay of Kentucky and Stephen A. Douglas of Illinois proposed the Compromise of 1850. In return for California, northerners offered the admission of several western territories as neither free nor slave states. They also accepted the Fugitive Slave Law, which required northern states and their citizens to apprehend and transport back to the South all escaped slaves living in northern states.

The Fugitive Slave Law of 1850 forced Henry Bibb to consider immediately what he would do to prevent reenslavement. In an abolitionist meeting, he stated, "If there is no alternative but to go back to slavery, or die contending for liberty, then death is preferable." Soon after the passage of the Fugitive Slave Law, Bibb and his wife slipped away to Canada, beyond the reach of slave-hunting marshals.

In Canada, Bibb worked hard to establish communities of escaped slaves from the South. He also encouraged free blacks from the North to emigrate. His efforts were centered in the Canadian province of Ontario, where he had taken up residence. In time, large communities of U.S. blacks would spring up in the Ontario cities of Sandwich, Chatham, and Windsor.

Soon Bibb decided to establish a newspaper that would express the ideas of this black immigrant community. In 1851, he founded *Voice of the Fugitive,* Canada's first black newspaper, which was also distributed in the United States. On a regular basis Bibb personally greeted and interviewed newly arrived American black immigrants to Canada and featured these interviews in *Voice of the Fugitive.*

Bibb was overjoyed when in 1852 three of his brothers escaped from slavery and joined him in Canada. By this time, he had also begun to work with MARTIN ROBISON DELANY to recruit fugitive slaves to immigrate to Canada. He also founded the American Continental and West India League, one of the first pan-African organizations, whose purpose was to unite all black people in the Americas to achieve an end to slavery and greater social justice.

Henry Bibb died suddenly at the age of 39 in the summer of 1854.

Further Reading

Bibb, Henry. *The Life and Adventures of Henry Bibb: An American Slave.* Madison: University of Wisconsin Press, 2000. Available online. URL: http://docsouth.unc.edu/neh/bibb/bibb.html. Downloaded July 15, 2009.

Cooper, Afua. "The Fluid Frontier: Blacks and the Detroit River Region: A Focus on Henry Bibb." *Canadian Review of American Studies* 30, no. 2 (2000): 129–149.

Dictionary of Canadian Biography Online. Henry Bibb. Available online. URL: http://www.biographi.ca/009004-119.01-e.php?&id_nbr=3786&&PHPSESSID=ychzfqkvzape. Downloaded July 15, 2009.

Hite, Roger W. "Voice of a Fugitive: Henry Bibb and Antebellum Black Separatism." *Journal of Black Studies* 4 (March 1975): 269–284.

Bolin, Jane Matilda

(1908–2007) *lawyer, community activist, judge*

The daughter of a lawyer, Jane Bolin became the first African-American female judge in the United States. Jane Matilda Bolin was born on April 11, 1908, in Poughkeepsie, New York, located on the Hudson River north of New York City. Bolin's father, Gaius Bolin, maintained a law practice, and Bolin was influenced by him to try her hand at law.

A good student, Bolin graduated from high school early and enrolled in Wellesley College, an elite women's college located in Wellesley, Massachusetts. Bolin was the only African American in her class and felt isolated. She later recalled that although Wellesley was "beautiful and idyllic," she developed

> few sincere friendships [and] on the whole, I was ignored outside the classroom. I am saddened and maddened even nearly half a century later to recall many of my Wellesley experiences, but my college days for the most part evoke sad and lonely personal memories. These experiences perhaps were partly responsible for my lifelong interest in the social problems, poverty and racial discrimination rampant in our country.

After graduation from Wellesley in 1928, Bolin enrolled in the law school at Yale University. There she was one of only three women and the only African American in her class. She was the first African-American woman to graduate from Yale Law School.

After graduating from Yale in 1931, Bolin clerked at her father's law office and passed the New York bar exam. She soon moved to New York City and married Ralph Mizelle, another lawyer. Bolin and her husband opened a law practice together. They had one son, Yorke, born in 1941. Bolin, a member of the Republican Party, ran unsuccessfully for a seat in the New York State Assembly in 1936. In 1937, Mayor Fiorello LaGuardia appointed her counsel for the City of New York to serve on the city's Domestic Relations Court. Two years later Mayor LaGuardia appointed Bolin judge on the Domestic Relations Court.

As a judge, Bolin helped make the Domestic Relations Court a better, more democratic organization. She made sure that race played no role in the cases that were assigned to probation officers, and she also required that private child-care agencies that received funds from the city could not reject children because of their race or ethnicity.

Bolin served as a Domestic Relations Court judge for 40 years. Her first husband, Ralph Mizelle, died in 1943; she married Walter P. Offutt, Jr., a minister, in 1950. She retired as a judge in 1979. Bolin served on the boards of the Child Welfare League of America, United Neighborhood Houses, and Neighborhood Children's Center and was a member of the Committee on Children of New York City, the Scholarship and Service Fund for Negro Students, and the Committee against Discrimination in Housing. She died at age 98 in Long Island City, New York, on January 7. 2007.

Further Reading

Hine, Darlene Clark, ed. *Black Women in America.* New York: Oxford University Press, 2005.

Martin, Douglas. "Jane Bolin, the Country's First Black Woman to Become a Judge, Is Dead at 98." *New York Times,* 10 January 2007. Available online. URL: http://www.nytimes.com/2007/01/10/obituaries/10bolin.html?_r=1&scp=1&sq=%22jane%20bolin&st=cse. Downloaded July 16, 2009.

Wellesley University. "Jane Bolin." Available online. URL: http://www.wellesley.edu/Anniversary/bolin.html. Downloaded July 16, 2009.

Bowles, Eva Del Vakia

(1875–1943) *social worker, community organizer*

An activist who sought to improve interracial relations and carve out a niche for black women in the executive decisions of the Young Women's Christian Association (YWCA), Eva Bowles helped several generations of black women through her work with the YWCA.

Eva Del Vakia Bowles was born in Albany, Ohio, on January 24, 1875, into a distinguished African-American family. Her grandfather, the Reverend John Randolph Bowles, was one of the first black public school teachers in Ohio. During the Civil War John Bowles served as the chaplain of Massachusetts's 55th Regiment. Eva Bowles's father, John Hawes Bowles, was the first black teacher and principal in Marietta, Ohio. Later he broke another racial barrier when he became one of the first railway postal clerks, a position he held in Columbus, Ohio.

Eva Bowles grew up in Columbus, the state capital of Ohio as well as the home of Ohio State University, the state's largest public institution for higher learning. She attended public schools in Columbus and after graduation from high school enrolled at Ohio State. She also later studied at Columbia University in New York City.

Bowles studied to be a music teacher for blind students. However, in most of the jobs of her youth she held regular teaching positions. She was first hired by the American Missionary Association, which sent her to one of its schools, the Chandler Normal School in Lexington, Kentucky. She was the first black teacher at Chandler. After several years in Kentucky, she moved to Raleigh, North Carolina, where she taught at Saint Augustine's school. She later taught at Saint Paul's Normal and Industrial Institute in Lawrenceville, Virginia.

While she taught in these schools, Bowles got to know a large number of women who worked for church organizations. In 1906, when she was 31, Bowles was called upon by some of these women who were active in the YWCA to move to New York to run a community house for young women in Harlem. Within a few years, this organization had become a new chapter of the YWCA, the 137th Street Branch YWCA. For a long period, it was the largest predominantly African-American YMCA group in the country. Again, Bowles had broken a barrier. In taking this position, she had become the first black woman to be hired as a YMCA branch head. She remained at his job and in New York for two years.

In 1908, Bowles decided to return to her hometown, Columbus, where she took a position as a caseworker for the Associated Charities group of that city. Working with the black community, Bowles stayed in Columbus until 1913. She then returned to New York City, where she took a job with the National Board of the YWCA. She was given responsibility for overseeing the nationwide YWCA program in branches whose clientele were mainly African-American girls and women. She would remain in this position until her retirement in 1932.

At the YWCA, Bowles pushed for the inclusion of more black women at all levels of the organization. She believed that the YWCA was in a unique position to foster integration and understanding between whites and African Americans. The YWCA, she told the *New York World* in 1930, was "the pioneer in interracial experimentation." This could be accomplished, she believed, both at the local level of the local YWCA branches and at the national level at the New York headquarters.

In 1917, at the beginning of World War I, Bowles was appointed to be the leader of the YWCA's Colored Work Committee, a section of the War Work Council. Her main task was to aid black women who were entering the workforce in major American cities. These women were filling positions left by men who had enlisted in the army. For many women, these jobs marked their first experience working in an industrial plant.

On a budget of $200,000, Bowles set up YWCA facilities near factories and army camps throughout the nation. These places offered women opportunities for recreation and study in the evenings after work. Drawing from her wide circle of friends, Bowles also organized a lecture circuit that featured successful black women who talked

to the black women who lived and worked near these YWCAs. The former president Theodore Roosevelt was so impressed with what he saw at the Camp Upton, New York, YWCA that he awarded Bowles a grant of $4,000.

Bowles continued to work for the YWCA until 1932. In that year she resigned her job in protest over a change in the organization that she believed cut out black women from decisions that were being made by the National Board. The *Woman's Press* lamented Bowles's departure from the YWCA and praised her for her "vision of a truly interracial movement in the YWCA."

Eva Bowles died of cancer on June 14, 1943, and was buried in Columbus, Ohio.

Further Reading

Brown, Nikki. *Private Politics and Public Voices: Black Women's Activism from World War I to the New Deal.* Bloomington: Indiana University Press, 2007.

Robertson, Nancy Marie. *Christian Sisterhood, Race Relations, and the YWCA, 1906–46.* Champaign: University of Illinois Press, 2007.

Boykin, Keith O.

(1965–   ) *author, commentator, presidential assistant, gay rights activist*

Best-selling author and current affairs commentator Keith Boykin is a leading activist in the African-American gay and lesbian community. Born on August 28, 1965, he grew up in Florissant, Missouri. His family moved to Clearwater, Florida, when Boykin was a sophomore in high school. He graduated from Countryside High School and attended Dartmouth College. He wrote articles for the college newspaper, *The Dartmouth*, and served as its editor in chief during his junior year. Boykin graduated in 1987 with a degree in government. He was awarded the Barrett All-Around Achievement Cup, presented to the college's most outstanding graduating senior.

After graduation, Boykin worked as a press aide on Michael Dukakis's 1988 presidential campaign. The following year, he began classes at Harvard Law School, where future president Barack Obama was already enrolled as a student. Boykin came out of the closet—publicly acknowledging his homosexuality—at Harvard Law School. He served as an editor of the *Harvard Civil Rights—Civil Liberties Law Review* and graduated in 1992.

After working briefly at a San Francisco law firm, he joined Bill Clinton's 1992 presidential campaign. He served as Midwest press director. After Clinton's election, Boykin moved to Washington, D.C., taking a job in the White House's communications department. He was soon promoted to special assistant to the president and director of news analysis. As special assistant, in 1993, he helped organize the historic first meeting between leaders of the American gay and lesbian community and a U.S. president. Boykin was the highest-ranked openly gay official in the Clinton administration.

In 1995, Boykin left the White House, accepting a position as executive director of the National Black Justice Coalition (NBJC), which he had helped establish. The only nationwide African-American gay civil rights organization, the NBJC is a leader in advancing the rights of black gay, lesbian, bisexual, and transgender people. Boykin headed the NBJC until 1998, helping the organization further its mission to end discrimination based on race and sexual orientation.

Boykin spoke at the Million Man March in October 1995. Organized by the Nation of Islam leader LOUIS FARRAKHAN, the massive gathering drew black men from across the United States to Washington, D.C., to pledge to improve their own lives and restore their struggling communities. The following year, Boykin's first book, *One More River to Cross*, was published. It explored the issues faced by black homosexuals and examined the common ground between African Americans and homosexuals. In 1997, President Clinton appointed Boykin to serve on a U.S. trade delegation to the African nation of Zimbabwe. He accompanied Jesse Jackson and Coretta Scott King on the mission. Boykin published his second book, *Respecting the Soul*, in 1999 and taught political science courses at American University in Washington, D.C.

As an authority on African-American gay issues, Boykin has a regular column that appears in regional gay publications nationwide. He has also appeared on such TV news and talk shows as *Anderson Cooper 360*, the *Montel Williams Show*, and the *Tyra Banks Show*. His third book, *Beyond the Down Low*, was published in 2005. Boykin edits the Daily Voice, an online news site focused on gay issues, and works as a regular panelist on *My Two Cents*, a current affairs talk show aired by the Black Entertainment Network. He received the Gay Men of African Descent's Angel award in 1998, and *Out Magazine* selected him as one of its most intriguing people in 2004.

Further Reading

Harvard Gay and Lesbian Caucus. "An Interview with Keith Boykin." Available online. URL: http://www.hglc.org/extras/keith_boykin_interview.pdf. Downloaded August 3, 2009.

keithboykin.com. "Biography." Available online. URL: http://www.keithboykin.com/bio/. Downloaded August 3, 2009.

Santiago, Roberto. "One More River to Cross: Gay and Black in America" [review]. *American Visions* 5, no. 11 October 20, 1996: 30.

Brock, Roslyn McCallister
(1965–) *civil rights leader, health care administrator, and activist*

A nationally recognized expert on health care, Roslyn Brock is the youngest person and fourth woman ever elected as chairman of the National Association for the Advancement of Colored People (NAACP). Born in 1965, Brock graduated magna cum laude from Virginia Union University in 1986. She earned a master of sciences degree in health services administration from George Washington University in 1989. Her thesis focused on developing a health outreach program for minorities for the NAACP. She later earned a master of business administration degree from Northwestern University and a master of divinity degree from the Samuel DeWitt Proctor School of Theology at Virginia Union University.

As an administrator, she managed health care programs for the U.S. Agency for International Aid and the New York State Department of Health. Between 1991 and 2001, she developed

Before being elected as chairman of the national board of directors for the NAACP in February 2010, Roslyn Brock served as vice chairman, the first woman to hold the position. *(NAACP)*

health care programs at the W. K. Kellogg Foundation. One of the world's largest charitable foundations, the Kellogg Foundation provides grants for projects that benefit children in the United States and abroad. Brock currently works as director of fund system development at Bon Secours Health Systems, a nonprofit company that operates hospitals and other health care facilities around the country.

Brock joined the NAACP during her freshman year in college. She served in various regional and national leadership positions in the organization. As vice chairperson of the NAACP's health committee, she helped secure grants to fund many NAACP health programs and publications, including health seminars at the NAACP's annual convention and a widely distributed brochure, "HIV/AIDS and You."

In 2001, she was elected the first-ever female vice chairman of the NAACP's national board of directors. Brock has helped the civil rights organization to fulfill its mission of abolishing racial discrimination and ensuring equal rights for all people. Brock has focused on increasing the organization's membership among young African Americans. In 2005, she helped create the Leadership 500 Summit, which developed a strategy to attract a new generation of civil rights leaders to the NAACP. On February 20, 2010, Brock was elected chair of the NAACP.

Her role as a young leader in the NAACP has allowed Brock to participate in programs to expand her knowledge and perspectives. She served on the National Committee on United States—China Relations, joining other rising American leaders in meeting young Chinese leaders to foster professional relationships and greater cultural understanding. In 2008, she participated in the U.S. Department of Defense's civilian orientation conference, which provides information about military and national defense to leaders from private businesses and nonprofit organizations.

Brock has served on the board of directors of many health care and faith-based community organizations. She has received many awards for her community service and leadership, including *Network Journal's* 40 Under 40 award, *Good Housekeeping* magazine's 100 Young Women of Promise Award, and *Ebony* magazine's Future Leaders award.

Further Reading

NAACP. "National Directors." Available online. URL: http://www.naacp.org/about/leadership/directors/rbrock/. Downloaded July 10, 2009.

NAACP and Crisis Publishing. *NAACP: Celebrating 100 Years.* Layton, Utah: Gibbs Smith, 2008.

National Journal. "40 Under 40 Awards: Roslyn M. Brock." June 2004. Available online. URL: http://www.tnj.com/archives/2004/june2004/cover_story/132.php. Downloaded July 10, 2009.

Brown, Hallie Quinn

(ca. 1845–1949) *educator, civil rights leader*

A teacher in high schools and colleges, Hallie Brown dedicated her life to the education of African-American students and to the achievement of full rights for blacks and women. Born on March 10, probably in 1845, Hallie Quinn Brown was the daughter of Thomas and Frances Jane Brown, former slaves who had moved to Pittsburgh, Pennsylvania. When Brown was still young, perhaps in response to the passage of the Fugitive Slave Law, her family moved to Ontario, Canada, where they lived on a small farm. Brown remained in Canada until her early 20s.

Around 1870, after completing her secondary education, Brown moved from Canada to Ohio to attend Wilberforce University, a college for African Americans in Wilberforce, Ohio, that had been founded in 1856 by the African Methodist Episcopal (AME) Church. Brown received a bachelor's degree from Wilberforce in 1873, then continued her education by studying elocution, or the art of speech making and verbal persuasion, for a number of years at the summer school of the Chautauqua Lecture School in Chautauqua, New York.

After her graduation from Wilberforce, Brown took the first of several positions as a teacher of recently freed slaves and their children in the South. Brown's first job, probably with the Freedmen's Bureau, was on a plantation in South Carolina. She later taught on a plantation in Mississippi and at public schools in Yazoo, Mississippi, and Columbia, South Carolina.

The first seven years of Brown's teaching work in the South must have been particularly exciting. The Reconstruction era, which began in 1865 with the passage of the Freedmen's Bureau Act shortly before the assassination of Abraham Lincoln, was in full force. Not only had the Emancipation Proclamation freed millions of enslaved African Americans, but the federal government during the two administrations of President Ulysses S. Grant also guaranteed that blacks would have the right to vote and to receive an education. The rights were enforced by federal troops until 1877, when federal troops were pulled out of the South after a political compromise with southern Democrats that gave the presidency to Rutherford B. Hayes.

By 1885, Brown was back in Columbia, South Carolina, where she had taken a job as dean of students at Allen University. She later served as dean of women students at Tuskegee Institute. In 1894, she returned to Wilberforce University to become a professor of speech and elocution.

Brown had always had a great interest in the art of public speaking. She had earlier studied public speaking at the Chautauqua Institute, and during the late 1880s, while she was teaching in Dayton, she polished her speaking style with a teacher from the Boston School of Oratory. During her summer vacations and other times when she was not teaching, she began making speaking tours, mostly of the South. A typical program she presented probably included readings from popular works of literature as well as the Bible. Eventually she expanded her range of topics to include speeches she had written about women's rights and the civil rights of African Americans.

In 1894, Brown made her first trip to Europe on an extended speaking tour of Great Britain. This booking went so well that she decided not to return to Wilberforce in the fall of that year. Instead, for the next six years she remained for the most part in England to pursue her speaking career. The highlights of this time included a speech she made in London before the Women's Christian Temperance Union in 1895 and an engagement in which she spoke to an audience that included the Princess of Wales in 1899.

Brown had been an advocate of women's rights, especially women's right to vote, since she had been an undergraduate at Wilberforce and heard Susan B. Anthony address a student group there. By the late 1890s, Brown had begun to participate in the women's movement. She spoke on behalf of women's emancipation at the International Conference of Women in London in 1899. She carried this struggle back to the United States in 1900, when she unsuccessfully sought election as secretary of education of the AME Church.

From 1905 to 1912, Brown served as president of the Ohio chapter of the Federation of Women's Clubs, and from 1920 to 1924, she was president of the National Association of Colored Women. At a 1925 meeting of the International Council of Women in Washington, D.C., Brown sharply criticized the sponsoring organization for segregating African-American women by assigning them seats in a separate part of the auditorium. "This is a gathering of women of the world here," she told the audience, "and color finds no place in it."

By 1906, Brown had returned to full-time teaching at Wilberforce, where she remained for the duration of her career. She died on September 16, 1949, in Ohio, at the age of 103 or 104.

Further Reading

Anderson, Greta. *More Than Petticoats: Remarkable Ohio Women.* Guilford, Conn.: Globe Pequot, 2005.

Brown, Hallie Q. *Homespun Heroines and Other Women of Distinction.* Available online. URL: http://docsouth.unc.edu/neh/brownhal/brownhal.html. Downloaded July 15, 2009.

Dunlap, Mollie E. "A Biographical Sketch of Hallie Quinn Brown." *Alumni Journal* (Central State University) (June 1963).

Brown, William Wells

(ca. 1814–1884) *abolitionist, Underground Railroad conductor, temperance activist*

Born into slavery in about 1814 on a plantation in Kentucky, William Wells Brown managed to escape servitude just before his 20th birthday and later became an active participant in the struggle to end slavery. The first two years of his life were spent near Lexington, Kentucky, on the farm of John Young, a physician. According to William's mother, Elizabeth, his father was George Higgins, a cousin of John Young.

When William was two, he, his mother, and his seven siblings moved to St. Louis, Missouri, when Dr. Young decided to work as a doctor in that thriving Mississippi River city. William, who was sold twice to new owners, remained in the St. Louis area for the next 18 years. He apparently remained with Dr. Young long enough to learn the rudiments of medicine and became fascinated with the subject.

Young leased William's labor to a number of people in St. Louis: at various times, he worked as a field hand, house servant, copyboy in a printing shop, and helper in a tavern. During his stint working in the tavern, he acquired a lifelong revulsion for drink and drunkards. At some point, he began working for James Walker, a well-known slave trader. William made three trips with Walker to New Orleans to assist Walker in the purchase of slaves for sale in Missouri.

By 1834, he had been sold to Enoch Price, a St. Louis merchant and steamboat owner. As he had with James Walker, William made frequent trips up and down the Mississippi and Ohio Rivers with Price. On January 1, 1834, while staying with Price in Cincinnati, William made an escape from bondage. While heading across central Ohio toward Canada, he met up with a friendly Quaker, William Wells, who helped him and gave him shelter. Until then, he had had no surname. Grateful to the Quaker for his friendship, William took the names Wells Brown as his middle and last names.

After landing on his feet in Ohio, Brown changed his mind about moving to Canada and settled in Cleveland instead. There he began to educate himself and married Elizabeth Schooner, a woman he met there in the summer of 1834. They would have three daughters, two of whom would survive to become adults.

In 1836, Brown and his family moved to upstate New York. For nine years, he lived in Buffalo, where he worked for several Lake Erie steamship companies. It was during this period that Brown became active as a temperance worker and speaker against slavery. In a much less public way, Brown also became a "conductor" in the Underground Railroad, the network of abolitionists who led escaped slaves from the South to freedom and safety in Canada. Because of his job working on steamships, he was able to place escaped slaves on these vessels for the final leg of the journey to freedom. In 1842 alone, he ferried 69 fugitives to Canada.

By 1843, Brown had become so active in the abolitionist movement that the Western New York Anti-Slavery Society hired him as a public speaker. In this capacity, he began to travel widely to towns and cities throughout New York and Ohio, at each stop giving riveting talks about his own experiences with slavery. Brown then moved to Boston, where he took up a job as lecturer and organizer for the Massachusetts Anti-Slavery Society. Except during sojourns to Europe, Brown would live in Boston for the rest of his life.

In New England, Brown found himself in the middle of the growing abolitionist movement. He met the prominent white abolitionists William Lloyd Garrison and Wendell Phillips, and he later joined Garrison in the American Anti-Slavery Society (AAS). In 1849, Brown was sent abroad by American abolitionists to represent their interests at the International Peace Congress in Paris. There he met French liberals such as the great writer Victor Hugo and Alexis de Tocqueville.

In September 1849, Brown crossed the channel to England, where he would remain for the next five years. There he delivered hundreds of lectures across the British Isles in an effort to win British public support for the abolition of slavery. Fearful of returning to the United States after the passage of the Fugitive Slave Law in 1850, Brown stayed in Britain until sympathetic English friends formally purchased his freedom from Enoch Price, the man who had been his last owner.

From 1854, when he returned to the United States, until the end of the Civil War, Brown continued to write and speak against slavery. Although not a trained historian, Brown wrote several works about African-American history in the 1850s, including *The Negro in the American Rebellion*, the first book about the military history of American blacks. He is also credited with being the first African American to write a novel, *Clothel*, about a fictional daughter of Thomas Jefferson and Sally Hemmings, who was one of Jefferson's slaves.

After the war, Brown apprenticed as a physician and became a doctor in Boston. Until his death on November 6, 1884, he divided his time between the practice of medicine and writing and lecturing in support of the temperance movement.

Further Reading

Brown, Josephine. *Biography of an American Bondsman, by His Daughter.* Boston: R. F. Wallcut, 1856.

Brown, William W. *A Fugitive Slave.* Available online. URL: http://docsouth.unc.edu/neh/brown47/brown47.html. Downloaded July 15, 2009.

Brown, William Wells, and Ezra Greenspan. *William Wells Brown: A Reader.* Athens: University of Georgia Press, 2008.

Farrison, William Edward. *William Wells Brown: Author and Reformer.* Chicago: University of Chicago Press, 1969.

Burroughs, Nannie Helen

(1883–1961) *educator, clubwoman, civil rights leader*

A teacher and administrator with a special empathy for working-class black women, Nannie Burroughs channeled her efforts toward spiritual and economic improvement of the African-American community through the Baptist Church. The eldest daughter of John and Jennie Burroughs, Nannie Helen Burroughs was born in Orange, Virginia, near Charlottesville in the Shenandoah Valley, on May 2, 1883. That year, after the death of her father, Burroughs moved with her mother to Washington, D.C., a place where her mother could more easily find work.

Burroughs, an intelligent and determined young woman, excelled in Washington's segregated school system. After graduating from high school in 1896, she moved to Louisville, Kentucky, where she worked as a bookkeeper and editorial assistant for the black National Baptist Convention's Foreign Mission Board. In Louisville, Burroughs began her career as a community organizer by founding a woman's school, the Women's Industrial Club, where courses in secretarial work and domestic labor were taught. The school also provided low-cost lunches for black women who worked in downtown offices.

Burroughs, a devout Baptist, always conducted her organizing work in association with the National Baptist Convention, the largest black Baptist group in the United States. She believed that there was a special need for practical, work-related training schools for poor black women and that these schools should be based on the ideas of racial pride, a hard-nosed work ethic, and Christian moral conduct.

In 1900, Burroughs helped found the Woman's Convention, a group for women within the National Baptist Convention. She was corresponding secretary of this group from 1900 to 1947 and president from 1948 until her death in 1961. Between 1900 and 1909, Burroughs worked tirelessly through the Woman's Convention to raise money for a national industrial school that would train African-American women. She finally achieved success when the National Training School for Women and Girls opened in Washington, D.C., in October 1909. Burroughs served as the school's first president.

Sited in Lincoln Heights on the edge of urban Washington, the National Training School was to be a place where young black women from across the nation could learn how to comport themselves properly as well as take lessons in typing and running a household. Under the motto "We specialize in the wholly impossible," Burroughs stressed what she called the "3 B's—the Bible, bath, and broom." Realizing that many of her students would be unable to find clerical or teaching jobs, Burroughs made sure that they would be well equipped to handle the stresses of working as maids or laundrywomen in a segregated society.

Perhaps because of her own difficult youth with her widowed mother in Washington, Burroughs always identified with working women. She did not tolerate any notion that middle-class black women were in any way superior to ordinary working women. As she wrote in a magazine article in 1902:

> Our high-toned notions as to the kind of positions educated people ought to fill have caused many women who cannot get anything to do after they come out of school to loaf rather than work for an honest living, declaring to themselves and acting it before

others, that they were not educated to live among pots and pans. None of us may have been educated for that purpose, but educated women without work and the wherewithal to support themselves and who have declared in their souls that they will not stoop to toil are not worth an ounce more to the race than ignorant women who have made the same declarations.

By the end of the school year in 1910, Burroughs had attracted 31 students to the National Training School. By 1935, more than 2,000 women had received either a high school or a junior college diploma from the school.

Nannie Helen Burroughs ca. 1910. A leader in the education of working-class black women, Burroughs founded the National Training School for Women and Girls in 1909. *(Library of Congress, Prints and Photographs Division, LC-USZ62-79903)*

The Great Depression of the 1930s was an especially trying time for Burroughs. As a result of lack of funds, the National Training School was forced to shut its doors for a brief time. In the northern cities especially, African Americans were especially hard hit, as hundreds of thousands were thrown out of work. Burroughs responded in Washington, D.C., by starting a group called Cooperative Industrial, Inc., which provided free medical care as well as a hairdressing salon and a small department store for poor women.

Burroughs contributed to several women's groups outside the realm of the Baptist Church. She was a member of the National Association of Colored Women and a founder of the National Association of Wage Earners. This latter group focused mainly on educating the public about the plight of black working women. She continued to be outspoken: In a 1934 article, "Nannie Burroughs Says Hound Dogs Are Kicked but Not Bulldogs," she is quoted as advising African Americans not to waste "time begging the white race for mercy." Instead she advocated "ballots and dollars" to fight racism.

Well into her 70s, Burroughs continued to be active in the black community of Washington, D.C., and the nation. For many years, she edited the *Worker,* the publication of the Baptist Women's Auxiliary. Nannie Helen Burroughs died in Washington on May 20, 1961, at the age of 82.

Further Reading

Easter, Opal V. *Nannie Helen Burroughs.* New York: Garland, 1995.

Higginbotham, Evelyn Brooks. *Righteous Discontent: The Women's Movement in the Black Baptist Church, 1880–1920.* Cambridge, Mass.: Harvard University Press, 2003.

Wolcott, Victoria W. "'Bible, Bath, and Broom': Nannie Helen Burroughs's National Training School and African-American Racial Uplift." *Journal of Women's History* 9 (Spring 1997): 88–110.

Butts, Calvin Otis, III

(1949–) *minister, community activist*

Pastor of the renowned Abyssinian Baptist Church in New York City, Calvin Butts is internationally known as a religious leader and community activist. Butts was born in Bridgeport, Connecticut, in 1949 but grew up in the Lillian Wald Projects on Manhattan's Lower East Side. His father was a cook, and his mother was a city welfare department administrator. The family moved to Queens when Calvin was eight years old. After graduating from Flushing High School, where he was elected president of the senior class, he attended Morehouse College in Atlanta, Georgia. He majored in philosophy and minored in religion. Butts was at Morehead when Martin Luther King, Jr., was assassinated in 1968. Along with other Morehead students, he joined in the rioting in Atlanta that followed the civil rights leader's assassination.

Butts had planned to become a teacher, but when he graduated in 1972, he decided that the ministry was his calling. He enrolled at Union Theological Seminary in New York. During his first year, he was hired as an assistant pastor at Harlem's Abyssinian Baptist Church. A group of African Americans and Ethiopian merchants had founded the historic church in 1808. They had tried to attend services at a downtown church but had been instructed to sit in the balcony, separate from white worshippers. Rather than agree to segregated seating, they built their own church. They named it after Abyssinia, a former name for Ethiopia. Under the leadership of Adam Clayton Powell, Sr., the church grew rapidly during the early 20th century. In 1924, the congregation moved into an enormous new house of worship on 138th Street, next door to the headquarters of Marcus Garvey's black nationalist movement. With its membership topping 14,000, Abyssinian Baptist Church soon became a center of African-American religious and intellectual activity in the New York City region.

Calvin Butts III endorsed Hillary Clinton for president in 2008, despite objections from some of his Harlem community. *(© Peter Foley/epa/CORBIS)*

By the time Butts accepted the assistant pastor position, Pastor Samuel Proctor was in the process of rebuilding the church. Membership had dropped to about 6,000, and the church was in deep financial trouble. Butts helped Proctor create new religious programs and community outreach services. In 1975, he received his master of divinity degree in church history. He would later earn a doctorate of ministry degree in church and public policy at Drew University. The church promoted Butts to executive pastor in 1977. He was selected as Abyssinian's new pastor when Proctor retired in 1989.

In one of his first initiatives as pastor, he encouraged the congregation to start rebuilding their own neighborhood. Economic hardship and years of neglect had transformed the once thriving neighborhood around Abyssinian into a slum. Abandoned buildings dotted many blocks, and drug dealers openly conducted their business on the streets. Under Butts's leadership, the church created the Abyssinian Development Corporation (ADC), a community-based, nonprofit organization that develops affordable housing and commercial properties in Harlem. One of ADC's first projects was to transform two abandoned buildings across the street from the church into temporary lodgings for homeless families, a daycare center, and housing for low- and middle-income families. ADC's other projects included erecting a $9 million apartment building for senior citizens and renovating a condominium building for moderate-income families. Butts also supervised the creation of many of the church's service programs, including an AIDS prevention program aimed at teens, a tutoring program to improve the math and science skills of students, and athletic and afterschool programs.

Throughout his career, Butts has joined in efforts to eliminate racial discrimination. In his role as president of the Organization of African-American Clergy, he led the battle against police brutality against African Americans by the New York Police Department. He also spoke out against negative messages in rap and hip-hop music.

In addition to his duties as pastor at Abyssinian, Butts has preached in Africa, the Caribbean, Europe, and the Middle East. He has also taken an active role in education. He serves as the president of SUNY College at Old Westbury. He has taught urban affairs at New York's City College, where he also served as an adjunct professor of African studies. He taught church history at Fordham University and gives lectures and speeches at colleges and universities throughout the United States and the world. He helped establish the Thurgood Marshall Academy for Learning and Social Change, a public middle and high school in Harlem, and the Thurgood Marshall Academy Lower School.

Reverend Butts has been presented with several honorary degrees, including from Tuskegee University and Trinity College in Connecticut.

Further Reading

Abyssinian Baptist Church. "Pastor Biography." Available online. URL: http://www.abyssinian.org/index.php?l=101. Downloaded July 7, 2009.

My Hero Project. *My Hero: Extraordinary People on the Heroes Who Inspire Them.* New York: Simon & Schuster, 2005.

C

Carmichael, Stokely
(Kwame Ture, Kwame Toure, Kwame Touré)
(1941–1998) *civil rights activist, pan-African activist*

A leading civil rights activist during the 1960s, Stokely Carmichael (who later changed his name to Kwame Ture) represented a more militant branch of the Civil Rights movement as it evolved during the late 1960s and 1970s. The last of three siblings, Carmichael was born on June 29, 1941, in Port-of-Spain, Trinidad. When Carmichael was about six years old, his father (a carpenter), mother, and two sisters moved to the United States, leaving him in the care of two aunts and a grandmother in Trinidad. He studied at a traditional British elementary school until he moved to New York City in 1952 at the age of 11. There he was reunited with his family.

For a brief time, Carmichael was active in a gang called the Morris Park Dukes in his Bronx neighborhood. This changed when he was admitted into the Bronx High School of Science, a prestigious New York public school. As Carmichael later recalled in a magazine interview, "I broke from the Dukes. They were reading funnies while I was trying to dig Darwin and Marx."

Handsome and outgoing, Carmichael was popular with fellow students of all races at Bronx Science. He was not interested in politics or the Civil Rights movement until 1960, his senior year of high school. After seeing photographs of blacks sitting-in at lunch counters in the South, he became politically active. As he later described this transformation in a magazine interview, "When I first heard about the Negroes sitting in at lunch counters down South, I thought they were just a bunch of publicity hounds. But one night when I saw those young kids on TV, getting back up on the lunch counter stools after being knocked off them, sugar in their eyes, ketchup in their hair—well, something happened to me. Suddenly I was burning."

As a sign of his evolving political consciousness, Carmichael decided to reject scholarships from several mainly white universities and enroll instead at Howard University, a historically black college, in Washington, D.C. Carmichael studied philosophy at Howard, but his real love quickly became politics and civil rights work. During his freshman year he took part in Freedom Rides, integrated bus trips to the South, which challenged segregated interstate travel.

Upon graduating in 1964, he became an organizer for the Student Nonviolent Coordinating Committee (SNCC), one of the mainstream civil rights organizations fighting Jim Crow segregation laws in the South. He was elected president of SNCC in 1966.

Carmichael entered the Civil Rights movement in the South as an organizer at a time when the universally recognized leader of this movement was Dr. MARTIN LUTHER KING, JR., the head of the Southern Christian Leadership Conference (SCLC). Dr. King was a staunch and unapologetic advocate of the tactic of nonviolent resistance, pioneered by Mohandas Gandhi in India. The core idea behind nonviolent resistance was the belief that the moral power of nonviolent protesters would win the support of moderate whites, who would back changes in laws that discriminated against African Americans.

For a while, Carmichael followed King's non-violent-resistance tactics. During frequent trips to the South to register blacks to vote, he was arrested more than 25 times and once was sentenced to 49 days in Mississippi's infamous Parchman Penitentiary, where he was beaten almost daily.

Eventually Carmichael's encounters with white violence changed his belief in the effectiveness of nonviolent resistance. In a SNCC protest march in Mississippi in June 1966, Carmichael coined the term *black power*, and he soon began to put forward the idea that blacks should not be afraid to use force and violence to protect themselves and further their cause. As he later explained in an interview, "[Dr. King] saw nonviolence as a principle, which means it had to be used at all times, under all conditions. I saw it as a tactic. If it was working, I would use it; if it isn't working, I'm picking up guns because I want my freedom by any means necessary."

In 1967, Carmichael quit SNCC and joined the Black Panthers, a much more militant organization, which was involved in organizing poor blacks in urban ghettos. For a while, he held the position of prime minister of the Black Panther Party. By 1969, he viewed even the Black Panthers as too moderate and berated some of that group's leaders for working with white radicals. That year, he decided to leave the United States for good and move to Africa.

With his South African–born wife, the singer and political activist Miriam Makeba, Carmichael established a home in Guinea, which he had visited in 1967. He changed his name to Kwame Toure (Touré), the first part taken from the name of Kwame Nkrumah, an early pan-African leader, the surname borrowed from Ahmed Sekou Toure, the president of Guinea.

In 1970, Carmichael founded the All-African People's Revolutionary Party. He used this organization to call for African Americans to return to Africa, an idea that had its roots in the late 1700s. "The black man should no longer be thinking of transforming American society," he told a reporter. "We should be concerned with Mother Africa." In addition, Carmichael continued to work to oppose what he called "American imperialism," to advocate socialism as a political system, and to work against Israel, a nation he believed had been imposed on Arabs by Western powers. By the mid-1970s, his influence in the United States was virtually nil.

Carmichael died of prostate cancer in Conakry, Guinea, on November 15, 1998. Documents released by the Central Intelligence Agency (CIA) in 2007 showed that CIA agents kept track of Carmichael after he dropped from public view. They recorded his travels from the 1970s into the 1990s.

Further Reading

Carmichael, Stokely. Black Power speech. Available online. URL: http://www.americanrhetoric.com/speeches/stokelycarmichaelblackpower.html. Downloaded July 17, 2009.

Carmichael, Stokely, and Michael Thelwell. *Ready for Revolution: The Life and Struggles of Stokely Carmichael.* New York: Scribner, 2003.

Goldman, John. "Stokely Carmichael, Black Activist, Dies: The Fiery Leader Who Coined the Slogan 'Black Power' Was 57 and Living in Africa." *Los Angeles Times* Online. Available online. URL: http://articles.latimes.com/1998/nov/16/news/mn=43406. Downloaded July 17, 2009.

Carson, Benjamin S.
(1951–   ) *surgeon, education activist*

One of the nation's leading pediatric neurosurgeons, Ben Carson is well known for his efforts to help young students excel. Carson was born in Detroit, Michigan, on September 18, 1951. He grew up in a poor neighborhood, and his parents divorced when he was eight years old. His mother, Sonya, had only a third-grade education. She worked at two jobs to provide for Ben and his older brother. At school, Ben and his brother fell behind in their schoolwork. By the fifth grade, Ben's scores were at the bottom of his class. Some classmates taunted him, calling him "Dummy" and other names. Ben got into many fights.

To improve her sons' grades, Mrs. Carson enforced strict new rules to ensure that they studied. The boys could not go out to play until they finished their homework. The boys could only watch a small amount of television. They had to read two library books each week and write book reports on them. This new regimen helped build Ben's confidence in himself and his intellect. He began to excel at school, and within a year, he had climbed to the top of his class. Ben became an avid reader and decided that he wanted to become a doctor.

After graduating from high school with honors, Carson enrolled at Yale University. He graduated in 1973 with a degree in psychology. He entered the University of Michigan Medical School, where he focused on neurosurgery. After earning his medical degree, he won a neurosurgery residency at the prestigious Johns Hopkins Hospital in Baltimore, Maryland. He became the hospital's director of pediatric neurosurgery at age 32. In 1987, Carson gained worldwide acclaim for successfully separating a pair of conjoined twins who were joined at the back of the head. It was the first surgery of this type in which one of the twins did not die. He also developed several surgical innovations and cofounded Angels of the OR, an organization that provides grants to help neurosurgery patients pay for medical care expenses not covered by their insurance. Carson teaches oncology, plastic surgery, and pediatrics at Johns Hopkins University School of Medicine.

Shocked when he read that the United States ranked next to last in science and math in a study of student proficiency in 22 wealthy countries, Carson decided to do something to improve educational opportunities, particularly in poor neighborhoods like the one of his childhood. In 1994, Carson and his wife, Candy, established the Carson Scholars Fund. It awards $1,000 scholarships to students who demonstrate academic excellence. Students can reapply each year in order to accumulate money to help pay for college. The fund awards nearly 600 scholarships each year and has helped nearly 2,000 students afford a college education. The fund also manages another program, the Ben Carson Reading Projects. This initiative finances innovative reading rooms so students can benefit from independent reading. More than 40 reading rooms have been built across the country.

Carson has written three books: *Gifted Hands* (1990), *The Big Picture: Getting Perspective on What's Really Important in Life* (1999), and *Think Big: Unleashing Your Potential for Excellence* (2005). He has received many awards and honors. *Time* magazine named him as one of the nation's 20 foremost physicians and scientists. He received the 2006 Spingarn Medal, the highest honor bestowed by the National Association for the Advancement of Colored People. In 2008, he was awarded the Presidential Medal of Freedom, the nation's highest civilian honor, and *U.S. News & World Report* magazine named him one of America's Best Leaders in 2008. He once said, "My story is really my mother's story—a woman with little formal education or worldly goods who used her position as a parent to change the lives of many people."

Further Reading
Academy of Achievement. "Benjamin S. Carson, M.D." Available online. URL:http://www.achievement.

org/autodoc/page/car1bio-1. Downloaded July 10, 2009.

Carson, Ben, and Cecil B. Murphey. *Gifted Hands: The Ben Carson Story.* Grand Rapids, Mich.: Zondervan, 1990.

Carson Scholars Fund. "Dr. Ben Carson: General Information." Available online. URL: http://carson scholars.org/. Downloaded July 10, 2009.

Comarow, Avery. "America's Best Leaders: Benjamin Carson, Surgeon and Children's Advocate." Available online. URL: http://www.usnews.com/ articles/news/best-leaders/2008/11/19/americas-best-leaders-benjamin-carson-surgeon-and-childrens-advocate.html. Downloaded July 10, 2009.

Carver, George Washington
(ca. 1864–1943) *educator, scientist, community activist*

Born into slavery, kidnapped as a child, and employed as a traveling farmhand as a youth, George Washington Carver—through his determination, talent, and curiosity—became an internationally known scientist and community organizer. Carver was born in Diamond Grove, Missouri, probably in the spring of 1864 to a woman known as Mary, who was the slave of Moses and Susan Carver, Union supporters who lived on the wild borderlands of southwest Missouri during the Civil War.

The Carvers were a curious couple. Although they lived in a region heavily populated with southern sympathizers, they backed Abraham Lincoln's war on the South. Even though they professed to dislike slavery, they owned slaves. Southwest Missouri at that was plagued not only by common bandits but by roving bands of northern and southern militias who frequently robbed people they thought to be supporters of their political opponents. During the war, Moses Carver's farm was robbed three times.

Not much is known about George Washington Carver's father, although it is thought that he was a slave who lived on a nearby farm. This man is believed to have been killed in a farm accident soon after Carver's birth. During his childhood, Carver probably had three siblings, a brother, Jim, and two sisters. The sisters died in infancy, and Jim lived to his early 20s, when he succumbed to smallpox.

At the end of the Civil War, when George Washington Carver was an infant, southern raiders attacked the Carver farm for the last time, taking Mary and George as captives. The raiders had ridden across the state line in Arkansas. For at least a year after the end of the war, they kept mother and child. As a result of the arrival of federal troops and the intervention of a neighbor, George was returned to Moses Carver at the end of 1865. Mary had disappeared and nothing was heard from or about her again.

Moses and Susan Carver assumed the task of raising George and Jim. During his captivity in Arkansas, George had contracted whooping cough, an illness that left him weak for many years. Because of his illness, he was unable to participate in field work. Instead he became proficient in cooking, cleaning, and sewing.

As a child, he displayed the personality he would carry into the rest of his life. He was a dreamy loner who, in his own words, preferred "talking to flowers" to engaging with other people. Later in his life, in a brief autobiographical account, he described himself as a child:

> I had an inordinate desire for knowledge and especially music, painting, flowers, and the sciences. Day after day, I spent in the woods alone in order to collect my floral beauties, and put them in my little garden I had hidden in the bush not far from the house, as it was considered foolishness in that neighborhood to waste time on flowers.

Using a weather-beaten copy of *Webster's Elementary Spelling Book,* Carver learned to read during the time that he still lived with Moses and

Susan Carver. Soon he asked to attend a segregated school in nearby Neosho. After a year or two, when he was probably around 14, he was forced by necessity to begin work.

For the next five or six years, he wandered through the Great Plains states—Kansas, western Missouri, possibly Oklahoma—harvesting wheat, chopping wood, and working as a cook. Whenever he could, he would study at local schools, and he finally managed to earn a high school diploma at Minneapolis, Kansas.

In 1886, when he was about 21, Carver became a homesteader in Kansas. He worked his plot of land for two years before selling out his claim for $300. He then opened a laundry in Winterset, Kansas, and enrolled at Simpson College in nearby

George Washington Carver around 1925. Carver, a teacher at the Tuskegee Institute, won renown for his botanical studies and education courses that helped southern farmers develop cash crops from peanuts and yams. *(Moorland-Spingarn Research Center, Howard University)*

Indianola, Kansas. At Simpson, Carver was lucky enough to befriend his art teacher, Etta Budd, who soon discovered his intense interest in plants. Budd directed Carver to Iowa State University, where her brother, J. L., taught botany. Carver enrolled at Iowa State in 1891.

Guided by two professors who would soon became U.S. secretaries of agriculture (James C. Wilson, agricultural secretary under President McKinley, and Henry Wallace, secretary under Presidents Harding and Coolidge), Carver excelled in botany, earning an B.S. in 1894 and an M.S. in 1896. In accomplishing this goal, he became the first African American to earn a degree from Iowa State University.

On the completion of his master's degree, Carver was contacted by BOOKER TALIAFERRO WASHINGTON, the noted African-American educator who had founded the Tuskegee Institute, an all-black college in Alabama. "I cannot offer you money, position, or fame," Washington wrote. "The first two you have; the last... you will no doubt achieve. . . . I offer you in their place work—hard, hard work—the task of bringing a people from degradation, poverty, and waste to full manhood." Replying, "Of course, it has always the one great ideal of my life to be of the greatest good to the greatest number of 'my people'... and to this end I have been preparing myself for these many years," Carver accepted Washington's offer.

Having won a yearly grant of $1,500 from the state of Alabama for an agricultural experiment, Carver began the task of revolutionizing southern agriculture. He quickly realized that much of the soil of southern farms was exhausted from the continual cultivation of a single crop, cotton. Poor farmers, black and white, were in desperate need of know-how to restore their farms from the edge of bankruptcy.

At the Tuskegee experimental farm, Carver began a careful study of simple techniques that could be used to reinvigorate soils with nutrients. He devised ways to convert organic wastes such as leaves, paper, and grass in to nutrient-rich compost. He also discovered that farmers could boost the nitrogen content of soils simply by planting cover crops such as cowpeas and peanuts.

The peanut, especially, became a crop that was tied to Carver's name. In the peanut, Carver saw a golden nugget where all others before him had seen a weed. He devised several ways to process the peanut—into a food product called peanut butter and into milk, cheese, shampoos, ink, and wood stains—that multiplied the value of the crop. Carver later applied the same logic to sweet potatoes and clays from the South's clay-rich soils, extracting numerous products from these simple goods.

Carver never rested from his task of educating farmers. In 1899, he founded what he called the "Movable School," a traveling teaching display on mule-drawn wagons. By 1918, he had replaced this contraption with a gasoline-powered truck. In the 1950s and 1960s, Carver's movable school idea was duplicated in developing countries such as China and India.

For his inventions and dedication to helping poor farmers, Carver won worldwide renown. In 1916, he was made a fellow of the British Royal Society of Arts; the National Association for the Advancement of Colored People awarded him its Spingarn Medal in 1923; and in 1941 he received an honorary doctorate from the University of Rochester.

Uninterested in material gain, Carver in 1940 used his life savings of $60,000 to start the George Washington Carver Research Foundation, which today employs more than 100 faculty and staff. Carver died on January 5, 1943, and was buried on the campus of Tuskegee Institute. In 2005, the American Chemical Society designated Carver's research at Tuskegee a National Historic Chemical Landmark. That same year, the Missouri Botanical Garden in St. Louis opened a George Washington Carver garden in his honor. A life-size statue of Carver stands in the garden.

Further Reading

"George Washington Carver, Chemurgist." Available online URL: http://www.black.scientists.com/component/content/article/3/7. Downloaded July 17, 2009.

Iowa State University E-Library. "The Legacy of George Washington Carver." Available online. URL: http://www.lib.iastate.edu/spcl/gwc/home.html. Downloaded July 17, 2009.

Kremer, Gary R. *George Washington Carver in His Own Words.* Columbia: University of Missouri, 1987.

McMurray, Linda. *George Washington Carver.* New York: Oxford University Press, 1981.

National Park Service. "George Washington Carver National Monument." Available online. URL: http://www.nps.gov/archive/gwca/expanded/main.htm. Downloaded July 17, 2009.

Chambers, Julius Levonne
(1936–) *civil rights lawyer, educator, administrator*

Julius Chambers is a veteran civil rights lawyer and legal educator who has litigated many key civil rights lawsuits since the 1960s. Born on October 6, 1936, in Mount Gilead, North Carolina, he grew up in rural western North Carolina. He attended segregated schools and experienced the many other anguishes of racial inequality during the Jim Crow era. One childhood incident particularly haunted Chambers. His father, William, who owned an auto repair business, had fixed a man's truck. His parents had planned to use the customer's payment to send Julius, then 12 years old, to a boarding school. The man, however, refused to pay his bill. Mr. Chambers approached several lawyers, seeking to sue the customer to recover the money owed him. None of the attorneys would consider taking on a case involving a black man suing a white man. Chambers would later point to this episode as the motivation for his becoming a civil rights lawyer.

After graduating from high school, Chambers enrolled at North Carolina College (now N.C. Central University), a historically black public college that the state had established for African-American students. The U.S. Supreme Court had ruled in *Plessy v. Ferguson* (1896) that creating separate public facilities, such as schools and restrooms, for whites and blacks was constitutional as long as the facilities were equal. This became known as the separate but equal doctrine, which states and individuals used to justify racial segregation. The public facilities provided for black citizens were almost always lower in quality.

Chambers graduated summa cum laude in 1958 with a degree in history. He applied for admission to the University of North Carolina School of Law, which had been desegregated since 1951. Chambers was one of the few black students admitted that year. He excelled in his classes and was selected to be editor in chief of the school's law review during his third (and final) year. He was the first African-American student to serve in the post. Chambers graduated in 1962. Ranking first in his class of 100, he was elected to the Order of the Coif and Order of the Golden Fleece, two prestigious honorary societies.

Chambers went to New York City to pursue an advanced degree at Columbia University School of Law. While earning his master of laws degree, he taught law courses at the school. He was selected as a the NAACP's Legal Defense and Educational Fund's first-ever intern and worked for legendary civil rights lawyer THURGOOD MARSHALL. (Marshall would be appointed to the U.S. Supreme Court in 1967.)

In 1964, Chambers returned to North Carolina. Despite his stellar academic record and experience working with Marshall, he was unable to find a law firm willing to hire a black lawyer. Chambers decided to set up a law office in Charlotte. His one-person practice soon grew into Chambers, Stein, Ferguson, and Atkins, the state's first integrated law firm. Chambers and his partners worked with the NAACP's Legal Defense and Educational Fund on many major civil rights cases. In *Swann v. Charlotte Mecklenburg Board of Education* (1971), Chambers and his cocounsel successfully argued for a federal mandate that required public school systems to bus students in order to achieve integrated schools. In *Griggs v. Duke Power Co.* (1971), the U.S. Supreme Court ruled that a utility company's test designed to prevent black employees from being promoted was unconstitutional. Because of his involvement in such high-profile desegregation cases, Chambers received many death threats from people opposed to integration. In separate incidents over the years, his office and home were firebombed, and his car was set on fire.

In 1984, Chambers left his law firm, moving to New York City to become director counsel of the NAACP's Legal Defense and Educational Fund. In this position, he supervised a staff of 24 in-house attorneys and provided guidance to more than 400 attorneys handling civil rights cases nationwide. Under his leadership, the Legal Defense and Educational Fund dealt with a wide variety of civil rights cases, ranging from discrimination cases in the areas of education, employment, and housing to lawsuits involving prisons and capital punishment.

After nine years at the NAACP, Chambers returned to North Carolina to serve as chancellor (administrative head) of his alma mater, North Carolina Central University. He continued to provide legal counsel in civil rights cases. Chambers returned to his law firm when he retired as chancellor in 2001. He continues to handle employment discrimination and other civil rights cases.

Throughout his career as a lawyer, Chambers made time in his busy schedule to teach law students. He served as an adjunct professor at several leading law schools, including University of Virginia Law School (1975–78), Columbia University Law School (1984–92), University of Michigan Law School (1985–92), and University of North Carolina School of Law (2001–   ).

In 2002, Chambers helped establish the University of North Carolina Center for Civil Rights. Its mission is to ensure the civil rights for all North Carolinians. He continues to serve as the center's first director. In 2006, Chambers received the American Bar Association's Thurgood Marshall award, which was established to honor people who have made major contributions to civil and human rights in the United States. He also received the 2009 Spirit of Excellence award from the American Bar Association Commission on Racial and Ethnic Diversity in the Profession. Chambers has also been awarded many honorary LL.D. (doctors of laws) degrees.

Further Reading

Chambers, Julius. "Black Americans and the Courts: Has the Clock Been Turned Back Permanently?" In *The State of Black America 1990*, edited by Jane Dewart. New Brunswick, N.J.: Transaction, 1990.

Schwartz, Bernard. *Swann's Way: The School Busing Case and the Supreme Court.* New York: Oxford University Press, 1986.

University of North Carolina School of Law. "Julius Chambers." Available online. URL:http://www.law.unc.edu/faculty/directory/details.aspx?cid=13. Downloaded July 16, 2009.

Chase, William Calvin
(1854–1921) *lawyer, publisher*

An influential lawyer and founder and publisher of the *Washington Bee*, William Calvin Chase kept the issues most important to his readership in the news and at the same time made his paper into a profitable business. Chase was born free in Washington, D.C., in 1854. His father, William H. Chase, was a well-to-do blacksmith, and his mother, Lucinda Seaton Chase, was a member of a middle-class black family who lived in Alexandria, Virginia, just across the Potomac River from Washington.

The second of six children, Calvin Chase grew up in a respectable, integrated neighborhood. He attended an elementary school that was housed in the basement of a Presbyterian church near his house, and later he enrolled at a public high school. He did not attend college as an undergraduate but did attend classes at the Howard University Law School in 1883–84. In 1889, Chase passed the bar exams for the state of Virginia and the District of Columbia.

Even though Chase maintained an active law practice, he is best remembered for his other profession, and probably his most consuming passion, his stewardship of the *Washington Bee*. Chase founded the *Bee* in 1882, the year before he began the study of law. For the first 13 years of its existence, the *Bee* was a four-page publication. In the beginning, at least half of the front page and half of the remaining space of the paper were given over to advertising. Chase, of course, sought out African-American advertisers, but he also took advertisers where he found them; a good half of the businesses that advertised in his periodical were white.

By 1895, Chase expanded the *Bee* to eight pages. There was always an editorial page, which Chase used to express his well-known corrosive wit, especially against white institutions that blocked access to full political and civil rights for African Americans. The *Bee*'s motto, "Honey for Friends, Stings for Enemies," accurately summarized Chase's editorial philosophy.

The late 1800s and early 1900s was a golden age for African-American newspaper publishing. Besides Chase's *Bee*, a handful of other city papers vied for the attention of the black community and tried to set its political agenda. One of these was the *New York Age*, a weekly begun in 1888 that was co-owned and edited by TIMOTHY THOMAS FORTUNE, a strong supporter of BOOKER TALIAFERRO WASHINGTON. Another prominent paper was the *Cleveland Gazette*, which was established in 1883. Edited by HARRY CLAY SMITH, the *Gazette* threw its weight behind the Republican Party and resisted Booker T. Washington's philosophy of striking a bargain with white segregationists.

Chase constantly reported about politics within and pertaining to the African-American community. As Booker T. Washington rose in prominence in national politics, Chase reported on him, often unfavorably. Chase criticized Washington's Atlanta Exposition Address, in which Washington had proposed that blacks should not push for greater civil and political rights but should instead pull themselves up by the bootstraps through moral and economic self-improvement. Chase called this speech "a bait of southern fancy." When Washington dined with President Theodore Roosevelt, Chase labeled the get-together "a political decapitation dinner." After a money crisis at the *Bee* in 1906, Chase backed off his criticism of Washington in order to receive financial help from Washington and his circle.

Even though Chase began to offer mild support for Booker T. Washington, he did not hesitate to report the frequent lynchings and race riots that were occurring throughout the nation in the early part of the 20th century. The *Bee* ran extensive coverage of lynchings and violent riots in which white mobs attacked blacks in Pennsylvania in 1911; in East Saint Louis, Illinois, and Houston, Texas, in 1917; and in Washington, D.C., and Chicago, Illinois, in 1919. He also was sharply critical of the federal government's discriminatory hiring and promotion practices against African Americans.

Chase ran his paper every day until he was felled at his desk by a heart attack on January 3, 1921. The *Bee* outlived him by only a year, its door and pages closing forever in 1922.

Further Reading

Cultural Tourism DC. "African American Heritage Trail Database: Washington Bee Newspaper Office." Available online. URL:http://www.culturaltourismdc.org/info-url3948/info-url_show.htm?doc_id=206740&attrib_id=7967. Downloaded July 17, 2009.

Gatewood, Willard B. *Aristocrats of Color: The Black Elite, 1880–1920.* Fayetteville: University of Arkansas Press, 2000.

Howard University. "William Calvin Chase." Howard University Archives. Available online. URL: http://www.huarchivesnet.howard.edu/0011huarnet/battle5.htm. Downloaded July 17, 2009.

Penn, I. Garland. *The Afro-American Press and Its Editors.* 1891. Reprint, New York: Arno Press, 1969.

Chester, Thomas Morris
(1834–1892) *educator, lawyer, journalist*

A teacher in Africa, newspaper correspondent who traveled with the Union forces during the Civil War, and lawyer and politician in postwar Louisiana, Morris Chester lived a full and engaged life in which he pursued his potential to the fullest extent possible. Thomas Morris Chester was born on May 11, 1834, in Harrisburg, Pennsylvania, to George Chester, a freeman, and Jane Chester, an escaped slave from Maryland.

Chester's parents must have been relatively prosperous because they were able to send him to Avery College, a trade school near Pittsburgh, when he was 17. He remained at Avery for two years, and in 1853, possibly with his parents, he journeyed to Monrovia, Liberia. In Monrovia, he continued his education at Alexandria High School. Chester remained in Liberia for only a year and returned to the United States in 1854. He finished his high school education at the Thetford Academy in Thetford, Vermont, from which he graduated second in his class in 1856.

After his graduation, Chester decided to return to Liberia to teach. One of his first jobs was as a teacher of Africans who had been liberated, probably by the British navy, from slave ships.

Liberia was the colonial stepchild of the American Colonization Society, a group of mostly white Americans who advocated sending free African Americans back to Africa. At the time of Morris's second arrival in Liberia, the colony had only recently declared its independence (in 1847). The president was an African American from Virginia, Joseph Jenkins Roberts. Only about 3,000 resettled African Americans remained (many had returned to the United States). Most of the population were members of a number of different tribal groups.

By 1860, Morris had begun his career as a journalist when he founded a newspaper called the *Star of Liberia.* He also served as the Liberian correspondent for the *New York Herald* and seems to have been active in Liberian politics.

The start of the Civil War drew Chester back to the United States in 1861. In 1862–63, he worked with FREDERICK DOUGLASS to lobby for all-black federal army units to fight the Confederates. When federal authorities approved this, he helped recruit African Americans to join the Massachusetts 54th and 55th Infantry Regiments, two all-volunteer units. Chester had wanted to volunteer to help lead one of these regiments, but when he discovered that federal army regulations barred any African American from holding a rank higher than sergeant, he decided not to enlist.

After learning shorthand so that he could quickly write down some of the inspiring speeches he heard given by other African Americans during his recruitment work, Chester landed a job in 1864–65 as a war correspondent for the *Philadelphia Press.* Writing under the pen name "Rollin," he chronicled the combat and day-to-day existence experienced by units of the Army of the James, a subgroup of General Ulysses S. Grant's Army of the Potomac that had been assigned the job of pushing up the banks of the James River toward the Confederate capital of Richmond. It is said that he wrote a dispatch about the federal army's capture of Richmond while seated at the desk of the deposed Confederate president, Jefferson Davis.

After the war, Chester began work as a fundraiser for a Pennsylvania group that sent money and teachers to help freed slaves in the South. From 1866 to 1871, he traveled across Europe soliciting funds from wealthy individuals and European governments. Chester spent the winter of 1866–67 in Russia as a guest of the czar, then settled in London, where he studied law and was admitted into practice as a lawyer in 1870.

Chester returned to the United States in 1871, this time to New Orleans, which was under the protection of federal troops and controlled by political forces loyal to the national Republican Party. Even though he was a northerner born and bred, Chester immediately took a liking to the South, believing that in spite of the virulent racism of many whites there, it was a place where African Americans and whites could learn to live together in peace and with respect.

Chester set up a law practice in Louisiana and became active in politics. In 1873, the governor appointed Chester a brigadier general in the state militia, and in 1875–76, he was appointed as a superintendent of education for a number of parishes in and around New Orleans. After the end of the Reconstruction governments in 1877, Chester supported himself through his law practice and various federal appointments.

One of his later positions was as an investigator on behalf of the U.S. attorney general looking into voting fraud in East Texas, a dangerous job for any African American at that time. Chester filed a report that chronicled the problems that blacks were having in voting, but little was done to change this situation.

Chester lived in Louisiana until ill health forced him back to Pennsylvania in 1892. He died of a heart attack at his mother's house in Harrisburg on September 30, 1892, at the age of 58. In September 2002, a refurbished marker was installed at Chester's gravesite in Harrisburg, Pennsylvania.

Further Reading

Afrolumens Project. "Chester Tombstone Dedication." Available online. URL: http://www.afrolumens.org/

rising_free/lincoln/chester02.html. Downloaded July 17, 2009.

Blackett, R. J. M., ed. *Thomas Morris Chester: Black Civil War Correspondent: His Dispatches from the Virginia Front*. New York: DaCapo, 1991.

Chester, T. Morris. *Negro Self-Respect and Pride of Race; Speech of T. Morris Chester, Esq., of Liberia, Delivered at the Twenty-Ninth Anniversary of the Philadelphia Library Company, December 9, 1862*. Philadelphia: Historic Publications, 1969.

Cinque, Joseph

(Sengbe Pieh, José Cinque, Joseph Cinquez)
(ca. 1817–ca. 1879) *slave revolt leader*

Sengbe Pieh, later named José Cinque by his Spanish captives, was born in Mani, Sierra Leone, around about 1817. By his account, he was a member of the Mende people, was a rice farmer, and was married with three children when another tribal group captured him and sold him into slavery to Spanish slave traders on the island of Lomboko, just off the coast of Sierra Leone. The Spanish in turn sold him to the captain of a Portuguese slave ship.

Cinque survived the torment of the notorious Middle Passage, the journey across the Atlantic from Africa to the Americas. According to Cinque, he was among the one-half of the captives who survived this journey. The rest died of disease or malnutrition in the crowded hold beneath deck.

By 1839, the importation of slaves into Cuba was illegal, although an underground trade in slaves still flourished. Cinque and the other slaves who survived the Middle Passage were unloaded in Havana, given Spanish names so that they would appear to have been born in Cuba, and resold. A Cuban planter named José Ruiz bought Cinque and 47 other Africans and chartered a sailing vessel, captained by a man named Ramon Ferrer, to take them to his farm near Puerto Principe, some distance from Havana.

During the journey from Havana, the ship's cook may have indicated by sign language to Cinque and the others that they were going to be killed and eaten. This probably was a cruel joke by the cook with no relation to reality. Slaves were much too valuable to be dispensed with in this way. In any event, Cinque—either because he believed that he and the others were about to be killed or because he sensed that the cook's gestures would motivate the other slaves—urged a mutiny. "We may as well die in trying to be free," he told the others, "as be killed and eaten."

Waiting until night, Cinque used a loose nail to pry apart the iron clasp that held his chain to the wall. In short order, he freed the others as well. The Africans armed themselves with knives, that they found in the hold that were used to cut sugar cane then stormed onto the deck. The Africans were fortunate that the vessel, called the *Amistad*, did not have a large crew. After a brief but furious

Joseph Cinque ca. 1839. Enslaved in West Africa and sent to Cuba, Cinque was the leader of a slave revolt aboard the sailing ship *Amistad*. He was freed by a ruling of the U.S. Supreme Court in 1840. *(Library of Congress, Prints and Photographs Division, LC-USZ62-12960)*

struggle, they killed the cook and Captain Ferrer. Several sailors threw a lifeboat into the ocean and made an escape. The rebels managed to capture Ruiz, the man who had bought them, along with a friend of Ruiz's, Pedro Montes.

By force of his personality, Cinque immediately assumed command of the ship. He made Ruiz and Montes help the slaves learn how to sail the vessel and ordered Montes, who knew about seagoing navigation, to chart a course back to Africa. Montes pretended to guide them eastward, but because a sailing vessel often has to tack, or zigzag, to use the prevailing winds, Montes was able to set their course to the northeast toward the southern United States without raising suspicion.

Instead of making landfall in Georgia or the Carolinas as he had hoped, Montes instead guided the ship toward Long Island, New York. In late September, after nearly a six-week voyage, the Africans spotted land. Not knowing where they were, some of them set out on a launch to go ashore to scout for food and water. While this crew was ashore, the *Amistad* was discovered and stormed by sailors from a U.S. Coast Guard vessel. All of the Africans, including those on shore, were captured and taken to New Haven, Connecticut, where they were held in prison pending a court hearing that would decide their fate.

On August 30, the *New York Journal of Commerce* described the arrival of the Africans in New Haven:

> On board the brig we also saw Cinques, the master spirit and hero of this bloody tragedy, in irons. He is about five feet eight inches in height, 25 or 26 years of age, of erect figure, well built, and very active. He is aid to be a match for any two men on board the schooner. His countenance… is unusually intelligent, evincing uncommon decision and coolness, with a composure characteristic of true courage, and nothing to mark him as a malicious man.

The discovery of the *Amistad* set off a furor in the United States. Abolitionists, whose antislavery cause had been gaining strength in the North, demanded that the slaves be freed. With equal conviction, southern slaveholders demanded that the slaves be returned to Cuba.

From September 1839 until February 1840, Cinque and the other Africans were held in prison in New Haven. A group of abolitionists, headed by Lewis Tappan and James Pennington, insisted that the Africans be freed and returned to Africa. President Martin Van Buren, a northerner who for political reasons did not want to alienate southern voters, declared that they be tried for murder.

A judge in Connecticut ruled that the Africans had been kidnapped; thus they had been justified in using violence to free themselves. The federal government disagreed and appealed the case to the U.S. Supreme Court. To argue their case in the Supreme Court, the abolitionists retained John Quincy Adams, the former president of the United States, who was then a member of the House of Representatives. In February 1840, the court ruled that all of the Africans should be set free.

Between 1840 and 1842, Cinque toured the North lecturing to audiences about his brush with slavery. After his return to Sierra Leone in 1842, he vanished from the sight of Western eyes. Decades later, in 1879, an old man showed up at a coastal mission in Sierra Leone that was run by the American Missionary Association. The man claimed to be Cinque. Old and in ill health, he asked to be buried in the mission cemetery. There he died and was laid to rest, a man, in the words of the *Colored American*, who had "risen only against the worst of pirates, and for more than life—for liberty, for country and for home."

A statue of Cinque stands outside New Haven's City Hall. In the 1997 movie *Amistad*, the actor Djimon Hounsou portrayed Cinque.

Further Reading

Famous American Trials. "Amistad Trials 1839–40." Available online. URL: http://www.law.umkc.edu/faculty/projects/ftrials/amistad/AMISTD.HTM. Downloaded July 17, 2009.

Kromer, Helen. *Amistad: The Slave Uprising aboard the Spanish Schooner.* Cleveland: Pilgrim Press, 1997.

Martin, B. Edmon. *All We Want Is Make Us Free: La Amistad and the Reform Abolitionists.* Lanham, Md.: University Press of America, 1986.

National Portrait Gallery. "The Amistad Case." Available online. URL: http://www.npg.si.edu/col/amistad/. Downloaded July 17, 2009.

Owens, William A. *Black Mutiny: The Revolt on the Schooner* Amistad. Philadelphia: Pilgrim Press, 1968.

Cleaver, Eldridge
(1935–1998) *black nationalist leader, Christian evangelist*

Author of the first and probably best-known black nationalist book of the 1960s and a leader of the Black Panther Party, Eldridge Cleaver later in life regretted his radicalism and embraced the Republican Party and Christianity. Born on August 31, 1935, in Wabbaseka, Arkansas, Cleaver moved with his family to Phoenix, Arizona, in the 1940s. By the 1950s, the Cleavers had moved farther west to Los Angeles, where the teenaged Cleaver began getting into trouble with the law for petty theft and selling marijuana. In 1957, he was convicted of assault with intent to murder and sent to San Quentin and Folsom prisons.

In prison, Cleaver began to read books on history and politics. He developed a liking for communist and socialist political philosophies and kept himself up to date about revolutionary events in the newly independent developing nations of Africa and Asia. By the early 1960s, he began to write essays that reflected the rage

Eldridge Cleaver ca. 1968. A radical turned conservative Republican in his later life, Cleaver was a prominent leader of the Black Panthers during the 1960s and 1970s. *(Library of Congress, Prints and Photographs Division, LC-U9-20018)*

he felt about his own experiences as a black man in the United States as well as his ideas about revolutionary violence. These essays, first published in the radical magazine *Ramparts*, were later collected in a book published in 1968, *Soul on Ice.* Cleaver's disdainful attitude toward whites and moderate black civil rights leaders would set the tone for what became known as the Black Power movement.

In *Soul on Ice*, Cleaver described his rape of a white woman as an act of black liberation, "an insurrectionary act. It delighted me that I was defying and trampling upon the white man's law . . . defiling his women." In a letter that appeared in

Ramparts, Cleaver bragged that he "wanted to send waves of consternation through the white race." Referring to the Vietnam War, which was then raging between the U.S. armed forces and the communist army of North Vietnam, he continued, "I'm perfectly aware that I'm in prison, that I'm a Negro, that I've been a rapist. My answer to all such thoughts lurking in their split-level heads, crouching behind their squinting bombardier eyes, is that the blood of Vietnamese peasants has paid off all my debts."

Released from prison in 1966, Cleaver helped found the Black Panther Party, a small radical group in Oakland, California. With Cleaver as their information minister, the Panthers were soon able to garner news headlines as a result of Cleaver's outrageous statements. On one level the Panthers presented themselves as guardians of blacks who lived in America's inner-city ghettos, but as Cleaver later confessed, they were deeply involved in drug dealing, intimidation, and murder.

Cleaver made a run for president in 1968 on the Peace and Freedom Party ticket. Before he had much time to campaign, he and other Panthers found themselves involved in a shoot-out with Oakland, California, police. At the time, the Panthers claimed that the police had targeted them for assassination. Later, however, Cleaver admitted that the police were going to arrest the Panthers because Cleaver and other Panther leaders had ordered an attempt to assassinate Oakland police officers.

After a bloody raid on Panther headquarters in which one Panther was killed, Cleaver was arrested and charged with attempted murder. Out on bond, he fled the country and spent most of the following decade on the run in Algeria, Cuba, and other countries whose regimes were at odds with the U.S. government. While in exile, Cleaver denounced his former associate, Huey P. Newton, as a traitor to the struggle for black liberation. Some of the people whom Cleaver organized from his exile would later become key figures in the short-lived Black Liberation Army.

Returning to the United States in 1975, Cleaver announced himself a changed man. Declaring that he had experienced a religious conversion, he announced his faith in the U.S. justice and political systems, saying that it was "better to be in jail in America than a free man in most other countries." Attempted murder charges against Cleaver were dropped, and he struck a plea bargain with government prosecutors in which he was convicted of parole violations. He spent five years in prison and was released in 1980.

During the 1980s, Cleaver preached that he was a born-again Christian. Looking back on his days as a Black Panther leader, he commented, "If people had listened to Huey Newton and me in the 1960s, there would have been a holocaust in this country." He ran in the Republican primary for a U.S. Senate seat in California in 1986 but lost. By the late 1980s, his drug addiction had surfaced again. He was arrested for cocaine possession in 1992 and almost killed by a fellow addict at a drug rehabilitation center in 1994. He was working as a diversity counselor at the University of LaVerne in Southern California at the time of his death of a heart attack on May 1, 1998.

Further Reading

Cleaver, Ahmad Maceo Eldridge. *Soul on Islam.* New York: Seaburn, 2006.

Cleaver, Eldridge. *Soul on Ice.* New York: McGraw-Hill, 1968.

CNN News. "'He Was a Symbol': Eldridge Cleaver Dies at Sixty-two." Available online. URL: www. cnn.com/US/9805/01/cleaver.late.obit/. Downloaded July 17, 2009.

PBS. *Frontline.* "The Two Nations of Black America: Interview with Eldridge Cleaver." Available online. URL: http://www.pbs.org/wgbh/pages/ frontline/shows/race/interviews/ecleaver.html. Downloaded July 17, 2009.

Rout, Kathleen. *Eldridge Cleaver.* Boston: Twayne, 1991.

Cobb, James Adlai

(ca. 1876–1958) *lawyer, judge, civil rights activist*

A contentious and highly regarded lawyer who often quarreled with officials at his alma mater, Howard University, James Cobb worked to overturn laws in several states that discriminated against African Americans. The circumstances of Cobb's birth and childhood are not well documented. It is believed that he was born James Adlai Cobb around 1876 in Louisiana, probably in or near Shreveport. Cobb's mother is thought to have been Eleanor J. Pond, a white woman. The identity of his father is unknown.

Cobb was orphaned as a child, and next to nothing is known of his upbringing. He must have been given a secondary education in Louisiana because he enrolled as an undergraduate in Fisk University in Nashville, Tennessee, sometime around 1890. He transferred to Straight University (now Dillard University) in 1893 and studied there for two years but did not earn a degree. Cobb then moved to Washington, D.C., where he began to attend the Howard University School of Law. He was awarded a bachelor of law degree in 1899 and a doctor of law in 1900 from Howard.

On graduation from Howard, Cobb was admitted into the bar in Washington, D.C. He is likely to have worked as a lawyer in a solo practice, or perhaps as an assistant for a firm, until 1907. In that year, Cobb got a break in his career when he was appointed to the position of special assistant in the U.S. Department of Justice. This appointment was likely the result of Cobb's active involvement in Republican Party politics.

Cobb began working for the federal government during the second term of President Theodore Roosevelt. On many issues, the Roosevelt administration embraced political reform and progressive ideas. During his term as governor of New York, Roosevelt had worked to enact bills that would allow the state government to enforce rules about the safety and purity of medicines and foods. He carried this idea with him to the White House, and James Cobb began work at the Justice Department related to the process. From 1907 to 1915, Cobb prosecuted a number of cases under the Food and Drug Act, which had been passed by the U.S. Congress in 1906. During this time, he acquired a reputation as a zealous prosecutor and as a Republican Party stalwart.

After resigning from the Justice Department in 1915, Cobb returned to private practice in Washington, D.C. He continued to be active in Republican Party politics and as a delegate attended the Republican national conventions in Chicago in 1920 and Cleveland in 1924.

In his private practice after 1915, Cobb began to take on cases that had important constitutional implications. One of his first cases was *Buchanan v. Warley*, a suit brought by an African American against the city of Louisville. Before the Supreme Court, Cobb argued that a law passed by the city of Louisville created and maintained segregation in housing in that city, a process that was unconstitutional under the Fourteenth Amendment of the Constitution. The court, striking down the Louisville law, ruled in favor of Cobb's client in this instance.

Beginning in 1916, Cobb taught at Howard University's law school, a position he would hold until 1938. Cobb's teaching position was always part-time, and until 1929 he taught in the evening because until that year the Howard law school held classes only at night.

By 1929, Cobb had little extra time to give to the law school. As reward for his political work on behalf of the Republican Party, he had been appointed a municipal judge in Washington, D.C., in 1926. With his work as a judge and his continuing private practice, Cobb was extremely busy in the late 1920s and early 1930s.

Cobb continued to take on high-profile constitutional cases after he was appointed a District of Columbia judge. In 1927, he was a counsel on *Nixon v. Herndon*, a case that challenged laws enacted by the Texas legislature that excluded blacks from voting in Democratic primaries. The Supreme Court once again ruled in favor of Cobb's clients, stating that the Texas law was a "direct and obvious infringement" of the Fourteenth Amendment. Five years later, Cobb returned to the Supreme Court to challenge another Texas law, which gave political parties in Texas the right to determine whom they would accept as members. This law allowed the Democratic Party in that state to exclude blacks from party membership. With Cobb's assistance, this law was also struck down.

In 1935, when Cobb's term of office as municipal judge expired, President Franklin Roosevelt did not reappoint him. After his loss of the judgeship, Cobb returned to full-time private practice as a partner in Cobb, Howard, and Hayes, one of Washington's most prestigious private black law firms. He continued to teach part time at the law school at Howard until 1938, when the Howard president, Johnson, finally succeeded in firing him, allegedly because of Cobb's insubordination. Cobb retaliated against Johnson by testifying before the House Un-American Activities Committee that Johnson had once been a member of the Communist Party. The firing ended Cobb's official connection with the school at which he had studied law. Unofficially, however, he would continue to be active in affairs at Howard.

Up to his death, Cobb was active in the white and black communities in Washington. He served on the local Selective Service Board, which oversaw drafts into the U.S. armed forces. He was also a trustee of the Washington Public Library and a board member of the National Association for the Advancement of Colored People (NAACP) and the Urban League. He died on October 14, 1958, ironically the day that he was finally admitted into what had previously been the all-white D.C. Bar Association.

Further Reading

Fleming, G. James, and Christian E. Burckel. "James A. Cobb." *Who's Who in Colored America.* Yonkers, N.Y.: Christian E. Burckel, 1950.

Howard University. Archives. "Cobb, James Adlai, 1876–1958: Papers, 1897–1958." Available online. URL: http://www.founders.howard.edu/moorland-spingarn/Colla-c.htm. Downloaded July 17, 2009.

Smith, J. Clay. *Emancipation: The Making of the Black Lawyer, 1844–1944.* Philadelphia: University of Pennsylvania Press, 1999.

Connerly, Ward

(1939–) *businessman, opponent of affirmative action*

An outspoken opponent of affirmative action, Ward Connerly has overcome a youth spent in poverty to become a successful businessman and conservative political activist in the Republican Party. Connerly was born in Louisiana in 1939. His father deserted the family when Ward was two, and his mother died when he was four. His part-Irish and part-Choctaw grandmother and an uncle in California then raised him.

Connerly's family was poor but they always encouraged him to excel in school. He did well in high school and entered American River Community College in 1958. He was elected president of the American River student body in his second year. In 1960, Connerly transferred to Sacramento State University; he earned a bachelor's degree in political science from that institution in 1962.

At Sacramento State, Connerly was only one of 50 African-American students in a student body of 2,000. While attending Sacramento State, Connerly was active in the Young Democrats, a student arm of the Democratic Party. He was also elected vice president of the Sacramento State student body, then president during his senior year.

During Barry Goldwater's losing campaign for the presidency in 1964, Connerly decided to become a Republican. In the mid-1960s, he began working for the California state housing department, and in 1968 he made the leap from state

Ward Connerly, University of California regent and chairman of the American Civil Rights Institute. A conservative, Connerly led the challenge to affirmative action programs in California. *(Courtesy American Civil Rights Coalition)*

bureaucracy to politics when he was hired as an aide to the California State Assembly's Committee on Urban Affairs. His boss was a Republican representative named Pete Wilson, later to become governor.

After his stint as a legislative aide, Connerly moved to the private sector, in which he forged a successful business as a real estate developer and land consultant. In 1993, he accepted the then-governor Pete Wilson's offer of an appointment to a 12-year term as regent of the University of California.

Connerly used his position as university regent to oppose the policy of affirmative action, a stance that resulted in the approval of California Proposition 209, which abolished affirmative action programs in the University of California system in 1996. Begun in the early 1970s by the federal and many state governments, affirmative action has granted special treatment to women and members of minority groups in employment and education as a way to overcome the legacy of past discrimination against these groups. At the University of California, for instance, places were set aside for minority students whose grades and Scholastic Aptitude Test (SAT) scores were lower than those of most of the student body.

In numerous interviews and speeches Connerly has defended his opposition to affirmative action.

> It is wrong for us to discriminate against white people and Asians when we give others preferences. . . . We're not trying to eliminate preferences because we want to take opportunities away from women and minorities. . . . We believe the hard-working, high-achieving women and minorities should not have to live under the cloud of affirmative action, and it's an insulting premise that we are incapable of winning in an open competition. We want a better America, and we're convinced that affirmative action, as we know it, is now standing in the way of that objective.

In 1996, Connerly cofounded the American Civil Rights Institute (ACRI). The organization provides information on the harms of racial and gender preferences. Connerly and the ACRI have worked to get anti–affirmative action measures onto state ballots. In 2003, California voters rejected Proposition 54, which would have prohibited the state from classifying any person by race, color, ethnicity, or national origin. In 2006, Michigan voters passed the Michigan Civil Rights Initiative, which prevents the state from considering race or sex in public education, employment, or contracting.

Further Reading

Connerly, Ward. *Creating Equal: My Fight against Race Preferences.* San Francisco: Encounter, 2000.

———. *Lessons from My Uncle James: Beyond Skin Color to the Content of Our Character.* San Francisco: Encounter, 2008.

Lewin, Tamar. "Race Preferences Vote Splits Michigan." *New York Times.* 31 October 2006. Available online. URL: http://www.nytimes.com/2006/10/31/us/31michigan.html?scp=2&sq=michigan%20civil%20rights%20initiative&st=cse. Downloaded July 18, 2009.

Lynch, Michael W. Reason Online. "Ward Connerly's New Cause." Available online: URL: http://reason.com/ml/ml053101.shtml. Downloaded July 17, 2009.

Watters, Ethan. "Ward Connerly Won the Battle; Now He's Facing the War." *Mother Jones,* 21 November 1997. Available online. URL: http://motherjones.com/politics/1997/11/ward-connerly-won-battle-now-hes-facing-war. Downloaded July 17, 2009.

Copeland, John Anthony

(1836–1859) *militant abolitionist*

John Anthony Copeland was among the 22 original members of John Brown's raiders who stormed the U.S. arsenal and munitions factory at Harpers Ferry (then Harper's Ferry), Virginia. He was born into a family of free African Americans in Raleigh, North Carolina, in 1836. Probably fearing for their freedom in a South that was increasingly hostile to free blacks, the Copeland family moved to Ohio in either the late 1830s or the early 1840s.

Copeland received a high school education in Ohio, and around 1854 he enrolled as an undergraduate at Oberlin College. Copeland was probably active in the Underground Railroad, the network of abolitionists who helped runaway slaves resettle in the North or make a passage to the safety of Canada. While attending Oberlin, he was arrested and jailed for aiding a fugitive slave.

In the summer of 1859, Copeland and his uncle, Lewis Leary, were recruited by John Kagi, a close associate of John Brown, to be part of the group of men who would raid the federal arsenal at Harpers Ferry. Brown hoped to seize the well-stocked arsenal, send out riders to alert slaves in the vicinity, and provoke a general slave uprising. Brown was counting on slaves from around Harpers Ferry to abandon their masters and go to the arsenal, where he would arm them with the plentiful rifles and ammunition that were stored there. If all went well, this force could hold off state and federal troops and provoke a slave rebellion that might spread through the rest of Virginia and the South.

By late September, Copeland and the other conspirators had gathered at a farm about five miles from Harpers Ferry. There they secretly trained for their assault on the arsenal. On the morning of October 16, 1859, the members of Brown's party gathered to pray for the liberation of slaves. That night, they marched into Harpers Ferry and seized a guard at the railroad bridge and a watchman at the armory without firing a shot. However, townspeople had heard a commotion and started firing at members of Brown's party. An alarm was sent out to state and federal authorities.

The next day as the counterattack on Brown's party intensified, John Kagi, John Copeland, and the others at the rifle factory attempted to escape across the river bridge. Most were killed, but Copeland, who had fallen into the river and whose wet rifle would not fire, was captured. A small force of U.S. Marines, under the command of Robert E. Lee, later commander of the southern army during the Civil War, finished off the federal assault and captured Brown and a handful of men who were still alive.

Copeland, along with the other survivors, was held in prison and tried for murder and treason. Copeland's integrity and courage won him the respect of even his prosecutors. One of the government attorneys remarked that "he behaved with as much firmness as any of them, and with far more dignity. . . . I regretted [as much if not more, at seeing him executed than] any other of the party."

Found guilty, Copeland, Brown, and the rest were hanged on December 16, 1859. "I am dying for freedom," Copeland is reported to have said as his final words. "I could not die for a better cause. I had rather die than be a slave."

Further Reading

Anderson, Osborne P. *A Voice from Harpers Ferry.* 1861. Reprint, Atlanta: Worldview, 1980.

Earle, Jonathan. *John Brown's Raid on Harper's Ferry.* New York: Bedford, 2008.

PBS. Africans in America, Resource Bank. "John Brown's Black Raiders." Available online. URL: http://www.pbs.org/wgbh/aia/part4/4p2941.html. Downloaded July 18, 2009.

Rossbach, Jeffery. *Ambivalent Conspirators: John Brown, the Secret Six, and a Theory of Slave Violence.* Philadelphia: University of Pennsylvania Press, 1982.

Corbin, Joseph Carter

(1833–1911) *journalist, educator*

Joseph Corbin was a leading educator in the South after the Civil War. He was born Joseph Carter Corbin in Chillicothe, Ohio, on March 26, 1833. Both of his parents, William and Susan Corbin, were born free. Corbin attended small primary and secondary schools in Ohio and in 1850 enrolled as an undergraduate in Ohio University in Athens, Ohio. In 1853, Corbin became the third African American to graduate with a bachelor's degree from Ohio University. He immediately enrolled in the graduate program at Ohio University and earned a master's degree in 1856.

After receiving his master's degree, Corbin took a job as a teacher in Louisville, Kentucky. At the outbreak of the Civil War, he moved to the somewhat safer haven of Cincinnati, where he edited that city's local African-American newspaper, the *Colored Citizen.* After the war, he married Mary Jane Ward. The couple would have six children.

In 1872, during the Reconstruction period in the South when federal troops were stationed in the former rebel states, Corbin and his family moved to Little Rock, Arkansas, where he became editor of the *Daily Republican.* A Republican Party activist, Corbin was rewarded with his party's nomination for superintendent of the state school system. He narrowly won election in the Republican primary and was easily elected in the general race. However, he held this office for only two years; in 1874, he was ousted when segregationist Democrats came to power.

After being removed from office, Corbin moved to Missouri for a year; there he held a teaching job in Jefferson City. The following year, the same Democratic politicians who had defeated him at the polls summoned him back to Arkansas. Impressed with his accomplishments as state superintendent, they offered Corbin the presidency of the newly created Branch Normal College in Pine Bluffs, an all-black school.

Corbin remained at the Branch Normal College (later the University of Arkansas at Pine Bluff) until 1902. He was to encounter difficulties with funding and continuing hostility about his political beliefs during his entire tenure. From 1875 until 1883, he was the only teacher at the school, which began with a class of seven students. After 1883, he was authorized to hire one assistant.

Because of his Republican Party activity, Corbin was investigated by the Arkansas legislature in 1893. The legislative committee, citing alleged financial irregularities, called for his dismissal. The board of trustees did not fire him but reassigned many of his responsibilities to a white employee. The legislature finally succeeded in firing Corbin in 1902. Thereafter, he became principal of Merrill High School in Pine Bluff. Corbin died in Pine Bluff on January 9, 1911.

Further Reading

Encyclopedia of Arkansas. "Joseph Carter Corbin." Available online. URL: http://www.encyclopedia ofarkansas.net/encyclopedia/entry-detail.aspx? entryID=1624. Downloaded July 18, 2009.

Rothrock, Thomas. "Joseph Carter Corbin and Negro Education in the University of Arkansas." *Arkansas Historical Quarterly* 30 (Winter 1971): 277–314.

Cornish, Samuel Eli

(1795–1858) *abolitionist, editor*

A reformer and fierce opponent of slavery, Samuel Cornish was one of the early leaders of the American abolitionist and moral reform movements. Samuel Eli Cornish was born to free parents in Delaware in 1795. Not much is known about his childhood and youth before the age of 20. In 1815, he moved to Philadelphia, where he seems to have been given his first formal education and received training as a minister from John Gloucester, the minister of Philadelphia's First African Church, a Presbyterian house of worship.

By 1819, he had been ordained, and he spent the better part of that year as a missionary to slaves on the Eastern Shore of Maryland. Cornish moved to New York City in 1821 and, minus a few brief sojourns elsewhere, would make the city his home until his death.

Cornish's first six years in New York were spent organizing the New Demeter Street Presbyterian Church, which he founded the year of his arrival in the city. He built up a congregation and also was intensely busy in missionary work, which he took outside the church and onto the streets, directing his efforts toward New York City's black population. During this time, he married Jane Livingston, and they had four children.

By 1827, Cornish had decided to branch out into a different kind of secular missionary activity. That year, he and JOHN BROWN RUSSWURM founded the first African-American newspaper in the United States, *Freedom's Journal*, which was based in New York City. Cornish lasted as editor only six months but picked up the publication again under his sole editorship after it had gone out of business in 1829. He relaunched the paper as *The Rights of All* and managed to keep it in business in New York's hypercompetitive market for a year.

Also beginning in 1827, Cornish began to get involved in work with other nonchurch organizations. That year he became a board member of the New York African Free Schools, which was organized to educate black children in the city. In 1833, along with William Lloyd Garrison, Arthur and Lewis Tappan, and others, Cornish founded what was arguably the most important abolitionist group, the American Anti-Slavery Society (AAS). He served on its executive committee for five years. He also served on the New York City Vigilance Committee, a group that aided runaway slaves; the American Moral Reform Society, which advocated abstinence from alcoholic drink among other issues; the American Bible Society; the Union Missionary Society; and other organizations.

Conservative in his core beliefs, an advocate of blacks' and whites' working together for the good of all, and intensely religious, Cornish fell out with many of his black colleagues in the antislavery struggle in the 1840s. This new breed of activists were much more militant and aggressive than Cornish and advocated a form of separatism from whites and even emigration out of the United States and establishment of African-American colonies abroad. Cornish always believed that the African-American homeland was the United States. It was in that country, he felt, that blacks should remain and make their case for full rights under the Constitution.

Cornish died in Brooklyn, New York, at the age of 63 on November 6, 1858.

Further Reading

New-York Historical Society. The New York African Free School Collection. "Samuel E. Cornish."

Available online. URL: https://www.nyhistory.org/web/afs/bios/samuel-cornish.html. Downloaded July 18, 2009.

Pease, Jane H., and William H. Pease. "The Negro Conservative: Samuel Eli Cornish." In *Bound with Them in Chains: A Biographical History of the Antislavery Movement.* Westport, Conn.: Greenwood, 1972.

Quarles, Benjamin. *Black Abolitionists.* New York: Oxford, 1969.

Crosswaith, Frank Rudolph

(1892–1965) *labor organizer, editor*

An important union activist in New York City, Frank Crosswaith helped African-American workers organize in a number of industries and gain a foothold in formerly segregated union organizations such as the American Federation of Labor (AFL). Born in Fredericksted in the Danish West Indies (now part of the U.S. Virgin Islands), Frank Rudolph Crosswaith was the son of William and Anne Eliza Crosswaith. After graduating from high school in Fredericksted, he headed for New York City, where he studied at the Rand School of Social Sciences (later the New School for Social Research). In 1915, just as he was beginning his career as a union organizer, he married Alma Besard. They had three children.

When Crosswaith began his organizing career, he must have drawn considerable inspiration from two other pioneering African-American organizers, ASA PHILIP RANDOLPH and CHANDLER OWEN, a team who published and edited the militant socialist magazine *Messenger* during the late teens and early 20s in New York City. With Randolph, Crosswaith helped found in 1925 a group devoted exclusively to organizing black workers. Called the Trade Union Committee for Organizing Negro Workers, the group adopted the to-the-point slogan "Union Hours, Union Conditions, and Union Wages for the Negro Worker in New York City." Crosswaith served as executive secretary of this group for several years until he became a full-time organizer for Randolph's Brotherhood of Sleeping Car Porters (BSCP).

During the 1930s and 1940s especially, mainstream white union organizers controlled most unions. Following the sentiments of most of their membership, these activists tried to keep black workers out of higher-paying union jobs. Thus Crosswaith had two goals in his organizing drives: to integrate white unions and to gain better wages and working conditions for black workers from the companies they worked for.

To accomplish these twin aims, Crosswaith organized the Harlem Labor Committee in 1934. Because he had already won a position as an organizer in the mainly white International Ladies Garment Workers' Union (ILGWU), Crosswaith felt well positioned to open up other American Federation of Labor unions. In New York City, he concentrated on local unions that represented building service workers, motion-picture operators, and workers in the garment industry such as clothes cleaners, dyers, hat makers, and cloth cutters. He was successful in integrating most of these jobs.

During the following year, Crosswaith organized the first Negro Labor Conference, a nationwide group, which met at New York's Madison Square Garden. Twenty thousand workers and organizers showed up to hear Crosswaith and A. Philip Randolph speak to urge the adoption of resolutions calling for a 40-hour week, solidarity of black and white workers, and the passage of a child-labor bill by the New York State legislature. The Negro Labor Committee, with Crosswaith as chair, grew out of this conference. This committee established the Harlem Labor Center, which in Crosswaith's words served as "the pivotal point [for] . . . constructive efforts affecting the work-a-day life of Negro labor in Harlem and greater New York."

During the 1930s and 1940s Crosswaith, who was a socialist, was also active in party politics in New York State. Through the Harlem Labor Committee, he sought to counter the activities of the American Communist Party, of which he was deeply suspicious. Crosswaith advocated democratic socialism, which was a much different animal from the totalitarian communism of the Communist Party. He ran for several political offices in New York City as well as New York State, including the city council and the offices of secretary of state and lieutenant governor. Even though he was not elected to any of these positions, Crosswaith kept his issues alive in the public's imagination by his political activities. His high profile won him an appointment from the mayor of New York, Fiorello LaGuardia, to the New York City Housing Authority in 1942.

In 1941, as war enveloped Europe and Asia, Crosswaith and Randolph organized the March on Washington by African-American workers, which was aimed at pressuring the administration of President Franklin D. Roosevelt into opening up American industry to black workers. Faced with massive civil protest at a time when it appeared that the United States was being drawn into a world war, Roosevelt, in exchange for cancellation of the March on Washington, agreed to issue an executive order making the exclusion of black workers from defense plants illegal. This was a huge victory for black workers and for Frank Crosswaith.

Crosswaith continued his organizing work into the 1950s and edited a publication called the *Negro Labor News*. During the 1960s, he retired and moved to Chicago. He died in Chicago on June 17, 1965, and was buried in New York City.

Further Reading

Appiah, Kwame Anthony, and Henry Louis Gates, Jr. "Frank Rudolph Crosswaith." In *Africana: Civil Rights: An A-to-Z Reference of the Movement That Changed America.* Philadelphia: Running Press, 2005.

Franklin, Charles Lionel. *The Negro Labor Unionists of New York.* New York: Columbia University Press, 1936.

New York Public Library. "Inventory of the Frank R. Crosswaith Papers, 1917–1965." Available online. URL: http://www.nypl.org/research/manuscripts/scm/scmcrosw.xml. Downloaded July 18, 2009.

Seabrook, John H. "Black and White Unite: The Career of Frank R. Crosswaith." Ph.D. dissertation, Rutgers University, 1980.

Cuffe, Paul

(1759–1817) *businessman, civil rights activist*

A wealthy ship captain and ship owner, Paul Cuffe was also a political activist who sought full rights in his home state of Massachusetts for African Americans and Indians and who later worked to establish colonies of free American blacks in Sierra Leone.

Cuffe was born on Cuttyhunk Island, which is located on Buzzards Bay offshore of the port city of New Bedford in southern Massachusetts. His father, Cuffe Slocum, was a freed slave, and his mother, Ruth Moses, was an Indian who belonged to the local Wampanoag tribe. Cuffe was one of 10 children and the youngest boy in the family. On reaching maturity, he took his father's Christian name.

Sometime during his youth, Paul Cuffe became acquainted with the members of the Society of Friends, the Quakers, and, finding himself attracted to their faith, soon joined them. Southern Massachusetts and neighboring Rhode Island had proved to be hospitable places for Quakers who had settled there in the late 1600s after having been persecuted by Puritans in and around Boston.

Growing up on an island, Cuffe learned to love the sea. He probably began working as a hand on fishing ships in his early to mid teens. He may have been part-owner of a fishing ketch as early as 1783, when he was 24. In that year he also married Alice Pequit, who, like Cuffe's mother, was Wampanoag. The couple settled in Westport, Massachusetts, a small port town about 10 miles west of

New Bedford, and had eight children, six of them daughters.

Cuffe's association with the Quakers was not only in line with his moral beliefs and spiritual practice but beneficial financially. By their hard work and frugality, many Quakers by the late 1700s had managed to become wealthy through shipping ventures, and Cuffe was able to tap into their business networks to aid his own ambitions.

With other Quakers, Cuffe invested in more ships and began making whaling and coastal trade runs. Eventually he was full or part-owner of so many ships that he could not captain each one individually, leading him to hire out captains and crews. By the mid-1790s, he had begun to acquire a fortune in cod fishing through the use of U.S. government subsidies. He later made considerable amounts of money by smuggling goods from Canada during the trading embargoes and crises that resulted from the wars between Britain and Napoleonic France in the early 1800s.

By 1797, Cuffe had acquired enough wealth to buy a large farm on the banks of the Westport River. Even though he was frequently at sea for long periods, this would remain his home for the rest of his life.

Cuffe's first recorded political activity on behalf of himself and other African Americans in Massachusetts occurred in 1780, when he was 21. In that year, he and his brother refused to pay state taxes on the grounds that they were not permitted the right to vote. They also organized a group of like-minded African Americans and Indians to petition the Massachusetts legislature.

Cuffe's complaint was directed against a section of the Massachusetts Constitution of 1778 that prohibited Indians and blacks living in the state from voting. Cuffe used the powerful argument that American colonists had leveled against the British at the beginning of the American Revolution: no taxation without representation. As a citizen who had been deprived of the vote, Cuffe argued, he had no representation. Thus he should not have to pay taxes.

The legislature declined to amend the constitution in the way Cuffe wanted. However, three years later, in 1783, a Massachusetts court ruled that the offending provision was unconstitutional and threw it out. Indians and blacks were then able to vote.

By 1810, Cuffe had amassed a fleet of about 10 ships, which included a schooner, the *Ranger*; a brig, *Hero*; and his flagship, the brig *Traveller*. His closest business partner was the white Quaker merchant William Rotch, Jr. In 1810, Cuffe made his first voyage to Sierra Leone, on the western coast of Africa, to scout the territory as a possible site for a settlement of free American blacks. He was backed financially and politically by Quakers in Westport and Philadelphia and by the African Institution, an abolitionist group in London.

Cuffe was pleased by what he saw in Sierra Leone. In spite of his own success, he may have come to believe that most African Americans would not be able to advance themselves in the United States. He almost certainly believed that African Americans living in Africa could carry out Christian missionary work to convert heathen Africans, and that this work alone would have justified a colony. An astute businessman, he also saw potential to make money through three-way trade among Sierra Leone, Europe, and the United States.

Cuffe's 1810 mission was widely and favorably publicized when he stopped in London on his way back to the United States. Back home, Cuffe organized the Friendly Society to enlist African Americans to resettle in Sierra Leone. He sailed one more time to Africa in 1815 on the *Traveller* with 38 settlers. This was to be his last trip. He died on September 9, 1817, before he was able to expand the settlement he had founded only two years before.

Further Reading

Harris, Sheldon H. *Paul Cuffe: Black America and the African Return*. New York: Simon & Schuster, 1972.

PBS. Africans in America, Resource Bank. "Memoir of a Captain: Paul Cuffe, Liverpool *Mercury*." Available online. URL: http://www.pbs.org/wgbh/aia/part3/3h485t.html. Downloaded July 18, 2009.

Salvador, George Arnold. *Paul Cuffe, the Black Yankee: 1759–1817*. New Bedford, Mass.: Reynolds-DeWalt, 1969.

Vaughn, Leroy. "Paul Cuffe: America's Richest African American." University of North Carolina at Charlotte. Available online. URL: http://www.ccds.charlotte.nc.us/vaughn/diversity/cuffe.htm. Downloaded July 18, 2009.

D

Dancy, John Campbell, Jr.
(1888–1968) *community leader, Urban League executive*

Born into a relatively affluent family in Salisbury, North Carolina, John Dancy grew up to serve the African-American community in New York City and, for 42 years, in Detroit. John Campbell Dancy, Jr., was the son of John and Laura Dancy. The senior Dancy had been born a slave but by hard work and determination had put himself through college at Howard University in Washington, D.C., after the Civil War. He then moved to North Carolina, where he edited several journals of the African Methodist Episcopal Church and held the position of collector of customs in Wilmington twice.

John Dancy, Jr., attended private schools in Salisbury and later was a high school student at the Phillips Exeter Academy. He enrolled in the University of Pennsylvania in Philadelphia in 1906 and graduated with a B.A. in 1910. After graduating, Dancy worked as a principal of a West Virginia school for a year, then took a job as secretary of the Negro Young Men's Christian Association (YMCA) in Norfolk, Virginia, in 1911. He remained at that job for five years; in 1916, he moved to New York City, where he worked as a probation officer for juvenile offenders and for the Urban League.

In 1918, Dancy was hired to be the executive director of the Urban League of Detroit, Michi-

gan. As had other major northern industrial cities, Detroit had become a focus of African Americans who were migrating from the South in search of work. During World War I, especially, many jobs that had previously been off-limits to black workers because of racial discrimination opened as a result of personnel shortages.

Slowly and patiently, Dancy worked behind the scenes to secure jobs for as many blacks as he could in Detroit, and he also worked to open up the local political process to African Americans. A member of innumerable boards, including the Board of Education, the Metropolitan Planning Commission, the American Red Cross, and the Parkside Hospital, Dancy met over and over again with white business and civic leaders in Detroit to gain access to jobs for newly arrived southern blacks.

On Dancy's retirement from his position as director of the Detroit Urban League, the *Detroit Free Press* wrote, "Dancy has had possibly the greatest impact of any individual on race relations in Detroit. Others have been momentarily more militant, more dramatic, but none has been more effective." Dancy died on September 10, 1968, at the age of 80.

Further Reading
Detroit African-American History Project. "John Dancy, Jr." Available online. URL: http://www.

daahp.wayne.edu/biographiesDisplay.php?id=103. Downloaded July 19, 2009.

Logan, Rayford, and Michael Winston. *Dictionary of American Negro Biography*. New York: W. W. Norton, 1982.

Davis, Angela

(1944–   ) *Black Power leader, educator*

A controversial participant in the Civil Rights movement of the 1960s, Angela Davis has remained a committed activist who has spoken out for economic justice and prison reform. Davis was born in Birmingham, Alabama, on January 26, 1944, to Frank and Sally Davis. Hers was a solidly middle-class family; her father was a businessman and her mother a teacher.

A bright student, Davis graduated from high school at age 17 in 1961. She enrolled as an undergraduate at Brandeis University but spent a few years in Europe studying at the University of Paris. Returning home in 1964, Davis completed her undergraduate studies in political science at Brandeis University in Massachusetts. She was awarded a B.A. from Brandeis in 1965.

After her graduation, Davis spent a year in Germany studying under the German Marxist professor Theodor Adorno. She returned to the United States in 1966 and enrolled as a graduate student at the University of California at San Diego (U.C. San Diego), where Herbert Marcuse, a German-born political philosopher who was a friend and colleague of Theodor Adorno, influenced her.

In San Diego, Davis concentrated her studies on Marxist philosophy, which she saw as the best approach for solving the many economic and social ills of the United States. Around 1968, at the same time she received her master's degree from U.C. San Diego, she joined the U.S. Communist Party and became active in the Black Panthers, one of the most radical of the civil rights organizations to spring up in the late 1960s.

The Black Panthers (also known simply as the Panthers) advocated black power, a form of black separatism. The Panthers were active in many of the urban ghettos of California and the North, and their message was aimed especially at poor blacks who lived in the ghetto. They urged African Americans to form their own organizations separate from white society. They preached in favor of socialism, or state control of many business enterprises, and advocated resisting the police with violence if necessary.

Davis quickly became a symbol of a new style of militant black woman. In 1970, because of her political affiliations, the regents of the University of California fired her from her teaching position. That same year, she was caught up in an armed escape attempt that had gone bad in Marin County, California. Several imprisoned Black Panthers who were having a court hearing at the Marin County Courthouse somehow were slipped weapons and tried to escape. The event ended in a bloody shoot-out in which a judge and one of the inmates were killed. Davis was charged as a conspirator in this case and for about three weeks was on the run. She was captured in August 1970 and in a trial in 1972 was found not guilty of the charges against her.

By the mid-1970s, Davis was again employed as a teacher, this time at San Francisco State University. She later became a professor at the University of California at Santa Cruz. She is the author of a number of books, including *Women, Race, and Class* (1981), *Are Prisons Obsolete?* (2003), and *The Meaning of Freedom* (2009). She continues to be politically active and has focused much of her attention on prisoner rights. Currently, she is a board member of the Prison Activist Resource Center. Davis is a frequent speaker at college campuses, discussing issues involving racism, feminism, class, prisons, and the legacy of slavery. She began teaching at Syracuse University as a visiting professor of women's and gender studies and African-American studies in 2010.

Further Reading

Davis, Angela. *Angela Davis: An Autobiography.* New York: Random House, 1974.

James, Joy, ed. *The Angela Y. Davis Reader.* Hoboken, N.J.: Wiley-Blackwell, 2006.

PBS. *Frontline.* "The Two Nations of Black America. Interview with Angela Davis." Available online. URL: http://www.pbs.org/wgbh/pages/frontline/shows/race/interviews/davis.html. Downloaded July 1, 2009.

Davis, Benjamin Jefferson, Jr.

(1903–1964) *lawyer, community activist*

A lawyer and civil rights activist who defended black communists in the South and later became a Communist Party official in New York City, Benjamin Davis believed that discrimination against African Americans could be overcome only by a revolutionary change in the American political and social system. He was born Benjamin Jefferson Davis, Jr., on September 8, 1903, in Dawson, Georgia. In 1909, Davis's father, Benjamin, Sr., moved his family to Atlanta and founded a weekly newspaper, the *Independent,* directed at the African-American community.

After graduating from high school in Atlanta in 1920, Davis attended Morehouse University for a year, then transferred to Amherst College in Massachusetts. A member of Amherst's football team, band, and debating society, Davis graduated with honors in 1925 and entered Harvard Law School. He earned a law degree from Harvard in 1929.

In 1932, Davis returned to Atlanta to practice law. In June of that year, he defended a young black communist activist named Angelo Herndon, who had been arrested in Atlanta for organizing a labor protest. He was charged under an 1861 Georgia law that outlawed slave insurrections. The law had been amended in 1871 to include whites as well as blacks who fomented "insurrection." The maximum sentence for a

guilty verdict under this law was the death sentence. The prosecutors argued that merely by possessing communist literature, Angelo Herndon was guilty of insurrection against the state government.

In court, Davis argued that under the U.S. Constitution his client had the right to organize workers to strike and make demands of their employers. Furthermore, Davis said, Herndon had the right to protest peaceably and organize others to protest with him. The Georgia statute that Herndon was charged with violating, David argued, was unconstitutional because it was based on a slave ordinance. Also, Davis noted, Herndon could not receive a fair trial in Georgia because he would not be tried by a jury of his peers: African Americans were not allowed to serve on juries.

After an ugly trial—in which the judge frequently turned his back on Davis as he was making arguments to the jury and in which the prosecutors were allowed to use racial pejoratives when referring to Davis and Herndon—Herndon was found guilty by an all-white jury. However, realizing that the maximum sentence was inappropriate for this case, the jurors asked the judge to spare Herndon's life. Herndon was sentenced to 18 to 20 years in prison, but on appeal, he was finally released from prison after serving five years.

Davis was deeply shocked by his experience with the white justice system in the Herndon trial. "It was the turning point of my life," he was to say later. "[I wanted] to hit this thing, this Jim Crow system. I considered that the best thing I could do was join the Communist Party."

Davis made good on his convictions, and in 1935, he left Atlanta and went to New York City to work at the U.S. Communist Party's headquarters. He became editor of the *Liberator,* the party paper that was aimed at African Americans. He also began working on the editorial staff of the main Communist paper, the *Daily Worker.*

In the 1940s, Davis jumped into New York City electoral politics. After losing a race for a seat on the city council, Davis ran again in 1943 and became the city councilman from a district in Manhattan. He ran again in 1945 and won by an even bigger margin. As a councilman, Davis demanded investigations into allegations of police brutality against blacks, overcrowding in Harlem hospitals, and segregated housing. Davis's tenure as a councilman ended in 1949, when he failed to win reelection.

By this time, Davis had become a target of the anticommunist hysteria that was to consume American politics during the late 1940s and early 1950s. He was indicted by a federal grand jury in 1948 for violation of the Smith Act, which made it illegal for anyone to advocate the overthrow of the U.S. government. As a Communist Party member, the government argued, Davis was automatically guilty of this charge. In September 1949, Davis was convicted and served three years of a 10-year sentence in a federal prison.

During the 1950s, and 1960s, Davis remained active in Communist Party activities. He was again indicted by a federal grand jury in 1962, but he died on August 22, 1964, before he was to be brought to trial.

Further Reading

Patterson, William L. *Ben Davis: Crusader for Negro Freedom and Socialism.* New York: New Outlook, 1967.

Record, Wilson. *The Negro and the Communist Party.* 1951. Reprint, New York: Atheneum, 1971.

Smith, J. Clay. *Emancipation: The Making of the Black Lawyer, 1844–1944.* Philadelphia: University of Pennsylvania Press, 1999.

Day, William Howard

(1825–1900) *abolitionist, editor, educator*

A leader in demanding civil rights for African Americans and the abolition of slavery, William Day pursued a long career as a newspaper editor, civil rights organizer, and educator. William How-ard Day was born on October 19, 1825, in New York City. His parents, John and Eliza Day, were wealthy enough to be able to send Day to private schools in Massachusetts. While a high school student in Northampton, Massachusetts, Day learned to be a printer, a trade that would help him in later years, at the *Northampton Gazette.*

After graduating from a public high school in Northampton in 1842, Day passed a rigorous examination in mathematics, Greek, and Latin and was admitted to Oberlin College, a progressive university in Ohio. The only African American in his class of 50, Day excelled at Oberlin and was able to pay his tuition by working as a printer for a newspaper. He graduated in 1847 and moved to Cleveland. He was married in 1852 to Lucy Stanton, another Oberlin graduate.

In Cleveland, Day began a lifelong career of civil rights work on behalf of the African-American community. To confront racist laws in Ohio and other states that discriminated against blacks, in 1848 he organized a convention of free blacks, called the National Convention of Colored Freeman. Along with FREDERICK DOUGLASS, Day spoke to the convention about working for full rights for free blacks in the North. He was chosen by the convention as the spokesman to address the Ohio legislature in an effort to repeal Ohio's so-called Black Laws. These laws banned free blacks from settling in Ohio unless the migrants could show proof of freedom and obtain financial backing from two free Ohio citizens. Blacks were also banned from public schools and could not testify against a white person in a trial. Day's speech before the Ohio legislature and his continued lobbying of legislators eventually resulted in the removal of these laws from the Ohio statutes.

Day continued to live and work in Cleveland until 1856. In 1851, he began working as a printer and editor at the *Cleveland Daily Democrat.* By 1853, he was working as an editor at another Cleveland newspaper, the *Aliened American,* which was marketed to African Americans and strongly supported the abolition of slavery. In

1854, Day won appointment as librarian of the Cleveland Library Association, which served as the city's only library until the public library was founded a few years later.

During his time as newspaper editor and librarian in Cleveland, Day continued his civil rights work. In 1852, he organized a commemoration of the deeds of black veterans of the War of 1812. By 1857, strained by overwork, Day's health began to fade. When a doctor recommended that he spend time on a farm to recover, Day left Cleveland for Elgin, a small town of African Americans who had fled the United States for Canada. Near the larger town of Buxon, Ontario, Elgin offered Day peace and rest. He soon recovered and returned to organizing work.

Day supervised the printing in Canada of John Brown's new constitution for the United States, which Brown hoped would be established in the event that his uprising in Harpers Ferry was successful. In 1858, Day was elected president of board of commissioners of the Colored People of Canada and the United States. Accompanied by a Canadian clergyman, Day decided to travel to the British Isles to raise money for a church and school for the Elgin community. Within a few years, he had helped raise $35,000 for this effort.

Possibly as a result of his involvement with John Brown's failed raid on Harpers Ferry, Day would remain in Britain for five years. As president of the Colored People of Canada and the United States, he authorized MARTIN ROBISON DELANY to travel to the Niger Valley on the west coast of Africa and scout it as a site for a possible colony for African Americans. With Delany, he formed the African Aid Society. In an effort to win over British public opinion, Day also lectured about the evils of slavery throughout the British Isles.

In 1863, with the Civil War well under way and any possible criminal charges against him as a result of his involvement in John Brown's raid forgotten, Day returned to the United States. For a time, having won an appointment as inspector general of schools for the Freedmen's Bureau, Day lived in Delaware and Maryland to work at this job. After the war, Day remained in Delaware, where he organized black voters and succeeded in achieving election of African Americans to the Delaware House of Representatives.

In 1872, Day moved to Harrisburg, Pennsylvania, where he would remain until the end of his life. Appointed a clerk in the state auditor's office, in 1878 he was elected to the Harrisburg school board. He was reelected several more times and eventually would serve as school board president from 1891 to 1893. Day was Harrisburg's first African-American school board president and possibly the first black school board president of a predominantly white public school system in the country.

On his death on December 3, 1900, Day was remembered by the *Harrisburg Telegraph* as "one of the leading men of his race."

Further Reading

Davis, Russell H. *Black Americans in Cleveland from George Peake to Carl B. Stokes, 1796–1969.* Washington, D.C.: Associated Publishers, 1972.

Pennsylvania Center for the Book. "William Howard Day." Available online. URL: http://pabook.libraries.psu.edu/palitmap/bios/Day__William_Howard.html. Downloaded July 19, 2009.

De Baptiste, George

(1814–1875) *abolitionist, civil rights leader, business leader*

An important "conductor" on the Underground Railroad, George De Baptiste became one of the wealthiest men in Detroit, Michigan. Born in 1814 to William and Eliza De Baptiste, free blacks from Fredericksburg, Virginia, George De Baptiste moved as a youth to Richmond, where he learned the trade of barber. For a few years during his 20s, De Baptiste traveled throughout the South as the personal valet to a professional gambler.

By 1838, De Baptiste had married his first wife, Lucinda Lee, and moved with her to Madison, Wisconsin, to open a barbershop. They would eventually have 10 children. On moving to Wisconsin, De Baptiste, as were all free blacks who moved into the state, was required by the state government to post a $500 bond. He sued to overturn this law and won in the state supreme court.

The next year, De Baptiste became the personal valet of William Henry Harrison, the former governor of Indiana Territory. He remained with Harrison through his successful campaign for the presidency in 1840. On Harrison's death after only one month in office, De Baptiste moved back to Wisconsin to resume his barbering business. As a result of the hostility of the white population, he left Wisconsin in 1846 for Detroit.

In Detroit, De Baptiste continued to have success as a businessman. Besides owning a barbershop, he opened a bakery, several catering businesses, and a restaurant. He would eventually also own a steamboat that ferried passengers between Detroit and Sandusky, Ohio.

From the beginning of his residence in Detroit, De Baptiste was active in the Underground Railroad, the organization that helped escaped slaves from the South establish a new life for themselves in the North and Canada. In Detroit, blacks, under De Baptiste's leadership, formed several secret associations, such as the African-American Mysteries and the Order of Emigration, to provide food and shelter to fugitive slaves.

In 1859, De Baptiste was one of a small number of African-American leaders who met with John Brown and FREDERICK DOUGLASS to hear of Brown's plans for a slave uprising in the South. De Baptiste supposedly suggested that a terror campaign accompany Brown's revolt, through the bombing of white churches in various spots in the South on a particular Sunday. This idea was never carried out.

After the Civil War, De Baptiste continued to work for the civil rights of blacks in Michigan. He served on the first Negro jury in 1870 and also successfully pushed the Detroit city government to desegregate the public schools.

De Baptiste died on February 25, 1875, characterized by one Detroit newspaper as "a bold, uncompromising advocate of right and justice [and] a firm friend of the poor and oppressed."

Further Reading

City of Detroit. "George [D]e Baptiste Home." Available online. URL: http://www.ci.detroit.mi.us/ historic/districts/depaptiste_hse.pdf. Downloaded July 19, 2009.

Clarke Historical Library. "Death of George De Baptiste." Available online. URL: http://clarke.cmich. edu/undergroundrailroad/georgedebaptiste.htm. Downloaded July 19,2009.

Katzman, David M. *Before the Ghetto: Black Detroit in the Nineteenth Century.* Urbana: University of Illinois Press, 1972.

Ripley, C. Pete. *Black Abolitionist Papers.* Vol. 1. Chapel Hill: University of North Carolina Press, 1985–1992.

Delany, Martin Robison

(1812–1885) *abolitionist, emigration leader, physician*

A leader in the movement to end slavery, Martin Delany later became an advocate of the mass migration of African Americans out of the United States. One of five siblings, Martin Robison Delany was born on May 6, 1812, in Charles Town, Virginia. Delany was the son of Samuel Delany and Pati Peace Delany. His father was for a time a slave; his mother was born free.

Because both of Delany's grandfathers had been born in Africa, Delany grew up with a close connection to that continent through the stories passed down by his elders. During his childhood, Delany and his brothers and sisters were taught to read by a northern traveling salesman. Teaching blacks to read was a crime in Virginia at that time, and the family had to move when a white neighbor discovered this act of kindness.

To avoid prosecution, the Delanys settled in Chambersburg, Pennsylvania, in 1822. They were followed there a year later by Samuel Delany, who had purchased his freedom. Delany finished primary school in Chambersburg, and in 1831, at the age of 19, he left for the larger city of Pittsburgh, where he worked on his secondary education in a night school that was housed in the basement of the city's African Episcopal Methodist Church. He also apprenticed himself to a white doctor and began working as a physician's assistant.

By the mid-1830s, Delany had become active in the Pittsburgh Anti-Slavery Society and helped escaped slaves settle in the northern Pennsylvania area through the network known as the Underground Railroad. In 1843, Delany married Catherine Richards. The couple had seven children who survived into adulthood.

In 1844, Delany began publishing the *Mystery*, the first African-American paper to the west of the Allegheny Mountains. A weekly newspaper, the *Mystery* reported local meetings and social events and kept the local black populace abreast of news about politics and the antislavery movement. Delany was able to keep the paper afloat for three years before debts forced the paper's closure in 1847.

Almost immediately after the collapse of the *Mystery*, Delany launched another paper, the *North Star*, with the collaboration of the famed abolitionist leader FREDERICK DOUGLASS. Though the *North Star* was based in Rochester, New York, Douglass's home at the time, for a year and a half Delany was coeditor. Traveling often through Ohio and Michigan to give speeches for abolitionist organizations, Delany also wrote dispatches back to the *North Star* that described the African-American communities of the Midwest. During one of these trips, he narrowly escaped lynching by a hostile crowd in an Ohio town.

By June 1848, Delany had resigned his editorship of the *North Star* to return to the study of medicine. Because of his race, his applications to several schools in the Northeast were rejected. However, possibly because the faculty thought he was white, he was admitted to Harvard in 1850. Because of protests by white students, Delany was able to remain for only one term. After being thrown out of Harvard, Delany returned to Pittsburgh. Because at the time there were no licensing requirements for doctors, he began calling himself a physician and set up a practice.

In his free time, Delany threw himself into the controversy surrounding the passage of the

A painting of Martin Robison Delany from the mid-1800s. A committed abolitionist, Delany was one of the first African Americans to endorse a black nationalist political position. (*Moorland-Spingarn Research Center, Howard University*)

Fugitive Slave Law of 1850. After the Congress passed this piece of legislation, every fugitive slave living in the North was subject to rearrest and a return to slavery by U.S. marshals. Free blacks were fearful of false accusations that they were escaped slaves. Few African Americans in the North felt safe.

By 1852, Delany had begun to have doubts about whether blacks could consider the United States home. His experience at Harvard and the uncertain conditions that resulted from the Fugitive Slave Law had caused him to rethink the position of African Americans in the United States. To express his doubts, he wrote *The Condition, Elevation, Emigration and Destiny of the Colored People of the United States,* a pamphlet that was published in 1852 by a firm in Philadelphia. In this publication, Delany urged blacks to depend only on themselves for their salvation. This rejection of white society, including rejection of the help of white abolitionists, marked the beginning of a political stance called black nationalism. To Delany, African Americans were "a nation within a nation. We must go from our oppressors."

Throughout the 1850s, Delany worked on schemes to arrange a mass migration of African Americans out of the United States. He conducted research on the suitability of places such as Central America, Hawaii, Haiti, and West Africa. Feeling threatened by the Fugitive Slave Act, Delany moved with his family to Canada, where more than 10,000 other U.S. blacks had moved since 1850. In 1854, he organized the National Emigration Convention in Cleveland, which had the purpose of gathering together African Americans to discuss emigration.

In 1859, Delany finally was able to travel to Liberia and the area around the Niger River Valley in what is now the nation of Nigeria. He negotiated a treaty with the king of Abbeokuta in the Niger River area for a colony of refugee American blacks, and during a stay in England on his way home gave talks to English groups about his plans and experiences in Africa.

By the time Delany returned to the United States in 1861, the North and South were at war. By 1863, Delany suspended his emigration plans and began to help the U.S. government recruit black soldiers for the army. He raised troops for all-black outfits in Massachusetts, Rhode Island, and Connecticut and was commissioned a major in the army.

Delany ended the war commanding two regiments of former slaves in Charleston, South Carolina. With war's end, he won a civilian appointment as assistant commissioner of the Freedmen's Bureau in Hilton Head, South Carolina. Fearing for the safety of his family, he installed his wife and children in Wilberforce, Ohio, while he worked in South Carolina. He remained at this job until 1873, when he became a lieutenant colonel in the state militia and a member of the Republican Party executive committee.

Delany remained in South Carolina until 1880. By then, the state had returned to the rule of the white-controlled Democratic Party. Toward the end of his South Carolina sojourn, he again attempted to revive the idea of emigration back to Africa by forming the Liberian Exodus Joint Stock Exchange Company. However, this venture ended in bankruptcy and Delany returned to Ohio to join his family. He died in Wilberforce at age 73 on January 24, 1885.

Further Reading

Adeleke, Tunde. *Without Regard to Race: The Other Martin Robison Delany.* Jackson: University of Mississippi Press, 2004.

Levine, Robert S. *Martin Delany, Frederick Douglass, and the Politics of Representative Identity.* Chapel Hill: University of North Carolina Press, 1997.

Martin Delany Homepage. "To Be More Than Equal: The Many Lives of Martin R. Delany." Available online. URL: http://www.libraries.wvu.edu/delany/home.htm. Downloaded July 19, 2009.

Sterling, Dorothy. *The Making of an Afro-American: Martin Robison Delany.* New York: Da Capo, 1996.

Derricotte, Juliette Aline
(1897–1931) *Young Women's Christian Association (YWCA) organizer, educator*

An educator and passionate advocate of interracial understanding, Juliette Derricotte worked during her life to bridge the gap between whites and African Americans in the United States. Born on April 1, 1897, in Athens, Georgia, Juliette Aline Derricotte was one of five children of Isaac and Laura Derricotte. She studied at public elementary and secondary schools in Athens.

When she was young, Derricotte learned first-hand about racial discrimination when she was denied admission to the Lucy Cobb Institute, a private all-white school in Athens. Much of her later life was devoted to tearing down the walls built by racial segregation.

After graduating from high school in 1914, Derricotte attended Talladega College in Alabama. Graduating from Talladega in 1918, she moved to New York City, where she studied for a summer at the national training school of the Young Women's Christian Association (YWCA). After finishing this course of study, she was hired as traveling secretary for the YWCA's National Council. Her job was to lecture about the goals of the YWCA and organize YWCA forums on college campuses.

As traveling secretary, Derricotte was sent overseas twice—in 1924 to England, where she represented the YWCA at the World Student Christian Federation conference, and in 1928 to India, China, and Japan, where she gave a series of lectures. In 1929 Derricotte accepted an offer from Fisk University in Nashville, Tennessee, to become dean of women students.

Derricotte held her position at Fisk for only three years. On November 6, 1931, she was involved in an automobile accident in Dalton, Georgia, that left her critically injured. Because the local hospital in Dalton did not take black patients, she had to be moved by ambulance the next day to Chattanooga, Tennessee. She died soon after arriving at the Chattanooga hospital. She was only 34 years old.

Further Reading
Jeanness, Mary. *Twelve Negro Americans*. 1936. Reprint, Freeport, N.Y.: Books for Libraries Press, 1969.

Robertson, Nancy Marie. *Christian Sisterhood, Race Relations, and the YWCA, 1906–46*. Champaign: University of Illinois Press, 2007.

Desdunes, Rodolphe Lucien
(1849–1928) *community activist*

An energetic chronicler of the life of blacks in New Orleans, Rodolphe Desdunes was deeply involved in protecting the civil liberties of African Americans in his native city. Born in New Orleans, Louisiana, on November 15, 1849, Rodolphe Lucien Desdunes was the oldest child of Jeremiah and Henrietta Desdunes. The Desdunes family history is interesting and typical of the cosmopolitan mix found in New Orleans. His mother was originally from Cuba, and his father's family emigrated from Haiti, probably after the revolution on that island in the 1790s. The family, which owned a tobacco plantation and cigar factory, was wealthy, and Desdunes was well educated by private tutors and later at the Bernard Convent school.

Not wanting to work in the family businesses, Desdunes got a job at the busy New Orleans customs house as a messenger in 1879. The job was political and given to patrons of whichever political party was then in power in Washington, D.C. Except for a lapse of six years in the late 1880s when the Democrats controlled the White House, Desdunes worked at the customs house until 1912. In 1899, he was promoted to weigher.

Desdunes was always proud of his native city and especially of its black citizens. During the 1890s, he wrote articles for the *Daily Crusader*, an African-American publication. He became a director of the Bernard Convent School, and in

1890 he was instrumental in organizing the Comité des Citoyens (the Citizen's Committee), whose goal was to protect African Americans in New Orleans from newly enacted laws that tightened racial segregation in public institutions and places and that deprived blacks of their voting rights. The Comité was instrumental in bringing the famous *Plessy v. Ferguson* lawsuit, which it hoped would kill the segregated Jim Crow system. Instead, the U.S. Supreme Court used *Plessy* to give an official blessing to racial segregation laws.

In 1911, Desdunes was partially blinded when dust from granite blocks that were being unloaded at the New Orleans docks blew into his eyes. As a result of his injury, he was forced to take early retirement from his customs house job in 1912. In spite of his blindness, he wrote a book about famous African Americans in New Orleans, published in French in 1912 as *Nos Hommes et notre histoire*. This work was translated into English in 1973 and published as *Our People and Our History*.

Desdunes died of cancer in New Orleans on August 14, 1928. He was laid to rest in the city's old and famous Saint Louis Cemetery.

Further Reading

Battle, Karen. "New Orleans Creoles of Color." Loyola University Web site. Available online. URL: http://www.loyno.edu/history/journal/1991-2/battle.htm. Downloaded July 19, 2009.

Medley, Keith Weldon. *We as Freemen*: Plessy v. Ferguson. Gretna, La.: Pelican, 2003.

Douglass, Frederick

(Frederick Washington Bailey)
(ca. 1817–1895) *abolitionist, journalist, civil rights activist*

One of the most important African-American leaders of the 19th century, Frederick Douglass, a former slave, worked for the abolition of slavery before the Civil War and the full extension of civil rights to black citizens after the war. He was born Frederick Washington Bailey on or around February 14, 1817, although the exact date and year of his birth are not known for sure. His mother was Harriet Bailey, a slave who worked on the plantation of Aaron Anthony, located in Tuckahoe, Maryland. Although Frederick never knew his father, he believed that he may have been Anthony.

In his childhood, Frederick Bailey was a companion of Aaron Anthony's acknowledged son. At age eight, Bailey was sent from the country to Baltimore, where he was taught to read and write and worked as a house servant. He worked in Baltimore for seven years, then returned to the Anthony plantation when he was 15.

Bailey, who had had a relatively carefree existence during his time in Baltimore, resented the tight restrictions that were imposed on the slaves in the country. In 1836, at the age of 19, he tried to escape from Anthony's plantation but was caught. Although the punishment for attempted escape could be severe, including being branded on the forehead and sold to another owner in the Deep South, Bailey seems to have been given a warning and sent back to Baltimore. He worked as a caulker at a shipyard for two years until, using the papers of a sailor he had befriended, he made a successful escape by sea to New York City.

In New York City, DAVID RUGGLES, a free black man who was active in the New York Vigilance Committee, hid Douglass and reunited him with Anna Murray, a free woman of color with whom Douglass had become romantically involved while working in Baltimore. After they were married, the Douglasses moved to New Bedford, Massachusetts, to start a new life.

Douglass took whatever jobs he could get in New Bedford while he acclimated himself in his new surroundings. He quickly made himself familiar with the movement to abolish slavery, called abolitionism, which was fast gaining converts in the northern states. In August 1841, he was drafted into the movement after he gave a riveting

Frederick Douglass ca. 1890. Perhaps the most important African-American leader of the 19th century, Douglass was an abolitionist before the Civil War and a civil rights leader later in his life. *(Moorland-Spingarn Research Center, Howard University)*

and informative speech at a meeting of the Massachusetts Anti-Slavery Society in Nantucket.

Douglass worked for four years as a speaker with the Massachusetts group, and during that time he became well acquainted with the white abolitionists William Lloyd Garrison and Wendell Phillips. Although he was naturally eloquent, Douglass became an even better speaker the longer he worked at it. Mixing his own experiences as a slave into a well-reasoned argument against the institution of slavery, Douglass won over audiences, in the words of one newspaper editor, with an "enunciation quite elegant" and a presentation that alternated "wit, argument, sarcasm, and pathos."

In May 1845, Douglass published a written account of his life as a slave and his escape from bondage. Called *Narrative of the Life of Frederick Douglass*, this book created a sensation in the United States. Because his whereabouts had been revealed, it also exposed Douglass to the possibility of being kidnapped and returned to slavery. To prevent this, Douglass traveled to the United Kingdom for an extended lecture tour in August 1845.

Douglass spent almost two years in England and made friends with English slave trade reformers such as John Bright and Thomas Clarkson. His English friends raised a fund to purchase his freedom, which allowed him to return safely to the United States. They also gave him $2,000 with which to start a newspaper.

On his return to his native country, Douglass moved with his family to Rochester, New York, to start a newspaper, the *North Star*, dedicated to ending slavery and promoting civil rights for blacks. The next year, 1848, he was chosen president of the Colored Convention Movement, an association of free northern blacks who protested discrimination against blacks, especially in employment, in the North. In the meantime, he used his Rochester newspaper offices personally to help more than 400 slaves escape to Canada. Douglass roundly attacked the Fugitive Slave Law, passed by the U.S. Congress in 1850, declaring that the "true remedy for the Fugitive Slave Bill . . . [was] a good revolver, a steady hand, and a determination to shoot any man attempting to kidnap."

As confrontation between the North and South seemed increasingly likely, Douglass threw his support to the newly created Republican Party. In 1860, despite some misgivings about the willingness of Abraham Lincoln to use federal power to free the slaves, Douglass backed Lincoln in his effort to win the presidency.

During the subsequent Civil War, Douglass became a paid recruiter for all-black Union army outfits made up of volunteers from the North.

Simultaneously, Douglass pushed northern states to drop laws that restricted the right of poor blacks to vote. At the end of the war, Douglass continued to pressure federal officials such as President Andrew Johnson to give African Americans the right to vote in the South as well. The Fifteenth Amendment, passed in 1870, secured this right.

In 1872, Douglass moved with his family from Rochester to Washington, D.C., where he would live for the rest of his life. He was rewarded for his loyal support of the Republican Party in 1877 when President Rutherford Hayes appointed him marshal of the District of Columbia. In 1881, he was appointed recorder of deeds for the District of Columbia, a position he held until 1886.

After the death of his first wife, Douglass remarried in 1884—this time a white woman, Helen Pitts, who had worked with him in the District of Columbia's Recorder's Office. In 1889, after campaigning hard for the Republicans again, Douglass was appointed ambassador to Haiti, a position he would hold until 1891.

During his years as a federal officeholder, Douglass did not temper his advocacy of full civil rights for African Americans. He went out on frequent speaking tours, always calling for the enforcement of existing voting laws and an end to the racial discrimination that was becoming known as Jim Crow. This system was based on laws, mainly but not exclusively in the South, that barred blacks from eating in certain restaurants, drinking at public water fountains, sitting with whites on trains, and holding certain jobs.

Douglass was an integrationist and a conciliator. He wanted blacks and whites to live together peacefully. He did not, as some of his contemporaries did, believe that blacks should build a society in the United States separate from whites.

Frederick Douglass died on February 20, 1895, of a heart attack in his home in Anacostia, District of Columbia. In the 1950s, Douglass's home was made a national shrine by the U.S. Department of Interior.

Further Reading

Foner, Philip S. *Frederick Douglass.* New York: Citadel, 1964.

McFeely, William S. *Frederick Douglass.* New York: Norton, 1991.

Meltzer, Milton, ed. *Frederick Douglass: In His Own Words.* San Diego, Calif.: Harcourt Brace, 1995.

PBS. Africans in America, Resource Bank. "Frederick Douglass." Available online. URL: http://www.pbs.org/wgbh/aia/part4/4p1539.html. Downloaded July 19, 2009.

Stauffer, John. *Giants: The Parallel Lives of Frederick Douglass and Abraham Lincoln.* New York: Twelve, 2008.

DuBois, W. E. B.

(William Edward Burghardt DuBois)
(1868–1963) *educator, writer, civil rights activist, pan-African leader*

One of the most important African-American leaders of the 20th century, W. E. B. DuBois created the intellectual framework and organizational support that helped all Americans conceptualize their race problems and aided black Americans in overcoming them. Born on February 23, 1868, William Edward Burghardt DuBois was the son of Alfred and Mary Silvina Burghardt DuBois. After his father deserted the family when DuBois was still a child, his mother was left with the task of working to earn a living and raising her son. She died shortly after his graduation from high school in Great Barrington, Massachusetts, in 1884.

DuBois seems to have experienced little racial prejudice directed toward him during his youth in Great Barrington. It was only when he ventured south in 1885 to study at Fisk University in Nashville, Tennessee, that he encountered racism firsthand. At Fisk, he earned a B.A. and edited the school newspaper. He also taught in rural schools during his summer vacations. His contact with southern racism caused him to reassess his place in his native country. He then believed that "a new loyalty and allegiance replaced my Americanism; henceforth I was a Negro."

After receiving his undergraduate degree from Fisk, DuBois enrolled as an undergraduate junior in Harvard University, the school that had been his first choice all along. He studied with such well-known thinkers as William James and George Santayana, and he concentrated on social sciences and history. DuBois graduated with honors from Harvard in 1890 and was chosen to be one of five student commencement speakers. His speech was about Jefferson Davis, president of the Confederacy; the topic was the history and legacy of slavery.

DuBois then studied at Harvard for another year, gaining a master's degree, before winning a grant to study at the University of Berlin in Germany while he worked to finish his doctoral dissertation. He remained in Germany from 1892 to 1894 and during that time finished his dissertation, entitled *The Suppression of the African Slave Trade,* a detailed and well-researched look at the rise and fall of the trade in human commerce between Africa and the Americas. This work was published as a book in 1896.

In 1895, after he had earned his Ph.D. from Harvard, the first African American to do so, DuBois began a long teaching career. He worked first at Wilberforce University, a predominantly African-American school, where he taught languages, including Greek and Latin. In 1897, he took a year off to do a sociological study of blacks in Philadelphia. He then went to Atlanta University in Georgia, where he would spend 13 productive years as an educator, thinker, activist, and writer.

During his time in Atlanta, DuBois taught history and economics and made the acquaintance of the main African-American leader of that time, BOOKER TALIAFERRO WASHINGTON, head of the Tuskegee Institute in Alabama and prominent spokesman for the aspirations of American blacks. For most of these years, the two men got on fairly well, even though the older leader resented and criticized DuBois's more militant approach to race relations between blacks and whites. For instance, Washington opposed the goals of the Niagara Movement, a group organized by DuBois in 1905, which was a forerunner of the National Association for the Advancement of Colored People (NAACP), of which DuBois was also a founder in 1909. DuBois, in numerous articles and through the Niagara Movement and NAACP, demanded full rights for African Americans and prescribed legal challenges to any laws or actions that denied blacks their rights.

W. E. B. DuBois ca. 1930. A leading intellectual in the early 20th century, DuBois was a driving force in the founding of the National Association for the Advancement of Colored People (NAACP) in 1909. *(Library of Congress, Prints and Photographs Division, LC-USZ62-84495)*

During his time in Georgia, DuBois wrote one of his best-known and most enduring books, *The Souls of Black Folk* (1903), a collection of essays that examined the meaning of being African American at the turn of the 20th century. He later published a novel, *Quest of the Silver* (1911). In a paper published by Atlanta University he pithily summarized the great question confronting African Americans then as now: "Am I an American or a Negro? Can I be both? Or is my duty to cease to be a Negro as soon as possible and be an American?"

In 1910, feeling that he had made his mark in Atlanta and as a teacher and university researcher, DuBois ventured beyond the university by moving to New York City to become the NAACP's director of research and editor of that organization's magazine, the *Crisis*. He would remain in New York City working at the NAACP for 24 years, during which time he essentially inherited Booker T. Washington's role of chief advocate for the hopes and aspirations of his people. Among the important causes he took up were his investigation on behalf of the NAACP of racial discrimination in the U.S. army during World War I and his championing, through articles in the *Crisis*, of African-American art and culture as it emerged during the Harlem Renaissance of the 1920s.

In 1934, after a squabble with other directors of the NAACP over whether that organization should pursue the policy of integration of blacks into the broader American society or instead champion all-black institutions and pursue a society apart from white Americans (which DuBois was coming to favor), he resigned as editor of the *Crisis* and returned to Atlanta University. He would stay in Atlanta until 1944, when he was invited back to New York to be director of special research at the NAACP.

From 1900, when he attended the Pan-African Conference in London, DuBois was interested in the fate of black people on a worldwide scale. This interest continued throughout the rest of his life. He would attend subsequent Pan-African Conferences in 1911, 1919, 1921, 1927, 1929, and 1945.

DuBois was also intensely interested in left-wing politics, especially socialism and communism. He attended socialist meetings in Germany during his days as a student in Berlin and joined the U.S. Socialist Party in 1911. Gradually during the 1930s and 1940s, he tilted even further leftward, eventually becoming an official member of the U.S. Communist Party in 1961, although he was unofficially a communist long before that, possibly by the mid-1930s.

DuBois paid a price for his radical politics. In 1948, he was fired from his job at the NAACP after the U.S. government indicted him on the charge that he was "an agent of the Soviet Union." DuBois was eventually found not guilty of this charge, but it made his life in the 1950s difficult. The federal government would not issue him a passport until 1958, thus denying him the ability to travel overseas. In his 80s, he was still active, running for the U.S. Senate in New York on the Progressive Party ticket in 1950 and serving as cochair of a private institution, the Council on African Affairs, from 1948 to 1956.

In 1961, with his passport again in hand, DuBois moved to Ghana, where he had been offered a guesthouse by Kwame Nkrumah, that country's new president. DuBois became a citizen of Ghana in 1963. He died, ironically, on August 27, 1963, the day before another black leader, MARTIN LUTHER KING, JR., would assume the mantle of spokesman of his people with a legendary speech from the steps of the Lincoln Memorial.

Further Reading

DuBois, W. E. B. *Dusk of Dawn*. Millwood, N.Y.: Kraus-Thomson Organization, 1975.

———. *The Souls of Black Folk*. New York: Vintage Books, 1990.

Greenberg, David. "W. E. B. DuBois: The Writer Who Traveled Backward." Available online. URL: http://slate.com./id/104910. Downloaded June 20, 2009.

Lewis, David Levering. *W. E. B. DuBois: Biography of a Race.* 2 vols. New York: Holt, 1993, 2001.

———. *W. E. B. DuBois: The Fight for Equality and the American Century, 1919–1963.* New York: Macmillan, 2000.

New Georgia Encyclopedia. "W. E. B. DuBois in Georgia." Available online. URL: http://www.georgia encyclopedia.org/nge/Article.jsp?id=h-905. Downloaded June 20, 2009.

Wager, Jennifer. "W. E. B. Du Bois: Freedom Fighter." Available online. URL: http://www.udel.edu/soe/deal/WEBDuBois.html. Downloaded June 20, 2009.

Dunjee, Roscoe

(1883–1965) *editor, civil rights activist*

A courageous and pioneering activist for African-American civil rights, Roscoe Dunjee was directly responsible for pushing forward racial integration in housing, university admittance, and jury selection in his home state of Oklahoma. Born in Harpers Ferry, West Virginia, on June 21, 1883, Dunjee was the son of John William and Lydia Ann Dunjee. His father was a minister and official at Storer College in Harpers Ferry. Later the Reverend John William Dunjee was sent to Oklahoma to organize churches by the American Baptist Missionary Society.

Roscoe Dunjee came of age in turn-of-the-century Oklahoma Territory and received his education at Langston University, an all-black college in Langston, Oklahoma. In 1815, when he was 32, Dunjee founded the *Black Dispatch* in Oklahoma City. Begun originally as a local newspaper for the Oklahoma African-American community, the *Black Dispatch* soon grew into a nationwide publication with a circulation of approximately 20,000 subscribers.

Adopting the slogans "Mouthpiece for All Better Thinking Colored People" and "A Message from the Black Fold," the *Black Dispatch* reported news of interest to African Americans in Oklahoma and throughout the nation. Of particular interest were the lively editorials by Dunjee and his sister, Drusilla. Dunjee personally traveled to sites where African Americans had been lynched in Texas and Oklahoma to report on these violent incidents.

Dunjee also focused on the issue of voting and urged calm determination and patient persistence of blacks working to obtain the right to vote. His strategy of laying a foundation of state court cases against voting restriction against blacks for later challenges in federal court was applied successfully by lawyers of the National Association for the Advancement of Colored People (NAACP).

In 1935, Dunjee reported on and publicized the case of Jess Hollins, a black man who had been convicted of a crime by an all-white jury. This case was overturned because African Americans had been excluded from the Hollins jury. Dunjee also successfully led the legal and press battle in 1948 to force open the doors of Oklahoma State University to African Americans.

Dunjee was active in many business and civil rights organizations, including the national and Oklahoma branches of the NAACP, the Oklahoma Youth Legislature, the National Negro Democratic Association, and the National Negro Business League. He died in Oklahoma on March 1, 1965.

Further Reading

Oklahoma Historical Society. Encyclopedia of Oklahoma History & Culture. "Dunjee, Roscoe." Available online. URL: http://digital.library.okstate.edu/encyclopedia/entries/D/DU007.html. Downloaded July 20, 2009.

Simmons, Charles A. *The African American Press: A History of News Coverage during National Crises, with Special Reference to Four Black Newspapers, 1827–1965.* Jefferson, N.C.: McFarland, 1998.

Teall, Kaye M. *Black History in Oklahoma: A Resource Book.* Oklahoma City, Okla.: Oklahoma City Public Schools, 1971.

Eagleson, William Lewis
(1835–1899) *journalist, homestead movement leader*

The publisher of the first black-owned newspapers in two Plains states, William Eagleson also was a booster of plans for massive African-American immigration into Kansas and Oklahoma. Born on August 9, 1835, in Saint Louis, Missouri, William Lewis Eagleson spent a good part of his youth learning to be a barber and working as a printer for newspapers in Saint Louis.

When he was 30, he married Elizabeth McKinney and lived with her for 10 years in Missouri and across the river in Illinois. In 1877, Eagleson moved with his wife and growing family (he would have nine children) to Fort Scott, a town in southeast Kansas, about 80 miles from Kansas City. In January the following year, he founded the *Colored Citizen,* the first newspaper owned by an African American in Kansas. Within months, Eagleson had moved again, this time to the larger town of Topeka, and set up the paper's office in that town. He also became deeply involved in Republican Party politics, for which he was rewarded with a job as a doorman at the Kansas House of Representatives.

Around 1878, Eagleson became active in the Colored State Emigration Board of Kansas, and through the *Colored Citizen* he promoted Kansas as a worthwhile destination for African Ameri-

cans who wanted to leave the South. Unfortunately, the newspaper was unable to support itself and went out of business in 1880.

After the bankruptcy of the *Colored Citizen* in 1880, Eagleson was forced to return to barbering for nine years to support his family. In 1889 he was swept up by the land fever that was gripping the territory of Oklahoma. Eagleson and EDWIN MCCABE formed the Oklahoma Immigration Society, and Eagleson joined McCabe in Langston, Oklahoma, a new all-black town that McCabe had founded.

In Langston, Eagleson founded the *Langston City Herald,* the first African-American newspaper in Oklahoma. He was also elected justice of the peace and city councilor in Langston. He was not to stay long in Langston, however. After McCabe sold his share in the paper, Eagleson returned to Topeka. Fed up with the Republican Party, Eagleson became a Democrat. He was appointed messenger for the governor when the Democrats came into power in 1896.

Eagleson died on June 22, 1899, almost at the age of 64. He was remembered in Kansas and Oklahoma as "the old warhorse" because of the straightforward editorials that he wrote for the *Colored Citizen* and *Langston City Herald.*

Further Reading
Franklin, Jimmy Lewis. *Blacks in Oklahoma.* Norman: University of Oklahoma Press, 1980.

Kansas State Historical Society. "William Eagleson." Available online. URL: http://www.kshs.org/cool2/coolpape.htm. Downloaded July 21, 2009.

Teall, Kaye M. *Black History in Oklahoma: A Resource Book.* Oklahoma City, Okla.: Oklahoma City Public Schools, 1971.

Edelman, Marian Wright

(1939–   ) *civil and children's rights advocate*

An activist during the Civil Rights movement of the 1960s, Marian Wright Edelman is the founder of the Children's Defense Fund, an organization that works to improve the lives of children in the United States. Marian Wright was born on June 6, 1939, the youngest of five children of a Baptist minister. After completing her secondary education in South Carolina, she enrolled in Spelman College in Atlanta in 1956 and graduated with a B.A. from the school in 1960. She then enrolled in the Yale Law School and earned a juris doctor degree in 1963.

Wright spent the summer of 1963 registering African-American voters in Mississippi and in the fall of that year moved to New York City, where she worked as an attorney for the Legal Defense and Education Fund of the National Association for the Advancement of Colored People (NAACP). She returned to Mississippi the following year, settling in Jackson, and became the first African-American woman to pass the Mississippi bar exam.

She maintained a private law practice that handled civil rights cases at the same time as she directed the Mississippi NAACP's Legal Defense and Education Fund. During her tenure as head of the Legal Defense and Education Fund in Mississippi, Wright concentrated on trying to improve the living conditions of poor people, both African Americans and whites, in that state. She pushed for a larger Head Start program for poor black and white children, for an expanded Food Stamp pro-

Marian Wright Edelman is the founder of the Children's Defense Fund, an advocacy group working to improve the lives of poor children in the United States and other countries. *(Courtesy Children's Defense Fund, photo by Michael Collopy)*

gram to deal with poverty and malnutrition, and for increased funding for education.

Wright remained in Mississippi until 1968. Early in that year, she moved to Washington, D.C., to work as a coordinator for the March on Washington, which was being organized by the Reverend MARTIN LUTHER KING, JR. After Dr. King was assassinated in Memphis in April, Wright carried through on her commitment to the March on Washington, which occurred that summer. With several other activist lawyers, she formed the Washington Research Project, a public-interest law firm that helped poor clients with their legal problems.

Marian Wright Edelman founded the organization for which she is best known, the Children's Defense Fund, in 1973. Around that same time, she also married Peter Edelman, a former staff member for Senator Robert Kennedy whom she had met in Mississippi in the late 1960s.

The Children's Defense Fund is committed to pressing the federal and various state governments to pass legislation that will protect children from neglect, abuse, and poverty. "It is time for the richest nation on earth to do what we know works to help all of our children," Edelman has said:

> Children who are homeless, hungry, neglected, abused, without health care, in unsafe communities and schools are not acts of God. They are our moral and political choices as a nation. We can change these choices and meet the needs of all our children. It is shameful and unnecessary that 12 million children are poor and 10.8 million children lack health insurance. We know how to solve these problems. Now we must build the political and civic will to do so.

Besides forging alliances with a number of other organizations to achieve results, the Children's Defense Fund, under Edelman's leadership, provided support for the Leave No Child Behind Act of 2001. Edelman is a frequent speaker on college campuses and at conferences.

Edelman has received the Albert Schweitzer Humanitarian Award and the MacArthur Foundation Prize. In 2000, President Bill Clinton awarded her the Medal of Freedom, the highest civilian honor bestowed by the U.S. government.

Further Reading

Children's Defense Fund. Homepage. Available online. URL: http://www.childrensdefense.org/. Downloaded July 17, 2009.

Edelman, Marian Wright. *Lanterns: A Memoir of Mentors.* Boston: Beacon Press, 1999.

———. *The Measure of Our Success: A Letter to My Children and Yours.* Boston: Beacon Press, 1992.

Gilbert, Geoffrey, ed. *Rich and Poor in America: A Reference Handbook.* Santa Barbara, Calif.: ABC-CLIO, 2008.

PBS. *Tavis Smiley.* "Marian Wright Edelman." Available online. URL: http://www.pbs.org/kcet/tavissmiley/archive/200703/20070327_edelman.html. Downloaded June 29, 2009.

Evers, Medgar Wiley
(1925–1963) *civil rights leader*

A civil rights leader in Mississippi at a time of intense conflict between southern white leaders and southern African Americans, Medgar Evers was murdered before he could witness the civil rights successes of the late 1960s and 1970s. Medgar Wiley Evers was born on July 2, 1925, in Decatur, Mississippi, a small town in the eastern part of the state, to James and Jessie Evers. The family was hard-working but not wealthy. His father was a farmer and worked in a local sawmill, while his mother did domestic work and laundry.

Evers attended primary and secondary schools in Decatur and graduated in 1943. After graduation, he was drafted into the U.S. Army and served in Europe during World War II. After the war, he returned to Mississippi to attend Alcorn State University, an all-black college located in Lorman, Mississippi. Evers was active in sports and served for two years as editor of the Alcorn State student newspaper. During his senior year, he married his fellow student Myrlie Beasley. They would have three children.

After his graduation from Alcorn State in 1952, Evers moved to Mound Bayou, Mississippi, where he worked as an insurance salesman. Evers joined the National Association for the Advancement of Colored People (NAACP) the year he graduated and worked as a part-time NAACP organizer in Mound Bayou. His first acts were to organize boycotts by black customers of white-owned gas stations that refused to let African Americans use their bathrooms.

Momentous changes in race relations began to occur in the United States in the early 1950s. In 1954, the U.S. Supreme Court declared in its landmark *Brown v. the Topeka Board of Education* ruling that segregation in public schools is unconstitutional. Prompted by this court ruling, Evers applied for admission to, and was rejected by, the University of Mississippi. This effort was noticed by the NAACP's state board, who decided to appoint Evers its statewide executive director.

With his appointment to the directorship of the Mississippi NAACP, Evers and his family moved to Jackson, the state capital. With the backing of the NAACP organization, he began investigations into the murders of blacks in Mississippi and an enlarged program of boycotts by African Americans and a few sympathetic whites against businesses that discriminated against black customers.

The aim of Evers and the NAACP was to tear down the system known as Jim Crow that had placed blacks in a second-class role in the South. Under this system, African Americans were denied their right to vote, could not eat in the same sections as whites in restaurants, could not attend schools with whites, could not sit with whites in movie theaters, and were in many other ways separated from whites and not allowed to work with whites in many kinds of jobs.

By the early 1960s, the scale of protest against Jim Crow had risen enormously. Not only was the NAACP organizing protests against discriminatory race laws in Mississippi and other southern states, but the Reverend MARTIN LUTHER KING, JR., had also organized marches in Alabama that were met with violence by white police and were televised around the world. Impressed with King's tactics, Evers joined King's Southern Christian Leadership Conference (SCLC) while continuing to work for the NAACP.

Evers's most important efforts during the early 1960s were the drives he organized to register African-American voters and his effort to integrate the University of Mississippi, known as Ole Miss. In October 1962, Evers backed the application of James Meredith, a black student, to Ole Miss. When Meredith was physically blocked at the doors of the university by state officials, U.S. marshals, under orders from the U.S. attorney general, Robert Kennedy, forced Meredith to be admitted. A resulting riot forced the Kennedy administration to call out National Guard troops to restore order. Four people were killed in the chaos.

Evers's successful organizing aroused fear and hatred toward him, especially among the Ku Klux Klan, the leading white hate group in the South. On the morning of June 12, 1963, as he was getting into his car to leave for work, Evers was shot and killed by a sniper in Jackson. A Klansman named Byron de la Beckwith was charged with his murder but released after two all-white juries failed to reach verdicts in the 1960s. In the 1990s, de la Beckwith was finally convicted and given a life sentence.

In an article he wrote shortly before his death, Evers explained what he was working for. "It may sound funny," he wrote, "but I love the South. I don't choose to live anywhere else. There's land here, where a man can raise cattle, and I'm going to do it some day. There are lakes where a man can sink a hook and fight the bass. There is room here for my children to play and grow, and become good citizens—if the white man will let them."

Further Reading

Evers, Myrlie B., with William Peters. *For Us, the Living.* Jackson: University Press of Mississippi, 1996.

Evers-Williams, Myrlie, and Manning Marable. *The Autobiography of Medgar Evers: A Hero's Life and Legacy Revealed through His Writings, Letters, and Speeches.* New York: Basic Civitas, 2006.

The Mississippi Writers Page. "Medgar Evers." Available online. URL: http://www.olemiss.edu/mwp/

dir/evers_medgar/index.html. Downloaded July 22, 2009.

Nossiter, Adam. *Of Long Memory: Mississippi and the Murder of Medgar Evers.* New York: De Capo, 2002.

Vollers, Maryanne. *Ghosts of Mississippi: The Murder of Medgar Evers, The Trials of Byron de la Beckwith, and the Haunting of the New South.* Boston: Little, Brown, 1995.

Williams, Juan. *Eyes on the Prize: America's Civil Rights Years, 1954–1965.* New York: Viking Penguin, 1987.

F

Fard, Wallace D.

(W. D. Fard, Wallie D. Fard, Wali Farad
Muhammad)
(unknown–ca. 1934) *community leader,
Nation of Islam founder*

The mysterious founder of the Nation of Islam
(NOI), Wallace D. Fard, usually referred to by
his initials, W. D., created a religious organization and political movement that would grow
enormously in the years after his disappearance
in 1933. Nothing of substance is known about
Fard's origins. In the folklore of the Nation of
Islam, it is said that he was born variously in
Mecca, Saudi Arabia; Lebanon; even Polynesia,
probably in 1877. Other sources list his birth as
1891. Various sources also list his original name
in a number of ways. It is not even known with
certainty whether he was white or of mixed racial
parentage. What is known is that he was very
light skinned and that he appeared in Detroit
around 1930.

Fard first became known in the Detroit ghetto
of Paradise Valley when he began selling silk gar-
ments and raincoats door to door. Along with the
sales pitch for his products, he seems to have been
quite skillful in offering a pitch about a new religion that he had "rediscovered" and of which he
also was a prophet. This new religion he named
Nation of Islam. To spread the word, Fard founded

a storefront church called Temple Number One,
which soon began to attract believers.

Fard mixed a contempt for white people (calling them "white devils") with a call for racial pride
among African Americans. He claimed that
blacks were the "original people" of God and that
whites had been created from them in an experiment that had gone wrong. He stated that Christianity was the "white man's religion" and that
blacks should follow Islam, their true faith. Fard
also demanded justice and equal treatment for
blacks in the United States.

Fard's brand of Islam, which had little to do
with Islam as practiced in the rest of the world,
and his call for blacks to separate from white society resonated with poor African Americans living
in the Detroit ghetto, many of whom had been
fired before whites at the beginning of the Great
Depression in the early 1930s. By 1933, Temple
Number One had growth to perhaps as many as a
thousand people, and Temple Number Two was
established in 1934 in Chicago.

Just as the Nation of Islam was beginning to
grow in membership, Fard disappeared in 1934,
not to be seen again. The circumstances of his
disappearance are mysterious. He may have been
murdered, died of natural causes, or simply moved
to another city or country, although the odds are
great that he died. In any event, leadership of the
Nation of Islam passed to his main disciple, Eli-

jah Poole, a poor man from Georgia and, like most of the blacks in Detroit, a recent immigrant from the South. Following Fard's advice, Poole changed his name to ELIJAH MUHAMMAD after his conversion to Islam. Elijah Muhammad would lead the Nation of Islam for 40 years and increase its membership from 1,000 or so in 1934 to more than 50,000 by the time of his death in 1975.

Further Reading

Curtis, Edward E. *Black Muslim Religion in the Nation of Islam, 1960–1975.* Chapel Hill: University of North Carolina Press, 2006.

McCloud, Aminah Beverly. *African American Islam.* New York: Routledge, 1995.

Muslim Historical Society of Chicago. "Early Studies in Black Nationalism, Cults, and Churches in Chicago by the WPA circa September, 1941." Available online. URL: http://www.geocities.com/Heartland/Woods/4623/wpa.htm. Downloaded July 17, 2009.

Farmer, James Leonard, Jr.

(1920–1999) civil rights leader, Congress of Racial Equality founder

Founder of the Congress of Racial Equality (CORE) and leader of the Freedom Rides of the summer of 1961, James Farmer was the architect of the strategy of nonviolent disobedience that was so successful for the Civil Rights movement during the 1960s. Born on January 12, 1920, in Marshall, Texas, James Leonard Farmer, Jr., was the son of Pearl Houston and James Leonard Farmer, Sr. The elder Farmer was a staunch Methodist and a university professor of theology and Old testament studies who taught at a number of historically black colleges, including Wiley College in Marshall, the East Texas city where Farmer was born.

Raised in a family for whom learning and religion were supremely important, Farmer excelled in school and was himself deeply religious. He graduated from high school at the age of 14 in 1934 and entered Wiley College in Texas. Farmer received a bachelor's degree from Wiley in 1938 and continued his studies at Howard University in Washington, D.C. He graduated from Howard's divinity school in 1941.

After receiving his divinity degree, Farmer decided that he would not become an ordained Methodist minister. Even though the United States was gearing up to do battle with the Japanese and Germans in World War II, Farmer refused to join the U.S. armed forces because of the government's policy of racial segregation in the army, navy, and marines. He was disappointed to find out that he was automatically granted an exemption because of his divinity degree.

In 1941, Farmer became director of race relations for a Quaker-sponsored group, the Fellowship of Reconciliation (FOR). Then living in Chicago, Farmer organized FOR's efforts at combating racism and destroying the Jim Crow system, state and federal laws that discriminated against African Americans.

In 1942, Farmer and several other pacifist organizers decided to form their own group, the Congress of Racial Equality (CORE), which would focus specifically on issues of race. Impressed with the tactics of nonviolent confrontation pioneered by Mohandas Gandhi in India against the British, Farmer was determined to use the strategy of peaceful but direct protest to break down the barriers of racial discrimination in the United States. CORE would be the first group to use nonviolent confrontation in the United States.

Farmer's first organized protests occurred in 1947 and were directed at restaurants in Chicago that discriminated against African Americans. Groups of integrated protesters, blacks and whites, would sit together in the targeted restaurants and, when asked to leave, would refuse. Within months, most of the targeted restaurants changed their racial policies and began to serve blacks.

In 1947, CORE, under Farmer's leadership, also organized what it called a Journey of Reconciliation, in which racially integrated groups sent out by CORE would ride in buses through the upper South. This project, which defied the commonly accepted practice of seating all blacks in the back of a bus, was designed to test the Irene Morgan case, a decision handed down by the U.S. Supreme Court in 1946 that banned segregated seating on interstate transport. Unfortunately, the country was not yet ready in 1947 to pay attention to this issue. A number of the protesters were arrested, the group garnered little press coverage, and some participants even served time on a North Carolina chain gang.

By 1961, the mood of the country had changed. CORE had continued to use its tactic of nonviolent confrontation in integrating restaurants. MARTIN

James Farmer ca. 1960. Farmer founded the Congress of Racial Equality (CORE) in 1942 and was one of the leaders of the Freedom Rides of the summer of 1961. *(Library of Congress, Prints and Photographs Division, LC-U9-11814)*

LUTHER KING, JR., also had picked up on CORE's method and used it well to protest racial integration on city buses in Birmingham, Alabama.

In 1961, Farmer decided to try again the idea of sending teams of racially integrated CORE volunteers, called Freedom Riders, on bus rides through the South. On May 4, 1961, Farmer and others left the Trailways and Greyhound bus terminals in Washington, D.C., bound for New Orleans, which they hoped to reach by May 17, the anniversary day of the *Brown v. the Board of Education of Topeka* decision that ordered the integration of public schools. Farmer knew that they would face trouble: "We felt we could count on the racists of the South to create a crisis so that the federal government would be compelled to enforce the law. When we began the ride I think all of us were prepared for as much violence as could be thrown at us. We were prepared for the possibility of death."

In Anniston and Birmingham, Alabama, on May 15 and 20, Freedom Riders were savagely attacked by white mobs as they left buses at terminals in those cities. In Anniston, the Greyhound bus on which Freedom Riders had seats was set on fire. In Birmingham, a mob of a thousand whites beat up Freedom Riders, sending them scattering for safety. Several Freedom Riders were knocked unconscious and left in the street for as long as a half-hour.

This time, unlike in 1947, the press was watching. News and television footage of these attacks was flashed around the world, putting pressure of the newly installed Kennedy administration to act. Kennedy was forced to call up National Guard troops to protect CORE protesters in Birmingham and secured an agreement with state officials in Alabama and Mississippi that the Freedom Riders would not again be attacked. As promised, no further attacks occurred, but CORE continued to send volunteers into the South all summer. None made it to New Orleans, and many, including Farmer, spent most of the summer in southern jails. But an unstoppable momentum, which would eventually culminate in the destruction of the Jim

Crow system, had been gained. The South, and the country, would never be the same again.

In 1966, Farmer resigned as head of CORE to begin a nationwide literacy program. Distancing himself from the growing militancy of the Civil Rights movement, he joined the Republican Party and in 1968 ran for a seat in Congress. He lost the race but joined the new Nixon administration as undersecretary of health, education, and welfare.

Beginning in 1971, he worked for the Council on Minority Planning and Strategy, a think tank that advises about tactics to achieve gains for African Americans, Hispanics, and women. He taught at several universities, including Lincoln University and Mary Washington College. In 1985, he wrote a memoir, *Lay Bare the Heart*, recounting the events of his life. For his achievements, Farmer was awarded the Medal of Freedom, the nation's highest civilian honor, by President Clinton, in 1998. He died on July 9, 1999.

Further Reading

CORE. "James Farmer." Available online. URL: http://www.core-online.org/History/james_farmer_bio.htm. Downloaded July 22, 2009.

Farmer, James. *Lay Bare the Heart: An Autobiography of the Civil Rights Movement.* Fort Worth: Texas Christian University Press, 1998.

Greensboro Voices. "Oral History Interview with James Farmer." Available online. URL: http://library.uncg.edu/depts/archives/civrights/detail-iv.asp?iv=41. Downloaded July 22, 2009.

University of Mary Washington. James Farmer Scholars Program. "Who Is James Farmer?" Available online. URL: http://www.umw.edu/cas/jfscholars/who/default.php. Downloaded July 22, 2009.

Farrakhan, Louis
(Louis Eugene Walcott)
(1933–   ) *black nationalist, Muslim leader*

One of the successors of the Nation of Islam (NOI) leader ELIJAH MUHAMMAD, Louis Farra-khan has headed an organization that is most faithful to Muhammad's beliefs and teachings. He was born Louis Eugene Walcott in Queens, New York, on May 11, 1933, the son of immigrants from the West Indies. Before he was born, his father and mother split up, and Louis moved with his mother and brother, Alvin, to the Roxbury section of Boston. As a child, he displayed a talent for music. He learned to play the violin and as a young teenager occasionally played with symphonies in Boston. He attended English High School in Boston and graduated in 1949.

After graduation, Louis Walcott moved to North Carolina to study at Winston-Salem Teacher's College, where he had been given an athletic scholarship as a track runner. Majoring in English, he graduated from Winston-Salem in 1953. That same year he married. After finishing college, he and his wife moved back to Boston, where he earned a living as an entertainer. Known as "the Charmer," Walcott worked as a singer in a calypso band and as a violinist and dancer.

Walcott would only work as an entertainer for a year and a half. In February 1955, after an engagement in Chicago, he was invited to hear a talk by Elijah Muhammad at the Nation of Islam's Temple Number Two. Impressed with what he heard, Walcott moved to New York and began attending meetings at the Nation of Islam's Harlem temple, then headed by MALCOLM X. After joining the NOI and changing his name, Farrakhan quit the music business and was sent back to Boston to work for the NOI there. By 1956, he headed the NOI's temple in that city, a position he would hold until 1965.

Farrakhan was attracted to the Nation of Islam because its angry response to white racism appealed to his temperament. Elijah Muhammad referred to Caucasians as "white devils" and branded them "an evil race." In his sermons Farrakhan would pick up this theme, singling out Jews especially. He would call Judaism a "gutter religion" and refer to Israel as an "outlaw state." He also called Hitler a "great man." The NOI's strict code of discipline—no drinking, drug taking, or use of profanities—also must have appealed to Farrakhan as a desirable alternative to the rough-and-tumble life on the streets.

After the assassination of Malcolm X, which some commentators have said Farrakhan played a part in, Farrakhan was appointed to head Malcolm's old Harlem temple. He also edited the NOI paper *Muhammad Speaks* and increasingly became part of the NOI inner circle.

After the death of Elijah Muhammad in 1975, Muhammad's seventh son, Wallace, was designated successor as leader of the Nation of Islam. Wallace quickly began to change the NOI, first admitting whites to its membership, then rejecting all of the old race-based mythology that had been used by his father. By 1977, Walid Muhammad (he had changed his name from Wallace) aligned the NOI with traditional Islamic beliefs as practiced in the Middle East. He also changed the name of the organization to the American Muslim Mission.

Alarmed at Walid Muhammad's transformation of the old NOI, Louis Farrakhan broke with his mentor's son in 1977. He picked up the original name of the group, the Nation of Islam; established a new organization with the former NOI beliefs; and appointed himself the NOI leader.

Louis Farrakhan's NOI still emphasizes that African Americans are superior to whites, that blacks should live separately from whites in the United States, that a homeland for blacks should be created by the U.S. government, and that blacks and whites should not marry.

Farrakhan has achieved some triumphs. In 1995, he served as one of the principal organizers of the Million Man March on Washington, D.C., which was intended as a show of black male pride and self-affirmation. In 1996, he made a tour of Africa and the Middle East, visiting 18 nations in that region.

To celebrate the fifth anniversary of the Million Man March, Farrakhan organized the Million Family March, which was held in Washington, D.C., on October 16, 2000. Fewer people attended this event than the original march. A Millions More March was held in 2005 to mark the original march's 10th anniversary. In 2007, Farrakhan underwent abdominal surgery, spending five weeks in a hospital. After recovering, he resumed his duties as head of the NOI. In October 2008, he presided over the rededication of the Maryam Mosque after extensive renovations. The Chicago mosque serves as the headquarters of the NOI.

Further Reading

Curtis, Edward E. *Islam in Black America: Identity, Liberation, and Difference in African-American Islamic Thought.* Albany: State University of New York Press, 2002.

Magida, Arthur J. *Prophet of Rage: A Life of Louis Farrakhan and His Nation.* New York: Basic Books, 1996.

Nation of Islam. "Bio Sketch of the Honorable Minister Louis Farrakhan." Available online. URL: http://www.noi.org/mlfbio.htm. Downloaded June 30, 2009.

Forbes, George Washington
(1864–1927) *editor, civil rights leader, community activist*

From the early 1890s until the early 1900s, George Forbes owned and edited two African-American newspapers in Boston. Through them, he developed a local and national reputation as a proponent of full rights of citizenship for blacks in the United States.

George Washington Forbes was born in Shannon, Mississippi, in 1864 (the exact date is unknown), just before the end of the Civil War. His parents had been slaves and must have encouraged him to follow his desire to study and leave Mississippi. For a while, Forbes, who probably received little education in Mississippi, worked at laboring jobs and on farms. Sometime around 1878, he left Mississippi permanently, traveling first to Ohio, where he studied for a while at Wilberforce University.

In the mid-1880s, Forbes moved to Boston. For three or four years, he worked as a laborer at Harvard University. Having saved enough money to continue his education, Forbes left Boston in 1888 to enroll in Amherst College. He graduated from Amherst in 1892, his graduation attended by a friend he had met in Boston, W. E. B. DuBois, who would later become one of the most important African-American leaders of his day.

After graduation, Forbes returned to Boston. He became a member of an informal group of black Boston activists, known as the "radicals," whose most prominent member was WILLIAM MONROE TROTTER. In the autumn after his graduation, Forbes founded the *Boston Courant*, the second African-American paper in Boston. Knowing that he would not be making much money as an editor of a fledgling newspaper, Forbes also worked as a librarian at the Boston Public Library.

Forbes edited the *Courant* for five years. When the *Courant* folded in 1897 as a result of financial problems, Forbes kept working at his library job while he waited to see whether he and his friends could found another newspaper to take the *Courant*'s place. In 1901, he and Trotter founded the *Guardian*, through which Forbes quickly made a name for himself by writing editorials that attacked BOOKER TALIAFERRO WASHINGTON, the most prominent African-American leader of that time.

Forbes and his partner Trotter took issue with Washington's forgiving stance toward racist laws that segregated African Americans from whites in public places and made it difficult for blacks to vote. Both men believed that a much more confrontational style opposing such laws was needed and faulted Washington as too timid.

After a personal dispute between Forbes and Trotter in 1903, Forbes left the paper. He participated to a small degree with his old friend W. E. B. DuBois in the founding of the Niagara Movement, the forerunner of the National Association for the Advancement of Colored People (NAACP). However, from about 1910 Forbes withdrew from politics and devoted himself to working at the Boston Public Library and writing a book, which was never published, about African-American literature. George Forbes died on March 10, 1927.

Further Reading

Campbell, Georgetta Merritt. *Extant Collections of Early Black Newspapers: A Research Guide to the Black Press, 1880–1915, with an Index to the Boston Guardian, 1902–1904*. Troy, N.Y.: Whitston, 1981.

Fox, Stephen R. *The Guardian of Boston: William Monroe Trotter*. New York: Atheneum, 1970.

Horne, Gerald, and Mary Young, eds. *W. E. B. DuBois: An Encyclopedia*. Westport, Conn.: Greenwood, 2001.

Ford, Barney Launcelot
(ca. 1824–1902) *Underground Railroad conductor, civil rights leader*

A wandering adventurer, Barney Ford eventually made his home in Colorado, and he made important contributions to that state's politics in the mid- to late 1800s. Barney Launcelot Ford was born into slavery in Virginia sometime in 1824. Little is known about his childhood. By his early 20s, he was living along the Mississippi River, where he had been hired out as a riverboat hand. In 1848, at age 24, he jumped ship at Quincy, Illinois, escaping slavery for good.

Probably soon after his escape, he married a woman named Julia, whom he possibly met when he fled bondage to Chicago. They would have three children. In Chicago, Ford taught himself to read and write, and he established a lifelong friendship with another black man, Henry Wagoner. For a number of months, both men were active in Underground Railroad activities in

Chicago and helped escaped slaves settle in the city or pass through to Canada.

Late in 1848, with news of the discovery of gold in California, Ford and his wife left Chicago by ship for the gold fields around the American River. However, landing in Nicaragua for the trek from the Caribbean to the Pacific, Ford discovered business opportunity in the Caribbean port town of Greytown. From 1851 to 1854, he owned the American Hotel in that City. During that time control of Greytown was disputed by the United States and Great Britain. When American gunships shelled the town in 1854 and destroyed the American Hotel, Ford built a new hotel a few miles inland at Virgin Bay. He remained there a few more years before selling out for a tidy profit and returning to Chicago around 1857.

In 1858, Ford, along with his friend Wagoner, finally made it to a new gold strike, this time in Colorado. Neither had much luck finding gold, but Ford again showed his talent for entrepreneurship by starting a number of barbershops, restaurants, and hotels in the booming city of Denver. Ford successfully fought the proposed Colorado constitution, which barred African Americans from voting, when the state sought admission to the Union in 1865. He personally traveled to Washington, D.C., to lobby senators against admission for Colorado. Colorado was not admitted until 1876, and African Americans were expressly given the right to vote by the Fifteenth Amendment, which was ratified in 1870 and for which Ford also fought.

Between 1867 and 1882, Ford lived in Cheyenne, Wyoming, and San Francisco, California, in both places supported by businesses he founded. He and his wife returned permanently to Denver in 1882. Active in Republican Party politics, he became the first black man to serve on a Colorado grand jury and he also had success pushing for the passage of a state bill that outlawed racial segregation in public places.

Barney Ford died at the age of 76 in 1902 in Denver.

Further Reading

Colorado Historical Society. "Barney L. Ford." Available online. URL: http://www.coloradohistory.org/kids/Barney%20Ford.pdf. Downloaded July 22, 2009.

Wood, Richard E. *Here Lies Colorado: Fascinating Figures in Colorado History.* Helena, Mont.: Farcountry, 2005.

Forman, James
(1928–2005) *reporter, civil rights leader*

Head of a major civil rights organization during the most turbulent part of the Civil Rights movement in the 1960s, James Forman has since worked as a housing advocate for poor people and an academic. Born in Chicago on October 24, 1928, Forman joined the United States Air Force after his graduation from high school in 1946. He served in Korea during the Korean War, and in the early 1950s he returned to the United States.

In 1954, Forman entered Roosevelt University in Chicago. He graduated with a B.A. from Roosevelt in 1957. After graduation, Forman worked for the *Chicago Defender,* Chicago's leading African-American newspaper. By the late 1950s, Forman's beat was the Civil Rights movement, which was picking up momentum in the South. Under the leadership of the Reverend MARTIN LUTHER KING, JR., demonstrators against segregation in public facilities and institutions in the South, a system known as Jim Crow, publicly challenged laws that they saw as discriminatory and unfair. Demonstrators were frequently met with violence by police and white mobs.

As he reported on demonstrations in Birmingham, Alabama, and other southern cities, Forman felt himself being drawn into the Civil Rights movement, not as a reporter but as a participant. As a result, in 1960 he quit his job at the *Defender* and joined the Congress of Racial Equality (CORE). With CORE, he worked to help poor southern farmers who had lost their land. Later in

1960, he took a position as an organizer with the Student Nonviolent Coordination Committee (SNCC), a group that was formed in the wake of a series of sit-ins at restaurants in Raleigh, North Carolina.

In 1961, SNCC volunteers, mostly college students, were divided about which direction they should take. One group favored continuing the sit-ins, which generated considerable white sympathy through press coverage of the sometimes violent ways that southern police broke up these demonstrations. Another faction wanted to devote their energies to registering African-American voters in the South. Forman suggested that SNCC do both.

Before he could launch this two-pronged offensive against southern racism, Forman joined other activist volunteers from SNCC on the dangerous Freedom Rides on buses throughout the South in the summer of 1961. By stepping in at a crucial time when many of the original Freedom Riders had been arrested, Foreman and the other volunteers carried the Freedom Rides forward throughout the summer.

In 1962, the SNCC, at the urging of Forman, joined the Voter Education Project, a joint effort of SNCC, the Urban League, the National Association for the Advancement of Colored People (NAACP), and the Southern Christian Leadership Conference (SCLC). For slightly less than two years, Forman and the SNCC attempted to register voters in Louisiana and Mississippi in "saturation" campaigns during which SNCC volunteers would enter a town and inform black voters of what they had to do to register to vote. This effort met with little success until Forman and others suggested that the volunteers had to remain longer in each town. The SNCC did this type of more complex organizing through the Council of Federated Organizations.

Appointed executive director of the SNCC in 1964, Forman was deeply involved in these voter registration efforts. A more militant organizer than those of most mainstream groups, Forman angered many moderate supporters of the Civil Rights movement when he suggested that the federal government should pay African Americans $500 million as compensation for the injustices of slavery and racism.

Forman quit the SNCC in 1968 and formed his own group, the Unemployment and Poverty Action Council, which tried to organize programs to provide jobs for poor African Americans. In the late 1970s, Forman returned to academic studies. He received a master's degree from the African-American Studies Department of Cornell University in 1980 and a Ph.D. from the Union of Experimental Colleges and Universities in Washington, D.C., in 1982. He settled in Washington, D.C., where he served as president of the Unemployment and Poverty Action Committee. He became active in Democratic Party politics and joined the battle for statehood for the District of Columbia. He died in 2005.

Further Reading

Carson, Clayborne, and Penny Russell. "James Forman." Available online. URL:http://www.stanford.edu/~ccarson/articles/left_2.htm. Downloaded July 22, 2009.

Forman, James. *The Making of Black Revolutionaries.* Seattle: University of Washington Press, 1997.

Hogan, Wesley C. *Many Minds, One Heart: SNCC's Dream for a New America.* Chapel Hill: University of North Carolina Press, 2007.

Forten, James

(1766–1842) *abolitionist, entrepreneur, social reformer*

A wealthy, self-made man, James Forten used his position of social and financial prominence to speak out against slavery and oppression of women and to fund organizations that agitated for social change. Forten was born in 1766 in Philadelphia to parents who were free. His parents do not seem to have been wealthy, although they had enough money to send him for a year or so to a Quaker school run by Anthony Benezet, an abolitionist.

When Forten was still young, his father died and he had to begin working to support his family. He worked for a while in a grocery store, and in 1781, when he was 15, he signed up as a gunpowder handler aboard the *Royal Louis*, a privately owned gunboat that fought for the American side during the Revolutionary War. Forten was taken prisoner when the British navy captured the *Royal Louis*. After a year spent partly in jail and partly in freedom in England, he returned to Philadelphia in 1782.

Back in Philadelphia, Forten began working for Robert Bridges, who ran a well-respected sail-making company. By 1786, the hard-working Forten had become foreman of Bridges's company. When Bridges retired in 1798, Forten arranged for loans to buy the company. He steadily built up the company's assets during the rest of his life. Forten's sail-making business would eventually employ 40 African-American and white workers, and Forten himself at his death would be worth more than $100,000, a huge fortune in those days.

Forten began to get involved in politics and social causes in 1800, when he and other Philadelphia abolitionists proposed changes in a fugitive slave bill that had been adopted by Congress in 1793. Congress rejected Forten's proposed changes, which would have made it easier for fugitive slaves to live in the North. In 1813, Forten organized resistance to a bill that was before the Pennsylvania legislature, one that barred immigration of free blacks from other states into Pennsylvania.

In the early 1800s, some African Americans and white abolitionists began to argue that American blacks should return to Africa to live. In Africa, the argument went, African Americans could live in complete freedom without the oppression they daily encountered in predominantly white America. Forten argued strongly against this idea, which was known as the Colonization Movement, because he believed that the United States was the homeland of American

blacks and that they should stay there and fight for the full rights that were guaranteed to Americans by the Constitution. At the Negro Convention of 1830, Forten stated that black leaders had "to devise ways… for the bettering of our conditions" and spoke out in favor of funds being used, not for colonization schemes but for the education of blacks, especially education in the trades.

In 1831, Forten bankrolled the *Liberator,* William Lloyd Garrison's publication, which was one of the first nationwide abolitionist periodicals. Two years later, Forten hosted at his house in Philadelphia a meeting of a group that organized the American Anti-Slavery Society, which would become the most important abolitionist organization.

While he was becoming perhaps the most important early leader among American abolitionists, Forten also spoke out in favor of rights for women. He also organized the American Moral Reform Society, a group that was composed exclusively of black members and that advocated temperance, abolition of slavery, and repeal of fugitive slave laws.

Forten died on February 24, 1842, at the age of 76.

Further Reading

Aptheker, Herbert. *Abolitionism: A Revolutionary Movement.* Boston: Twayne Publishers, 1989.

Independence Park Institute. "The Forten Household." Available online. URL: http://www.independenceparkinstitute.com/inp/forten/forten_family.htm. Downloaded July 23, 2009.

Winch, Julie. *A Gentleman of Color: The Life of James Forten.* New York: Oxford University Press, 2002.

Fortune, Timothy Thomas
(1856–1928) *journalist, civil rights leader*

The best-known African-American journalist in the North as the 19th turned into the 20th century, T. Thomas Fortune lived a full and tumultuous life that he dedicated to stirring agitation in support of full rights for blacks in the United States. Timothy Thomas Fortune was born into slavery in Marianna, Florida, on October 3, 1856, to Emanuel and Sarah Jane Fortune. At the end of the Civil War, Fortune's father served as a representative in the Constitutional Convention and in the state legislature. The resumption of white rule to the South ended the elder Fortune's career, and the family was forced to flee to the larger city of Jacksonville.

Fortune was able to attend a Freedmen's Bureau school in Florida for only a year and a half. He then apprenticed in a printing shop and became a type compositor. Using this skill, he accumulated enough money to move to Washington, D.C., in 1876. There he attended Howard University's Preparatory School for about a year, but he was forced by lack of money to work full time as a printer again. For a few years, he worked for the *Washington Advocate,* a black-owned newspaper in that city. He also married Carrie Smiley; they would have five children and live together until their separation in 1906.

Fortune moved to New York City with his family in 1879 and quickly founded a tabloid newspaper, the *Rumor.* The *Rumor* was renamed the *Globe* in 1881. Fortune edited this periodical until its bankruptcy in 1884. Fortune then immediately founded another paper, the *New York Freeman,* which became the *New York Age* in 1887. The *Age* was a great critical, although not commercial, success for Fortune. Through it, he became the one of the best-known journalists and editors in the country.

In the pages of the *Age,* Fortune pushed relentlessly for full voting and citizenship rights for all African Americans. Through most of the 1880s, he abandoned the Republican Party, which was then, in the eyes of most African Americans, the natural ally of blacks and their ambitions. Fortune savaged the Republicans for letting white Democrats regain power in the South, but he ultimately returned to the Republican Party in 1889.

In the 1890s, Fortune was very active in organizing nationwide black political organizations, which, he hoped, would have the power to arouse blacks and intimidate or shame whites into granting full rights to the nation's black citizens. The first of these groups was the National Afro-American League, founded in 1890. When the league collapsed in 1893 as a result of poor funding and a lack of popular support, Fortune waited a few years before trying again, this time helping to found the National Afro-American Council in 1898. Fortune was elected president of the council and served until 1904.

Fortune engaged in ego battles with many of the African-American leaders of his day, especially with WILLIAM MONROE TROTTER and W. E. B. DuBois. Fortune found DuBois especially annoying and accused him of stealing his own ideas when DuBois founded the Niagara Movement in 1905.

Fortune was on somewhat better terms with BOOKER TALIAFERRO WASHINGTON, who was arguably the best-known black leader of that time. To supplement his meager income from the *New York Age,* Fortune semisecretly took money from Washington in return for providing him with advice, speechwriting services, and ghostwritten articles. Washington also lent money to Fortune to subsidize the *Age,* and though the *Age* was never a mouthpiece of Washington's views, it never attacked him.

In 1907, Fortune suffered a nervous breakdown brought on by alcoholism. For nearly a decade, he was virtually a street person and unemployed. Bit by bit, he recovered, and by 1919 he was working again as a journalist—this time writing editorials at the *Norfolk Journal and Guide.* In 1923, he moved back to New York City to become the editor of the *Negro World,* a periodical published by MARCUS GARVEY's Universal Negro Improvement Association (UNIA). Fortune would never wield the kind of influence he once possessed as owner and editor of the *Age,* but he was at least working and in relatively good health.

Fortune suffered a stroke in New York in April 1928 and was taken to the hospital in which his son, Frederick, worked. He died in Philadelphia on June 2, 1928. He was remembered by colleagues in the African-American press as "the best journalist that the Negro race has produced in the Western world."

Further Reading

PBS. "T. Thomas Fortune." Available online: URL: http://www.pbs.org/blackpress/news_bios. Downloaded July 23, 2009.

Salley, Columbus. *The Black 100: A Ranking of the Most Influential African-Americans, Past and Present.* New York: Citadel Press, 1999.

Thornbrough, Emma Lou. *T. Thomas Fortune, Militant Journalist.* Chicago: University of Chicago Press, 1972.

Freeman, Elizabeth

(Mumbet)
(ca. 1742–1829) *abolitionist*

A married slave whose husband had died during the Revolutionary War, Elizabeth Freeman initiated a lawsuit that effectively ended slavery in Massachusetts. Born around 1742, probably in Massachusetts, to parents who were taken into slavery in Africa, Freeman and her sister were purchased when they were young by Colonel John Ashley.

Freeman and her sister lived with the Ashleys for at least 10 years. It was not an easy place for them to be. Mrs. Ashley had a hot temper and frequently scolded the sisters. Physical abuse seems to have been common.

Two events would soon end her days as a slave. While waiting on the table of the Ashleys, Freeman overheard a discussion about the Bill of Rights and the new Massachusetts state constitution. The concept that "all men were created free and equal" was discussed among the Ashleys with Freeman silently listening.

When, sometime later, Mrs. Ashley attempted to hit Freeman's sister with a red-hot shovel, and Freeman took the blow with her outstretched arm, she decided that she could no longer remain with the family. Freeman left the Ashleys and refused to return. She also retained a lawyer, Theodore Sedgwick, and sued the Ashleys for illegally holding her in bondage. Since "all men were created free and equal," according to the Constitution, the Ashleys had no right to hold her.

In 1783, Sedgwick convinced a jury in Stockbridge, Massachusetts, that Freeman should not return to the Ashleys. The verdict in her favor, which was upheld, ended slavery in the state of Massachusetts.

After her victory, Freeman worked for a while as a paid housekeeper for the Sedgwicks. She later moved into her own house and made her living through a variety of domestic positions.

Elizabeth Freeman died on December 28, 1829, in Massachusetts.

Further Reading

Kaplan, Sidney. *The Black Presence in the Era of the American Revolution: 1770–1800.* Amherst: University of Massachusetts Press, 1989.

Massachusetts Historical Society. African Americans and the End of Slavery in Massachusetts. "The Legal End of Slavery in Massachusetts." Available online. URL: http://www.masshist.org/endof slavery/?queryID=54. Downloaded July 23, 2009.

Roberts, Cokie. *Founding Mothers: The Women Who Raised Our Nation.* New York: HarperCollins, 2004.

Swan, John. "The Slave Who Sued for Freedom." Available online. URL: http://www.american heritage.com/articles/magazine/ah/1990/2/1990_2_51.shtml. Downloaded July 23, 2009.

Garnet, Henry Highland

(1815–1882) *abolitionist, political activist, minister*

One of the leaders of the movement to abolish slavery before the Civil War, Henry Highland Garnet also campaigned against economic and social injustices and in favor of women's rights, temperance, and world peace. Garnet was born a slave in 1815 in New Market, Maryland, to enslaved parents. When Garnet's father, George, escaped from slavery in 1824, he took Henry, then only nine, with him. Father and son ended up in New York City, where George Garnett worked as a shoemaker and Henry began his education at the African Free School Number 1, one of what would become a number of schools established by the New York City African-American community for the education of their children.

A bright child, Garnet enrolled in the Noyes Academy in Canaan, New Hampshire, in 1834, when he was 19. Noyes offered an experiment in interracial education: 28 of the students at Noyes were white, and 14 were African Americans. Garnet attended Noyes for only a year. The school was literally torn down during the summer of 1835 by neighbors who did not approve of the interracial schooling of children. Garnet then enrolled in the Oneida Theological Institute, located near Utica in upstate New York.

After graduation from Oneida with a degree in divinity in 1840, Garnet moved to Troy, New York, where he was appointed pastor of an African-American Presbyterian church in that city in 1842. He married Julia Williams that year. They had no children.

Even before he became a minister in Troy, Garnet was already active in the abolitionist movement. In 1842 and 1843, he worked as an editor on the *Troy National Watchman,* a newspaper that called for the abolition of slavery. In 1843, he electrified the National Negro Convention, held in nearby Buffalo, with a speech in which he called for an armed rebellion to overthrow slavery. Garnet's speech was narrowly rejected, by one vote, from being adopted as the official resolution of the conference. Four years later, in 1847, it was adopted as the resolution of this convention.

With his speech, Garnet ushered in a new era of confrontational abolitionism among free northern African Americans. By the late 1840s, Garnet had also begun to explore the idea of colonizing liberated slaves and even free northern blacks in Africa. He thought emigration might be a desirable alternative to staying in the United States because he believed that African colonies might be able to produce enough cotton to threaten the economic base of the South and thus bring down the slave system. He also felt that Africa could offer a freer environment for American blacks to live in. "I would rather see a man free in Liberia," he said in one speech, "than a slave in the United States."

The speech to the National Negro Convention in 1842 made Garnet famous. As a result of his newfound fame, he was invited to attend the World Peace Congress in Frankfurt, Germany, in 1850. Garnet remained in Europe through 1851, giving lectures to audiences in Great Britain about the evil of slavery in the United States. The Presbyterian Church of Scotland was so impressed with Garnet's talks that they offered him a job as pastor of the Stirling Presbyterian Church on the island of Jamaica. He traveled to Jamaica in 1853 and remained on the island until 1856.

In 1856, Garnet returned to the United States. He was active as an abolitionist through the Civil War. At the start of the war, Garnet in a number of speeches and articles publicly urged President Lincoln to enlist African-American troops into the Union army.

Toward the end of the war, Garnet moved to Washington, D.C., where he took up the position of pastor of the Fifteenth Street Presbyterian Church. In 1864 while in that position, he became the first black minister to deliver a sermon to the U.S. House of Representatives. After the war, Garnet worked for a short time as an official in the Freedmen's Bureau. His experiences with the bureau and with the resumption of white political power in the South at the end of Reconstruction left him disenchanted with political involvement.

Throughout most of the 1870s, he was semiretired and lived in New York City. He married SARAH GARNET in 1879, and in 1881, he accepted an appointment as the American ambassador to Liberia. He had been in Liberia less than three months when he died, on February 12, 1882.

Further Reading

PBS. Africans in America, Resource Bank. "Henry Highland Garnet." Available online. URL: http://www.pbs.org/wgbh/aia/part4/4p1537.html. Downloaded July 23, 2009.

Hutchinson, Earl Ofari. *Let Your Motto Be Resistance: The Life and Thought of Henry Highland Garnet.* Boston: Beacon Press, 1972.

Quarles, Benjamin. *Black Abolitionists.* New York: Oxford, 1969.

Rodriguez, Junius P., ed. *Encyclopedia of Slave Resistance and Rebellion.* Westport, Conn.: Greenwood, 2007.

Garnet, Sarah
(Sarah J. Smith; Sarah Thompson)
(1831–1911) *educator, community leader, women's suffrage advocate*

A pioneering African-American teacher and principal in the New York public schools, Sarah Garnet spent her life as an educator in the New York black community. She was born Sarah J. Smith in Queens County, on Long Island, New York, on July 31, 1831, to Sylvanus and Annie Smith, and she grew up on her parents' farm. The Smiths were successful and prosperous farmers and were able to send Sarah to schools in New York City after she had received her elementary education from her maternal grandmother.

In 1845, when she was 15, Smith went to New York City to study to become a teacher at the same time that she began teaching at the Manumission Society, an African-American institution in the Williamsburg section of Brooklyn. For 18 years, she taught in several free schools organized by the New York City African-American community for the education of their children. In the early 1850s, she married the Reverend James Thompson. She had two children with Thompson, neither of whom lived to adulthood. After Thompson died in the late 1860s, she married HENRY HIGHLAND GARNET, a well-known minister and abolitionist leader.

In 1863, Sarah Garnet was appointed the principal of an elementary school that became P.S. 80 in New York City. On her appointment, she became the first African-American principal of a New York public school. Garnet would remain at this school as principal until her retirement at age 69 in 1900.

In the late 1880s, Garnet founded and became the leader of the Equal Suffrage Club, a group of African-American women who met at Garnet's home in Brooklyn to discuss gaining voting rights for women, black women in particular. Garnet was also active in the National Association of Colored Women and spoke out against the discrimination against African-American teachers in the New York City school system.

At age 80, Garnet attended the first meeting of the Universal Races Conference in London. She returned to New York full of new ideas about how to attack the continuing problem of suffrage for women and passed out papers that she had received at the conference to members of the Equal Suffrage Club.

Garnet died shortly after she returned from England, on September 17, 1911.

Further Reading

Brown, Hallie Q. *Homespun Heroines and Other Women of Distinction.* Freeport, N.Y.: Books for Libraries Press, 1971.

Mjagkij, Nina, ed. *Organizing Black America: An Encyclopedia of African American Associations.* New York: Taylor & Francis, 2001.

Neyland, Leedell. "Sarah J. Smith Thompson Garnet." Available online. URL: http://www.awoman aweek.com/garnet.htm. Downloaded July 23, 2009.

Garvey, Marcus

(1887–1940) *black nationalist leader, Universal Negro Improvement Association founder*

A pioneer of the idea of uniting black people around the world in one movement, Marcus Garvey headed the Universal Negro Improvement Association (UNIA), one of the strongest organizations for black pride and self-help in the early 20th century. Garvey was born on August 17, 1887, in Saint Ann's Bay, Jamaica, to Marcus and Sarah Garvey. Garvey, whose father was a stonemason, grew up in a poor family. One of 11 siblings, he was able to attend a local elementary school and probably studied for a few years at the local secondary school. By his 16th birthday, he was forced to quit school and take a job to help support himself and his family. He apprenticed himself to a printer and began to learn the newspaper trade.

In 1904, when Garvey was 17, he had learned his trade well enough to move to Kingston, the capital of Jamaica. He worked there as a printer for three years, and he became involved in local labor and electoral politics. As a union activist, he polished his oratorical skills and became a skilled public speaker.

After participating in an unsuccessful printers' union strike in 1907, Garvey left Jamaica and kicked around the Caribbean, working for a while on a banana plantation in Costa Rica, then for English-language newspapers in Panama. Racial discrimination against blacks in these countries upset Garvey. After appealing to British authorities for help to counter this discrimination, and receiving little sympathy, Garvey began to believe that blacks would not receive fair treatment from whites.

In 1912, Garvey moved to London to further his education. He studied for several years at Birkbeck College and began to meet people from other parts of the world who lived under British colonial rule. Garvey also became aware of BOOKER TALIAFERRO WASHINGTON for the first time after reading Washington's autobiography *Up from Slavery.*

Garvey's growing awareness that racial discrimination was a worldwide problem led him to return to Jamaica in 1914 and found the Universal Negro Improvement Association. In its literature, the UNIA announced that its purpose was to "[draw] the peoples of the race together." Garvey hoped to do this by encouraging racial pride, fostering education, and supporting businesses owned by blacks that would sell to blacks.

Marcus Garvey ca. 1920. Garvey was an important early 20th-century black nationalist leader and the head of the Universal Negro Improvement Association (UNIA). *(Library of Congress, Prints and Photographs Division, LC-USZ62-109626)*

Garvey started a trade school in Jamaica that was similar to Booker T. Washington's Tuskegee Institute, but, because of little funding, the school was bankrupt within a year or two. Sensing that he would have a greater chance of success in a larger country, Garvey moved to New York City in 1916. He had hoped to convince Booker T. Washington to support his efforts, but Washington died shortly before Garvey arrived in the United States.

Completely unknown and alone, Garvey opened up a storefront office and began delivering his message at black churches in Harlem and in other churches around the country. His call for racial pride and self-sufficiency was warmly received both by the immigrant West Indian community of Jamaicans and Bahamians who lived and worked in New York City and by African Americans who were tired of the second-class treatment they were receiving from many whites and the U.S. government.

By 1918, Garvey had founded his own paper, *Negro World*. Within a year and a half it had achieved a circulation of 50,000 subscribers. Garvey expanded on the U.S. base of *Negro World* by founding Spanish- and French-language editions of the paper that were circulated in Latin America and Africa. The paper was full of calls by Garvey for blacks to lift themselves up by founding their own businesses and political organizations; he also urged Africans living under French or British colonial rule to work for independence for their countries. British and French authorities responded by banning *Negro World* from their colonies.

In 1919, Garvey began one of his most ambitious enterprises, the founding of the Black Star Line, an international fleet of steamships. His idea was to create a fleet of freight and passenger ships that would link black-owned enterprises in the Americas with similar businesses in Africa. This would promote trade that would help raise the standard of living for blacks in both the Americas and Africa. The passenger ships of the Black Star Line would ferry African Americans and blacks who lived in the Americas back to Africa, where Garvey planned to start colonies for these refugees. Garvey married Amy Ashwood in 1919; after his divorce from Ashwood in 1922, he married Amy Jacques. He and Jacques had two children.

Garvey raised money to buy ships for the Black Star Line by selling stock in the company only to blacks for $5 a share. In 1919 alone, he raised more than $600,000 and was able to buy three ships: a small cargo ship called the *Yarmouth*; the *Kanawha*, a yacht that was converted into a passenger ship; and the *Shadyside*, a Hudson River steamer.

Another part of Garvey's scheme to create a black-owned financial empire was the founding of the Negro Factories Corporation, a financial institution that would lend money to African Americans and other blacks who wanted to start their own businesses. By 1921, the Negro Factories Corporation, which also raised money by selling stock at $5 a share, had funded a number of small businesses, including a restaurant, publishing company, laundry, and chain of grocery stores.

To consolidate and promote his many ideas for black self-improvement, Garvey held the first international UNIA convention in New York City in 1920. More than 2,000 delegates, representing local UNIA organizations from 48 states and a dozen countries, attended. *Negro World* printed Garvey's summation of the achievements of the conventions. For African Americans and other blacks, Garvey said, there would be

no more fear, no more cringing, no more sycophantic begging and pleading; but the Negro must strike straight from the shoulder for manhood rights and for full liberty. Africa calls now more than ever. She calls because the attempt is now being made by the combined Caucasian forces of Europe to subjugate her. . . . This convention of August left us full-fledged men; men charged to do our duty, and by the God Divine, . . . we have pledged ourselves to bring the manhood of our race to the highest plane of human achievement. We cannot, and we must not, falter. There is absolutely no turning back. . . . Destiny leads us to liberty, to freedom; that freedom that Victoria of England never gave; that liberty that Lincoln never meant; that freedom, that liberty, that will see us men among men; . . . that will make of us a great and powerful people.

Unfortunately for Garvey and his supporters, as a result of mismanagement and financial irreg-

ularities, his business enterprises, especially the Black Star Line, were on the edge of bankruptcy. In 1922, the U.S. government indicted Garvey and several associates for fraud. Garvey was found guilty in 1923 and began serving a five-year jail term in 1925.

After President Coolidge commuted his sentence in 1927, Garvey was deported from the United States. Garvey spent eight years in Jamaica trying to restore the vigor and credibility of the UNIA. However, without his presence, the UNIA chapters in the United States dwindled, as did those in other countries.

Garvey moved to London in 1935 and lived there for the rest of his life. The worldwide economic depression had diverted attention from financial self-improvement schemes. Now most people had their hands full simply trying to stay alive. UNIA conferences organized by Garvey in Toronto, Canada, in the late 1930s were poorly attended, and Garvey barely managed to scratch out a living in London through a new publication, *Black Man*, and correspondence courses he offered through a business called the School of African Philosophy. He died, at the age of 52, in London on June 10, 1940.

Further Reading

Cronon, Edward David. *Black Moses: The Story of Marcus Garvey and the Universal Negro Improvement Association.* Madison: University of Wisconsin Press, 1955.

Grant, Colin. *Negro with a Hat: The Rise and Fall of Marcus Garvey and His Dream of Mother Africa.* New York: Oxford University Press, 2008.

PBS. *The American Experience.* "Marcus Garvey." Available online. URL: http://www.pbs.org/wgbh/amex/garvey. Downloaded July 23, 2009.

University of California at Los Angeles. Marcus Garvey Project. Available online. URL: http://www.isop.ucla.edu/mgpp. Downloaded July 23, 2009.

Wintz, Cary D., ed. *African American Political Thought, 1890–1930: Washington, DuBois, Garvey, and Randolph.* Armonk, N.Y.: M. E. Sharpe, 1996.

Gates, Henry Louis, Jr.

(1950–) *scholar, educator, author, social commentator*

Well known as a scholar, educator, author, and social commentator, Henry Louis Gates, Jr., has worked hard to broaden and deepen the understanding of and the appreciation for the African-American experience. He was born on September 16, 1950, in Keyser, West Virginia. His father worked at a local paper mill. His mother suffered from a mental illness, which complicated his childhood. In 1968, Skip, as his friends called him, graduated at the top of his high school class. He enrolled at a local college, Potomac State College. Recognizing his student's talents, one of Gates's professors encouraged him to apply for admission to Ivy League schools. He was accepted by Yale University, where he majored in history. Gates graduated summa cum laude in 1973.

Winning a fellowship to study at Cambridge University in England, Gates earned master and doctorate degrees in English literature. He returned to the United States and began teaching at Yale University in 1979. He was soon promoted to associate professor of English and was named as director of the Afro-American studies department. In 1985, he left Yale to become a full professor at Cornell University. After a one-year stint at Duke University, in 1991, Gates accepted a position as a professor of humanities and as director of the African American studies department at Harvard University. He currently holds the Alphonse Fletcher University professorship at Harvard and serves as the director of the university's W. E. B. Du Bois Institute for African and African American Research.

A prolific writer, Gates has published many major books on African-American literature, history, and culture. His 31-volume Oxford-Schomburg Library of Nineteenth-Century Black Women Writers (1991) popularized interest in African-American women writers. He has also edited the *Norton Anthology of African American Literature* (1996) and coedited *Africana: The Encyclopedia of the African and African American Experience* (1999), *The African-American Century: How Black Americans Have Shaped Our Country* (2002), and *The African American National Biography* (2008). He has written several critically acclaimed books that examine the role of blacks in American society, including *Thirteen Ways of Looking at a Black Man* (1997), *America behind the Color Line: Dialogues with African Americans* (2004), and *The Future of the Race* (1996), which he coauthored with scholar CORNEL WEST. *Colored People: A Memoir* (1994) chronicles his childhood experiences. He has produced and hosted several PBS series that looked at the African-American experience, including *Wonders of the African World*, *America beyond the Color Line*, and *African American Lives*. In 2010, Gates hosted the

Educator and author Henry Louis Gates, Jr., hosted *African American Lives* in 2006 and 2008, a PBS television miniseries that explored the genealogy of prominent African Americans. *(© Marc Brasz/Corbis)*

four-part PBS series *Faces of America,* which explored the genealogy of 12 noted North Americans.

Gates serves as editor in chief of the Oxford African-American Studies Center, a scholarly online resource that provides comprehensive information and research in the field of Africana and African-American studies, and as editor in chief of the *Root,* a daily online magazine that provides news commentary from a wide range of black perspectives.

In 2009, Gates became the focus of a major news story when he was arrested for disturbing the peace. After returning home from a trip abroad, he discovered that the front door of his Cambridge, Massachusetts, house was jammed. His attempts to open the door prompted an observer to report a possible break-in to the police. By the time the police arrived, Gates had entered his home through the back door. An argument between Gates and the responding officer ensued, resulting in Gates's arrest. Although prosecutors quickly dropped the charges, the arrest sparked a media frenzy and a heated public debate about race and police procedures. To defuse the situation, President Barack Obama invited Gates and the arresting officer to the White House to discuss the incident.

Gates has received many honorary degrees, including a MacArthur Fellows Program Award (known popularly as the "Genius Award") and a George Polk Award for Social Commentary. He has been named as one of *Time* magazine's 25 most influential Americans and as one of *Ebony* magazine's 100 most influential black Americans.

Further Reading

Gates, Henry Louis, Jr. *Colored People: A Memoir.* New York: Knopf, 1994.
PBS. *African American Lives.* "Henry Louis 'Skip' Gates, Jr." Available online. URL: http://www.pbs.org/wnet/aalives/profiles/index.html. Downloaded July 30, 2009.
W. E. B. Du Bois Institute. "Henry Louis Gates, Jr." Available online. URL: http://dubois.fas.harvard.edu/henry-louis-gates. Downloaded July 30, 2009.

Green, Shields

(ca. 1825–1859) *abolitionist, Harpers Ferry raid participant*

Born into slavery in South Carolina, Shields Green was one of five African Americans and 16 whites who made the raid with John Brown on the U.S. government arsenal at Harpers Ferry on October 16, 1859. Very little is known about Green's early life. The year and date of his birth are not known; nor is the location of the plantation where he grew up.

Sometime around his 13th birthday, Green managed to escape from slavery in South Carolina, which was not an easy task because of that state's location in the Deep South. Aided by the Underground Railroad, the informal alliance of abolitionists in the North who helped fugitive slaves, Green ended up in Rochester, New York, where he contacted FREDERICK DOUGLASS, a well-known African-American abolitionist leader.

Instead of proceeding on to Canada and certain freedom, Green apparently remained in Rochester for several years, working for Douglass and other abolitionists. In one of his memoirs, Douglass remembered Green as "a man of few words… speech singularly broken; but his courage and self-respect made him quite a dignified character."

John Brown, a white abolitionist who had waged war against slaveholders in Kansas, had been planning a raid on a federal arsenal in slave territory in the late 1850s. His idea was to seize an arsenal where huge amounts of weapons and ammunition were stored, send out runners to rouse the surrounding slave population, then, with their aid, ignite a general slave revolt that would spread throughout the entire South. He had even written a new constitution that was to become the supreme law of the land on the success of this revolution.

Sometime in early 1859, Green met John Brown at Frederick Douglass's house in Rochester. Brown told Douglass and Green about his plans, and by then he had singled out Harpers Ferry, an armory that was located in what was then Virginia (now West Virginia). Brown was looking for volunteers and wanted to know whether Douglass or Green would join him. Douglass, seeing disaster, declined; Green accepted.

In August 1859, Green and John Brown's son, Owen, traveled south from New York to Virginia. Dodging slave patrols in northern Virginia, they worked their way to the farm near Harpers Ferry where the assault team was staying and training. On Sunday night, October 16, the attack began, first with the seizure of a railway bridge across the Potomac River, then with the taking of the weakly defended armory itself.

Within hours, local and federal troops began to descend on Harpers Ferry to confront and defeat Brown's men. Slowly, the members of Brown's party were separated and picked apart by the U.S. troops, who were under the command of Robert E. Lee, later the chief commander of Confederate forces during the Civil War. Green stuck by Brown's side, but by Tuesday, October 18, they had run out of ammunition and were captured.

Like the other captured members of Brown's party, Green was charged with treason, murder, and insurrection of a slave rebellion. His lawyer argued that Green, who was still legally a slave and thus not a citizen, could not be charged with treason. The court dropped that charge, but a jury found him guilty of murder and insurrection. He was hanged on December 16, 1859.

Further Reading

Anderson, Osborne P. *A Voice from Harpers Ferry.* 1861. Reprint, Atlanta: Worldview, 1980.

Douglass, Frederick. "Last Meeting between Frederick Douglass and John Brown." Available online. URL: http://www.iath.virginia.edu/jbrown/fdlife. html. Downloaded July 23, 2009.

Nudelman, Franny. *John Brown's Body: Slavery, Violence, & the Culture of War.* Chapel Hill: University of North Carolina Press, 2004.

Greener, Richard Theodore
(1844–1922) *educator, lawyer, diplomat*

The first African-American graduate of Harvard College, Richard Greener began his career as an educator before turning to law, diplomacy, and politics. Richard Theodore Greener was born in Philadelphia on January 30, 1844, to Richard Wesley and Mary Ann Greener. When he was a child, his family moved to Cambridge, Massachusetts.

Because the Greeners were a middle-class family who could afford to send their son to private schools, Richard was able to attend prep schools in Ohio and Massachusetts before enrolling in Harvard College in 1865. Greener excelled at Harvard and won prizes in oratory and for his senior dissertation. On his graduation in 1870, he became the first African American to earn a degree from that institution.

After graduation, Greener worked as a high school educator for three years. He returned to his hometown of Philadelphia to serve as principal at the Institute for Colored Youth, then took a job as principal of the Preparatory High School for Colored Youth in Washington, D.C.

In 1873, benefiting from the integrated politics in the South during the Reconstruction era, Greener was hired as a philosophy professor at the University of South Carolina. He also taught Latin, Greek, and U.S. constitutional and international law. At the end of his first year in South Carolina, he married Genevieve Ida Fleet.

While teaching in South Carolina, Greener also studied law. He completed a law degree from the University of South Carolina in 1876 and was admitted to the South Carolina bar that same year. In 1877, he was admitted to the bar in Washington, D.C.

After Reconstruction ended in South Carolina in 1877 and the state reverted to white, conservative rule, Greener was forced to give up his position at the university and move to Washington, D.C. In 1877, he became a professor of law at Howard University's law school; he would hold that position until 1880, when the law school was temporarily disbanded.

During his time at Howard University, Greener educated a generation of law students. He also became a voice in the racial and political debates of the day, defending in articles against FREDERICK DOUGLASS the movement to encourage former slaves from the South to relocate as homesteaders to Kansas and other Plains states.

When the Howard University law school shut down, Greener began a law career in Washington and worked as a campaigner for the Republican Party in the Midwest and upper South. For his political work, he was awarded several patronage jobs, notably that as chairman of the Grant Monument Association in New York City in 1885. He moved to New York City and also held a job there as a bureaucrat on the city's civil service board.

By 1892, because of shifting political fortunes, Greener had lost his jobs in New York City. For several years, he was faced with poverty as he tried unsuccessfully for an appointment in the foreign service. He finally secured a foreign service posting in 1898 on the election of President William McKinley, a Republican. He was sent to the unpromising city of Vladivostok, a port town on the Sea of Japan in the far eastern part of Russia.

Greener seems to have enjoyed Vladivostok. He served not only as American counsel but as the trade representative there. In 1900, he was pivotal in aiding victims of the Boxer Rebellion and the Shansi famine in nearby China and was awarded the Order of the Double Dragon by the Chinese government in appreciation of his services.

Greener retired from the foreign service in 1906. On his return to the United States, he lived in Chicago and became a friend of BOOKER TALIAFERRO WASHINGTON. Greener attended several meetings of the Niagara Movement and reported secretly about the participants, especially about W. E. B. DuBois, to Washington. Greener died in Chicago on May 22, 1922.

Further Reading

University of South Carolina Bicentennial. "A Brief Biography of Richard Greener." Available online. URL: http://www.sc.edu/bicentennial/pages/greenerpages/greenerbio.html. Downloaded July 23, 2009.

Guinier, Lani
(1950–) *lawyer, voting rights advocate*

A groundbreaking constitutional scholar and teacher, Lani Guinier also has been involved in efforts to bridge the racial divide in the United States. Born in Queens, New York, in 1950, Guinier attended integrated public schools. Encouraged to excel in her education by her father, Ewart, and her mother, Eugenia, Guinier was offered a scholarship to Radcliffe College after graduating from high school in 1967. In 1971, she graduated from Radcliffe and enrolled in the Yale Law School, where she earned her degree in 1974. After her graduation, Guinier worked as a law clerk for Damon J. Keith, the senior judge at the U.S. District Court in Detroit. Later she worked for several years as a referee at the Wayne County Juvenile Court before taking a job as a special assistant in the Civil Rights Division of the Justice Department in Washington, D.C. During this time, she married Nolan Bowie, a professor of communications. They have one child.

Guinier knew that she wanted to be a civil rights lawyer from the age of 12, when she watched on television as Constance Baker Mott, a black lawyer working for the National Association of

Lani Guinier, a professor at Harvard Law School, is a scholar of voting law rights and an activist in racial reconciliation. *(Courtesy Harvard Law School Communications)*

Colored People (NAACP), escorted James Meredith, the first African-American student at the University of Mississippi, through a mob of howling white students. Therefore, it was with great pleasure that she took a job as a civil rights lawyer for the NAACP's Legal Defense Fund in 1981.

From 1981 to 1988, Guinier worked for the NAACP as a lawyer and political adviser in Washington and the South. In Washington she took part in the successful effort in 1981 to extend the 1965 Voting Rights Act, a law that had forced southern states to allow black voters to participate in the electoral process for the first time. In the South, Guinier tried voting rights cases and defended clients who were being harassed because of their efforts to get blacks to vote.

In 1988, Guinier joined the faculty of the University of Pennsylvania law school in Philadelphia. There she began to explore other systems of voting that allowed a broader range of representation than the winner-take-all system used in most parts of the United States. She began writing articles advocating "proportional representation," a concept whereby minority voters could be more fairly represented than under the winner-take-all system. In one form of proportional representation, for instance, the one used in South Africa, voters vote not for individual candidates but for parties. If one party wins 20 percent of the vote, then it is guaranteed 20 percent of the seats in the Congress.

In 1993, Guinier was nominated by President Clinton to head the Justice Department's Civil Rights Division. Her nomination created a firestorm. Conservative opponents of the Clinton administration, and some middle-of-the-road newspapers such as the *New York Times*, questioned Guinier's commitment to the idea of majority rule. The *Times* accused Guinier of wanting to "[segregate] black voters in black districts." The *Wall Street Journal* dubbed her a "quota Queen," meaning that she thought that African Americans were entitled to a set number of representatives in elections based on their percentage of the population. Although these accusations did not accurately reflect Guinier's actual beliefs, they caused the Clinton administration to withdraw her nomination before she had a chance to defend herself in Senate hearings.

In the mid-1990s, Guinier helped found Commonplace, an organization that, in Guinier's words, sought

> to transform public discourse, particularly about issues of race. . . . There is a breakdown in our ability to talk to each other on a number of issues. . . . We're trying to rethink the nature of this conversation so that the focus is . . . on listening, mutual understanding and mutual respect. We think that, through genuine conversation, collaboration will emerge.

She also wrote *Lift Every Voice,* a book that explains her beliefs and chronicles her aborted Justice Department nomination.

In 1998, Guinier was hired as a full professor by Harvard Law School. She continues to teach at Harvard and is working on issues such as finding new, nondiscriminatory ways of determining how students are admitted to colleges and universities. In 2003, she cowrote *The Miner's Canary: Enlisting Race, Enlisting Power, Transforming Democracy,* which called for cross-racial coalitions to increase public participation in politics and reform of the current power structure in the United States.

Further Reading

Guinier, Lani. *Lift Every Voice.* New York: Simon & Schuster, 1998.

———. *The Tyranny of the Majority: Fundamental Fairness in Representative Democracy.* New York: Free Press, 1994.

Harvard Law School. "Lani Guinier Home Page." Available online: URL: http://www.law.harvard.edu/faculty/guinier/. Downloaded August 1, 2009.

PBS. *Charlie Rose.* "Lani Guinier." Available online. URL: http://www.charlierose.com/guest/view/3645. Downloaded August 1, 2009.

H

Hall, Prince
(ca. 1735–1807) *abolitionist, community activist*

An early civil rights leader in Boston and crusader for the abolition of slavery, Prince Hall also established the first African-American Masonic lodge in the United States. Not much is known of Hall's early life, including his place of birth, his parents, and details about his childhood. However, it seems likely that he was born in Boston sometime around the year 1735. Public records show that in his early teens Hall was listed as the slave of the owner of a Boston leather goods business named William H. Hall. Hall's parents were probably slaves as well. Records in Boston also show that Hall joined a Congregational church in 1762 and that he was married for the first time, to Sarah Ritchie, in 1763. Hall would later marry two more times and have at least two children.

In 1770, around Hall's 35th birthday, his owner, William Hall, freed Hall from slavery. By this time, Hall must have been an experienced leather tanner and artisan. He probably either set up his own small business or continued to work, now as a paid employee, for William Hall.

Hall is best known for his ceaseless work promoting the ideas of Masonism among African Americans in the United States. Masonic lodges originated in Europe, where they had begun to be organized in the 1600s. Masons had many secret rituals, but they were also known to encourage ideas such as the universal brotherhood of humankind, mutual assistance among Masons, tolerance, and sober and moderate behavior.

Hall was one of 15 African Americans who were initiated into a Masonic lodge attached to a British army unit stationed in Boston in March 1775. The outbreak of war between the colonists and the British army at Bunker Hill and Lexington in April of that year must have put Hall in a tight spot. There is no record that Hall served with the Revolutionary army, although he did make supplies such as drumheads for the Americans.

By July 1775, the original 15 blacks of the British army lodge formed their own group, African Lodge No. 1. Prince Hall was elected master, or leader, of this group. The members of African Lodge No. 1 had to wait another 12 years, until 1787, for official recognition of their lodge by the Masonic headquarters, which was located in London. In 1797 and 1798, Hall helped organize two more African-American lodges, one in Providence, Rhode Island, the other in Philadelphia.

Lodges appealed to African Americans of this period and later because they were institutions in which black men could meet among themselves and make decisions for their community outside the domain of the white society. The lodges served as incubators of early African-American leadership. Masonic rules encouraged self-help and mutual support among lodge members, valuable commodities at a time when there were no old-age pensions or disability benefits. Plus they also encouraged respectful, sober behavior among their members. Lodges produced leaders, and Prince Hall soon became a leader of the Boston African-American community.

One of Hall's first acts of leadership was to organize in 1777 a petition drive in Boston urging the Massachusetts legislature to abolish slavery. Hall pointed out that slavery was not consistent with the patriot cause of liberty and self-determination. The legislature took Hall's petition under consideration but did not act on it. Slavery was abolished through a court case in 1783.

Hall was the first African American to propose that American blacks should leave the United States and return to Africa. In 1787, citing "the very disagreeable and disadvantageous circumstances" of African Americans, Hall asked the Massachusetts legislature to provide funds for blacks to return to Africa. The idea was that American blacks would found a colony somewhere on the west coast of Africa, would set up their own government and churches, then would set out to Christianize "those nations [of Africa] who are now sunk in ignorance and barbarity." When the legislature ignored this request, Hall decided to focus on improving the plight of African Americans in Massachusetts instead.

Later in 1787, Hall again petitioned the legislature, this time requesting money for schools for African-American children in Massachusetts. Hall argued that because blacks were taxed as other citizens were, they should also reap the benefit of this taxation in the form of schools. Again, the legislature ignored Hall's request. However, a school for black children was finally established in 1800 after Hall convinced Boston city officials to pay for teachers. From 1800 to 1806, this school was held in Hall's house. The first two teachers were Harvard students.

In 1788, Hall and his Masonic lodge successfully organized a protest campaign to free three black Bostonians who had been kidnapped from the streets of Boston and taken aboard a ship to the French island of Saint Bartholomew, where they were sold into slavery. In March 1788, the legislature passed an act that forbade the trade of slaves in Massachusetts. Letters from the Massachusetts governor, John Hancock, motivated by Hall's persistent pressure, freed the three men. Their return to Boston in July 1887 was the occasion of a huge community celebration organized by Hall and African Lodge No. 1.

Prince Hall died on December 4, 1807, in Boston. According to local papers, "a very large procession of blacks" accompanied his body to his gravesite, a mark of the respect with which he was held.

Further Reading

Cass, Donn A. *Negro Freemasonry and Segregation: An Historical Study of Prejudice against American Negroes as Freemasons, and the Position of Negro Freemasonry in the Masonic Fraternity.* Chicago: E. A. Cook, 1957.

PBS. Africans in America, Resource Bank. "Prince Hall." Available online. URL: http://www.pbs.org/wgbh/aia/part2/2p37.html. Downloaded July 23, 2009.

Wesley, Charles H. *Prince Hall: Life and Legacy.* Washington, D.C.: United Supreme Council, Prince Hall Affiliation, 1977.

Hamer, Fannie Lou
(Fannie Lou Townsend)
(1917–1977) *civil rights activist, Mississippi Freedom Democratic Party founder*

Risking her life for the cause of basic civil rights and justice for African Americans in the South, Fannie Lou Hamer was an important leader who helped blacks in Mississippi get the right to vote. One of 20 children, Fannie Lou Townsend was

Fannie Lou Hamer ca. 1964. Hamer led civil rights campaigns in Mississippi during the 1950s and 1960s and spearheaded the Mississippi Freedom Democratic Party in 1964. *(Library of Congress, Prints and Photographs Division, LC-U9-12470B)*

born on October 6, 1917, to Jim and Lou Ella Townsend in Montgomery County, in north central Mississippi. As a child, she contracted polio, which left her a slight disability.

Fannie Lou's parents worked as sharecroppers on a cotton plantation. The pay was poor, and the Hamers usually worked for more than eight hours for as little as $2 a day. Beginning at age six, Fannie Lou was obliged to work in the fields to earn money for the family. Also at age six, she began to study in a local school, but local authorities did not encourage black children to stay in school. In an interview, she later recalled, "My parents tried so hard to do what they could to keep us in school,

but school [for black children] didn't last but four months out of the year and most of the time we didn't have clothes to wear. I dropped out of school [in the sixth grade] and cut cornstalks to help the family."

In 1944, when she was 27, Fannie Lou married Perry "Pap" Hamer. The couple moved to Ruleville, about 30 miles away from where she grew up. As her parents had, Fannie Lou Hamer and her husband became sharecroppers. Living on the Marlow plantation, she worked as a time-keeper while her husband worked in the fields. Unknowingly sterilized by white doctors, and therefore unable to conceive children, Hamer adopted four daughters. Seeing injustice all around her, Hamer yearned for a way to help African Americans who could not vote and were denied education, as well as full access to public facilities such as restaurants, movie theaters, hospitals, and even bathrooms.

Hamer's chance to help occurred in 1962, when the Student Nonviolent Coordinating Committee (SNCC) went to Ruleville and began to instruct African Americans about registering to vote. After receiving instruction from SNCC volunteers, Hamer tried to register. The first time, she was asked detailed questions about the Mississippi state constitution that few, white or black, could answer. Not surprisingly, she failed this rigged "test." She kept returning until she finally was allowed to register.

When word of Hamer's persistence reached Marlow, the plantation owner, he fired her and threw her off the plantation. Hamer then volunteered for the SNCC, working to help register other black voters. She told an interviewer, "I am determined to become a first-class citizen. . . . I am determined to get every Negro in the state of Mississippi registered."

Hamer suffered terribly for her determination. In 1963, she was arrested in Winona, near where she was born. She was taken to the county jail, where a state policeman, telling her "he was going to make me wish I was dead," ordered several black prisoners to beat her. "They made me lay down on my face and they ordered two Negro prisoners to beat me with a blackjack," Hamer later told an interviewer. "That was unbearable. The first prisoner beat me until he was exhausted, then the second Negro began to beat me. . . . They beat me until I was hard, 'til I couldn't bend my fingers or get up when they told me to."

Even after this ordeal, Hamer refused to give up her work. She continued to register voters, and the next year, 1964, she organized the Mississippi Freedom Democratic Party, a challenge to the regular Democratic Party in the state, which refused to allow black delegates to attend the Democratic National Convention in Atlantic City, New Jersey. Hamer took her own delegation to Atlantic City and stopped the proceedings until President Lyndon Johnson arranged a compromise. In exchange for giving up her protest, Hamer was promised that Mississippi would never exclude black delegates again. The following year, President Johnson also succeeded in passing the Voting Rights Act, which gave federal agents the right to register voters in the South. Soon, hundreds of thousands of African-American citizens were for the first time able to vote.

During the late 1960s, Hamer worked on projects to help poor families get food and adequate housing. In 1968, she founded the Pig Bank, a livestock cooperative in Mississippi that provided low-priced meat to poor people. In 1969, she organized the Freedom Farm Cooperative, an organization that helped poor farmers buy land and grow food. In the 1970s, Hamer worked to desegregate schools in Mississippi and provide housing for low-income people.

Fannie Lou Hamer died in Ruleville, Mississippi, on March 15, 1977.

Further Reading

Lee, Chana Kai. *For Freedom's Sake: The Life of Fannie Lou Hamer.* Urbana: University of Illinois Press, 1999.

Mills, Kay. *This Little Light of Mine: The Life of Fannie Lou Hamer.* Lexington: University of Kentucky Press, 2007.

University of Southern Mississippi. Civil Rights in Mississippi Digital Archives. "An Oral History with Fannie Lou Hamer." Available online. URL: http://www.lib.usm.edu/~spcol/crda/oh/hamer.htm?hamertrans.htm~mainFrame. Downloaded July 23, 2009.

Hart, William Henry

(1857–1934) *lawyer, civil rights leader, philanthropist*

A longtime professor of law at Howard University in Washington, D.C., William Hart was also a pioneer in using the courts to advance the civil rights of African Americans. Born into slavery in Eufaula, Alabama, in 1857, to Henry and Jennie Hart, William Henry Hart probably received little if any education during his youth in that state. When he was around 20, he moved from Alabama to Washington, D.C., traveling at least part of the way by foot.

In Washington, Hart immediately set about catching up in his education. While working to support himself, he enrolled in the Preparatory School at Howard University; he graduated in 1880. Hart continued his studies at Howard, earning a B.A. in 1885, a law degree in 1887, and a master's degree in 1889. Soon after his arrival in Washington, Hart married. He and his wife, Mary, had three children.

Hart's intelligence impressed Senator William Evats of New York, who hired Hart as his private secretary in 1888. While still working for Evats, Hart was appointed special assistant to the U.S. district attorney in 1889, and in 1890 he started teaching law at Howard University, beginning a 32-year association with that institution. As a fund-raiser, he gathered a significant amount of money for the construction of the new Howard University Law School building in 1892.

Hart's main contribution to civil rights law occurred on the heels of his arrest on board a train bound from Washington, D.C., to New York City. Hart was arrested in Maryland for refusing to sit in the cars that were reserved for blacks only. He was tried, found guilty of violating Maryland's segregation laws, and fined $5. Hart fought the conviction by appealing the case to a federal court. The higher court reversed Hart's conviction by ruling that Congress had exclusive jurisdiction over interstate transportation, and Congress had not enacted segregation laws for transport.

Even though Hart won the case, *Hart v. the State of Maryland* (1905), segregation continued to be practiced on all in-state trains in the South and on most interstate trains to and from the South. Segregation on interstate transport such as trains and buses would not be completely abolished until the early 1960s.

Hart retired from Howard University in 1922 and moved to Brooklyn, New York. He died in Brooklyn on January 17, 1934.

Further Reading

Logan, Rayford. *Howard University: The First Hundred Years.* New York: New York University Press, 1969.

Logan, Rayford, and Michael Winston. *Dictionary of American Negro Biography.* New York: W. W. Norton, 1982.

Hastie, William Henry, Jr.

(1904–1976) *lawyer, civil rights activist, judge*

A lawyer who often worked for the National Association for the Advancement of Colored People (NAACP), William Hastie was one of the leaders of the legal fight against racial discrimination. He later had a distinguished career as a federal judge. Born on November 17, 1904, in Knoxville, Tennessee, William Henry Hastie, Jr., was the son of William Henry and Roberta Hastie. After attend-

ing primary school in Knoxville, Hastie moved with his family to Washington, D.C. He finished his secondary education at Dunbar High School in Washington in 1921.

After graduation from high school, Hastie enrolled in Amherst College in Massachusetts. An excellent student, he graduated first in his class in 1925. Hastie taught at a school in New Jersey for two years before being admitted to the Harvard Law School in 1927. While a student at Harvard, Hastie served on the staff of the *Harvard Law Review.* He earned a law degree from Harvard in 1930.

William Henry Hastie, a leader of the National Association for the Advancement of Colored People's (NAACP's) strategy of legal action against racial discrimination, became the first African-American federal judge in 1937. *(Moorland-Spingarn Research Center, Howard University)*

After his graduation from Harvard, Hastie moved back to Washington, D.C., where he began teaching law at Howard University's law school. He was admitted to the Washington, D.C., bar in 1931 and joined the firm of CHARLES HAMILTON HOUSTON, another of the NAACP's leading civil rights attorneys.

In the 1930s, Hastie began to help fashion the NAACP's slow and careful legal assault against racial discrimination in the United States. Guided by Hastie, Houston, and others, the NAACP selected state and federal laws and regulations that targeted black voters for discrimination and filed lawsuits challenging the constitutional validity of these laws.

With the election of Franklin D. Roosevelt in 1932, Hastie found that he had allies inside the government. His former law school professor Felix Frankfurter had become an adviser to Roosevelt, and through Frankfurter, Hastie became part of what was known as the "black cabinet," an informal group of African-American men and women who advised the president on race issues.

Hastie was appointed as a lawyer at the Interior Department in 1933 and served there until 1937, when Roosevelt appointed him judge of the Federal District Court in the U.S. Virgin Islands. With his confirmation by the U.S. Senate, Hastie became the first African American to serve as a federal judge. Hastie worked in this position for two years before returning to Washington to become dean of the Howard University law school.

For several years after the start of World War II, Hastie was an aide to Secretary of War Henry Stimson. However, in 1943, he resigned his position to protest the federal government's policy of segregation in the armed forces. The next year, Hastie worked with a group that was trying to eliminate the poll tax—a fee imposed by many, mostly southern, states—which greatly hindered the right of poor African Americans to vote. Hastie testified several times before Senate committees in favor of a bill to prohibit use of poll taxes.

After the war, Hastie returned to the Virgin Islands, this time as governor after his appointment by President Truman. He served in this position for three years, until his nomination by Truman as a judge on the Third Circuit Court of Appeals. Hastie was confirmed in this position, the first African American to attain such a high position in the U.S. judiciary. Hastie served as a U.S. appeals judge for 21 years, eventually becoming chief judge of this court.

Citing his "distinguished career as jurist and as an uncompromising champion of equal justice," the NAACP awarded Hastie the Spingarn Medal in 1943. William Hastie died on April 14, 1976, in Pennsylvania.

Further Reading

Fleming, Thomas C. *Columbus Free Press.* "The Black Cabinet." Available online. URL: http://www. freepress.org/fleming/flemng83.html. Downloaded July 23, 2009.

Tennessee State University. "William Henry Hastie." Available online. URL: http://www.tnstate.edu/ library/digital/hastie.htm. Downloaded July 23, 2009.

Vile, John, ed. *Great American Lawyers: An Encyclopedia.* Santa Barbara, Calif.: ABC-CLIO, 2002.

Ware, Gilbert. *William Hastie: Grace under Pressure.* New York: Oxford University Press, 1984.

Haynes, George Edmund

(1880–1960) *social worker, educator, Urban League founder*

A researcher into the problems encountered by African Americans after their arrival in northern cities, George Haynes put his knowledge of social conditions to work by founding the Urban League in 1910. George Edmund Haynes was born in the small Arkansas town of Pine Bluff in 1880. His father, Louis Haynes, was a laborer, and his mother, Mattie, worked as a domestic. Both of

Haynes's parents emphasized the importance of education as a tool for advancement and encouraged young George to pursue his interests in his studies.

Haynes attended elementary school in Pine Bluff, but when he was around 10, he and his sister were taken by their mother to Hot Springs, where the schools were better. Haynes first became aware that he could attend college while working for a white doctor in Hot Springs. Once he knew about this possibility, he made it his goal. In 1893, he attended the Chicago World's Fair, an event that opened his eyes to the world outside Arkansas.

After graduation from high school in Hot Springs in 1898, Haynes studied for a year in a college preparatory course at the Agricultural and Mechanical College in Normal, Alabama. He then transferred to Fisk University in Nashville, Tennessee. He was a good student and graduated from Fisk with a B.A. in 1903. After graduation, Haynes was admitted to Yale University and earned a master's degree from that institution in 1904.

In 1905, Haynes took his first job. Serving as secretary of the Colored Men's Department at the International Young Men's Christian Association (YMCA), he traveled frequently around the country as he visited historically African-American colleges and universities. His goal was to offer encouragement to black students and show them that there were rewards for hard study. During one of these tours he met Elizabeth Ross, who would become his first wife. They had one son. After Ross's death in 1953, Haynes would marry Olyve Love Jeter.

Haynes left the YMCA job in 1908 to continue his education. The more he saw of conditions in the big northern cities, the more interested he became in understanding the social conditions in those places. He enrolled as a student in Columbia University's New School of Philanthropy in 1908 and took his degree there in 1910. By 1912, he had completed a Ph.D. at Columbia, becoming the first African American to earn a doctorate from that university.

While Haynes was working on his degrees from Columbia, he also began working for organizations that were actively involved in helping newly arrived southern blacks get jobs and apartments in New York City. One of these organizations was called the Committee for Improving the Industrial Conditions of Negroes in New York (CIICNNY). Haynes worked as a researcher for CIICNNY, investigating working conditions of newly arrived African Americans, finding out how easy or difficult it was for them to join a union and how they were treated by white employers.

During his work for CIICNNY, Haynes met Mrs. William Baldwin, the wealthy widow of a railroad magnate, who was interested in helping the poor. Together, they founded the Committee of Urban Conditions among Negroes in 1910. A year later, this group merged with CIICNNY to become the National Urban League. George Haynes was the league's first executive director. In 1910, he also accepted the position of director of Fisk University's newly created social work department.

It had always been Haynes's vision that racial problems in America had to be solved through interracial cooperation. Mrs. Baldwin was white, Haynes black. Likewise the board of directors of the league was an interracial group. The league was founded just as a huge new wave of black migration from the South reached northern cities, especially during World War I, when shortages in northern factories lured blacks north. The goal of the league was to ease the way for these black workers. The league also tried to defuse racial tensions between whites and blacks whenever possible.

In 1917, Haynes quit his Urban League job to take a full-time position as director of Negro economics at the U.S. Department of Labor. He would remain at the Labor Department until 1921, heading studies of the working conditions of African Americans.

In 1921, Haynes left the government to become executive director of the Church of Christ's Department of Race Relations, a job he would hold until 1947. At this job, he developed the idea of holding Interracial Clinics, which would offer white and black leaders a chance to get to know each other personally, thus, Haynes hoped, opening up bridges of communication between the two communities. In 1930 and 1947, Haynes took one-year leaves of absence to travel to Africa, where he did surveys of the work of the Young Men's Christian Association (YMCA) there. This would lead to a job as African consultant for the YMCA from 1948 to 1950.

In the last decade of his life, Haynes served on the board of trustees of the State University of New York system and taught at the City College of New York. Haynes died in 1960 in New York City.

Further Reading

Haynes, George. "The Church and the Negro Spirit." Available online. URL: http://etext.lib.virginia.edu/harlem/HayChurF.html. Downloaded July 23, 2009.

Mjagkij, Nina, ed. *Organizing Black America: An Encyclopedia of African American Associations.* New York: Taylor & Francis, 2001.

Perlman, Daniel. "Stirring the White Conscience: The Life of George Edmund Haynes." Ph.D. dissertation, New York University, 1972.

Tennessee Encyclopedia of History and Culture. "George Edmund Haynes." Available online. URL: http://tennesseeencyclopedia.net/imagegallery.php?EntryID=H032. Downloaded July 23, 2009.

Height, Dorothy

(1912–2010) *foundation administrator, civil rights activist, women's rights activist*

An influential civil rights activist for more than 70 years, Dorothy Height fought tirelessly for equal rights and social justice for African Americans and women. Dorothy Irene Height was born on March 24, 1912, in Richmond, Virginia. Her father, James, worked as a building contractor, and her mother, Fannie, was a nurse. The Heights moved from Virginia to Rankin, Pennsylvania, near Pittsburgh, when Dorothy was four years old.

Although she attended integrated public schools, Height experienced the sting of segregation. One summer day, she and her friends went to a YWCA in Pittsburgh for a swim. Because the organization did not allow African Americans to use its facilities, the YWCA refused to allow Dorothy to swim with her white friends. Her involvement in civil rights began that day when the precocious 12-year-old demanded to speak to the YWCA's manager to protest being denied admission to the pool because of the color of her skin. As a teenager, Dorothy joined a local campaign that advocated voting rights for African Americans.

Dorothy excelled in high school. A gifted public speaker, she finished in first place at a national speech contest, winning a four-year scholarship. In 1929, Barnard College in New York City offered her admission, but the college would not let her enroll when she arrived there. In her 2003 autobiography, *Open Wide the Freedom Gates,* Height recalled, "It took me a while to realize that their decision was a racial matter: Barnard had a quota of two Negro students per year, and two others had already taken the spots." Barnard officials told her that she could enroll in the college's 1930 spring semester. One of the college's current black students would graduate at the end of the fall semester. Height instead applied for admission to New York University (NYU). Despite her late admission request, NYU admitted Height and allowed her to enroll for fall classes. To persuade NYU to accept her application, she had shown a dean her admission letter from Barnard. Height earned a bachelor's degree in education in 1933 and a master's degree in educational psychology the following year.

Height briefly considered pursuing a medical degree but decided that social work was her true calling. She became a caseworker in New York City's welfare department. In the late 1930s, she accepted a position as the assistant executive director of the YWCA in Harlem, an African-American neighborhood in New York City. Around the same time, Height became involved with the National Council of Negro Women (NCNW), an organization that MARY MCLEOD Bethune had founded in 1935. Height impressed the prominent educator and influential civil rights advocate, who soon became the younger woman's mentor.

In the early 1940s, Height moved to Washington, D.C., after accepting a position as director of a YWCA branch in the nation's capital. In 1944, she joined the organization's national board as a staff member. Two years later, she managed the desegregation of all YWCA programs and facilities throughout the United States. She would remain a YMCA staffer until she retired in 1975.

While working at the YWCA, Height also remained an active volunteer in the NCNW. When Bethune died in 1955, she became the organization's president and served as its leader until 1998. During her 40-year tenure, the NCNW developed programs to address a wide range of problems faced by African-American women and their families, from voting rights and unemployment to poverty and AIDS. In 1985, Height and the NCNW helped establish the Black Family Reunion Celebration, annual get-togethers that celebrate the traditions of African-American families. More than 10 million people have participated in these gatherings.

Through her leadership roles in the YWCA and the NCNW, Height became a key figure in the Civil Rights movement. In the 1950s, she urged President Dwight Eisenhower to desegregate public schools. In 1963, she was among the major civil rights leaders sitting behind Martin Luther King, Jr., as he delivered his momentous "I Have a Dream" speech in Washington, D.C. Three weeks later, King asked her to travel to Alabama to console and counsel the families of four African-American girls killed in a racially motivated bombing of Birmingham's 16th Street Baptist Church.

During the peak of the Civil Rights movement in the 1950s and 1960s, the NCNW, through Height's leadership, initiated social programs throughout the South. The organization conducted voter-registration drives and sponsored a program called Wednesdays in Mississippi, in which black and white women from around the country came to Mississippi to teach in alternative "Freedom Schools" in African-American communities throughout the state. In 1965, Height founded the YWCA's Center for Racial Justice and served as its director until her retirement.

Height was also active in the women's rights movement. As a prominent equal rights advocate, she was invited to the White House to witness President John Kennedy's signing of the Equal Pay Act in 1963. With Shirley Chisholm, Betty Friedan and other leading women's rights activists, Height helped found the National Women's Political Caucus in 1971.

Because of Height's efforts to guarantee social justice for all Americans, 10 U.S. presidents, from Eisenhower to Obama, sought her advice on civil rights issues. In 1993, she was inducted into the National Women's Hall of Fame. She received many honors for her life's work, including the nation's two most prestigious civilian awards: the Presidential Medal of Freedom (1994) and the Congressional Gold Medal (2004). Harvard, Princeton, and other universities awarded her honorary degrees. Barnard College, which had refused her admission 75 years earlier, named Height as an honorary graduate in 2004. When Barack Obama was sworn in as the nation's first African-American president in 2009, Height was among the special guests sitting on the podium to witness the ceremony.

Dorothy Height died on April 10, 2010. Upon learning of her death, President Obama called Height "the godmother of the Civil Rights Movement" and "a hero to so many Americans." He observed that she "devoted her life to those struggling for equality . . . witnessing every march and milestone along the way."

Further Reading

"Dorothy I. Height, Founding Matriarch of U.S. Civil Rights Movement, Dies at 98." *Washington Post,* 11 April 2010. Available online. URL: http://www.washingtonpost.com/wp-dyn/content/article/2010/04/20/AR2010042001287.html. Downloaded June 22, 2010.

Height, Dorothy. *Open Wide the Freedom Gates.* New York: Public Affairs, 2003.

National Women's Hall of Fame. "Dorothy Height." Available online. URL: http://www.greatwomen.org/women.php?action=viewone&id=75. Downloaded June 22, 2010.

Henry, Aaron

(1922–1997) *pharmacist, civil rights activist*

The son of a Mississippi sharecropper, Aaron Henry pursued an education to become a respected businessman in Clarksdale, Mississippi. During the 1950s, before civil rights had become a nationally important issue, Henry courageously organized civil rights activities in his home state. Born in 1922 on the Flowers plantation near the Mississippi Delta town of Clarksdale, Henry lived and worked on the plantation until he was about six years old. Around 1928, the Henrys moved to Clarksdale, where Aaron began his education. For his elementary education, he studied at a local school for African Americans set up in a Baptist church. He then attended the Coahoma County Agricultural High School.

After graduating from high school in 1941, Henry worked as a clerk in a motel while he saved money for college. After the United States entered World War II in December 1941, he was drafted into the army and from 1943 to 1946 lived in Camp Roberts in California. There he became active in the local chapters of the National Association for the Advancement of Colored People (NAACP) and informally helped to ease racial tensions in his army unit.

After the war, Henry returned to the South. He enrolled in the School of Pharmacy at Xavier University in New Orleans in 1946 and worked at a local pharmacy to learn his trade. On his graduation from Xavier in 1950, Henry returned to Clarksdale and opened up a drugstore. He married Noelle Michael that year. The couple would have two children.

Because he had grown up in Clarksdale, Henry knew how far the town had to go for blacks to achieve fair and honest treatment at the hands of white authorities. Henry first joined the Progressive Voters League, a group that encouraged blacks to register to vote. In 1951, he organized the first branch of the NAACP in Clarksdale, and that same year he organized the Regional Council of Negro Leadership (RCNL). In the early to mid-1950s, the RCNL organized a number of boycotts of white businesses that would not let African Americans use public facilities such as bathrooms. Under Henry, the RCNL also managed to register an ever-increasing number of voters in rural Mississippi.

By 1959, the board of the Mississippi NAACP was so impressed by Henry's work that they voted him state director of the organization. In 1961, Henry began working with ROBERT MOSES, of the Student Nonviolent Coordinating Committee (SNCC), and MEDGAR WILEY EVERS, a fellow Mississippian who was active in the NAACP, to devise strategies to end Jim Crow, the system of racial segregation common in the South. In 1961, Henry organized a boycott of stores in Clarksdale that discriminated against African-American customers. This boycott lasted for three years, until passage of the Civil Rights Act in 1964, which outlawed almost all forms of racial discrimination.

As a result of his efforts, Henry's home and business were both firebombed, and he was jailed repeatedly. In spite of these attempts to intimidate him, Henry did not quit his civil rights organizing work. In the late 1960s and through the 1970s, he worked with moderate black and white leaders to remake the Mississippi Democratic Party into a truly inclusive political party. He served as cochair of the party and in 1979 was elected as a representative to the state legislature.

After working for more than 35 years to change the politics and racial atmosphere of Mississippi, Aaron Henry died in Clarksdale on May 19, 1997.

Further Reading

Documenting the American South. "Oral History Interview with Aaron Henry." Available online. URL: http://docsouth.unc.edu/sohp/A-0107/menu.html. Downloaded July 23, 2009.

Henry, Aaron, and Constance Curry. *Aaron Henry: The Fire Ever Burning.* Jackson: University Press of Mississippi, 2000.

Mills, Kay. *Changing Channels: The Civil Rights Case That Transformed Television.* Jackson: University Press of Mississippi, 2004.

Higginbotham, Aloysius Leon, Jr.

(1928–1998) *lawyer, judge, civil rights advocate*

A leader in the African-American community in Philadelphia and the nation, A. Leon Higginbotham chose the law as the tool to advance the struggle of civil rights for African Americans. Aloysius Leon Higginbotham was born on February 15, 1928, in Trenton, New Jersey. His mother worked as a cleaning woman, and his father was a laborer. Both parents understood the value of education and encouraged Higginbotham to study.

After graduating from high school in Trenton in 1946, Higginbotham enrolled in the engineering program in Purdue University near Chicago.

He immediately discovered that black students were housed in an inferior, segregated dormitory, which he protested. After realizing that university officials were not going to change this policy, Higginbotham transferred to Oberlin College, which housed its African-American students in integrated dormitories. Higginbotham graduated from Oberlin with a B.A. in 1949.

After finishing his undergraduate degree, Higginbotham enrolled in the Yale Law School in 1950 and graduated in 1952. He then moved to Philadelphia, where he formed his own law firm with a law school classmate, Clifford Green. Unable to rent office space in downtown Philadelphia because they were black, Green and Higginbotham set up shop in an office near the downtown area. Higginbotham joined the Philadelphia chapter of the National Association for the Advancement of Colored People (NAACP) and worked without pay on many cases for poor members of Philadelphia's black community. According to Green, Higginbotham's "clientele was among the poorest people in Philadelphia, and he represented them with great sincerity and great dedication. And he was very successful in vindicating their rights." In 1956, he began his public law career by taking a job as a deputy state attorney general.

Higginbotham quickly established a reputation as an able and fair-minded lawyer as well as a Democratic Party stalwart. In 1962, President John Kennedy appointed him to the Federal Trade Commission. He served in this position for a year and was nominated by Kennedy to be a judge of the U.S. District Court in Pennsylvania. Because of his strong civil rights background, his nomination was held up for more than a year. Lyndon Johnson renominated him in 1964, and the Senate finally confirmed him after the Mississippi senator who had blocked his appointment withdrew his objection. At the age of 35, Higginbotham was one of the youngest judges ever appointed to the federal bench.

Higginbotham served on the Pennsylvania district court for 13 years. In the late 1960s, Higginbotham was appointed by President Johnson to the Kerner Commission, which produced the *Kerner Report,* one of the most famous studies of race relations and conflict of the 1960s. Higginbotham also wrote numerous legal opinions and scholarly articles in law journals, many related to race and the law in the United States. Beginning in 1970, he found time to teach university classes on both the sociology of race as well as race and the law at the University of Pennsylvania in Philadelphia. He traveled frequently to other colleges, including Harvard, Michigan, and New York University, to teach these courses, which dissected the long history of racial discrimination and unequal legal treatment based on race in the United States.

In 1977, President Jimmy Carter elevated Higginbotham to the federal court of appeals in Philadelphia. He would eventually become chief judge of that court and remain at that job until 1993.

After his retirement from the federal bench, Higginbotham moved to Cambridge, Massachusetts, to teach at Harvard Law School. Typically unable to slow down, he also took a position at Paul, Weiss, Rifkind, Wharton & Garrison, a law firm with offices in Washington, D.C., and New York City. He continued to write articles about racial politics and was critical of the Reagan and Bush administration efforts to roll back civil rights advances. He also testified to the House Judiciary Committee against the impeachment of Bill Clinton in 1998. In that testimony, Higginbotham engaged in a memorable exchange with a representative who favored Clinton's impeachment. When told that "real Americans" favored Clinton's impeachment, Higginbotham responded: "I am in profound dispute when you speak about the 'real America.' The 49 percent who voted for the President, were they not real Americans? Those who disagree with you about impeachment, are they not real Americans? Sir, my father was a laborer, my mother a domestic. I came up the hard way. Don't lecture me about the real America."

In spite of his heavy workload, Higginbotham found time to write two critically acclaimed books, *In the Matter of Color* (1978) and *Shades of Freedom* (1996). He died on December 14, 1998, at age 70, in Cambridge, Massachusetts.

Further Reading

Bill Moyers' Journal. "In the Matter of Color" [videorecording]. WNET/13. New York: Educational Broadcasting, 1979.

Diver, Colin. "A. Leon Higginbotham, Jr. (1928–1998): A Tribute." Available online. URL: http://www.upenn.edu/gazette/0399/higginbotham.html. Downloaded July 23, 2009.

Vile, John, ed. *Great American Judges: An Encyclopedia.* Santa Barbara, Calif.: ABC-CLIO, 2003.

Hill, Thomas Arnold

(1888–1947) *community activist, National Urban League executive*

A racial conciliator and community activist in Chicago, Thomas Arnold Hill worked for many years for the National Urban League. Born in Richmond, Virginia, on August 23, 1888, Thomas Arnold Hill was the son of Reuben and Irene Hill. Because Hill's parents were middle class and comparatively well-to-do, they could send him to a private school, the Wayland Academy, from which he graduated in 1906. Hill then attended a business school for a year before enrolling in Virginia Union University to study for a B.S. He graduated from Virginia Union in 1911.

Two years after his graduation, Hill landed a job at the newly established National Urban League, which was headquartered in New York City. A friend from Richmond, EUGENE KINCKLE JONES, had recently been appointed executive secretary of the league and needed an able assistant to help with publicity and organization. Hill was hired as Jones's assistant in 1914.

From 1914 to 1920, the league was extremely busy organizing new chapters in cities throughout the nation, but especially in industrial cities in the North. A wave of immigration of African Americans from the South during World War I had placed strains on the relatively small black communities in many northern cities, and league officials stepped in to help newly arrived blacks find jobs and challenge racial discrimination in housing, employment, and dealings with city officials.

From 1914 to 1916, Hill traveled often and worked long hours as a league organizer. Chicago was one of the cities that needed the Urban League most. With the possible exception of New York City, Chicago had the largest population of southern African Americans. Tens of thousands of blacks moved to Chicago to take jobs in its steel mills, stockyards, and meat-packing plants.

By 1916, Hill was in Chicago so often that Urban League executives decided to appoint him as the Chicago Urban League executive secretary. His first job was to solicit financial and organizational backing of wealthy white and African-American Chicagoans. Because of his energetic but nonconfrontational personality, Hill was able to pick up backing easily. He also met Sara Henderson, whom he married in 1917. They would have two children.

Hill faced his greatest challenge in Chicago in July 1919, when bloody race riots, which resulted in the deaths of 23 African Americans and 15 whites, broke out. What began as an attack by white mobs on blacks who swam at a beach commonly used by whites turned into a nearly weeklong raging battle between white and black gangs and police.

Under Hill's direction, the Urban League office was transformed into an emergency center. League officials quelled rumors and handed out relief to families whose housing had been burned. Hill insisted that the governor of Illinois appoint a commission to investigate the riot and recommend ways to prevent future disturbances.

In 1923, Hill ignored an Urban League policy about the need to stay out of party politics by running as an alderman from Chicago's South Side, a mostly African-American neighborhood. Although backed by some of Chicago's largest newspapers and wealthiest citizens, Hill lost the race to a candidate supported by Chicago's largest black-owned newspaper, the *Defender*. Hill stayed in Chicago two more years before returning to the national Urban League headquarters in New York City.

In 1925, Hill was made national director of industrial relations of the Urban League, a position he would hold until his resignation from the league in 1940. As director of industrial relations, Hill was instrumental in persuading the league to back the efforts of ASA PHILIP RANDOLPH, who had begun to organize African-American railroad workers in the Brotherhood of Sleeping Car Porters (BSCP). Hill also met frequently with officials of the mainly white American Federation of Labor (AFL) in an effort to persuade them to include more blacks in their unions. In this endeavor, he had only limited success.

In 1940, after a personality clash with the Urban League executive secretary, Jones, Hill left the league for a position with the National Youth Administration, a federal agency created in the 1930s by the administration of President Franklin D. Roosevelt. Hill remained with the federal government for several years, then began a career as a consultant on race relations for schools and colleges. He died, at age 59, in 1947.

Further Reading

Strickland, Arvarh. *History of the Chicago Urban League.* Columbia: University of Missouri Press, 2001.

Hilyer, Amanda Victoria Gray
(1870–1957) *community and civil rights leader*

A Progressive Era reformer, Amanda Victoria Hilyer was active in the African-American community of Washington, D.C., during the early 20th century.

Amanda Gray, was born on March 24, 1870, in Atchinson, Kansas, to Exoduster parents, blacks who had moved in the Great Migration from the South to homestead the High Plains after the Civil War. She received primary and secondary education in Kansas public schools. When she was 23, she married Arthur Gray, a pharmacist in Kansas.

Four years after her marriage, Amanda Gray moved with her husband to Washington, D.C. There she also studied pharmacology at Howard University, and she received a degree in that subject in 1903. After graduating, she helped her husband with the pharmacy business he had set up in one of the main African-American business districts of the city.

Excited to be in one of the major hubs of black culture of the United States, Gray began to get involved in community groups during evening and weekend hours. She was a progressive who wanted to provide after-work venues other than pool halls, movie houses, and bars for poorer African Americans. One of the first projects that she took up was the Phyllis Wheatley Young Women's Christian Association (YWCA), a branch of the YWCA that provided rooms and activities for black women in Washington. By 1905, Gray served as recording secretary of this group.

Through the YWCA, Amanda Gray Hilyer participated in other progressive causes that were typical of that era. She worked to oppose the opening of theaters on Sundays and petitioned the city government to appoint a matron to supervise youth activity at Washington's segregated African-American public beach.

Gray sold the pharmacy she had helped run when her husband died in 1917. Retired on a comfortable salary, she became active in efforts to support troops when the United States entered World War I in 1917. As a member of the War Work Council, she traveled to Camp Sherman in Ohio to oversee the Hostess House activities for black soldiers there.

Gray returned to Washington after the war. In 1923, she married ANDREW FRANKLIN HILYER, an inventor, civil rights activist, and prominent Washingtonian. Amanda Hilyer continued to be active in Washington's black community after her husband's 1925 death. Throughout the 1920s and 1930s, she was president of the Home for Unwed Mothers established by IONIA ROLLIN WHIPPER. She also served as president of Howard University's Women's Club, the Association for the Study of Negro Life and History, and a group that restored FREDERICK DOUGLASS's home in Washington, D.C. Hilyer died on June 19, 1957, in Washington.

Further Reading

Appiah, Kwame Anthony, and Henry Louis Gates, Jr. *Africana: The Encyclopedia of the African and African-American Experience.* New York: Oxford University Press, 2005.

Hine, Darlene Clark, ed. *Black Women in America.* New York: Carlson, 1993.

Hilyer, Andrew Franklin
(1858–1925) *community leader, inventor*

Trained as a lawyer, Andrew Hilyer worked as an accountant for several federal agencies at the same time that he invented several devices that would later earn him a considerable amount of money. A believer in self-help and entrepreneurship, he worked to help poorer African Americans climb the economic ladder.

Andrew Franklin Hilyer was born into slavery in Georgia on August 14, 1858. When he was still a child, he became an Exoduster, one of thousands of southern blacks who moved to High Plains states in search of a better life, when his mother took him to Nebraska. On the death of his mother, Hilyer moved with relatives to Minneapolis, where he eventually got to know several wealthy white families who helped him with his education. A good student, he enrolled in the University of

Minnesota in 1878 and graduated with a B.A. in 1882.

After his graduation, Hilyer moved to Washington, D.C., to study law at Howard University's law school. He received two degrees in law—an LL.B. in 1884 and an LL.M. in 1885. He was soon hired as a clerk at the Treasury Department, where he worked for a few years before transferring to the General Accounting Office, a branch of the Interior Department where he worked for many years. Hilyer married Mamie Nichols of Washington, D.C., in 1886. The couple would have three children. Several years after the death of his first wife in 1916, he married Amanda Gray (who thereafter was known as AMANDA HILYER).

Though he was a full-time employee of the federal government, the industrious Hilyer used his spare time to buy and sell real estate and tinker with inventions. Two of his inventions, a hot-air register and a water evaporator for a hot-air register, were widely used.

Hilyer worked to encourage African Americans to learn trades and create businesses. In 1892, he was one of the founders of the Union League of the District of Columbia, an association of black businessmen and businesswomen. Hilyer also attended the first meeting of BOOKER TALIAFERRO WASHINGTON's National Negro Business League in 1900.

Hilyer was a member of the Howard University Board of Trustees from 1913. He also frequently participated in the Hampton Institute conferences on industrial education. He died on January 13, 1925. His achievement is best summarized by the stated goals of the Union League: "to advance the moral, material, and financial interests of colored people . . . and to inaugurate and maintain a more fraternal feeling . . . among them."

Further Reading

Appiah, Kwame Anthony, and Henry Louis Gates, Jr. *Africana: The Encyclopedia of the African and African-American Experience.* New York: Oxford University Press, 2005.

Houston, Charles Hamilton
(1895–1950) *lawyer, civil rights leader*

An innovator in the field of civil and constitutional rights, Charles Hamilton Houston was the lead attorney for the National Association for the Advancement of Colored People (NAACP) during their slow but methodical assault on the legal foundations of segregation in the United States. Houston was born on September 3, 1895, in Washington, D.C., to Mary and William Houston. His mother was a hairdresser and his father an attorney. By all accounts, the Houstons were a warm and affectionate family, and Charles's parents gave their only son every cultural and educational advantage they could afford, including piano lessons, outings to the theater, and books, which Houston devoured at a prodigious pace.

Houston attended segregated schools in Washington, but he was fortunate to attend the M Street High School, Washington's best all-black secondary school. A hard worker, Houston did so well at M Street that he was offered a scholarship to Amherst College in Massachusetts in 1911. In his own words, "shy and proud," Houston did not make many friends at the mainly white Amherst. He did continue to excel academically, however, graduating from Amherst in 1915 as a member of Phi Beta Kappa and one of six valedictorians.

After graduation, Houston returned to Washington to teach undergraduate English for two years at Howard University. Houston was not thrilled with the U.S. entry into World War I in 1917, but he decided to enter an officer training program for African Americans rather than being "herded into the army" by the draft. He encountered many instances of racial discrimination during his tour of duty in army camps in Iowa and later in France. After witnessing black soldiers' being unfairly punished for violations of army rules they did not commit and having a close encounter with a lynch mob of American soldiers in France, Houston decided, "If luck was with me, and I got through this war, I would study law and use my time fighting for men who could not strike back. . . . My battleground [is] in America, not France."

The summer of 1919, the year Houston returned to the United States, was one of the worst times for race riots in U.S. history. From Longview, Texas; to East St. Louis, Illinois; to Washington, D.C., white-led rioters attacked black neighborhoods, killing black citizens and setting their homes and businesses on fire. Houston applied to and was accepted into Harvard Law School in the fall of that year. He again worked hard and earned high marks. His grades won him a place on the *Harvard Law Review*. He was among the top 5 percent of his class when he graduated in 1921.

After spending 1922–23 in Spain earning an advanced degree, Houston returned to Washington and entered private practice with his father. In the fall of 1924, he also began teaching law at Howard University. Since its founding in 1869, Howard's law school had produced three-fourths of all African-American lawyers in the United States, and Houston was determined that the standard of teaching at Howard would reach the highest possible level. By 1929, Houston had become vice dean of the school. He had ended the night school and tightened course requirements. He had also begun personally to train law students such as THURGOOD MARSHALL, William Bryant, and others who would eventually accomplish the goal that Houston had set for himself when he left the army in 1919. That goal was the complete destruction of the segregated system known as Jim Crow that assigned permanent second-class citizenship to African Americans.

In 1935, Houston took a leave of absence from his other duties to work as a full-time special counsel for the NAACP. At the NAACP, with the help of former students such as Thurgood Marshall, he worked out a strategy to begin dis-

mantling Jim Crow. Choosing his targets carefully, Houston began taking on the discriminatory admission practices of universities. His first victory was in 1938 against the University of Missouri law school, the only law school in that state, which under the ruling of *Missouri ex rel. Gaines v. Canada* was forced either to create a law school for black students or to admit them to its student body because there were no opportunities to obtain a similar education in that state.

Houston also represented several African-American defendants who had been given the death sentence by juries on which blacks were deliberately excluded. In both instances—one representing an Oklahoma man, the other a man from Kentucky—Houston convinced the Supreme Court to overturn the death penalty on the basis of the exclusion of blacks from the jury pool.

During the 1940s, Houston began representing the International Association of Railway Employees and the Association of Colored Railway Trainmen and Locomotive Firemen in cases involving racial discrimination in the workplace. In two cases, *Steele v. Louisville and Nashville R.R.* and *Tunstall v. Brotherhood of Locomotive Firemen and Enginemen*, Houston persuaded the U.S. Supreme Court to broaden the rights of minority workers. In *Steele* the court required a white union to include black workers who had been excluded from the union in any agreement that the union made with an employer. In *Tunstall* the court ruled that a white-dominated union could not discriminate against African-American workers by denying them the same seniority rights as white workers.

Houston would continue methodically to pick apart the racial segregation system a piece at a time. In 1945, he won a case in which an African-American woman was excluded because of her race from a librarian-training program in Baltimore. In 1948, he won two cases before the U.S. Supreme Court that struck down the exclusion of African Americans from residential neighborhoods through the use of restrictive covenants.

Houston's greatest triumph would occur four years after his death of a heart attack on April 22, 1950. The landmark *Brown v. the Board of Education of Topeka* ruling in 1954 overturned racial discrimination in American public schools, an important victory for the African-American community. Even though Thurgood Marshall, and not Houston, would argue this case before the U.S. Supreme Court, Houston had created the groundwork by setting the legal precedents that were used as buttresses in this case. And it was his team of lawyers, many of whom he had trained since law school, who took his 15 years of work to fruition.

Further Reading

Charles Hamilton Houston Institute for Race & Justice. "Charles H. Houston." Available online. URL: http://www.charleshamiltonhouston.org/Houston.aspx. Downloaded July 27, 2009.

Linder, Douglas O. "Before *Brown*: Charles H. Houston and the *Gaines* Case." Available online. URL: http://www.law.umkc.edu/faculty/projects/ftrials/trialheroes/charleshoustonessayF.html. Downloaded July 27, 2009.

McNeil, Genna Rae. *Groundwork: Charles Hamilton Houston and the Struggle for Civil Rights.* Philadelphia: University of Pennsylvania Press, 1983.

Vile, John, ed. *Great American Lawyers: An Encyclopedia.* Santa Barbara, Calif.: ABC-CLIO, 2002.

Hrabowski, Freeman A., III

(1950–) *mathematician, college administrator, education activist*

As president of the University of Maryland, Baltimore County (UMBC), Freeman Hrabowski has achieved national acclaim for his successful efforts in strengthening the education of minority students, particularly in math, science, and engineering. Hrabowski was born on August 13, 1950, in Birmingham, Alabama. Both of his parents were teachers, and they instilled in him a passion for academic excellence. A gifted student, he skipped two grades in elementary school and was attending high school by age 12.

Growing up in Birmingham placed Hrabowski in the center of some of the most violent episodes in the Civil Rights movement. In 1963, he participated in the Children's Crusade, a march by Birmingham's young people to protest the arrest of MARTIN LUTHER KING, JR., by the city's police. During the march, Hrabowski was among the many young people arrested. He spent five days in a juvenile detention facility. Racial tensions continued to rise in Birmingham. On September 15, 1963, a bomb exploded at the 16th Street Baptist Church, killing four young black girls. Hrabowski knew one of the victims.

The young scholar continued to excel at his studies and graduated from high school at age 15. He enrolled at Hampton Institute in Hampton, Virginia. In 1970, he graduated with highest honors in mathematics. The 19-year-old then moved to Champaign, Illinois, to pursue an advanced degree at the University of Illinois. While working hard to complete his master's degree in mathematics in only one year, Hrabowski set up a math tutoring program for minority students.

As he worked on his doctorate, Hrabowski began his career in education. He accepted a position as assistant dean for student services. He also taught statistics classes and served as the university's director of Project Upward Bound, a program that encouraged high school students from low-income families to attend college. Despite all of the demands on his time, Hrabowski received his doctorate in 1975 at the age of 24. His dissertation used statistical analysis to examine the effects of race on education.

Hrabowski moved to Normal, Alabama, working as associate professor of statistics at Alabama A&M University. The following year, he became professor of mathematics and dean of the arts and science division at Coppin State College in Baltimore, Maryland. He was promoted to vice president for academic affairs in 1981. Six years later, he accepted a position as vice provost at UMBC.

In 1988, he worked with a wealthy Baltimore family to create the Meyerhoff Scholarship Program. The program was designed to remedy the shortage of African-American students and professionals in the fields of math, science, and engineering. The program enables high school students who have excelled in math and science to work in research laboratories at colleges and businesses. These valuable experiences help them gain admission to many of the nation's colleges and universities.

UMBC promoted Hrabowski to president in 1993. In this role, he has focused his efforts on recruiting students interested in math and science to his university. Rejecting a proposal to start a university football team, he has used the university's funds to hire talented math and science professors, build up-to-date science labs, and sponsor a championship chess team. Under Hrabowski's leadership, UMBC has become one of the nation's leading universities in producing math and science graduates. His philosophy is that by holding minority students to the highest standards, they will meet and exceed those standards.

Hrabowski has written many articles on math and science education and coauthored two books, *Beating the Odds* (1998) and *Overcoming the Odds* (2002). He serves as chairman of the Science and Engineering Workforce Pipeline and the National Academies' Committee on Underrepresented Groups. He has been awarded honorary degrees from many universities. Hrabowski has been elected to the American Philosophical Society and the American Academy of Arts and Sciences. He received the McGraw Prize in Education, and the *Baltimore Sun* named him Marylander of the Year. *U.S. News & World Report* named him one of America's Best Leaders in 2008, and in 2009, *Time* listed him as one of the ten-best U.S. college presidents.

Further Reading

Clark, Kim. "America's Best Leaders: Freeman Hrabowski, University of Maryland—Baltimore County." *U.S. News and World Report,* 19 November 2008. Available online. URL: http://www.usnews.com/articles/news/best-leaders/2008/11/19/americas-best-leaders-freeman-hrabowski-university-of-maryland-baltimore-county.html. Downloaded on July 16, 2009.

Kessler, James H. *Distinguished African American Scientists of the 20th Century.* Westport, Conn.: Greenwood, 1996.

Hunton, Addie D. Waites
(1875–1943) *community leader, social worker*

A prominent official in the Young Women's Christian Association (YWCA), Addie Hunton was also involved in numerous community and civic organizations whose goal was to improve the lives of African-American citizens. She was born Addie D. Waites in Norfolk, Virginia, on June 11, 1875, the daughter of Jesse and Adelina Waites. Her father was a prosperous businessman and her mother a homemaker.

Addie did not live long in Virginia. After the death of her mother when she was still a young child, she was sent to Boston to be raised by a maternal aunt. She attended high school at Boston's Girls Latin School. After graduation, she attended a business college in Philadelphia, then moved to Normal, Alabama, to teach at the all-black vocational college located there, which later became Alabama Agricultural and Mechanical College.

She lived in Alabama for about a year before she married WILLIAM ALPHAEUS HUNTON, an official of the black Norfolk Young Men's Christian Association (YMCA). The couple lived in Norfolk from 1893 until 1899, when they moved to Atlanta, where William Hunton had taken another YMCA post. They would have four children.

Addie D. Waites Hunton (center) ca. 1917 with U.S. troops in France. Hunton was a top African-American official in the YWCA. *(Courtesy YMCA of the USA and the Kautz Family YMCA Archives)*

During the 1890s and 1900s, Addie Hunton joined a number of women's groups. In 1895, she attended the founding convention of the National Association of Colored Women, and she remained active in that group for many years. She was president of the International Council of the Women of Darker Races.

Thus, by 1906, when the Huntons moved to Brooklyn, New York, Addie Hunton had the experience as an organizer to become active in the YWCA. In 1907, the YWCA national board hired her as an organizer for its Council on Colored Work. She spent 1907–08 traveling through the South and Midwest on a tour of local YWCAs, and in 1909, she and her children spent a year in

Strasbourg, then a part of Germany, where she attended Kaiser Wilhelm University. She returned to the United States to find her husband very ill with tuberculosis. The family moved to the country in upstate New York but returned to New York City after the death of William Hunton in 1914.

Hunton was one of only three African-American women to be sent by the YMCA to France to help black soldiers serving in World War I. In northern France, she organized a literacy program for the soldiers as well as a Sunday evening discussion program. In southern France, she organized an array of religious, athletic, and cultural events for black soldiers on rest and relaxation leave from the war. Hunton wrote about her experiences in *Two Colored Women with the American Expeditionary Forces,* published in 1920.

After the war, Hunton worked as a vice president and field secretary of the National Association for the Advancement of Colored People (NAACP), and in 1926, she served as an observer of the American occupation of Haiti for the Women's International League for Peace and Freedom. Hunton died in Brooklyn on June 21, 1943.

Further Reading

Chandler, Susan. "Addie Hunton and the Construction of an African American Female Peace Perspective." *Afflia* 20, no. 3 (2005).

Mjagkij, Nina, ed. *Portraits of African American Life since 1865.* New York: Rowman & Littlefield, 2003.

Robertson, Nancy Marie. *Christian Sisterhood, Race Relations, and the YWCA, 1906–46.* Champaign: University of Illinois Press, 2007.

Hunton, William Alphaeus
(1863–1916) *community leader, social worker*

The first black man employed by the Young Men's Christian Association (YMCA) and the YMCA's first full-time African-American organizer, William Hunton combined a fervent Christian idealism with a pragmatic spirit that made him an effective leader in the African-American community in the 1890s and early 1900s. William Alphaeus Hunton was born in Chatham, Ontario, Canada, in 1863. His father, Stanton Hunton, an escaped former slave from Virginia, was an American citizen, though William was not. His mother, Mary Ann Hunton, died when he was four, and his father raised him.

Hunton attended public schools in Chatham. After his graduation from high school, he enrolled at Wilberforce Institute of Ontario and graduated from that college in 1884. After teaching in public schools and working as a clerk for a Canadian government agency for several years, Hunton took a job with the U.S. YMCA in 1888, its first black employee. From 1888 until 1899, he lived in Norfolk, Virginia, where he ran the black Norfolk YMCA. In 1893, he married Addie Waites (who was thereafter known as ADDIE D. WAITES HUNTON). They would have four children.

Hunton became a traveling organizer, or secretary, of the YMCA in 1891 and began extensive tours of YMCA facilities across the United States. In his reports to the YMCA's national committee, he noted the problem of segregation that existed in YMCAs in almost every part of the country. Not liking this segregation, but accepting it as a reality, he organized the Colored Men's Department of the YMCA in 1896 and served as its head. During this period, Hunton, as a delegate to the Golden Jubilee of the YMCA in London, made his first trip abroad.

In 1899, Hunton moved with his family to Atlanta, Georgia, a move that coincided with his decision to focus his energies on organizing YMCA student associations on black college campuses. Making dozens of trips to the campuses of historically African-American universities, by 1911 Hunton had organized more than 100 student associations of 7,000 members in 20 states.

After the devastating race riots in Atlanta in 1906, Hunton and his family moved to Brooklyn, New York. He continued to organize student YMCA events. Some were segregated, such as a conference of student associations he presided over in King's Mountain, North Carolina, in 1912, whereas others were integrated, such as the World's Student Federation Conference held in Lake Mohonk, New York, in 1913.

In 1914, Hunton was stricken by an acute case of tuberculosis that was complicated by a lingering condition of malaria that he had contracted during one of his tours of the South. He and his

William Alphaeus Hunton ca. 1910. Hunton, the first African-American man to serve as an organizer of the Young Men's Christian Association (YMCA), became a prominent figure in YMCA work at historically black colleges in the United States. *(Courtesy YMCA of the USA and the Kautz Family YMCA Archives)*

family retired to the countryside of upstate New York, but this retreat did not cure his illness. Hunton died of tuberculosis in 1916. His life's work is well expressed in words he spoke to the Lake Mohonk conference in 1913: "Pray with us that there shall come to the heart of the world not only the intellectual interpretation of the brotherhood of man, but a spiritual acceptance of it, so that . . . man shall not judge his fellow-man by color, race, tradition or any of the other accidents of life but righteousness and truth and unselfish service to humanity."

Further Reading

Hunton, Addie W. *William Alphaeus Hunton: A Pioneer Prophet of Young Men.* New York: Association Press, 1938.

Kautz Family YMCA Archives. "A Brief History of the YMCA and African American Communities." Available online. URL: http://special.lib.umn.edu/ymca/guides/afam/afam-history.html. Downloaded July 27, 2009.

Mjagkij, Nina, ed. *Light in the Darkness: African Americans and the YMCA, 1852–1946.* Lexington: University Press of Kentucky, 2003.

J

Jackson, Jesse
(Jesse Louis Burns)
(1941–) *civil rights activist, presidential candidate*

Perhaps the best-known African-American civil rights leader of the late 20th century, Jesse Jackson has had an up-and-down career that reflects the transformation of the Civil Rights movement during this period. Born Jesse Louis Burns on October 6, 1941, in Greenville, South Carolina, Jackson was the child of an unmarried mother and seldom saw his biological father. In 1956, when he was 15, he changed his surname to Jackson, his stepfather's name.

Jackson attended segregated public schools in Greenville and graduated from Sterling High School in 1959. A good student as well as an outstanding athlete, Jackson accepted a football scholarship to the University of Illinois but remained there only one year before transferring to North Carolina Agricultural and Technical College in Greensboro, North Carolina. In 1962, while still a student, Jackson married Jacqueline Lavinia Brown. They would eventually have five children (one of whom would go into politics himself).

Jackson returned to the South at the height of the Civil Rights movement. Leaders such as the Reverend MARTIN LUTHER KING, JR., and MEDGAR WILEY EVERS were organizing increasingly large and bold demonstrations to demand full civil and political rights for African Americans.

In Greensboro, Jackson found himself in the middle of a long-running protest organized by students from his college. In 1960, four students at North Carolina Agricultural and Technical College in Greensboro decided to integrate the F. W. Woolworth store. One day, they quietly sat down at the lunch counter and did not leave when they were not served; they remained seated until closing time. The next morning, 25 students showed up. Eventually, Woolworth's would be integrated, but the struggle to integrate other places such as movie theaters, restaurants, gas stations, and hotels, continued. Soon Jesse Jackson was in the thick of this struggle.

In trying to chart a course of civil disobedience, Jackson found a wise counsel in Samuel Proctor, president of North Carolina Agricultural and Technical College. Proctor had been a student with Martin Luther King at Boston University and was well versed in King's strategy of creative, nonviolent confrontation, which had been borrowed from Mohandas Gandhi in India. Proctor would later say, "[Jackson] thought somebody like King was the kind of thing he would like to be. He saw himself as embryonic to something bigger like that."

Jackson began to explore ways to dent the hard-core racist sentiment of the South. The "police finally were moving to arrest us," he explained about one demonstration,

> and we kneeled and started saying the Lord's Prayer. Police all took off their caps and bowed their heads. Can't arrest folks prayin'. We finished, they started for us again. We stood up and started singing "The Star-Spangled Banner." They stopped, put their hands over their heart. Can't arrest folks singing the national anthem. We were touching something bigger, see, that we both respected. Opening up the moral terms of the situation. Went on for, like, half an hour, until we got tired and let 'em arrest us.

After making a considerable name for himself during his three years in Greensboro, Jackson graduated with a B.A. in 1964. He then enrolled in the Chicago Theological Seminary, where he would study off and on for four years. However, bigger issues were calling him. In March 1965, after watching the bloody confrontation between Dr. King and his supporters and the Alabama state police on the Edmund Pettus Bridge in Selma, Jackson called King and asked to work for the Southern Christian Leadership Conference (SCLC). King immediately put him to work as the head of the Chicago chapter of Operation Breadbasket, a SCLC project to help feed poor people.

During the next three years, Jackson would expand SCLC efforts in Chicago. In the summer of 1966, he helped organize marches in white communities in Chicago that had excluded blacks, who were not allowed to rent apartments or buy houses. Some of these marches, such as one held in Cicero, a white, working-class Chicago suburb, turned bloody as residents pelted the marchers with rocks and bricks.

By the summer of 1967, Jackson had become the head of Operation Breadbasket. He had also become a close aide of King. Jackson was with King in Memphis when a sniper assassinated the older leader in April 1968.

The Civil Rights movement lost a powerful voice at King's death. Also, newer, more militant leaders such as ELDRIDGE CLEAVER and STOKELY CARMICHAEL had emerged to challenge the idea of trying to integrate blacks with whites. These newer leaders called instead for African Americans to separate themselves as much as possible from white society, creating a black constellation within the galaxy of white America.

Black separatism did not appeal to Jesse Jackson. His vision included all races, social classes, men, and women. The summer after King's assassination, Jackson finished his work at the Chicago Theological Seminary and became an ordained minister. By 1971, he had also resigned from SCLC, an organization that was disintegrating without the powerful leadership of its fallen leader.

That same year, Jackson created his own organization, Operation PUSH, the acronym standing for "People United to Save Humanity." The goals of Operation PUSH were ambitious: to create economic and educational opportunities for poor people and minorities.

Jackson's tactics in achieving these goals have come under fire. Typically, he and PUSH identify a corporation that they accuse of discriminatory practices, such as in hiring and promotions. They then organize a boycott against this corporation until it agrees to PUSH's agenda, which usually includes hiring more minority workers or promoting more minorities to higher positions in the company. Frequently, Operation PUSH has also been the beneficiary of sizable donations from the companies that have been targeted. Some critics say that once PUSH has received funding from the companies, Jackson then ignores the company's policies. In effect, this accusation implies that Operation PUSH is more interested in shaking down companies for money than in achieving real racial integration.

Jesse Jackson ca. 1980. Onetime aide to the Reverend Martin Luther King, Jr., Jackson ran for the presidency twice in the 1980s. *(Library of Congress, Prints and Photographs Division, LC-U9-41583)*

By 1984, Jackson had developed higher ambitions. In that year he formed the Rainbow Coalition, a political organization that supported his run for the presidency in the Democratic primary. Jackson lost that race but decided to run again in 1988. In that year, after a strong showing in Michigan in which he won that state's Democratic presidential primary, Jackson lost the nomination to Massachusetts's governor, Michael Dukakis.

Since the late 1980s, Jackson has taken on the mantle of elder statesman. He has frequently flown, often at the last minute and with little preparation, to crisis points in the United States and the world. In 1991, he won release of foreigners being held by Iraqi troops after the Iraqi invasion of Kuwait. Jackson visited Kenya in 1997 and 1998 in a fruitless mission to persuade Kenyan president Daniel Arap Moi to loosen the grip of his dictatorial rule of that country. Jackson's attempts to negotiate a compromise between Serbian president Slobodan Milosevic and the United Nations were ignored by both sides in that conflict.

In 2000, Bill Clinton awarded him the Presidential Medal of Freedom. The following year, however, Jackson's image as a moral leader was tarnished by revelations that he had fathered a child with a staff member who worked at his PUSH Rainbow Coalition office. Although his effectiveness as a leader of the civil and social rights struggle was diminished, he continued his social activism, giving lectures, providing counsel, and leading protests around the country. In 2003, he opposed the Bush administration's decision to invade Iraq. In 2007, Jackson was arrested for trespassing during a protest outside a gun store in Illinois. He had joined a community group to draw attention to the store, which local activists believed was selling guns to local gang members.

Jackson supported Barack Obama in the 2008 presidential election. On the night of November 4, 2008, he attended Obama's victory speech at Chicago's Grant Park. With tears in his eyes, he spoke with reporters about the significance of the election of the nation's first African-American president.

Further Reading

Domenico, Roy Palmer, and Mark Y. Hanley, eds. *Encyclopedia of Modern Christian Politics.* Westport, Conn.: Greenwood, 2006.

Frady, Marshall. *Jesse: The Life and Pilgrimage of Jesse Jackson.* New York: Random House, 1996.

PBS. *Frontline.* "The Pilgrimage of Jesse Jackson." Available online. URL: http://www.pbs.org/wgbh/pages/frontline/jesse/. Downloaded July 27, 2009.

Rainbow PUSH. "Rev. Jesse Jackson." Available online. URL: http://www.rainbowpush.org/about/revjackson.html. Downloaded July 27, 2009.

Jealous, Benjamin Todd

(1973–) *civil rights leader, foundation administrator*

Named as president of the National Association for the Advancement of Colored People (NAACP) in 2008, Benjamin Jealous is the youngest person to serve as the prominent civil rights organization's chief executive officer in its more than 100-year history. Born on January 18, 1973, Jealous grew up in Pacific Grove, California. His parents, Ann and Fred Jealous, are marriage and family counselors.

Jealous enrolled at Columbia University in New York City in 1991. He soon became a student leader, helping organize demonstrations and other activities to draw attention to various civic and university issues. He led efforts to support the rights of homeless people and a successful campaign to preserve admission and financial aid policies at Columbia that helped poor students attend the university. Off campus, he worked as a community organizer for the NAACP's Legal and Educational Defense Fund. He helped with voter registration drives and other civil rights projects in Harlem.

In early 1993, Columbia University suspended Jealous, along with three other students, for violating the school's student code of conduct. The students had participated in a protest over a government and university plan to turn the historic Audubon Theater and Ballroom, where MALCOLM X had been assassinated, into a medical research center. During his suspension, Jealous moved to Washington, D.C., where he directed a student campaign to save historically black public colleges.

Despite controversy over his election as president of the National Association for the Advancement of Colored People (NAACP), Benjamin Jealous remains committed to social justice and public service. *(NAACP)*

He soon moved to Mississippi to serve as a campaign field organizer to help stop the State of Mississippi from closing three historically black colleges in order to turn them into prisons.

While in Mississippi, he accepted a job as a reporter for the *Jackson Advocate,* an African-American newspaper based in the state's capital. He covered several major news stories, including one that exposed corruption at a state prison. His articles about a black farmer accused of arson helped lead to the man's acquittal at trial. The newspaper promoted him to managing editor. Jealous later resumed his studies at Columbia, graduating in 1997 with a degree in political science. He was awarded a prestigious Rhodes Scholarship, which allowed him to study at Oxford University in England. There, he earned a master's degree in comparative social research.

Returning to the United States, Jealous served as the head of several business and civic organizations. From 1999 to 2002, he worked as executive director of the National Newspaper Publishers Association (NNPA). The NNPA is a coalition of more than 200 African-American community newspapers. He spearheaded the association's efforts to increase the number of black-owned newspapers publishing online. Jealous next worked as director of the U.S. Human Rights Program at Amnesty International, an organization that advocates and helps protect human rights worldwide. In this position, he managed a campaign that drew public attention to the common practice in many states of sentencing teen offenders to life in prison without parole. In 2005, the Rosenberg Foundation hired Jealous to be its president. The private San Francisco–based charity provides funding for projects that improve the lives of immigrants and poor people.

With the support of renowned civil rights leader Julian Bond, Jealous was selected as the NAACP's 17th president in September 2008. His hiring was not without controversy. Several board members were upset because the 35-year-old Jealous was the only candidate presented to the board

of directors. Some NAACP members voiced their opinions that the new president was too young and inexperienced in the civil rights field to take on the challenging position. After assuming leadership of the organization, Jealous stated that he would focus the NAACP's efforts on employment discrimination, school segregation, inner city violence, and the nation's unusually high imprisonment rate for black males. He also planned to start programs to expand the organization's membership (numbering about 275,000), with an emphasis on attracting young members.

Jealous has received many awards, including the Clarion of Justice award from the National Rainbow Coalition & Operation PUSH, the Exceptional Communicator award from New California Media, and the Emerging Leader award from the National Coalition of Black Civic Participation. *Ebony* magazine named him as one of its 30 Leaders of the Future. He is married to Lia Epperson Jealous, a law professor and former civil rights lawyer with the NAACP's Legal Defense and Educational Fund.

Further Reading

Kuruvila, Matthai. "Next Wave of Black Leaders Find Fresh Voices." *San Francisco Chronicle.* 27 May 2008. Available online. ULR: http://www.sfgate.com/cgi-bin/article.cgi?f=/c/a/2008/05/27/BANG10QF1I.DTL. Downloaded July 27, 2009.

National Association for the Advancement of Colored People. "Benjamin Todd Jealous: President and CEO." Available online. URL: http://www.naacp.org/about/leadership/executive/jealous/index.htm. Downloaded July 27, 2009.

Johnson, Charles Spurgeon
(1893–1956) *educator, Fisk University president*

An outstanding educator, Charles Johnson was also a highly regarded sociologist and university president who built Fisk University into a first-class educational institution. Born in Bristol, Virginia, in 1893, Charles Spurgeon Johnson was one of six children of the Reverend Charles Henry Johnson and Winifred Johnson. Johnson's father, who was well educated, taught Charles to read at an early age and encouraged his intellectual curiosity. At age 14, Johnson left Bristol for Virginia, where he attended the Wayland Academy. He then attended Virginia Union University, he received a B.A. there in 1916.

After finishing his undergraduate work, Johnson enrolled in the graduate school of the University of Chicago. There he formed a close bond with sociologist Robert E. Park. Johnson's objective approach to race relations resulted from the influence of Park. Johnson's studies at Chicago were interrupted by the U.S. entry into World War I in 1917. Volunteering for the army, Johnson spent a year in France as a sergeant. He completed his Ph.D. in 1918.

Before he left for France, Johnson had begun working for the newly formed National Urban League as director of research and records for the Chicago office. In the summer of 1919 at his arrival back in the United States, Johnson witnessed firsthand the destructive race riots in Chicago. Hired as associate executive director of the Chicago Commission on Race Relations, Johnson was one of the principal authors of *The Negro in Chicago: A Study in Race Relations and a Race Riot,* the famous book about race in Chicago. In 1920, Johnson married Marie Antoinette Burgette; the couple would have four children.

In 1921, Johnson moved to New York City to become editor of the Urban League's magazine, *Opportunity.* As editor until 1928, Johnson helped define the Harlem Renaissance, that period in the 1920s when young African-American artists and intellectuals sought to portray a new view of what it meant to be black. In the pages of *Opportunity,* Johnson featured talented writers such as Claude McKay, Alain Locke, and Langston Hughes.

Johnson left the Urban League and New York City in 1928 to become director of the Social Sci-

ence Department at Fisk University, a historically black college in Nashville, Tennessee. At Fisk, he devoted himself to studies of race in the United States, eventually producing 31 books as author or coauthor and more than 60 articles. His best-known works are *The Negro in American Civilization* (1928), *Shadow of the Plantation* (1934), and *Monthly Summary of Events and Trends in Race Relations,* a bulletin that was read by President Franklin Roosevelt.

In the 1940s and 1950s, Johnson served on numerous international organizations and boards. In 1946, he spent a number of months in Japan as an adviser to the U.S. government on the restructuring of Japanese schools. As a member of the U.S. delegation, he attended two conferences held in 1946 and 1947 by the United Nations Educational, Scientific, and Cultural Organization (UNESCO), and he was a delegate to the World Conference of Churches meeting in Amsterdam in 1948. Johnson also doubled the educational budget of Fisk University and added a number of new buildings to the campus. He died of a heart attack on October 27, 1956.

Further Reading

Gilpin, Patrick J., and Marybeth Gasman. *Charles S. Johnson: Leadership beyond the Veil in the Age of Jim Crow.* Albany: State University of New York Press, 2003.

Tennessee Encyclopedia of History and Culture. "Charles S. Johnson." Available online. URL: http://tennesseeencyclopedia.net/imagegallery. php?EntryID=J021. Downloaded July 27, 2009.

Johnson, James Weldon
(1871–1938) *educator, civil rights activist, writer, song lyricist*

A song lyricist, journalist, fiction writer, civil rights leader, and educator, James Weldon Johnson led a full and varied life. Along with W. E. B. DuBois and Marcus Garvey, Johnson was one of the greatest African-American leaders of the early 20th century.

Johnson was born in Jacksonville, Florida, on June 17, 1871, to James and Helen Johnson. His father, a mixed race freeman from Virginia, worked as a waiter in Nassau in the Bahamas and New York City before venturing south to become headwaiter at a fashionable Jacksonville hotel. Johnson's mother was a native of the Bahamas, who taught at a segregated black grammar school in Jacksonville.

Johnson attended elementary and middle schools in Jacksonville, a town that he remembered in later years as being relatively tolerant of racial differences. When he was 16, Johnson was sent by his parents to finish his secondary education at the Atlanta University preparatory school. He finished these studies in 1890 and immediately enrolled in Atlanta University, where he earned a B.A. in 1894.

From an early age, Johnson had been exposed to the larger world outside the South. When he was 13, he made the first of several trips to New York City with his parents, and in 1893, he worked for a time as a carpenter at the World's Columbian Exposition in Chicago. During those months, he was fortunate enough to hear an elderly but still vital FREDERICK DOUGLASS give a speech about civil rights.

After graduation, Johnson took a job as principal of the Stanton School in Jacksonville, a position he would hold until 1901. Full of energy, Johnson did not confine himself to his duties as a high school principal. In 1895, he founded a newspaper in Jacksonville, the *Daily American.* He used this paper to expound on his views about race, endorsing a segregated black exhibit at the Atlanta Cotton Exposition in 1895 and at the same time calling for integration of private schools in the South. Johnson also was active in affairs at his former university. In 1896, he was secretary of the first Atlanta University Conference on Negro Life, and at that time he met W. E. B. DuBois, who had recently moved to Atlanta to teach.

James Weldon Johnson ca. 1930. A song lyricist and the author of "Lift Every Voice and Sing," Johnson also served as director of the National Association for the Advancement of Colored People (NAACP) for 14 years. *(Library of Congress, Prints and Photographs Division, LC-USZ62-42498)*

Already busy during the late 1890s Johnson also studied law with a white lawyer in Jacksonville and in 1898 was admitted to the bar in Duval County, the first African American allowed to practice law in that county. On top of that, Johnson began writing songs with his brother, John. Johnson wrote the words (and his brother the music) for his best-known song, "Lift Every Voice and Sing," in 1900.

In 1902, buoyed by the success of "Lift Every Voice" and discouraged by the increasingly segregationist racial and political climate in Florida, the Johnson brothers moved to New York City to pursue a career in show business. They signed a contract with the Joseph W. Stern Company, a music publishing business, and began writing songs for a living. They had a big hit in 1903 with "Under the Bamboo Tree," a song that was included in the popular musical *Sally in Our Alley*. Johnson followed this up with "Didn't He Ramble" and "The Old Flag Never Touched the Ground," a song that was written for Theodore Roosevelt's 1904 presidential campaign.

In Florida and New York, Johnson had been close with supporters of BOOKER TALIAFERRO WASHINGTON, the most popular black leader of that time. With Washington's political help, Johnson won an appointment as U.S. counsel to Venezuela in 1906. In 1908, he was given the consular assignment in Corinto, Nicaragua. Taking a break to return to New York City in 1910 to marry Grace Nail, Johnson remained in Nicaragua until 1913, when Woodrow Wilson, a Democrat, won the presidency. Because he was a Republican, Johnson knew he would not be reappointed, so he resigned and returned to New York.

In Nicaragua, the pace of his job had been slow enough to give Johnson time to write a book, *The Autobiography of an Ex-Colored Man*, about a light-skinned black man who passes for white. The book won favorable reviews at the time, but it was not really appreciated until the Harlem Renaissance of the 1920s.

Back in New York City, Johnson was appointed as editor of the *New York Age*, a paper aimed at the African-American community. From 1914 until 1916, Johnson ran the paper and wrote editorials about the issues of the day. As always, he supported race pride yet also insisted that the goal of the African-American community should be full integration with full rights into the American social and economic system. However, he occasionally took pragmatic views, such as his support of an integrated Young Men's Christian Association (YMCA) in Harlem, because he knew that was the only way a YMCA would be built for blacks in New York City at that time.

In late 1916, Johnson took a job as a field organizer for the relatively new National Association for the Advancement of Colored People (NAACP).

Johnson probably felt free to do this because of the death of Booker T. Washington in 1915. Washington and NAACP founder W. E. B. DuBois had been political enemies. Now that Washington was no longer alive, Johnson did not have to worry about losing a strong ally.

Johnson worked for the NAACP, first as a field organizer and later as the NAACP director, for 14 years. His first task was to organize NAACP chapters in the South. In early 1917, he was able to add 13 NAACP branches and more than 700 members in the South. In July 1917, Johnson organized a dramatic silent march in New York City to protest lynching in the South. Later that year, Johnson organized to protest the execution of 13 black soldiers accused of participating in riots in Houston, Texas, in August 1917.

Johnson became national director of the NAACP in 1920. During the 1920s, under Johnson's stewardship, the NAACP backed ASA PHILIP RANDOLPH's efforts to organize black railway workers into the Brotherhood of Sleeping Car Porters. He also urged blacks to abandon the Republican Party after President Harding and President Coolidge did little to further African-American civil rights. Under Johnson's leadership, the NAACP created a political strategy that cast black voters in the swing position for electoral races in the urban North. According to the strategy, whichever party promised to do more for broader black civil rights and workplace participation would be endorsed by the NAACP.

In 1930, exhausted by his intense schedule at the NAACP, Johnson accepted the position of professor of creative literature and writing at Fisk University in Nashville. For the next eight years, he was primarily an educator and writer, working at Fisk in the spring semester and frequently teaching at other universities in the fall. In 1933, he published his last book, his autobiography, *Along This Way*.

Johnson died on June 17, 1938, of injuries suffered in a collision between his car and a train at an unmarked train crossing in Massachusetts.

More than 2,000 people attended his funeral in Harlem to celebrate his life. In the words of one commentator, James Weldon Johnson was "a man of poise and dignity, of warm friendliness, of ironic humor in spite of fundamental seriousness . . . to him [fell] the purpose of [vindicating] the American idea of opportunity and recognition of merit. His own career [was] such a vindication."

Further Reading

Gates, Henry Louis, Jr., and Cornel West. *The African-American Century: How Black Americans Have Shaped Our Country.* New York: Simon & Schuster, 2002.

James Weldon Johnson Institute. "James Weldon Johnson." Available online. URL: http://www.james weldonjohnson.emory.edu/sub-james.htm. Downloaded July 27, 2009.

Johnson, James Weldon. *Along This Way: The Autobiography of James Weldon Johnson.* New York: Viking Press, 1933.

———. *The Autobiography of an Ex-Colored Man.* New York, Hill & Wang, 1960.

Levy, Eugene D. *James Weldon Johnson: Black Leader, Black Voice.* Chicago: University of Chicago Press, 1973.

Jones, Eugene Kinckle

(1885–1954) *Urban League official, civil rights activist*

For almost 40 years, Eugene Jones worked to improve the lives of African Americans and bridge the differences between whites and blacks in the United States. Born in Richmond, Virginia, on July 30, 1885, Eugene Kinckle Jones was the son of Joseph and Rosa Jones. His father was an ex-slave and one of the first African Americans in Virginia to earn a college degree.

Both parents were teachers, and Jones grew up in the liberal, racially mixed environment of Virginia Union University, where his parents taught. This friendly, multiracial setting destroyed the myth that blacks were inferior to whites. "I had seen my mother and father on mixed faculties of white and colored teachers where equality was recognized in the group," Jones wrote. "This contributed to my growing belief in the essential equality of men, and in the capacity of the Negro, with opportunity, to measure up, man to man, with any racial variety."

After graduating from high school in 1902, Jones enrolled in Virginia Union University. He won a B.A. degree from that institution in 1906, then enrolled in the social science graduate program at Cornell University. He was awarded an M.A. from Cornell in 1908. After his graduate work at Cornell, Jones taught in Louisville, Kentucky, for three years. In 1909, he married Blanche Watson. They would have two children.

In 1911, Jones was hired as a field researcher for the newly created Committee on Urban Conditions among Negroes, located in New York City. His boss was the pioneering African-American social worker GEORGE EDMUND HAYNES.

Jones conducted studies of the living conditions of blacks in New York City for the National Urban League, as it was soon renamed. He was one of the principal authors of a groundbreaking work, *The Negro Community in New York.* In 1917, after Haynes had been hired to head the social work department at Fisk University, Jones was promoted from field secretary to executive secretary. Under Jones's leadership, the league would grow rapidly because of his insistence that priority be placed on increasing the number of local Urban League boards across the country. By the time he retired as executive secretary in 1941, the Urban League had 58 locals and an annual budget of half a million dollars.

As executive secretary, Jones was instrumental in making the Urban League a major player in the civil rights community. He founded the Urban League's magazine, *Opportunity,* and hired its dynamic first editor, CHARLES SPURGEON JOHNSON. *Opportunity* quickly became an important outlet for young and talented black writers and poets, and it did much to set the tone of the Harlem Renaissance in New York City in the 1920s.

Jones also was responsible for the creation of the Schomburg Collection, one of the largest repositories of African-American books, manuscripts, oral histories, and photographs in the United States. When Arthur Schomburg approached Jones with an offer to give his collection to the Urban League, Jones instead induced the Carnegie Foundation to buy the collection and give it to the New York Public Library. The library then set up the collection as a separate entity, located in Harlem, within its organization.

The manner in which Jones dealt with the Schomberg Collection is indicative of Jones's style at the league. If a problem existed for African Americans in the nation as a whole or in a particular city, he would tell the league researchers and activists to investigate. Then, having produced a paper about the problem, the league would persuade the appropriate public or private social agency to do something about it. Jones also was in constant contact with white officials, whether they were union leaders or corporate leaders. He believed strongly in interracial cooperation as a means of solving problems.

Although Jones would talk cordially with white leaders, he did not hesitate to use stronger measures to help black people living in big cities. Under his leadership, the league boycotted firms that refused to employ blacks, pressured schools to expand vocational opportunities for young people, prodded Washington officials to include blacks in New Deal recovery programs, and worked to get blacks into previously segregated labor unions.

By 1941, as a result of years of hard work and illness, Jones had lost some of his vitality and decided to retire from day-to-day work for the Urban League. He was appointed general secretary of the league and served in that position until 1950. He died in New York City four years after he had retired, on January 11, 1954.

Further Reading

Mason, Skip. "Eugene Kinckle Jones." Available online. URL: http://skipmason.com/jones.htm. Downloaded July 28, 2009.

Parris, Guichard, and Lester Brooks. *Blacks in the City: A History of the National Urban League.* Boston: Little, Brown, 1971.

Weiss, Nancy J. *The National Urban League, 1910–1940.* New York: Oxford University Press, 1974.

Jones, Nathaniel R., Jr.
(1926–) *lawyer, federal judge*

After a career as a civil rights attorney, Nathaniel Jones was appointed to the federal judiciary, in which he has continued to seek remedies for racial discrimination. Born on May 13, 1926, in Youngstown, Ohio, Nathaniel R. Jones is one of four children of Nathaniel, Sr., and Lillian Jones. The elder Jones was a steelworker in the plants of Youngstown until he was laid off during the Great Depression. He then made a living as a janitor. Lillian Jones worked as a domestic servant and later a salesperson.

Jones attended public schools in Youngstown. Crediting his parents with encouraging him to study and excel in school, Jones graduated from high school in 1944. After his graduation, he served in the U.S. Army during World War II, and after the war, with the help of the GI Bill he attended Youngstown State University. He graduated with a B.A. in 1951 and worked for a few years at a printing company. In 1953, he enrolled in the law school at Youngstown State, where he was awarded an LL.B. in 1956.

Jones's first job after law school was as the executive director of the Youngstown Fair Employment Practice Commission. During this time J. Maynard Dickerson, a family friend and prominent member of the Youngstown African-American community, mentored the young attorney. According to Jones, through Dickerson, "I was able to sit in on strategy conferences and policy discussions with leaders of national repute, including THURGOOD MARSHALL . . . and others. CHARLES HAMILTON HOUSTON said it best: a minority lawyer must be a social engineer. I saw [law] as a way to effect meaningful changes in society and shape the destiny of individuals locked into second class status."

In 1961, the Kennedy administration appointed Jones as an assistant U.S. attorney for the northern district of Ohio. He served in that position until 1967, when he was appointed assistant general counsel for the Kerner Commission, the group created by President Lyndon Johnson to investigate the causes of the frequent race riots that erupted in the United States during the late 1960s. After the release of the Kerner Commission report, which declared that the United States was becoming "two societies, one black, one white—separate and unequal," Jones became general counsel of the National Association for the Advancement of Colored People (NAACP).

Jones worked at the NAACP for 10 years, during which he was most engaged with the issue of school desegregation in the North. In 1974, 1977, and 1979, Jones headed up efforts to desegregate public schools in Detroit, Michigan; Dayton, Ohio; and Columbus, Ohio. He would argue a few of these cases before the Supreme Court.

In 1979, President Jimmy Carter appointed Jones to the U.S. Sixth Circuit Court of Appeals in Cincinnati. In addition to his full-time work on the court, Jones has also worked as an adjunct professor at the University of Cincinnati College of Law, instructor in the trial advocacy program at the Harvard Law School, and adjunct professor at the Criminal Law Institute of Atlanta University.

Jones retired from the federal bench in 1999. He continues to work as an attorney in Cincinnati. In 2003, the U.S. Congress honored Jones by naming the federal courthouse in Youngstown, Ohio, the Nathaniel R. Jones Federal Building and U.S. Courthouse.

Further Reading

American Inns of Court. "The Honorable Nathaniel R. Jones." Available online. URL: http://www. innsofcourt.org/Content/Default.aspx?Id=353. Downloaded July 27, 2009.

Elected and Appointed Black Judges in the United States. Washington, D.C.: Joint Center for Political Studies, 1986.

Jones, Scipio Africanus
(ca. 1863–1943) *lawyer, civil rights activist*

A crusading civil rights lawyer, Scipio Jones continually challenged the white-dominated political establishment in Arkansas to include African Americans in the political process, and he protected blacks from unfair criminal prosecution. Born around 1863 in Tulip, Arkansas, a small town in the south-central part of the state, Scipio Africanus Jones was the son of Jemmima Jones, a slave, and an unknown white man. After emancipation, Jones's mother married Horace Jones, a black man. Scipio lived with his mother and Jones until he was 18 or 19, when he moved to Little Rock to attend the college preparatory school at Bethel University.

Around 1982, Jones entered Shorter College in Little Rock and studied to be a teacher. He received a B.A. from Shorter in either 1885 or 1886 and began teaching primary and secondary school courses in Sweet Home, a town near Little Rock. During the four or so years that he was a teacher in Sweet Home, Jones began to study law, probably on his own and with the help of a sympathetic local attorney, in the evening and on weekends. In 1889, when he was 26, he was admitted into the Arkansas bar.

After becoming a lawyer, Jones moved back to Little Rock and set up a practice. He dealt in the usual concerns of a general practice lawyer—wills, contracts, felony and misdemeanor criminal cases—and founded real estate, ice, and fuel businesses.

Jones quickly established a reputation as a protector of the civil and constitutional rights of African Americans in Arkansas. He successfully

Scipio Africanus Jones ca. 1900. A courageous southern attorney, Jones challenged racial segregation in his native state of Arkansas and won several important criminal trials of unjustly accused black clients. *(Courtesy Arkansas History Commission)*

argued for the right of black Shriners to use the name "Shriner," which was challenged by the white part of the Shriner organization. He also fought the "grandfather clause," a law often used in southern states to prevent blacks from voting because it stipulated that only persons whose grandfathers had voted in past elections could vote in current ones. Because at that time almost all of the grandfathers of living African Americans in the South had been slaves, and thus banned from voting, this law disenfranchised African-American voters.

Jones was also active in the so-called Black and Tan faction of the Republican Party, those mainly black Republicans who sought an integrated party. Beginning in 1902, Jones fought an almost 30-year running battle with white Arkansas Republicans, the "Lily Whites," about integrating the party. That he was partially successful can be seen in his choice as a Republican delegate from Arkansas to the 1908 and 1912 Republican National Conventions.

Jones is best remembered for his spirited appeal of 12 blacks sentenced to death for defending themselves against whites during a race riot in Elaine, Arkansas, in October 1919. Pointing out that the men were acting in self-defense and that they were tried by an all-white jury that convicted them in less than an hour, Jones, who spent six years on these cases, eventually was able to free all of the men. One of the cases went to the U.S. Supreme Court. Although Jones did not argue the case before the highest court, he prepared most of the briefings for these arguments.

Jones died in Little Rock in 1943 at the age of 80.

Further Reading

Arkansas Black Lawyers. "Scipio Africanus Jones." Available online. URL: http://www.arkansasblack lawyers.com/lawyers/sajones.html. Downloaded July 28, 2009.

Encyclopedia of Arkansas History and Culture. "Scipio Africanus Jones." Available online. URL: http://

www.encyclopediaofarkansas.net/encyclopedia/
entry-detail.aspx?search=1&entryID=2427.
Downloaded July 27, 2009.

Ovington, Mary White. "Scipio Africanus Jones."
Available online. URL: http://www.cals.lib.ar.us/
butlercenter/abho/docs/1927%20account%
20Scipio%20A%20Jones%20and%20Elaine.pdf.
Downloaded July 27, 2009.

Jordan, Vernon Eulion, Jr.

(1935–) *lawyer, civil rights activist, Urban
League director*

Beginning his career as a civil rights lawyer and
activist, Vernon Jordan later became a corporate
lawyer and lobbyist. His career has prompted some
critics to see him as more concerned with his own
wealth and success than with the broader struggle
for the civil rights of poor and working-class African Americans.

Born in Atlanta, Georgia, in 1935 to Vernon,
Sr., and Mary Belle Jordan, Vernon Eulion Jordan, Jr., lived in one of the first housing projects
for blacks in Atlanta. Though he lived in the
projects, he had a middle-class life. His father was
a postal worker, and his mother owned a catering
business. In spite of his relative material comfort,
Jordan had to endure the rigid Jim Crow segregation laws of the South at that time. As he later
told an interviewer, "You knew there was colored
water and there was white water, and you knew
you sat upstairs in the theater. It was a way of life,
and you understood that. It never meant you
accepted it."

After graduating from a segregated high school,
Jordan enrolled in DePauw University in Indiana
in 1953. In spite of being the only black student at
DePauw, Jordan was popular. He played on the
basketball team, was vice president of the campus
Democratic club, and won a number of oratorical
contests. After graduating with a B.A. in political
science in 1957, Jordan moved to Washington,
D.C., and enrolled in Howard University's law
school. He graduated from Howard with an LL.B.
in 1960.

After finishing law school, Jordan moved back
to Atlanta, at that time the intellectual center
for much of the Civil Rights movement then
sweeping the South. For his first year or two, he
served as a clerk in the law office of Donald Hol-
lowell, an experienced civil rights attorney. In
1961, Jordan made news when he escorted Charlene Hunter (later well known as Charlene
Hunter-Gault as a reporter for the Public Broadcasting System [PBS]) into the University of
Georgia, where she became that university's first
black student.

Vernon Eulion Jordan, Jr., ca. 1965. Jordan served as
director of the Urban League during the 1970s and is
currently a lobbyist and lawyer in Washington, D.C.
*(Library of Congress, Prints and Photographs Division,
LC-USZ62-105921)*

In 1964, Jordan was hired as a field secretary for the National Association for the Advancement of Colored People (NAACP) in Georgia. In that position, he organized a number of successful boycotts of businesses that did not hire blacks. Many of these businesses soon began adding blacks to their workforce.

Jordan moved to Arkansas in 1964 and opened a law firm there. However, by the late 1960s, he returned to Atlanta, where he began to lay the groundwork for a run for a U.S. congressional seat. Concluding that the race for Congress would be difficult, Jordan instead took a job as head of the United Negro College Fund, an organization that raises money for a number of historically black colleges and universities in the United States. In 12 months, Jordan raised $8 million for 36 colleges.

In 1971, after the accidental death of WHITNEY M. YOUNG, JR., executive director of the Urban League, Jordan was hired as the league's new director. Jordan continued and expanded the programs begun by Young—especially job training and early childhood development projects. Young's main emphasis was on raising money for the Urban League, and he was very accomplished at this work. Eventually, he would sit on a number of boards of corporations that donated money to the league. However, because the league also received a significant amount of money from the federal government, it was vulnerable to political shifts. One such shift occurred with the election of Ronald Reagan, a conservative Republican, in 1980. Under Reagan, federal funds that had gone to Urban League programs were radically reduced in the early 1980s.

On May 29, 1980, during a trip to an Urban League chapter in Fort Wayne, Indiana, Jordan was shot and seriously wounded by a racist gunman. While recovering in the hospital for four months, Jordan decided that it was time for him to move on to the next phase of his life. In 1981, he announced that he had taken a job with a well-connected law firm as a lobbyist in Washington, D.C. Jordan remained at this firm, Akin, Gump, Strauss, Hauer and Feld, through the 1990s and into the new millennium. In this position, he has acted as an adviser on race matters to several U.S. presidents, most notably Bill Clinton, who is a close friend.

Jordan reentered the spotlight in 1998 because of allegations that he got a high-powered job for Monica Lewinsky, the young White House intern who would be at the center of efforts to impeach President Bill Clinton in 1998.

In 2000, Jordan joined the powerful investment banking firm Lazard Ltd. as senior managing director. The following year, the NAACP awarded him its prestigious Spingarn Medal for outstanding achievement by an African American.

Further Reading

Jordan, Vernon E., with Annette Gordon-Reed. *Vernon Can Read! A Memoir*. New York: Public Affairs, 2001.

Jordan, Vernon Eulion, and Lee A. Daniels. *Make It Plain: Standing Up and Speaking Out*. New York: Public Affairs, 2008.

New Georgia Encyclopedia. "Vernon Jordan (b. 1935)." Available online. URL: http://www.newgeorgia encyclopedia.org/nge/Article.jsp?id=h-2518& pid=s-51. Downloaded July 23, 2009.

Karenga, Ron
(Ronald Everett, Maulana Karenga)
(1941–   ) *black nationalist leader, Kwanzaa founder, educator*

A controversial and divisive figure in his youth, Ron Karenga later became a professor of African-American studies in California. Born in 1941 in Baltimore, Maryland, Karenga, who was born Ronald Everett, is the son of a Baptist minister. After graduating from high school, he migrated west to California and settled in Los Angeles.

He attended colleges off and on in the Los Angeles area, but he was more interested in the evolving black protest movements that were springing up in the inner cities of Los Angeles and Oakland. By the mid-1960s, Ronald Everett had changed his name to Ron Karenga, the new surname an African-inspired name of his own creation. He would later drop his first name, Ron, and begin using *Maulana*, which is a Swahili word for "master teacher."

By 1965, Karenga earned a master's degree in political science at the University of California in Los Angeles. He also founded the group United Slaves, known as US, a militant, black nationalist organization that demanded an independent nation, created from several states of the United States, to be composed exclusively of African Americans. In 1966, Karenga invented a holiday called Kwanzaa. The term "Kwanzaa" is from the Swahili phrase *matunda yakwanza*, meaning "first fruit."

Originally, Karenga advertised Kwanzaa as a revolutionary, almost Marxist holiday, which, in his words, would create "conditions that would enhance the revolutionary social change for the masses of Black Americans" and provide a "reassessment, reclaiming, recommitment, remembrance, retrieval, resumption, resurrection and rejuvenation of those principles (Way of Life) utilized by Black Americans' ancestors." Karenga laid out seven principles—unity, self-determination, collective work and responsibility, cooperative economics, purpose, creativity, and faith—each of which is highlighted during one day of the week of Kwanzaa. The holiday was designed to be an alternative to Christmas. In one of his books, Karenga stated that Christianity (along with Judaism) "denies and diminishes human worth, capacity, potential and achievement." Karenga's current organization, Organization US, now downplays this earlier view of Christmas and Christians.

Karenga and US competed fiercely for the loyalties of black inner-city residents. US's most intense rival was the Black Panthers, another radical black group based mostly in the black ghettos of large cities. The two groups frequently clashed, sometimes violently. Neither attracted a large following among African Americans, and both groups would dwindle to a few members by the early 1970s.

In 1971, Karenga was indicted for the kidnapping and torture of two women whom he had accused of being government spies inside US. He was found guilty of these crimes in September 1971 and sent to prison, where he served four years of a 10-year sentence. After his release in 1975, Karenga began work on a Ph.D. in African Studies at the University of Southern California, which he earned in the late 1970s.

By the mid-1980s, Karenga had left violence in the past. He is currently a professor of Africana Studies at California State University in Long Beach.

Further Reading

Karenga, Maulana. *Kwanzaa: A Celebration of Family, Community and Culture.* Timbuktu, Mali: University of Sankore Press, 2007.

Mulshine, Paul. Frontpage. "Happy Kwanzaa." Available online. URL: http://www.frontpagemag.com/readArticle.aspx?ARTID=22181. Downloaded July 27, 2009.

Snow, Tony. "The TRUTH about Kwanzaa." Available online. URL: http://www.martinlutherking.org/kwanzaa.html. Downloaded July 27, 2009.

Travers, Len. *Encyclopedia of American Holidays and National Days.* Westport, Conn.: Greenwood, 2006.

King, Martin Luther, Jr.

(1929–1968) *civil rights activist, minister, Southern Christian Leadership Conference (SCLC) director*

A minister with a deep sense of social mission, Martin Luther King, Jr., became the most influential civil rights leader of the 20th century. The legacy of his career as a passionate advocate for racial and social justice is profound.

Born on January 15, 1929, in Atlanta, Georgia, Martin Luther King, Jr., was the son of Martin Luther and Alberta King. His father was a well-known minister at the Ebenezer Baptist Church in Atlanta. King, a diligent student, attended segregated public schools in Atlanta and in 1944 entered Morehouse College in that city at the age of 15. After graduating with a degree in sociology from Morehouse, King enrolled at the Crozer Theological Seminary in Chester, Pennsylvania, he graduated with a divinity degree with highest honors in 1951. He then moved to Boston, where he studied at Boston University for a doctorate, which he was awarded in 1955. While he was living in Boston, King married Coretta Scott in 1953.

In 1954, King was hired as the minister of the Dexter Avenue Baptist Church in Montgomery, Alabama. He arrived in Montgomery at the exact time that African-American residents of that city and the South in general were beginning to revolt against the legal system of racial segregation known as Jim Crow. A year after King moved to Montgomery, ROSA PARKS, a black seamstress, refused to give up her seat in the "white" section of a Montgomery bus. For this act of defiance, she was arrested. In response, King organized the Montgomery bus boycott, in which black residents, who made up a majority of Montgomery's bus riders, refused to use the city buses.

The boycott lasted for more than a year, during which King's house was firebombed and numerous black citizens were arrested. The confrontation was finally settled by a case before the Supreme Court. In November 1956, the court struck down Alabama laws that required racial segregation on buses. Federal injunctions were issued to the city on December 20. On December 21, King and the Reverend Glen Smiley, a white minister, shared a front seat during a victory ride on a city bus.

After the Montgomery boycott, King wrote *Stride toward Freedom* (1958), a book about the experience, and made two trips overseas. In 1957, he was invited to witness the ceremonies that marked the independence of Ghana, and in 1959 he went to India, where he met the Indian prime minister Nehru and Vinoba Bhave, a disciple of Mohandas Gandhi, the great Indian independence leader who was assassinated in 1948.

King's approach to protest was deeply influenced by Gandhi's idea of *satyagraha,* a Hindi word for "firmness in truth." As did Gandhi, King believed passionately in nonviolent civil disobedience. If laws were immoral and unjust, King would organize mass protests against them until they were repealed. His answer to violence was continued peaceful protest and love. It was a powerful message that would eventually resonate throughout the nation and the world, and it would result in major social and legal changes in the United States.

In 1960, at the request of African-American ministers in the South, King resigned his ministry of the Dexter Avenue Baptist Church and moved to Atlanta to head the Southern Christian Leadership Conference (SCLC). Now a full-time civil rights leader, King began to organize and participate in protests at segregated restaurants and stores in Atlanta. In October 1960, he was arrested with several dozen protesters for refusing to leave a segregated lunch counter. Instead of being taken to the county jail, King was secretly imprisoned in a Georgia state penitentiary. Subsequent outrage and the protest of John F. Kennedy, then the Democratic presidential candidate, won King's release.

King continued to organize protests against segregated facilities, this time in Albany, Georgia, throughout 1961 and 1962. In April and May 1963, King journeyed to Birmingham, Alabama, to lead protests against segregation in that city. There he and his fellow protesters were met with high-pressure water cannons, snarling police dogs, and police batons as they peacefully sought an end to segregation in restaurants, movie theaters, and schools. Scenes of the brutality against the protesters were flashed around the nation by television and began to sway public opinion in favor of the protesters. In his famous "Letter from Birmingham Jail," King defended his actions:

> You may well ask: "Why direct action? Why sit-ins, marches and so forth? Isn't negotiation a better path?" You are quite right in calling for negotiation. Indeed, this is the very purpose of direct action. Nonviolent direct action seeks to create such a crisis and foster such a tension that a community which has constantly refused to negotiate is forced to confront the issue. It seeks so to dramatize the issue that it can no longer be ignored. . . . I have earnestly opposed violent tension, but there is a type of constructive, nonviolent tension which is necessary for growth. Just as Socrates felt that it was necessary to create a tension in the mind so that individuals could rise from the bondage of myths and half-truths to the unfettered realm of creative analysis and objective appraisal, we must we see the need for nonviolent gadflies to create the kind of tension in society that will help men rise from the dark depths of prejudice and racism to the majestic heights of understanding and brotherhood.

On August 28, 1963, King and Asa Philip Randolph, a respected African-American labor leader, organized the March on Washington, in which speaker after speaker demanded an end to the Jim Crow system and full justice under law for black Americans. That day, King gave one of his most impassioned and famous speeches, in which he outlined his vision of a just America:

> There will be neither rest nor tranquility in America until the Negro is granted his citizenship rights. The whirlwinds of revolt will continue to shake the foundations of our nation until the bright day of justice emerges. . . .

I say to you today, my friends, that in spite of the difficulties and frustrations of the moment, I still have a dream. It is a dream deeply rooted in the American dream.

I have a dream that one day this nation will rise up and live out the true meaning of its creed: "We hold these truths to be self-evident: that all men are created equal."

I have a dream that one day on the red hills of Georgia the sons of former slaves and the sons of former slave owners will be able to sit down together at a table of brotherhood. . . .

I have a dream that my four children will one day live in a nation where they will not be judged by the color of their skin but by the content of their character. . . .

Later that year, King received the Nobel Peace Prize for his efforts as leader of an ever-growing civil rights crusade in the United States, and in January 1964 he was chosen *Time* magazine's Man of the Year, the first African American so honored by that publication.

In 1964, King paused to lay the foundations for further protest. He also held back as President Lyndon Johnson, through artful manipulation, persuaded the Congress to pass the landmark Civil Rights Act in July. This act, prodded by King's protests in the streets, and the sympathy it won especially from northern voters, created the foundation of the destruction of overt segregation in the United States. The Voting Rights Act, passed in August 1965, for the first time gave African Americans federal protection of their voting rights.

In March 1965, King led perhaps the major act of civil disobedience of his life. In response to the killing of a civil rights protester by an Alabama state trooper, black citizens in Marion, Alabama, asked King to help them organize a march from the nearby town of Selma to Birmingham, the state capital. Fearing violence and disorder, the Johnson administration's Justice Department asked a federal court to stop the march, and the court did. Saying, "We have the right to walk the highways, and we have the right to walk to Montgomery if our feet will get us there," King made it clear he was determined to hold the march anyway. Nonetheless, he flew to Washington to try to negotiate a compromise agreement. In his absence, the marchers attempted to walk over the Edward Pettus Bridge in Selma and were viciously attacked by sheriff's officers. The next day, King led marchers to the bridge again, but in a compromise brokered by the federal government, the state and local police allowed them across the bridge but not into the

Martin Luther King, Jr., founded the Southern Christian Leadership Conference, one of the most active civil rights organizations of the late 1950s and 1960s. King was assassinated in 1968. *(Library of Congress, Prints and Photographs Division, LC-U9-11696)*

town. King led thousands of marchers all the way to Birmingham 12 days later.

In 1966, King took his protests to the North, specifically Chicago. With the help of JESSE JACKSON, one of King's most trusted aides, and scores of other civil rights organizations, King and his supporters seized a tenement building and held the tenants' rent in trust until the landlord made repairs to the building. King and his family lived in the tenement for several days. King also led marchers into traditionally white neighborhoods, demanding that African Americans be allowed to live there. In Cicero, a tough, working-class neighborhood, King and his supporters were pelted with bricks, and King narrowly escaped injury. After the outbreak of a three-day race riot, King was forced to accept a compromise called the Summit Agreement, in which the problems he addressed—nondiscriminatory hiring for jobs, access to housing, integrated schools—were swept under the rug.

King's compromises angered younger, more militant black leaders such as STOKELY CARMICHAEL of the Student Nonviolent Coordinating Committee (SNCC) and ELDRIDGE CLEAVER of the Black Panthers. In June 1966, on a trip to Mississippi to help civil rights workers engaged in registering black voters, King was booed at a rally in Greenwood, and Carmichael was cheered when he called for "Black Power" and insisted that blacks should use violence to defend themselves.

Nonetheless, King continued his efforts, then focusing on opposition to the war in Vietnam and the economic underpinnings of inequality, which affected poor whites as well as poor blacks. He called for a $30 billion a year federal government effort to eliminate poverty through better schools, job training, and youth programs. In February 1968, he began organizing the Poor People's Campaign, a multiracial march on Washington by as many as 3,000 supporters that would dramatize the need for social and economic reforms to end the unequal distribution of wealth among haves and have-nots in the United States.

Although the march did occur in the summer of 1968, King did not live to make the march himself. On April 4, an assassin shot and killed him as he stood on the balcony of a motel in Memphis, Tennessee, a city he had visited to help support a strike of sanitation workers. King's assassination provoked a week of rioting in scores of cities in the United States, including Washington, D.C. However, even though the nature of the civil rights struggle had changed with the Civil Rights and Voting Rights Acts and with affirmative action, King's mission did not die with him. Of all of King's disciples, Jesse Jackson has been the most active in carrying on his struggle for racial and economic justice.

A Martin Luther King, Jr., National Memorial is being planned for the National Mall in Washington, D.C. Originally sponsored by the Alpha Phi Alpha fraternity, the project was approved by Congress in 1996. A nonprofit organization, the Martin Luther King, Jr., National Memorial Project Foundation continues to raise funds for the memorial's construction. Once built, the National Park Service will manage the memorial. It will be the first memorial on the National Mall to honor an African American.

Further Reading

Bill Moyers' Journal. *Andrew Young Remembers Martin Luther King* (videorecording). WNET/13, New York: Educational Broadcasting, 1979.

Branch, Taylor. *America in the King Years.* New York: Simon & Schuster, 1988.

Carson, Clayborne, Tenisha Armstrong et al., eds. *The Martin Luther King, Jr., Encyclopedia.* Westport, Conn.: Greenwood, 2008.

Garrow, David J. *Bearing the Cross: Martin Luther King, Jr., and the Southern Christian Leadership Conference.* New York: Morrow, 1986.

———. *The FBI and Martin Luther King, Jr.: From "Solo" to Memphis.* New York: W. W. Norton, 1981.

King Center. "Biography." Available online. URL: http://www.thekingcenter.org/DrMLKingJr/. Downloaded July 27, 2009.

Martin Luther King, Jr., Research and Education Institute. "About the Institute." Available online. URL: http://mlk-kpp01.stanford.edu/index.php/ about/article/about_keeping_the_dream_alive/. Downloaded July 27, 2009.

New Georgia Encyclopedia. "Martin Luther King Jr. (1929–68)." Available online. URL: http://www. georgiaencyclopedia.org/nge/Article.jsp?id=h-1009&sug=y. Downloaded July 27, 2009.

L

Leary, Lewis Sheridan
(ca. 1836–1859) *abolitionist, Harpers Ferry raid participant*

Lewis Leary took part in one of the most striking episodes in U.S. history, the raid by John Brown and his 22 followers on the Harpers Ferry arsenal in Virginia (now West Virginia) on October 16, 1859. This event signaled the end of an era and presaged the American Civil War.

Born sometime around 1836 in North Carolina, Lewis Sheridan Leary was the son of a black slave woman and her Irish owner, Jeremiah O'Leary. Soon after his birth, O'Leary freed Lewis Leary's mother and his siblings, all of whom seem to have been O'Leary's. The family then moved to Ohio, where Leary (he never used the O in his father's surname) worked as a harness maker.

Leary managed to spend some time as a student at Oberlin College in Ohio. In his early 20s, he also married Mary Patterson (who would become the grandmother of the Harlem Renaissance poet Langston Hughes). They had one child.

In early 1859, Leary eagerly signed up with the white abolitionist John Brown when Brown began secretly recruiting participants for a raid he planned to make on the federal arsenal in Harpers Ferry (then Harper's Ferry). Brown hoped to seize weapons at the arsenal and give them to slaves on nearby farms. He expected that this action would provoke a general uprising of slaves throughout the South and an overthrow of the political system that supported slavery. Brown had even written a new constitution to be put in effect when his uprising had swept away the opposition.

The actual raid, carried out in the last hours of Sunday, October 16, was a military disaster. Brown and his men seized the arsenal and a nearby railway bridge, but they encountered enough opposition to alert the townspeople that something was amiss. Within hours, reinforcements in the form of state militia and U.S. army troops arrived to surround the militants who were holed up inside the arsenal.

On Monday, October 17, troops attacked the arsenal, wounding Lewis Leary. He lived for a few hours before bleeding to death. The rest of the raiders, except one—Osborne Perry Anderson, who escaped the arsenal and fled to Canada—were captured and eventually executed.

Leary was buried in a cemetery at Harpers Ferry, but in 1899 his body was moved to lie beside that of John Brown in North Elba, New York.

Further Reading
Anderson, Osborne P. *A Voice from Harpers Ferry.* 1861. Reprint, Atlanta: Worldview, 1980.

Horton, Lois E. *Slavery and the Making of America*. New York: Oxford University Press, 2004.

PBS. Africans in America, Resource Bank. "John Brown's Black Raiders." Available online. URL: www.pbs.org/wgbh/aia/part4/4p2941.html. Downloaded July 3, 2009.

Lemus, Rienzi Brock
(1880–1969) *labor organizer*

A soldier and correspondent during the Philippine insurrection at the beginning of the 20th century, Rienzi Lemus later became an important labor leader who helped organize the Brotherhood of Dining Car Employees. Born on January 8, 1880, in Richmond, Virginia, Rienzi Brock Lemus was the son of Charles and Mamie Lemus. He attended Richmond's segregated schools and when he turned 18 volunteered for the U.S. Army.

A member of the 8th Volunteer Infantry and later the 25th Infantry, Lemus served in the army occupation force in the Philippines after the Spanish-American War. He wrote a number of informative articles for African-American newspapers such as the *Boston Chronicle* and the *New York Age* describing the life of a soldier in the Philippines. He also strongly opposed schemes to colonize African Americans on the Philippine Islands.

After he mustered out of the army in 1902, Lemus got a job as a Pullman porter on a railroad. Two years later, he switched jobs, becoming a dining car waiter. Beginning around 1917, Lemus led the movement to organize railroad dining car employees into a union. This effort gained momentum with the U.S. entry into World War I in 1917. After the declaration of war, the U.S. government took control of the nation's railroads and negotiated a contract with Lemus's Brotherhood of Dining Car Employees (BDCE). As president of the union, Lemus renewed this contract with six rail lines at war's end.

Lemus worked to expand union membership steadily during the 1920s. By 1929, the brotherhood included 2,700 members and half the black dining car workers on rail lines east of the Mississippi River. The Great Depression hurt the union's effectiveness and made it vulnerable to the organizing efforts of competing unions. In the late 1930s, the American Federation of Labor's (AFL's) Hotel and Restaurant Workers Union lured away many workers from the BDCE.

In 1941, Lemus was ousted from the presidency of the union as the BDCE merged with the Transport Workers Union. He continued to live in New York City for a number of years and moved to Baltimore later in his life. He died in Baltimore on June 6, 1969.

Further Reading
Anderson, Warwick. "Immunities of Empire." Available online. URL: http://muse.jhu.edu/demo/bhm/70.1anderson02.html. Downloaded August 28, 2001.

Arnesen, Eric. *Brotherhoods of Color: Black Railroad Workers and the Struggle for Equality*. Cambridge, Mass.: Harvard University Press, 2002.

Logan, Rayford, and Michael Winston. *Dictionary of American Negro Biography*. New York: W. W. Norton, 1982.

M

Malcolm X

(Malcolm Little, El-Hajj Malik El-Shabazz)
(1925–1965) *political activist, Muslim leader*

A political activist and religious leader especially popular among northern inner-city blacks, Malcolm X was one of the most controversial African-American spokesmen of the late 1950s and early 1960s. Born on May 19, 1925, in Omaha, Nebraska, Malcolm Little was the son of a Baptist minister Earl Little, who was deeply influenced by MARCUS GARVEY's Universal Negro Improvement Association (UNIA). The UNIA was an organization that demanded civil rights for blacks and promoted black self-determination through the creation of black-owned businesses and charitable institutions.

From Malcolm's earliest days, his family was traumatized by violence. Shortly before Malcolm was born, Ku Klux Klan members threatened to kill his father; the incident caused the family to move briefly to Milwaukee, Wisconsin, before heading to Lansing, Michigan.

The move did not end the cycle of violence against the Littles. Possibly because of Earl Little's continued involvement in the UNIA, arsonists burned the family house in Lansing, and the Littles were forced to move again—this time to nearby East Lansing. In 1931, when Malcolm was six, Earl Little died after being hit by a streetcar.

The death of Malcolm's father threw the family into a crisis. Louise Little, Malcolm's mother, slipped into depression, and Malcolm began to get into trouble with the local authorities. In 1937, when he was 12, Malcolm was placed in a juvenile detention center and his mother was committed to a state mental hospital. For a couple of years, Malcolm lived with a white family who worked at the detention center. In 1940, shortly after his 15th birthday, he moved to Boston to live with his half-sister, Ella.

After his arrival in Boston, Malcolm dropped out of school and took a job shining shoes at the Roseland Ballroom, one of Boston's largest jazz clubs. Like most establishments of its kind in both the North and the South, the Roseland was racially segregated. Malcolm quickly learned that he could boost his income by selling drugs to his white customers. He continued to work various street rackets after his move to Harlem in New York City in 1942.

By 1946, Malcolm had burned most of his bridges in New York City. He later described himself as "an uncouth, wild young Negro. I was really a clown, but my ignorance made me think I was sharp." Moving back to Boston to escape New York underworld figures who had turned on him, Malcolm was arrested for burglary in February 1946. After a short trial, he received a 10-year sentence.

Malcolm X was heir apparent to Elijah Muhammad in the Nation of Islam (NOI) until their split in 1964. He was assassinated at the Audubon Ballroom in New York City in 1965. *(Library of Congress, Prints and Photographs Division, LC-U9-11695)*

In prison, Malcolm slowly began to change. He met an older inmate who coaxed him into taking correspondence courses to improve his language skills. His brother, Reginald, now living in Detroit, visited him and introduced him to a new religion, called the Nation of Islam (NOI). Reginald told Malcolm about the group's leader, ELIJAH MUHAMMAD, and urged Malcolm to consider changing his life by joining them in this spiritual journey.

At first Malcolm, a man who never prayed and had only been on his knees, as he put it, to "[pick] a lock to rob someone's house," resisted. The Nation of Islam demanded a complete change of life. He would be required to abstain from pork, cigarettes, alcohol, and drugs. Sexual promiscuity was forbidden; courteous language and respectful behavior were required of all members.

In 1949, Malcolm converted to the NOI. "Every instinct of the ghetto jungle streets," he later wrote, "every hustling fox and criminal wolf instinct in me was struck dumb" by this religious experience. He changed his name to Malcolm X, the X in the creed's philosophy replacing the name that had been given the Little family by white slave owners.

The NOI also supplied Malcolm with a heightened political consciousness from which he evaluated his past life. He began to read voraciously about politics and history and created a picture in his mind of the influence of white society on his life—white Klan members who had chased the family out of Omaha, white institutions that excluded him from employment and schooling, white social workers who had committed his mother and held him in detention, white police officers who had hounded him in Michigan and New York.

This new awareness meshed well with the philosophy of the Nation of Islam that white people were "devils," unleashed onto the world by a mad scientist named Yacub. But, according to Elijah Muhammad, the oppressive world of these "white devils" was about to end. Guided by the Nation of Islam, blacks would build a separate society free of the control of whites.

Malcolm accepted the Nation of Islam's worldview completely and uncritically, and he became one of its most energetic organizers. He began converting prisoners at Norfolk Prison, where he was being held. After his release from prison in 1952, he moved to Detroit and continued his one-man recruitment campaign on the city's streets.

By 1954, Malcolm had worked his way up the organization and was sent to head the NOI temple in Harlem. From his base in Harlem, Malcolm worked feverishly to spread the word about the Nation of Islam and call for blacks to create their own society separate from whites. In 1958, Malcolm married Betty Shabazz; they would have five children.

Among Malcolm X's favorite targets in his fiery speeches were moderate black leaders who were working with sympathetic whites to persuade Congress and large corporations to pass meaningful civil rights legislation and hire more black workers. Malcolm called such black leaders "men with black bodies and white heads." He derided slow progress toward greater civil rights for blacks, saying, "You don't stick a knife in a man's back nine inches and pull it out six inches and say you're making progress."

By 1962, Malcolm seemed on the verge of taking over the leadership of the Nation of Islam from the elderly and ailing Elijah Muhammad. However, other NOI leaders began to conspire against him. By 1963, the power struggle within the Nation of Islam had reached a fever pitch. Elijah Muhammad suspended Malcolm from his work for 90 days after Malcolm made incendiary comments about white violence after the assassination of President John F. Kennedy.

In February 1964, Malcolm learned that someone at NOI headquarters in Chicago had given orders for his murder. Saying that he "felt like something in nature had failed—like the sun or the stars," he quit the Nation of Islam, even as he remained a devout Muslim and committed activist for African-American rights.

After his resignation from the Nation of Islam, Malcolm founded two organizations, Muslim Mosque, Inc., and the Organization of Afro-American Unity. He also made a pilgrimage to Mecca, the Muslim holy city in Saudi Arabia, and began to rethink his belief that all whites were his enemies. After holding long conversations with leading Muslim theologians, he began to understand that Elijah Muhammad's beliefs were not in line with traditional Muslim thought about the brotherhood of all humankind. On his return to the United States, he announced, "I can get along with any white people who can get along with me." During this trip, he also changed his name again, this time to El-Hajj Malik El-Shabazz.

For the rest of 1964 and 1965, Malcolm worked hard to get his new organizations off the ground. This was a period of intense effort by civil rights leaders in the South. Freedom Summer, a voter registration drive by white and black activists, had begun with violence directed against its volunteers. Riots erupted in New York, Chicago, and Philadelphia.

In 1964 and 1965, Malcolm X knew he was a marked man with a murder contract out on him by the NOI. Still he worked with his usual energy. He finished writing a book about his life and beliefs, *The Autobiography of Malcolm X,* and he began a campaign to persuade the United Nations to pass a resolution condemning U.S. racial policies.

On February 13, 1965, as he was giving a speech at Harlem's Audubon Ballroom, he was gunned down by several assassins. Despite evidence to the contrary, the Nation of Islam always denied any role in the killing.

Malcolm X's death removed from the scene one of the most articulate advocates for African-American civil and political rights at a time when his thinking about the relationship of whites and blacks was changing. But his death made him a larger-than-life figure and ensured that his ideas would not be forgotten. His energy and uncompromising devotion to black pride and self-sufficiency remain an inspiration to succeeding generations of African Americans.

In 2005, Columbia University opened the Malcolm X and Dr. Betty Shabazz Memorial and Educational Center. Located in the Audubon Ballroom, where Malcolm X was assassinated, the center promotes human and civil rights by sponsoring programs and services that increase knowledge and understanding of the African and African-American experiences.

Further Reading

Carew, Jan. *Ghosts in Our Blood: With Malcolm X in Africa, England, and the Caribbean.* New York: Lawrence Hill, 1994.

Dyson, Michael Eric. *Making Malcolm: The Myth and the Meaning of Malcolm X.* New York: Oxford University Press, 1995.

Malcolm X and Dr. Betty Shabazz Memorial and Education Center. "About Us." Available online. URL: http://theshabazzcenter.net/about_us.htm. Downloaded July 27, 2009.

Malcolm X Project at Columbia University. "The Life of Malcolm X." Available online. URL: http://www.columbia.edu/cu/ccbh/mxp/life.html. Downloaded July 27, 2009.

Rummel, Jack. *Malcolm X.* New York: Chelsea House, 1989.

Sales, William W., Jr. *From Civil Rights to Black Liberation: Malcolm X and the Organization of Afro-American Unity.* Boston: South End Press, 1994.

Marshall, Thurgood

(1908–1993) *lawyer, civil rights activist, Supreme Court justice*

As a longtime lawyer for the National Association for the Advancement of Colored People (NAACP) and later as a justice of the U.S. Supreme Court, Thurgood Marshall was instrumental in destroying legalized racial segregation in the United States. Born in 1908 in Baltimore, Maryland, Marshall was the son of William and Norma Marshall. Marshall's family was middle class; his father was a steward at an all-white country club and his mother was a teacher in Baltimore's segregated school system.

Marshall was encouraged to study and got good grades in public school. After his graduation from high school in 1926, he enrolled in Lincoln University in Pennsylvania, from which he graduated with honors in 1930. He then enrolled in the law school of Howard University in Washington, D.C., and he earned an LL.B. in 1933. Marshall married Vivian Burey in 1929. When she died in 1955, he would marry Cecelia Suyat, with whom he would have two children.

For a few years after his graduation from law school, Marshall maintained a private practice in Baltimore and specialized in civil rights cases. He took work for the Baltimore branch of the NAACP and developed a reputation as a diligent lawyer. By the mid-1930s, he moved to New York City and began working for CHARLES HAMILTON HOUSTON, the head of the NAACP's Legal Defense Fund.

Marshall succeeded Houston as head of the special counsel for the NAACP in 1938. In 1940, he was made legal director of the NAACP. As the lead lawyer for the NAACP, Marshall carried out the strategy he had developed with Houston. He began his attack on the system of legal segregation, known as Jim Crow, by first bringing cases that challenged racial segregation at graduate and professional schools. He and Houston believed that the court would be more sympathetic to these cases because they involved respectable middle-class African-American students. He also took on other types of civil rights cases as they presented themselves. Marshall hoped that after he had won enough of these cases to establish a precedent he would then be able to attack the more fundamental racial segregation found in public elementary and secondary schools.

Marshall won the first of 29 U.S. Supreme Court victories in 1940. By the mid-1940s, he had begun to argue and win major cases before the court. In 1944, he won *Smith v. Allwright,* in which the Supreme Court ruled unconstitutional Texas's exclusion of African-American voters from political primaries, especially the Democratic Party primary (Texas was at that time a heavily Democratic state). In 1948, Marshall argued *Shelley v. Kraemer,* a case that sought to ban real-estate covenants that excluded the resale of homes in certain neighborhoods to African Americans. In this case, as in *Smith v. Allwright,* Marshall convinced the court to overturn this race-based law.

In 1950, Marshall won two major cases that banned racial segregation at universities. In *Sweatt v. Painter,* the court ruled that the University of

Texas had to admit African-American students to its law school because the state's segregated law school was not "substantially equal" to that provided to white students. In *McLaurin v. the Oklahoma Board of Regents,* the court ruled that the University of Oklahoma had to offer black students access to the same facilities available to whites at the university.

As Marshall hoped, these cases set the stage for what would be his major case, a suit brought by a black family against the Topeka, Kansas, school system, which Marshall argued before the Supreme Court in 1954. *Brown v. the Board of Education of Topeka* was arguably the most important U.S. civil rights case of the 20th century. Marshall argued that the Topeka schools' segregated educational system did not provide an equal education to black children. The doctrine of "separate but equal," established in 1896 by another court case, *Plessy v. Ferguson,* Marshall told the court, created a system that provided unequal, second-class education to African Americans. During the court hearings, when asked by Justice Felix Frankfurter to define *equal,* Marshall had a straightforward reply: "Equal means getting the same thing, at the same time and in the same place." The court agreed and ordered Topeka to come up with a plan to desegregate its schools. Eventually 21 states would be required to dismantle their segregated school systems as well.

Brown v. the Board of Education of Topeka marked the beginning of the most intensive phase of the Civil Rights movement, which would last roughly from 1954 until 1965, the year the Voting Rights Act, giving African Americans federal voting protection, was passed. In 1961, President Kennedy, recognizing Marshall's accomplishments, appointed Marshall to the federal bench as a district judge. Marshall served four years as a federal judge then accepted an appointment in 1965 to be solicitor general of the Justice Department. He was solicitor general for only two years before President Lyndon Johnson nominated him

Thurgood Marshall headed the National Association for the Advancement of Colored People (NAACP) legal team that won a victory for the racial integration of public schools with *Brown v. the Board of Education of Topeka,* a 1954 Supreme Court decision. He later served as a Supreme Court justice. *(Library of Congress, Prints and Photographs Division, LC-U9-1027B)*

to be a justice on the U.S. Supreme Court. When the Senate confirmed the nomination in 1967, Marshall became the first African American to sit on the nation's highest court.

During Marshall's 24-year tenure, he promoted the policy that became known as affirmative action as a way to redress years of exclusion of blacks from the mainstream of American society. In numerous cases, the court, following Marshall's lead, upheld racial preferences and set-asides that allowed African Americans to attend colleges and universities they had not been able to study at before and to get work as contractors and on job sites where they had previously been excluded.

Marshall lived to see the court swing to a more conservative stance in the 1980s. Newer, more conservative justices appointed by Presidents Ronald Reagan and George H. W. Bush slowly began to reject the idea of affirmative action. His health failing, and disappointed by what was happening to the court, Marshall retired in 1991. He died on January 24, 1993.

Further Reading

Rowan, Carl T. *Dream Makers, Dream Breakers: The World of Justice Thurgood Marshall*. Boston: Little, Brown, 1993.

Supreme Court Historical Society. "Thurgood Marshall, 1967–91." Available online. URL: http://www.supremecourthistory.org/history/supreme courthistory_history_assoc_082marshall.htm. Downloaded July 2, 2009.

Tushnet, Mark, ed. *Thurgood Marshall: His Speeches, Writings, Arguments, Opinions, and Reminiscences*. Chicago: Lawrence Hill, 2001.

Williams, Juan. "Thurgood Marshall." Available online. URL: http://www.thurgoodmarshall.com/home.htm. Downloaded July 2, 2009.

———. *Thurgood Marshall: American Revolutionary*. New York: Times Books, 1998.

Matthews, Victoria Earle

(1861–1907) *journalist, women's club organizer, social worker*

Victoria Matthews was a pioneering journalist who worked for both predominantly white as well as black-owned publications. In her later years, she concentrated her energies on trying to help poor black women find respectable employment in northern cities.

Born into slavery in Fort Valley, Georgia, in 1861, Victoria Earle had a difficult childhood. For several years she was raised by a nurse when her mother escaped servitude during the Civil War.

The mother, Caroline Smith, lived in New York City until the end of the war, then returned to Georgia to get Victoria and her three siblings, who were still living with their white father. It is unclear whether the father was also their slave master, although this is likely.

In New York City, Victoria attended a public grammar school for several years but was soon forced to drop out to take jobs to help support her family. Working as a domestic servant, she was able to continue her education by reading books that were in the libraries of her employers. In 1879, at age 18, she married William Matthews, a coachman. After moving to Brooklyn, New York, she and her husband had one son.

In the 1880s, Victoria Matthews began to work as a reporter for a number of newspapers, most of them in the bustling New York market. At first she worked as a "sub" reporter, a sort of freelance position in which she did odd pieces of writing and filled in for other full-time reporters. However, she soon began to hold down full-time positions and worked for such leading black newspapers as the *Boston Advocate, New York Globe,* and *New York Age.* She also worked for the white-owned *New York Times* and *New York Herald.*

As a reporter, Matthews formed a close bond with TIMOTHY THOMAS FORTUNE, the owner of the *New York Age.* When her interest began to shift to organizing black women in the 1890s, Fortune introduced her to BOOKER TALIAFERRO WASHINGTON, who helped her get funding for the White Rose Industrial Association and White Rose Mission, two groups that Matthews founded to offer education for black women who wanted to enter domestic service.

Matthews also founded and became first president of the Women's Loyal Union of New York. She helped found the National Federation of Afro-American Women, and she organized the merger of the federation with the National Colored Women's League, which became the National Association of Colored Women (NACW). She served as the principal national organizer for the NACW from 1897 to 1899.

Matthews died of tuberculosis in 1907. Only 45 at her death, she left a void in the community of African-American women organizers.

Further Reading

Brown, Hallie M. *Homespun Heroines and Other Women of Distinction.* Xenia, Ohio: Aldine, 1926.

Garland, I. *The Afro-American Press and Its Editors.* Springfield, Mass.: Willey, 1891.

Kramer, Steve. "Matthews, Victoria Earle." Available online. URL: http://www.anb.org/articles/15/15-01315.html. Downloaded July 2, 2009.

Williams, Yolanda. *Encyclopedia of African American Women Writers.* Westport, Conn.: Greenwood, 2007.

Maynard, Nancy Hicks

(1946–2008) *journalist, publisher, educator*

Nancy Hicks Maynard blazed trails as a black female reporter and newspaper publisher and helped train hundreds of African-American journalists and newspaper editors. Nancy Alene Hall was born in New York City on November 1, 1946. Her father, Alfred, was a noted jazz musician, and her mother, Eve Keller, was a nurse. Nancy grew up in Harlem and became interested in journalism as a teenager. When a fire destroyed her former elementary school, the city's newspapers portrayed Harlem in a harshly negative light. The misleading depiction of her neighborhood angered Nancy. She decided that she could make a difference by becoming a journalist. After graduating from high school, she enrolled at Long Island University. During college, she worked as a copy girl on weekends at the *New York Post.* There, she met the noted black journalist Ted Poston, who became her mentor. She earned a journalism degree in 1966.

After graduation, Maynard began working as a reporter at the *New York Post.* Her reporting impressed editors at the *New York Times,* who offered her a job in 1968. She became the youngest reporter in the city news department at the time, as well as one of the first black female reporters at the paper.

One of Maynard's first assignments was to report on a controversial decentralization of school districts in Brooklyn. The process led to charges of racism against the city's department of education and sparked a citywide teachers' strike. Maynard's editors assigned her to cover stories involving African Americans. She covered race riots, black student protests at Cornell and Columbia Universities, and a memorial for slain presidential candidate Robert F. Kennedy. She later moved beyond reporting African-American issues. She began to focus on stories involving education and science and soon specialized in covering health care issues. She wrote major stories on the Apollo space missions and Medicare.

After her husband, Daniel Hicks, died, she met Robert C. Maynard, a columnist for the *Washington Post.* She transferred to the *New York Times* Washington news bureau the following year and married Maynard. In 1977, the couple quit their newspaper jobs. Along with seven other journalists, they created the Institute for Journalism Education, based in Berkeley, California. The institute's mission was to train minority journalists to increase newsroom diversity. Nancy Maynard served as the institute's first president. Since its founding, the Maynard Institute has trained hundreds of minority journalists, editors, and managers. (The institute would be renamed the Maynard Institute for Journalism Education following the death of Robert Maynard.)

In 1979, the *Oakland Tribune* hired Robert Maynard as its editor. Four years later, the Maynards bought the financially struggling newspaper. For nearly a decade, the couple worked as copublishers. They built a racially diverse staff and provided increased coverage of Oakland's large African-American community. Nancy wrote a regular column and focused on the business aspects of running the newspaper. She revamped operations in the circulation and advertising departments. She refused to run gun ads because of the city's rising murder rate. The newspaper again encountered financial difficulties, and the Maynards sold it in 1992. During their tenure, the newspaper won many journalism awards, including a Pulitzer Prize in 1990. It remains as the only major metropolitan newspaper ever owned by African Americans. Nancy Maynard would later say that publishing the *Tribune* was her greatest accomplishment.

Robert Maynard died in 1993. Following her husband's death, Nancy worked as a media consultant and writer. Her 2006 book, *Mega Media: How Market Forces Are Transforming News,* examined the factors that were rapidly changing the news business. Maynard remained a member of the board of directors of the Maynard Institute and continued as a tireless advocate for newsroom diversity and the social mission of journalism. Following a long illness, she died in 2008.

Further Reading

Hicks, Nancy Maynard. *Mega Media: How Market Forces Are Transforming News.* Bloomington, Ind.: Trafford, 2006.

Maynard Institute for Journalism Education. "Nancy Maynard, Famous Black Woman." Available online. URL: http://www.mije.org/nancy-maynard. Downloaded June 27, 2009.

Mays, Benjamin Elijah

(1894–1984) *civil rights leader, Morehouse College president*

An influential university president, Benjamin Mays was also an inspiring moral leader who influenced the direction of the 20th-century movement for African-American civil rights. Born on August 1, 1894, in Epworth, South Carolina, Benjamin Elijah Mays was encouraged by his family to study. After graduation from high school in the South, Mays enrolled in Bates College, a small liberal arts college located in Lewiston, Maine, in 1916. He graduated from Bates a member of Phi Beta Kappa in 1920.

After completing his undergraduate education, Mays returned to the South and for three years served as preacher of the Shiloh Baptist Church in Atlanta. In 1923, Mays was hired as an instructor of mathematics and as a debate coach at Morehouse College, one of the oldest historically black universities in that city. While teaching at Morehouse, Mays worked on a master's degree from the University of Chicago, which he earned in 1925. Mays was awarded a Ph.D. from the University of Chicago in 1935. In 1929, Mays married Sadie Gray, a teacher and social worker. They would remain together until her death in 1969.

In 1934, Mays was hired as the dean of Howard University's School of Religion. He would remain at Howard until 1940, when he returned to Atlanta to become president of Morehouse College. During his 27 years as president of Morehouse, Mays would transform the college. He upgraded the faculty and installed a Phi Beta Kappa chapter. Equally important, he served as a mentor and role model for a new generation of African-American leaders who were undergraduates at Morehouse during his tenure.

Mays was best known at Morehouse for his Tuesday morning talks at Sale Hall, a building on the Morehouse campus. There, he spoke eloquently and movingly to the students as he challenged them to find their purpose and goal in life. "It is not what you keep, but what you give that makes you happy," Mays once said. "We make our living by what we get. We make our life by what we give. Whatever you do, strive to do it so well that no man living and no man dead, and no man yet to be born can do it any better. As we face the unpredictable future, have faith that man and God will assist us all the way."

Arguably, Mays's best-known student was MARTIN LUTHER KING, JR., who credited Mays as his "spiritual mentor and intellectual father." It was through Mays that King first grasped the importance of nonviolence as a moral center for the civil rights crusade. King would take Mays's lessons on Mohandas Gandhi's doctrine of nonviolent civil disobedience and push the Civil Rights movement to important victories in the 1960s. Mays delivered the eulogy at Dr. King's funeral in 1968.

Mays retired as president of Morehouse in 1969 but did not retire from an active life in his community. From 1970 until 1981, he served on the board of Atlanta's public school system. Along with *Born to Rebel*, his autobiography, published in 1971, he wrote more than 2,000 papers and nine books. He died on March 28, 1984.

Further Reading

Dumas, Carrie M., and Julie Hunter, eds. *Benjamin Elijah Mays: A Pictorial Life and Times*. Macon, Ga.: Mercer University Press, 2006.

Howard University Divinity Library. "Dr. Benjamin Elijan Mays." Available online. URL: http://www.howard.edu/library/Divinity_Library/Benjamin_Mays.htm. Downloaded July 2, 2009.

Mays, Benjamin E. *Born to Rebel: An Autobiography*. 1971. Reprint, Athens: University of Georgia Press, 2003.

New Georgia Encyclopedia. "Benjamin Elijah Mays." Available online. URL: http://www.georgiaencyclopedia.org/nge/Article.jsp?id=h-2627. Downloaded July 2, 2009.

McCabe, Edwin

(1850–1920) *civil rights activist, founder of Langston, Oklahoma*

A land promoter and political operative, Edwin McCabe was the most influential African-American leader in Kansas and Oklahoma in the late 1800s. He was primarily responsible for the immigration of thousands of blacks from the South to Oklahoma Territory in the 1890s. Born in Troy, New York, on October 10, 1850, McCabe

was the son of Elizabeth McCabe and her husband, a man whose name is not known. He had a knockabout childhood and youth, moving with his parents first to Fall River, Massachusetts, then to Newport, Rhode Island; Bangor, Maine; San Francisco, California; and finally back to Newport. In spite of the instability of his family life, he seems to have acquired a basic education.

In the late 1860s while still in his teens, McCabe moved to New York City, where he got work as a clerk for a Wall Street investment firm. In 1872, he moved to Chicago and worked for a while as a clerk for a hotel. He soon moved up, taking a job in the Cook County's treasurer's office, where he worked until 1878.

By the late 1870s, the Exoduster movement—the migration of blacks to the Plains states where they were able to acquire homestead lands—was in full bloom. McCabe saw opportunity in these circumstances and in 1878 moved from Chicago to Nicodemus, Kansas, a small town in the northwest part of the state.

McCabe, an outgoing and intelligent man with a fair amount of prior office experience, was soon able to assert himself as a leader among Nicodemus's citizens, black and white. He was elected secretary of Nicodemus township and in 1879 was appointed county clerk. Feeling secure in his position, he returned to Chicago in 1880 to marry Sarah Bryant. They would have two children.

Returning to Kansas with his bride, McCabe, who was active in Republican Party politics, was elected in 1882 as state auditor. He was reelected in 1884 but lost this position in the election of 1886. During his tenure as auditor, McCabe held the highest political position of any African American in the North at that time.

After losing yet another political race in Kansas in 1888, McCabe looked to Oklahoma Territory, portions of which had recently been removed from Indian Territory and opened up to non-Indian settlement. He was made the federal representative of the Oklahoma Immigration Society, a group of African Americans from Kansas who were organizing a real estate venture and migration to Oklahoma. He was sent to Washington, D.C., where for a while he was in the running for an appointment as the Oklahoma territorial governor.

Failing to win any federal appointments in Oklahoma Territory, McCabe in 1890 moved to Guthrie, Oklahoma, then the capital of the territory. Soon thereafter, along with a white developer named Charles H. Robbins, McCabe founded the town of Langston, named after John M. Langston, Virginia's first black congressman. McCabe set up a real estate office and began promoting the

Edwin McCabe ca. 1900. A proponent of black settlement in the Plains states, McCabe was the founder of the all-black town of Langston, Oklahoma. *(Western History Collection, University of Oklahoma Library)*

town to blacks in the South who were now experiencing the harsh new Jim Crow laws after the end of Reconstruction.

McCabe advertised lots for sale in Langston through African-American newspapers and traveling salesmen. The purchase of each lot included a railway ticket to Oklahoma. Further, to discourage white speculators who might be tempted to pick up properties from ill-financed black settlers, each deed stipulated that resale of properties could only be to other African Americans. By 1891, Langston had a population of 200, which included a doctor, preacher, and schoolteacher.

With WILLIAM LEWIS EAGLESON, McCabe established the *Langston City Herald*. As in Kansas, he won the race for treasurer of Logan County, the district in which Langston was located. In 1893, McCabe established Liberty, another town not far from Langston. In 1895, he was appointed assistant chief clerk of the territorial assembly, a position he held until 1907.

After Oklahoma achieved statehood in November 1907, McCabe lost his political patronage position. Worse, blacks as a group also lost whatever liberties and rights they had held during the territorial period. The first bill introduced into the new state legislature required segregation in railroad stations and cars. Three years later an amendment to Oklahoma's constitution made it all but impossible for African Americans to vote in Oklahoma.

McCabe fought these destructive changes. He took the Atchison, Topeka, and Santa Fe Railroad to court over the segregation issue but lost when the U.S. Supreme Court upheld the Oklahoma law in 1914. McCabe had not waited until then to leave the state. In 1908, he sold his properties and moved to Chicago, where he would die penniless on March 20, 1920.

Further Reading

Logan, Rayford, and Michael Winston. "McCabe, E.P." In *Dictionary of American Negro Biography*. New York: W. W. Norton, 1982.

Soul of America. "Black Towns: Oklahoma." Available online. URL: http://www.soulofamerica.com/towns/7776.0.0.1.0.phtml./. Downloaded July 2, 2009.

Teall, Kaye M. *Black History in Oklahoma: A Resource Book*. Oklahoma City, Okla.: Oklahoma City Public Schools, 1971.

McGhee, Frederick Lamar

(1861–1912) *civil rights activist, lawyer*

A renowned criminal defense lawyer, Frederick McGhee was also an important civil rights leader in the later 1800s and early 1900s. Born into slavery in Aberdeen, a small town in northeast Mississippi, Frederick Lamar McGhee was the son of a slave who had taught himself to read and write and had become a Baptist preacher.

At the end of the Civil War, the McGhees moved to Knoxville, Tennessee, to begin a new life. Tragically, by 1873, when McGhee was 12, both parents had died, leaving him an orphan. McGhee was raised and educated by Episcopal missionaries and attended secondary school at Knoxville College. In 1879, when he was 18, he moved to Chicago, where he supported himself by working as a waiter while he studied law with an attorney. In 1885, he passed the bar exam and became a lawyer. One year later, he married Mattie Crane. They would have one daughter.

McGhee practiced law in Chicago for three years and then decided to move to the frontier state of Minnesota. Setting up a practice in St. Paul, the state capital, McGhee quickly made a name for himself as an able attorney. He won a number of headline-making criminal cases and had both blacks and whites as clients.

Though the racial climate in Minnesota was liberal and McGhee suffered little racial discrimination, he was well aware of the issue of racial discrimination and acted to stop it. In 1898, he was an organizer of the National Afro-American Council. He served as that organization's legal expert and directed its local affiliate in St. Paul. In 1904, he worked with BOOKER TALIAFERRO WASHINGTON on a lawsuit to overturn state laws in Maryland that made it difficult for African Americans in that state to vote. Unfortunately, this suit was thrown out of court by segregationist judges.

By 1905, McGhee, who was becoming increasingly militant in his opposition to racial discrimination, broke with Booker T. Washington. Washington's mild response to Jim Crow laws alienated McGhee, who joined W. E. B. DuBois in founding a new, more assertive organization, the Niagara Movement. McGhee served as the legal expert for this group, helping the Niagara Movement sue the Pullman Company in 1907 for discriminatory practices. As in the Maryland suit, McGhee lost the case.

When the Niagara Movement became the National Association for the Advancement of Colored People (NAACP) in 1910, McGhee was a founding member and the head of the NAACP's Saint Paul chapter. Exhausted from overwork, McGhee died of pleurisy on September 9, 1912.

Further Reading

Minnesota History Center. "Fredrick L. McGhee." Available online. URL: http://discovery.mnhs.org/MN150/index.php?title=Fredrick_L._McGhee. Downloaded July 2, 2009.

Nelson, Paul D. *Fredrick L. McGhee: A Life on the Color Line, 1861–1912*. Saint Paul: Minnesota Historical Society Press, 2002.

Spangler, Earl. *The Negro in Minnesota*. Minneapolis: T. S. Denison, 1961.

McKissick, Floyd

(1922–1991) *civil rights activist, black power advocate*

A onetime moderate civil rights leader, Floyd McKissick became a militant black power leader in the late 1960s. McKissick was born in Asheville, in the Appalachian Mountains of western

North Carolina, on March 9, 1922. After graduation from high school in Asheville, he enrolled in Morehouse College, a historically black school in Atlanta, in 1940. At the beginning of World War II, McKissick joined the U.S. Army and served as a sergeant. After the war, he finished his undergraduate education, then enrolled in the law school at the University of North Carolina, that institution's first African-American student.

After finishing law school, McKissick moved to Durham, North Carolina, where he established a law practice. Already a member of the National Association for the Advancement of Colored People (NAACP) and the Congress of Racial Equality (CORE), McKissick became active in organizing and defending demonstrators at sit-ins at segregated public facilities such as restaurants and stores in Durham in the early 1960s. He also sued a local of the Tobacco Workers Union, a branch of the American Federation of Labor-Congress of Industrial Organizations (AFL-CIO), seeking to force the local union to allow blacks to become members.

While he was participating in the larger public civil rights struggle, McKissick experienced a much more personal struggle at home. His daughters, who attended an integrated school, became the target of humiliation because of their race. As McKissick later recalled, they had "patches cut out of their hair, pages torn out of books, water thrown on them in the dead of winter, ink down the front of their dresses." This treatment, as well as his growing conviction that African Americans needed to form and run their own organizations separate from whites, caused McKissick to become more radical in his outlook about what direction blacks should take to achieve their potential.

In 1966, McKissick became the executive director of CORE, a moderate civil rights organization that included whites and blacks. Following the lead of STOKELY CARMICHAEL and other radicals, McKissick declared that CORE would become a "black power" organization. He discouraged whites from joining and steered CORE into a confrontational stance with white authorities. Within several years, the group had lost many members and much of its former clout.

McKissick remained the director of CORE until 1968. After his resignation from the group, he headed a new effort in the 1970s to found a mainly black town, called Soul City, in Warren County, North Carolina. Originally conceived as a town that would grow to 55,000, Soul City was funded by a Philadelphia bank and bonds issued by the U.S. Department of Housing and Urban Development. However, the project was poorly planned and never took off. It was dissolved in bankruptcy proceedings in 1980. McKissick was able to retain 88 acres, a mobile home park, and a large building that was intended as a factory.

McKissick remained in the remnants of Soul City, working as a preacher in a local church, throughout the 1980s. He died on April 28, 1991.

Further Reading

Congress of Racial Equality. "Floyd McKissick." Available online. URL: http://www.core-online.org/History/mckissick.htm. Downloaded July 2, 2009.

Marable, Manning, and Leith Mullings, eds. *Let Nobody Turn Us Around: Voices of Resistance, Reform, and Renewal.* Lanham, Md.: Rowman & Littlefield, 2003.

Martin Luther King Jr. Center. Martin Luther King, Jr. Encyclopedia. "McKissick, Floyd Bixler." Available online. URL: http://mlk-kpp01.stanford.edu/index.php/kingpapers/article/mckissick_floyd_bixler_1922_1991/. Downloaded July 2, 2009.

Mitchell, John R., Jr.

(1863–1929) *journalist, civil rights activist, business leader*

A leading, militant voice of southern African Americans in the late 19th century, John Mitchell later, through his business ventures, became part of the establishment that he had so vehemently criticized. John R. Mitchell, Jr., was born into slavery in Richmond, Virginia, in 1863. As a youth, he worked as a carriage hand for his family's former master. His parents, John, Sr., and Rebecca Mitchell, encouraged him to excel in school, and he became a fine student at the Richmond Normal and High School and graduated as the valedictorian in 1881.

For several years, Mitchell worked as a reporter for the *New York Globe* but decided to return to Richmond in 1884 when he 21. In that year, he became editor of the *Richmond Planet,* a paper that had been founded only the year before.

Between 1884 and 1921, the year the *Planet* was seized by U.S. postal inspectors because of Mitchell's reporting about poor treatment of black soldiers in World War I, Mitchell made the *Planet* one of the most controversial African-American newspapers in the United States. Mitchell placed a drawing of a strong black arm with flexed muscle and clenched fist at the top of the front page as the paper's logo. And he did not hesitate to criticize government policies or attitudes of whites that were discriminatory toward blacks.

In particular, Mitchell took on the practice of lynching, which was particularly prevalent in the South during the late 1800s and early 1900s. In 1890, he wrote that "the best remedy for a lyncher . . . is a 16-shot Winchester rifle in the hands of a Negro who has nerve enough to pull the trigger." Mitchell also relentlessly attacked laws aimed against African Americans, which were being passed with increasing frequency in southern states. These laws, known as Jim Crow laws, legislated an official policy of racial segregation in public places such as streetcars, railroads, restaurants, hotels, and movie theaters.

In spite of his militancy, Mitchell was elected several times to the Richmond city council, serving on that body from 1888 to 1896. He was finally defeated in 1896, probably in a corrupt election in which phony ballots for his white opponent were stuffed at various polling places. Even though he ran again for the city council and later for the governor of Virginia as a Republican, he never again held office.

In 1902, Mitchell began devoting his energies to accumulating personal wealth. That year he founded the Mechanics Savings Bank of Richmond, one of the few black-owned banks in the United States at that time. He later acquired a movie theater, cemetery, and other real estate properties in Richmond. However, his financial empire collapsed because of mismanagement and lack of capital in 1922, and Mitchell ended his days broke. He died on December 3, 1929.

Further Reading

Library of Virginia. "John Mitchell, Jr., and the Richmond Planet." Available online. URL: http://www.lva.virginia.gov/exhibits/mitchell/planhq.htm. Downloaded July 2, 2009.

Trotti, Michael Ayers. *The Body in the Reservoir: Murder & Sensationalism in the South.* Chapel Hill: University of North Carolina Press, 2008.

Morgan, Clement Garnett
(1859–1929) *civil rights leader, lawyer*

A former slave, Clement Morgan became a noted lawyer and community leader in Boston, and with his friend W. E. B. DuBois helped found the Niagara Movement, the forerunner of the National Association for the Advancement of Colored People (NAACP). Clement Garnett Morgan was born in Stafford County, Virginia, in 1859 to Clement and Elizabeth Morgan, both of whom were enslaved. After the Emancipation Proclamation in January 1863, the Morgans left Virginia for Washington, D.C. Young Clement attended Washington's Preparatory High School for Colored Youth, but after his graduation in the late 1870s he was forced by racial discrimination to work as a barber.

In the early 1880s, Morgan moved to Saint Louis, Missouri, where he was hired as a teacher.

Yearning to challenge himself, he left Saint Louis in 1885 to go to Boston, where he enrolled in the Boston Latin School, a college preparatory institution. Supporting himself as a barber, Morgan did well enough at Boston Latin to be admitted to Harvard College in 1886. He continued to work as a barber for his first two years at Harvard, by his third year he had won $1,200 in scholarship funds, just enough to support himself as a full-time student. During his junior year, Morgan won the Boylston Prize as Harvard's best orator. He graduated from Harvard in 1890.

Immediately after graduation, the ambitious Morgan enrolled in the Harvard Law School; he earned a LL.B. in 1893. After his admission to the bar, Morgan set up a law practice in Cambridge, Massachusetts, and immersed himself in local Republican Party politics and the cause of civil rights for African Americans.

Morgan joined several other black leaders in Boston in denouncing BOOKER TALIAFERRO WASHINGTON, the leading African-American figure of the day. Morgan, with WILLIAM MONROE TROTTER, Archibald Grimke, and others, spoke out against Washington's policy of not challenging newly enacted race laws that restricted the rights of African Americans. These laws, passed in many states in both the North and the South, segregated the races in schools, hotels, theaters, restaurants, and other public places, reserving inferior places for African Americans. Although Morgan and his friends shared Washington's ideas that blacks should work hard to improve their lives economically, they believed that the U.S. Constitution forbade racially discriminatory laws. Unlike Washington, they spoke out forcefully against these laws and organized protests against them.

In the mid- to late 1890s, Morgan served on the Cambridge city council as a Republican. During this period, he married Gertrude Wright, a native of Illinois. By 1905, he joined his school friend W. E. B. DuBois to form the Niagara Movement, an association of white and black liberals who sought to challenge racial discrimination on all levels. By 1909, the Niagara Movement had morphed into the NAACP. From 1912 to 1914, Morgan served on the executive committee of the Boston branch of the NAACP. He continued to be active as a civil rights leader until his death at age 70 in Boston in June 1929.

Further Reading

Logan, Rayford, and Michael Winston. *Dictionary of American Negro Biography.* New York: W. W. Norton, 1982.

Schneider, Mark. *Boston Confronts Jim Crow, 1890–1920.* Lebanon, N.H.: University Press of New England, 1997.

Sollors, Werner, Caldwell Titcomb, and Thomas A. Underwood, eds. *Blacks at Harvard: A Documentary History of African-American Experience at Harvard and Radcliffe.* New York: New York University Press, 1993.

Morial, Marc Haydel

(1958–   ) *lawyer, politician, foundation administrator*

A successful two-term mayor and president of a major civil rights organization, Marc Morial is a nationally recognized expert on economic, social, and political issues related to large cities. Morial was born on January 3, 1958, in New Orleans, Louisiana. He was the second of five children of Sybil and Ernest "Dutch" Morial. His mother was a teacher, and his father was a lawyer. When Marc was nine years old, Dutch was elected to the Louisiana state senate. He was the first African American to serve in the state legislature since Reconstruction. The elder Morial later became the first African American to serve on the Louisiana Court of Appeals.

Marc Morial graduated from Jesuit High School in 1976. He enrolled at the University of Pennsylvania, graduating in 1980 with a degree in economics. He then attended law school at Georgetown University, graduating in 1983. Morial started his legal career at a law firm in New Orleans. He practiced there for two years before opening his own law office. He handled civil rights cases and was soon named to the board of the Louisiana chapter of the American Civil Liberties Union.

While Marc had been away at college, his father had been elected as mayor of New Orleans. In 1978, Dutch Morial became the racially divided city's first black mayor. New Orleans voters reelected him to another four-year term in 1981. After his father's 1989 death, Marc decided to enter politics. He ran for an open seat in the U.S. Congress in 1990 but lost in the Democratic primary. Two years later, he was elected to serve in the Louisiana senate. As a state legislator, Morial received many accolades. He was named the Education Senator of the Year, the Conservationist Senator of the Year, and the Legislative Rookie of the Year.

Even after leaving his position as mayor of New Orleans, Marc Morial continues to support the city through community-based economic development through the National Urban League. *(© Najlah Feanny/CORBIS)*

In 1993, Morial decided to follow in his father's footsteps. He ran for mayor of New Orleans. Promising to clean up corruption in city government, he captured 54 percent of the vote. He was sworn in as mayor on May 2, 1994. Once in office, he introduced anticrime measures and policies to reform the city's police department. He also secured federal money for construction projects to improve the city's crumbling infrastructure. Boosted by a dramatic drop in crime rates, Morial easily won reelection in 1997. During his second term, he became president of the U.S. Conference of Mayors, helping develop the organization's recommendations for national urban policies. As his second term neared its end, Morial unsuccessfully tried to overturn a law limiting a mayor to two terms in office.

After leaving office in 2002, Morial was selected as president and chief executive officer of the National Urban League. Founded in 1910, the Urban League is the nation's oldest and largest civil rights organization. Its mission is to protect civil rights and to enable African Americans to become economically self-reliant. Morial began his tenure at the organization in May 2003. He spearheaded the organization's efforts to create new jobs and housing in urban areas and to extend the Voting Rights Act. In 2005, Hurricane Katrina devastated Morial's hometown, killing more than 700 and leaving tens of thousands of New Orleans residents homeless. The Urban League provided assistance to the residents of New Orleans and advice to government officials.

Morial has been named by *Non-Profit Times* as one of the top 50 U.S. nonprofit executives. *Ebony* magazine selected him as one of the 100 most influential black Americans. Xavier University and the University of South Carolina Upstate have awarded him honorary doctorates.

Further Reading

National Urban League. Mark Morial biography. Available online. URL: http://www.nul.org/marchmorial. html. Downloaded July 16, 2009.

PBS. *Tavis Smiley.* "Interview with Marc Morial." Available online. URL: http://www.pbs.org/kcet/tavis-miley/archive/200509/20050907_morial.html. Downloaded July 16, 2009.

Tisch, Jonathan M., and Karl Weber. *The Power of We.* Hoboken, N.J.: Wiley, 2004.

Morris, Robert, Sr.
(1823–1882) *lawyer, civil rights leader*

One of the first African-American lawyers in the United States, Robert Morris was known for his outspoken criticism of racial discrimination in his home state of Massachusetts. Born on June 8, 1823, in Salem, Massachusetts, Robert Morris, Sr., was the son of a man who had been taken from Africa to Boston in the late 1700s, but had later been freed. Morris acquired a basic education at a school in his hometown of Salem, but his real education did not begin until he moved to Boston to live and work with the family of Ellis Gray Loring, a Boston lawyer.

For several years after he moved to Boston in the early 1840s, Morris worked as a servant at the Loring home. Eventually he began to clerk in Loring's law office and apprenticed himself to Loring to study law. Morris was admitted to the bar in 1847.

By the early 1850s, Morris seems to have set up his own law practice and for many years represented both the Boston African-American and Irish communities. At about this time, he married Catherine Mason. They had one child, a son, Robert, Jr.

Morris made a name for himself early with the suit he brought against the city of Boston on behalf of black parents of that city. In 1849, these parents sued the Boston public schools, which maintained a segregated primary school system. On behalf of his clients, Morris argued that this segregated system was unfair to black children because it forced them to travel long distances to attend specially designated black schools. He added that this system also violated the Massachusetts constitution.

Morris lost this case, but Boston's schools were desegregated in 1855 by another state court case. In his arguments he stated that segregated schools were inherently unequal because they violated "the great principle" of both the Massachusetts and the U.S. constitutions ensuring that all persons, regardless of race or color, are equal before the law. With these ideas, Morris laid the foundations for later successful attacks on segregation in all states of the nation. The *Brown v. the Board of Education of Topeka* case in the early 1950s used much the same argument that Morris had employed in 1849.

In the 1850s, Morris became an activist in the abolitionist movement. He became a member of Boston's Vigilance Committee, an interracial group of Bostonians who worked to sabotage the Fugitive Slave Law of 1850s. This group aided fugitive slaves who were being sought by bounty hunters hired to capture them and take them back to the South and slavery. In 1851, Morris was arrested and tried for his part in freeing a fugitive slave named Shadrach who had been captured by a bounty hunter in Boston. Morris was found not guilty of that charge.

At the outbreak of the Civil War, Morris urged President Lincoln to accept black recruits into the army but only under terms that were equal to those for white recruits. Morris continued to work in his law practice into the 1880s. He died on December 12, 1882.

Further Reading

Horton, James Oliver, and Michele Gates Moresi. "Roberts, Plessy, and Brown." Available online. URL: http://www.oah.org/pubs/magazine/deseg/horton.html. Downloaded July 2, 2009.

Smith, J. Clay. *Emancipation: The Making of the Black Lawyer, 1844–1944.* Philadelphia: University of Pennsylvania Press, 1999.

Moses, Robert Parris
(Bob Moses)
(1935–   ) *civil rights activist, educator*

Robert Moses has had two intertwined careers: first as one of the principal organizers of "Freedom Summer," the dangerous but ultimately successful civil rights drive in Mississippi in 1964, and later as a passionate advocate of the power of education to improve the lives of poor black children.

Robert Parris Moses was born in Harlem in New York City on January 23, 1935. From a poor family, Moses was encouraged to take schooling seriously. A good and dedicated student, he was able to attend a private high school. On graduation in 1953, he enrolled in Hamilton College in Clinton, New York, a small upstate town. After earning a B.A. from Hamilton, Moses enrolled in the graduate school of Harvard University in 1957.

To deal with a family emergency, Moses dropped out of Harvard in 1959 and began to teach at the Horace Mann School, a private school in Manhattan. In 1960, moved by the idealism of the growing Civil Rights movement, Moses quit his teaching job to become an organizer for the Student Nonviolent Coordinating Committee (SNCC), a newly founded civil rights group that had become active in trying to change laws, especially in the South, that discriminated against African Americans.

Moses began his work with the SNCC in 1961 by organizing voter registration drives in Mississippi, Louisiana, and Georgia. In the states of the old South especially, blacks had been forced out of the voting process by the late 1800s. Although legally entitled to vote, blacks were effectively blocked from exercising this basic right through violence, economic intimidation, and discriminatory laws. To register black voters was dangerous work in states where whites did not hesitate to beat or kill African Americans who protested racial discrimination.

In 1961, Moses helped organize the Freedom Rides, interstate bus trips by white and black SNCC volunteers that challenged segregation laws in a number of southern states. These trips were marred by violence in Alabama, where mobs of whites beat SNCC volunteers on several occasions.

In the fall of 1963, in response to statements by southern politicians that southern blacks were not interested in voting, Moses organized Freedom Vote, a mock election held during the Mississippi general election. In this exercise, 80,000 disenfranchised African-American voters cast ballots for candidates of their choice, thereby disproving the notion that they were indifferent to their voting rights.

Moses followed up the Freedom Vote protest with Freedom Summer, a larger voter-registration drive in Mississippi and Louisiana in 1964. One aim of Freedom Summer was to prove to the nation that white authorities were still using physical threats to prevent blacks from registering to vote. The murder that summer of three SNCC volunteers—Michael Schwerner, James Chaney, and Andrew Goodman—provoked outrage and effectively demonstrated the point that the SNCC was trying to make: only the federal government had the power to enforce fair voting laws and procedures in the South.

During the summer of 1964, Moses also helped organize the Mississippi Freedom Democratic Party (MFDP), an integrated group of Mississippi voters who elected their own slate of delegates to the Democratic National Convention that was held in Atlantic City, New Jersey. The MFDP challenged the regular, all-white Democratic Party delegates from Mississippi. When representatives of President Lyndon Johnson offered a compromise, that only two of the MFDP's 44 delegates be seated with the regular all-white delegation, the MFDP walked out of the convention.

The activities of the SNCC and other civil rights groups put pressure on Congress to pass two landmark pieces of federal legislation. In 1964, Congress passed the Civil Rights Act, which outlawed all forms of legalized racial discrimination in public places and job hiring. In 1965, the Voting Rights Act was passed, giving federal guarantees of African-Americans voting rights in the United States. The effect of these new federal laws was powerful. For instance, in 1964, 6.7 percent of Mississippi's voting-age blacks were registered to vote; by 1969, that number had leaped to 66.5 percent.

By 1965, in the heat of this battle and before their efforts had borne fruit, many SNCC activists were becoming tired of taking beatings at the hands of southern white sheriffs and losing out in deals with northern white politicians. Increasingly the organization became more radical and militant. In 1967, STOKELY CARMICHAEL, an advocate of black power and violent resistance, was elected as head of the SNCC. With Carmichael's election, the nonviolent tradition of the SNCC, and of Robert Moses, ended.

Moses had quit the SNCC by the time of Carmichael's election. In 1966, after being drafted into the U.S. Army, Moses fled to Africa; eventually he settled in Tanzania. The Vietnam War was growing fiercer each year, and Moses, a pacifist, did not want to participate in that conflict.

Moses would remain in Tanzania, teaching high school, for 11 years. On his return to the United States in 1977, he reenrolled in Harvard and earned a Ph.D. Moses then founded the Algebra Project, an educational organization whose goal was to teach math skills to middle school students. The Algebra Project focused especially on students in poor families, who traditionally did not do well in math. Instead of sitting in a classroom trying to memorize equations, students learn math through real life experiences. They are often taken on a field trip and measure the distance they travel, use landmarks to find locations, and then map the journey.

For his work, Moses has been awarded the MacArthur Prize and the Heinz Award in the Human Condition. He continues to head the Algebra Project. In 2005, the Fletcher Foundation chose Moses as a Fletcher Fellow. The Fletcher Foundation awards grants to activists and scholars working on civil rights issues. The following year, Cornell University named him a Rhodes Class of '56 professor.

Further Reading

Bowser, Betty Ann. "The Algebra Project." PBS. Available online. URL: http://www.pbs.org/newshour/bb/education/jan-june00/algebra_6-9.html. Downloaded July 7, 2009.

Burner, Eric. *And Gently He Shall Lead Them: Robert Parris Moses and Civil Rights in Mississippi.* New York: New York University Press, 1994.

Moses, Robert P., and Charles E. Cobb, Jr. *Radical Equations: Civil Rights from Mississippi to the Algebra Project.* Boston: Beacon Press, 2002.

My Hero Project. "Teacher Hero: Robert Moses." Available online. URL: http://myhero.com/myhero/hero.asp?hero=robert_moses. Downloaded July 7, 2009.

Motley, Constance Baker
(1921–2005) *lawyer, federal judge*

A pioneering lawyer, Constance Motley represented the National Association for the Advancement of Colored People (NAACP) on a series of precedent-setting court cases and later pursued a distinguished career as a federal judge. Constance Baker was born on September 14, 1921, the daughter of Rachel and Willoughby Baker, immigrants from the Caribbean island of Nevis. The ninth of 12 children, she grew up in a working-class family. Her father was the chef of Skull and Bones, an exclusive club of Yale undergraduates.

A diligent student, Constance attended public schools in New Haven and, because of the small African-American population in that city, was usually one of only a few African Americans in her classes. Because her parents could not afford to send her to college, she worked for a short time as a domestic servant after her graduation from high school in 1939. She was lucky to meet Clarence Blakelee, a wealthy white building contractor, who was impressed with her intelligence and determination. Blakelee offered to pay for Baker's education.

Because she wanted to witness firsthand the conditions under which blacks lived in the South, Constance Baker attended Fisk University in Nashville for a year. Fisk is a historically black college, and its student body is nearly all black. Accustomed to a more racially integrated environment, she decided to transfer from Fisk to New York University (NYU). She graduated from NYU with a B.A. in economics in 1943.

In 1943, she entered Columbia University's law school. While a student there, she met THURGOOD MARSHALL, one of the main trial lawyers for the NAACP, who also taught as a visiting professor at Columbia. By her senior year, Baker had begun to work with Marshall at the Legal Defense and Education Fund, the legal arm of the NAACP. On her graduation from Columbia in 1946, she joined the Legal Defense Fund as a full-time lawyer. In 1948, she married Joel Wilson Motley, a real estate and insurance broker.

From 1946 to 1964, Constance Motley worked as one of the NAACP's frontline trial lawyers, arguing numerous cases before federal courts. At that time, the NAACP was pursuing a strategy of attacking state laws that singled out and discriminated against African Americans. This action was taken through the court system, with many cases being tried in federal court. These state laws were challenged by the NAACP lawyers on the grounds that they were in violation of the U.S. Constitution, which guarantees equal rights to all citizens regardless of their racial or ethnic identity.

Motley argued three general types of cases: those that attacked laws that legitimized racial discrimination in public facilities, in public educational institutions, and on juries. Many of Motley's first cases went after cities that denied African

Americans the right to live in low-income public housing projects. In suits against the cities of Detroit, Michigan; St. Louis, Missouri; Columbus, Ohio; Evansville, Indiana; Schenectady, New York; and Savannah, Georgia, Motley argued and won cases that challenged these cities' discrimination against blacks in public housing.

In 1961, Motley argued before the U.S. Supreme Court in *Swain v. Alabama* that the state of Alabama could not exclude blacks from juries in death-penalty cases. Even though she lost this case before the Supreme Court, one of her few losses, the Supreme Court upheld her argument a few years later in another case.

In 1962, Motley argued before the Supreme Court the case of James Meredith against the University of Mississippi. Meredith wanted to enter the university, which until then had been off-limits to black students. Motley won this case, and Meredith, after a riot on the campus of Ole Miss, was eventually admitted as a student.

In 1964, Motley left her job with the NAACP to run for the New York State Senate. She won that election and became the first African-American woman to serve in that legislative body. She used her tenure to push for tougher laws banning racial discrimination and for more low- and middle-income housing in New York State.

In February 1965 Motley was appointed to fill a vacancy in the presidency of the Borough of Manhattan in New York City. She was elected to this position in November 1965. However, she served in it for less than a year. In January 1966, President Lyndon Johnson nominated her to be a federal judge for the U.S. District Court for the Southern District of New York. She was quickly confirmed and has remained a federal judge since. She became chief judge of that court in 1982 and senior judge in 1986. Judge Motley continued to serve on the federal bench until she died on September 28, 2005.

Further Reading

Columbia Magazine. "A Columbian Ahead of Her Time: Constance Baker Motley." Available online. URL:

http://www.columbia.edu/cu/alumni/Magazine/
Spring2004/motley.html. Downloaded July 7,
2009.

Motley, Constance Baker. *Equal Justice under Law: An
Autobiography.* New York: Farrar, Straus & Giroux,
1998.

National Women's History Project. "Constance Baker
Motley." Available online. URL: http://www.nwhp.
org/whm/motley_bio.php. Downloaded July 7,
2009.

National Visionary Leadership Project. "Constance
Baker Motley." Available online. URL: http://
www.visionaryproject.com/motleyconstance
baker/. Downloaded July 7, 2009.

Vile, John, ed. *Great American Lawyers: An Encyclopedia.* Santa Barbara, Calif.: ABC-CLIO, 2002.

Muhammad, Elijah
(Elijah Poole)
(1897–1975) *black nationalist, Muslim leader*

A ferocious critic of whites and the white-
dominated mainstream establishment in the
United States, Elijah Muhammad took over a
small, fractured organization and built it into the
best-known and most influential black separatist
group of the 20th century.

Born in Sandersville, Georgia, on October 7,
1897, Elijah Poole was the seventh of 13 children
of William and Mariah Hall Poole, who were
sharecroppers. On Sundays after a week's work
in the fields, William Poole preached at a local
Baptist church in Sandersville. The family moved
to a farm near Cordele, Georgia, when Poole was
three. Again the elder Poole preached at a Baptist church. Young Elijah Poole seems to have
been captivated with Bible study and theological
questions. He also began to attend the local segregated schools, but because he was expected to
work in the fields to help his family, Poole left
school for good in the third or fourth grade.

From age 10, Poole chopped wood, picked cotton, and did other manual labor to support himself and help his family. In 1913, at age 16, Poole
left Cordele to strike out on his own. He ended up
in Macon, Georgia, where he worked in sawmills,
on railroad construction gangs, and as a hand at a
brick factory. He married Clara Evans in 1919.
They would have eight children.

Poole, who at age 10 had witnessed a lynching
of a friend by a white mob, observed another
lynching of a black man in Macon in 1921. Lynchings of African-American men by white mobs
were common occurrences in the South from the
1870s until as late as the 1950s. However, they
were especially common around the turn of the
century. In 1916 alone, 16 black men were lynched
in Georgia, often because they had been accused
with little supporting evidence of sexual assault
on white women.

This climate of extreme violence, coupled with
grinding poverty and no chance of advancement,
compelled Poole to leave Georgia for Detroit in
1923. He was not alone in this journey. Lured by
plentiful manufacturing jobs, hundreds of thousands of African Americans left the South for
northern cities during the 1910s and 1920s. Poole
was glad to be out of Georgia. He had seen, he
would later say, "enough of the white man's brutality in Georgia to last me 26,000 years."

In Detroit, Poole worked at whatever employment was available, mostly laboring jobs. He
soured on Christianity, believing it to be a religion that promised salvation in another life while
making black people servile in their life on Earth.
Poole became an admirer of MARCUS GARVEY
and Garvey's Universal Negro Improvement
Association (UNIA) during the 1920s. Garvey's
lesson that the black man could depend only on
himself, and not the white man, for self-improvement struck a chord with Poole. Because of
Poole's experience with whites, he accepted the
idea that the only way for African Americans to
advance economically, socially, and spiritually
was to separate themselves from white society.
However, Garvey was jailed on fraud charges in
1923 and deported from the United States in

Elijah Muhammad speaking at a rally ca. 1960. For more than 40 years, Muhammad headed the militant black separatist organization the Nation of Islam (NOI). *(Library of Congress, Prints and Photographs Division, LC-USZ62-116389)*

1927, leaving a void in the black separatist movement.

In 1931, Poole heard about WALLACE D. FARD, a door-to-door clothing salesman in the Detroit ghetto who had begun to preach at a newly established storefront church called the Temple of Islam Number One. Little is known about Fard, but the basic idea of his teaching, which was that the whites were "devils," and that the true religion of blacks was Islam, was absorbed and passed down through Elijah Poole. Soon after meeting Fard, Poole accepted Fard's beliefs and changed his name to Elijah Muhammad.

When Fard vanished without a trace in 1934, possibly as the result of a murder, Muhammad, Fard's most zealous disciple, assumed leadership of Temple Number One. Soon, however, because of

strife within the Detroit temple, Muhammad was forced to move to Chicago, where he set up Temple Number Two, which would remain his headquarters for the rest of his life.

Throughout the 1930s and 1940s, Muhammad elaborated a theology for the Nation of Islam (NOI), the name of this new religion. Even though Muhammad and Fard had incorporated the word *Islam* into the title of their organization, the beliefs of the Nation of Islam as spelled out by Muhammad had little relation to traditional Islam as practiced in Muslim countries. Instead, NOI doctrine became obsessed with the evil of the Caucasian race and developed an ornate theory of how whites and blacks had evolved. According to Muhammad, blacks were the "original" race, and whites were created by a certain Dr. Yacub, an evil scientist whose genetic experiment went horribly awry when whites gained ascendancy in the world, beginning with the age of exploration in the late 1400s. None of this is found anywhere in the Koran, the Islamic text equivalent to the Bible.

In spite of its racist theology, NOI attracted members at a slow but steady pace. Disenchanted and poorly educated African Americans who lived in poverty in northern ghettos found in the teachings of the Nation of Islam an explanation for their abject condition. Also, the rigid codes of conduct demanded of the NOI—such as abstinence from alcohol, premarital sex, and gambling—appealed to many blacks who were tired of the crime and chaos too often found in inner-city ghettos.

In the meanwhile, Muhammad was having problems with government authorities. He was put on a Federal Bureau of Investigation (FBI) watch list during World War II when he preached that his followers should refuse to enter the armed forces. He went even further when he preached that his followers should support the Japanese. Muhammad argued that the victorious Japanese would reward Nation of Islam members with a homeland on islands in the Pacific. In 1942, Muhammad was arrested on the charge of violating the Selective Service Act. He was jailed for four years and released in 1946.

In the 1950s and early 1960s, the NOI continued to grow, especially after it recruited an ex-convict named Malcolm Little who would change his "slave" name for a NOI-approved name, MALCOLM X. An impassioned speaker, Malcolm X converted scores of inner-city blacks in Boston, New York, and Los Angeles to the ranks of the Nation of Islam. Under Muhammad's leadership, the NOI developed a number of black-run businesses that gave jobs to many of its members. Many of these businesses proved to be successful and were a sign of Muhammad's commitment to racial solidarity and self-improvement.

In 1962, Malcolm discovered that Muhammad had fathered several children with NOI secretaries. This violated the strict rules of NOI conduct that had been established by Muhammad himself. Sensing that Malcolm was making a play for power within the group, and knowing that Malcolm knew of his illegitimate children, Muhammad expelled him from the Nation of Islam. Several NOI members assassinated Malcolm in New York City in February 1965. Though Elijah Muhammad was never tied to this murder, it is possible that he was the one who ordered it.

By the mid-1970s, Muhammad was beginning to show signs of frailty and had largely given up day-to-day control of the NOI to his son, Wallace Deen Muhammad. Elijah Muhammad died on February 25, 1975.

The Nation of Islam, Elijah Muhammad's legacy, quickly dissolved after Muhammad's death. His successor, Wallace Muhammad, changing the name of the organization to the World Community of Islam, quickly moved the Nation of Islam away from the race-based ideology developed by Elijah Muhammad and adopted traditional Muslim beliefs. A breakaway group under the leadership of LOUIS FARRAKHAN retained the name Nation of Islam, along with the racial ideology of Elijah Muhammad.

Further Reading

Asante, Molefi K., and Ama Mazama, eds. *Encyclopedia of Black Studies*. Thousand Oaks, Calif.: SAGE, 2005.

Curtis, Edward E. *Islam in Black America: Identity, Liberation, and Difference in African-American Islamic Thought*. Albany: State University of New York Press, 2002.

Evanzz, Karl. *The Messenger: The Rise and Fall of Elijah Muhammad*. New York: Pantheon, 1999.

Marable, Manning, and Leith Mullings, eds. *Let Nobody Turn Us Around: Voices of Resistance, Reform, and Renewal*. Lanham, Md.: Rowman & Littlefield, 2003.

Nation of Islam. "A Historical Look at the Honorable Elijah Muhammad." Available online. URL: http://www.noi.org/elijah_muhammad_history.htm. Downloaded July 7, 2009.

Muhammad, Khalid Abdul
(Harold Moore, Jr.)
(1948–2001) *Nation of Islam leader*

A self-admitted bigot and hate-monger, Khalid Muhammad was a top lieutenant to the Nation of Islam (NOI) leader LOUIS FARRAKHAN until his expulsion from that organization in 1994. He then formed his own group, the New Black Panther Party.

Khalid Abdul Muhammad was born Harold Moore, Jr., in Houston, Texas, in 1948. He grew up in that city, where he attended public schools and was a star quarterback at a predominantly African-American high school. After his graduation from high school in 1966, Moore attended Dillard University in New Orleans. After hearing Farrakhan speak at a gathering on campus, he became interested in Nation of Islam beliefs. By the 1970s, he had converted to that sect of Islam and changed his name.

When the original Nation of Islam organization disintegrated with the death of its founder, ELIJAH MUHAMMAD, in 1977, Khalid Muhammad followed Louis Farrakhan into a smaller splinter group, which kept the Nation of Islam name. The new Nation of Islam also retained much of the older organization's ideology: its distrust, even hatred of whites; its belief that blacks should segregate themselves from white society; and its quasi-military discipline.

In 1981, Khalid Muhammad was appointed Louis Farrakhan's chief deputy. He served as a speaker and organizer at the NOI's mosques in New York City and Atlanta, and he frequently traveled, making fiery antiwhite, anti-Semitic, and antihomosexual speeches. In 1993, one of Muhammad's speeches was videotaped and gained notoriety because of its harsh language. Portraying Pope John Paul II as "a no-good cracker," Muhammad went on to call for the murder of whites in South Africa:

> We don't owe nothing [to whites] in South Africa . . . we give him 24 hours to get out of town, by sundown. That's all. If he won't get out of town by sundown, we kill everything white that ain't right in South Africa. We kill the women, we kill the children, we kill the babies. . . . We kill the faggot, we kill the lesbian, we kill them all.

After the publicity generated by similar speech a few months later, Louis Farrakhan expelled Muhammad from the Nation of Islam, though Farrakhan expressed agreement with what he called Muhammad's "truths." Muhammad then formed the New Black Panther Party. With a dozen or so rifle-toting party members, he attended the trial of the murderers of James Byrd, a black man who had been dragged to death by white racists in Texas in 1998. That year, Muhammad organized what he billed as a "Million Youth March" in Harlem. Perhaps 6,000 people showed up. Another such gathering in 2000 attracted around 100 people.

Khalid Muhammad died of a brain aneurysm in Marietta, Georgia, on February 17, 2001.

Further Reading
New York Times. "K. A. Muhammed, 53, Dies; Ex-Official of Nation of Islam." Available online. URL: http://www.nytimes.com/2001/02/18/nyregion/ka-muhammad-53-dies-ex-official-of-nation-of-islam.html. Downloaded July 7, 2009.

Singh, Robert. *The Farrakhan Phenomenon: Race, Reaction, and the Paranoid Style in American Politics.* Washington, D.C.: Georgetown University Press, 1997.

Murphy, Carl
(1889–1967) *civil rights activist, journalist*

An academic and intellectual, Carl Murphy was persuaded by his father to leave his teaching job and take over the reins of the *Baltimore Afro-American*. He built this paper into one of the best-known African-American papers of the early to mid-20th century.

Murphy was born in Baltimore to JOHN HENRY MURPHY, SR., and Martha Howard Murphy on January 17, 1889. After distinguished service in the U.S. Colored Maryland Volunteers, the elder Murphy founded the *Baltimore Afro-American* in 1892. Although respecting his father's accomplishments, Carl Murphy, an excellent student, was more interested in pursuing a career as a teacher than as an editor. He enrolled in Howard University in Washington, D.C., in 1907, and earned a B.A. in 1911. After his graduation from Howard, Murphy entered Harvard University as a graduate student to study German language and literature. He studied for a summer at the University of Jena in Germany and earned an M.A. from Harvard in 1913. Murphy worked at Howard from 1913 to 1918 as a professor of German.

By 1918, the elder Murphy was searching for someone to replace him as head of the *Baltimore Afro-American.* As many other northern cities had, Baltimore had experienced a large growth in its black population as the great migration of African Americans from the South to the North began. Between 1910 and 1920, Baltimore's black population had grown by 27 percent, an increase that created opportunities for black-owned businesses such as the *Afro-American.*

After resisting his father's arguments for a number of years, Murphy finally returned to Baltimore in 1918 to become editor of the family paper. Under his editorship after his father's death in 1922, Murphy built the *Baltimore Afro-American* into one of the most popular black-owned newspapers in the country. Murphy took a strong stance for equal rights for the African-American community, and he was especially closely connected with the National Association for the Advancement for Colored People (NAACP). The *Afro-American* regularly reported on and supported NAACP actions in Baltimore and across the nation.

Murphy used the pages of the *Afro-American* to demand that Baltimore's police and fire departments hire blacks, to campaign for black representation in the state legislature, and to push for the establishment of a state-supported university to educate African Americans. The paper hired such notable black writers and artists as Langston Hughes and Romare Bearden. During World War II, the newspaper sent out correspondents to Europe and the Pacific to report on the condition of black troops and progress in the war.

Murphy began serving on the NAACP board of directors in 1931, but his most important role with that organization was his chairmanship of the NAACP legal redress committee, which oversaw the work of CHARLES HAMILTON HOUSTON and THURGOOD MARSHALL, the NAACP's two brilliant trial lawyers. Murphy played a crucial behind-the-scenes role of raising and directly contributing money for the NAACP's strategy of steadily attacking the foundation of legalized segregation through a series of court cases. With Murphy's backing, the NAACP began breaking down the system of racial segregation through a string of victories in the U.S. Supreme Court.

In 1954, Murphy was awarded the Spingarn Medal by the NAACP in recognition of his service to the advancement of civil rights for the African-American community. That same year, he was also elected president of the National Newspaper Publishers Association. He died on March 17, 1967. The *Afro-American* continues to be published in Baltimore.

Further Reading

BlackPressUSA. 2002 Gallery of Greats. "Carl J. Murphy." Available online. URL: http://www.black pressusa.com/history/GOG_Article.asp?NewsID =2049. Downloaded July 7, 2009.

Farrar, Hayward. *The Baltimore Afro-American, 1892–1950.* Westport, Conn.: Greenwood Press, 1998.

PBS. "Newspapers: The *Afro-American.*" Available online: URL: http://www.pbs.org/blackpress/news_bios/afroamerican.html. Downloaded July 7, 2009.

Murphy, John Henry, Sr.

(1840–1922) *publisher, journalist*

John Murphy was the founder of the *Baltimore Afro-American*, one of the most important black-owned newspapers of the late 19th and early to mid-20th centuries. Born into slavery in Baltimore on December 25, 1840, John Henry Murphy, Sr., was the only child of Benjamin and Susan Ann Murphy, who were also enslaved. The elder Murphy worked as a whitewasher and interior decorator, a trade taken up by John Murphy in his teens. Although Murphy clearly was literate, little is known about his education. The entire family was freed from slavery in 1863. Soon thereafter John Murphy joined the federal army fighting against the Confederates as a member of the U.S. Colored Maryland Volunteers. He eventually rose to the rank of sergeant.

After the Civil War, Murphy continued working in the home-decoration trade in Baltimore. He married Martha Howard in 1868. They would have 11 children, including their sons Daniel, who would later oversee the printing of the *Afro-American*; Arnett, who would become advertising director; and CARL MURPHY, who would eventually become the editor.

Active in the Bethel African Methodist Episcopal (AME) Church of Baltimore, Murphy had become superintendent of the Sunday school by the late 1880s. Seeking to unite all the Sunday schools of Maryland's AME churches, Murphy bought a small printing press in 1890 and began publication of the *Sunday School Helper*. In 1892, a Baltimore Baptist minister founded a paper called the *Afro-American* to publicize the activities of his church.

By 1896, the original *Afro-American* was up for sale and Murphy bought it for $200. Merging the *Sunday School Helper* with the *Afro-American*, Murphy changed the name to the *Baltimore Afro-American*. He also changed the focus. It would no longer be mainly a church-focused paper but would instead cover the full spectrum of events taking place in Baltimore's African-American community.

Initially, Murphy ran the *Baltimore Afro-American* as a family enterprise. Unpaid, his oldest son served as the typesetter, and his daughters worked as reporters. Eventually, as the *Afro-American*'s scope extended to include articles from other cities up and down the Eastern Seaboard, the staff grew. By 1920, the paper had a paid staff of more than 90 and a circulation of 14,000 subscribers.

John Murphy died on April 5, 1922, after having handed over leadership of the paper to his son Carl. His legacy is perhaps best expressed in the letter he wrote to his sons in 1920:

> A newspaper succeeds because its management believes in itself. . . . It must always ask itself whether it has kept faith with the common people; . . . Whether it is fighting to get rid of slums, to provide jobs for everybody; whether it . . . expose[s] corruption and condemn[s] injustice, race prejudice, and the cowardice of compromise.

Further Reading

Blackvoicenews. "The Afro-American Founded 1892." Available online. URL: http://www.blackvoice news.com/content/view/42460/28/. Downloaded July 7, 2009.

Farrar, Hayward. *The Baltimore Afro-American, 1892–1950*. Westport, Conn.: Greenwood Press, 1998.

PBS. "Newspapers: The *Afro-American*." Available online: URL: http://www.pbs.org/blackpress/news_bios/afroamerican.html. Downloaded July 9, 2009.

Myers, Isaac

(1835–1891) *labor organizer, entrepreneur*

Isaac Myers was a leading organizer of African-American workers, both in his native Maryland and nationwide, in the years following the Civil

War. He later became a successful businessman in Maryland. Born on January 13, 1835, Myers grew up free, the child of freeborn parents who lived in a slave state. Because Maryland offered no public education for African Americans, he received an elementary education at a private school for blacks run by a Baltimore minister.

In 1851, when he was 16, Myers became an apprentice ship caulker. This trade, in which the worker applied adhesive caulk to the cracks between timbers of a ship's wooden hull, was an important part of the shipbuilding industry in the years before steel-hulled, engine-driven ships. Myers worked on numerous sail-powered clipper ships built in Baltimore during the 1850s.

In 1865, at the end of the Civil War, white workers in Baltimore's shipyards went out on strike to demand that the shipyard owners fire all African-American workers. When this action succeeded, after receiving support from the city government and the police department, Isaac Myers stepped forward to propose a plan for new jobs for unemployed shipyard workers. Myers suggested that the African-American shipyard workers join in a cooperative venture, raise money among themselves, and buy an abandoned shipyard and railway. After gathering $10,000 and a further $30,000 from a ship captain, the workers founded the Chesapeake Marine Railway and Dry Dock Company.

By 1867, 300 black caulkers and carpenters were employed by this new cooperative venture. The next year, Meyers organized the Colored Caulkers Trade Union Society of Baltimore. He was elected its first president.

Myers's activism coincided with a gesture from the predominantly white National Labor Union (NLU), the largest coalition of labor unions in the nation at that time. In 1869 the NLU invited Myers and several other black union representatives to its annual conference, which was held in Philadelphia. Myers spoke at the convention and hailed the NLU for opening up its membership to African-American workers.

Later in 1869, Myers called on black unions to meet in Washington, D.C., to form a black NLU. This group met in August 1869 and named itself the Colored National Labor Union. Myers was elected the first president. In his speech to the delegates, Myers warned that black workers could only advance if they were united. Otherwise, he said, they would become "the servants, the sweepers of shavings, the scrapers of pitch, and the carriers of mortar."

The union between black unions and the white NLU lasted just a year and was broken up in 1870 when the NLU demanded that black unions desert the Republican Party for the newly formed Labor Reform Party. When the African-American labor leaders refused to do this, the two sides ended their cooperation.

Soon after this rupture, Myers dropped out of labor organizing. He secured a political patronage job as a detective for the U.S. Post Office, a position he held from 1872 to 1879. For most of the 1880s, he held another federal patronage job. However, by the 1890s, he seems to have become a business promoter, serving as president of the Maryland Colored State Industrial Fair Association and the Colored Businessmen's Association of Baltimore. Myers was also active in the Freemasons and was grandmaster of the Maryland Masons. He died on January 26, 1891.

Further Reading

Maryland Online Encyclopedia. "Myers, Isaac (1835–1891)." Available online. URL: http://www.mdoe.org/myersisaac.html. Downloaded July 7, 2009.

Smith, Jessie Carney, Millient Lownes Jackson, and Linda T. Wynn, eds. *Encyclopedia of African American Business.* Westport, Conn.: Greenwood, 2006.

N

Newton, Huey P.
(1942–1989) *Black Panther activist*

A founder of the Black Panthers, a black power group, Huey P. Newton was for a time a symbol of the most militant side of the African-American struggle for justice and self-respect. Born in Monroe, Louisiana, on February 17, 1942, Newton was one of seven children of Walter and Armelia Newton. When he was still a child the family moved from Louisiana to California, where the elder Newton found work in the busy port city of Oakland.

Newton attended public schools in Oakland, where he had a troubled youth. Arrested several times for minor criminal charges, Newton was convicted of assault in the stabbing attack of a man in Oakland in 1964. Around that time, he was a student at several local colleges, including Oakland Community College and Merritt College, where he met Bobby Seale, with whom he later founded the Black Panthers. Continuing to run street scams, Newton also burglarized homes in the Bay Area to get money to attend college.

Like Seale, Newton was disaffected with the mainstream black leadership of the Civil Rights movement as represented by figures such as MARTIN LUTHER KING, JR., and ROY OTTAWAY WILKINS of the National Association for the Advancement of Colored People (NAACP). Determined to add their own voice to the campaign for racial justice, Newton and Seale founded the Black Panther Party in 1966.

With Newton as its minister of defense, the Black Panther Party began to organize African Americans who lived in the poorest ghettos of America's big cities. Vowing to "defend the community against the aggression of the power structure, including the military and the armed might of the police," Newton created patrols of Panther members to follow police around the Oakland ghetto. Because they were armed, these patrols encountered much hostility from the Oakland police. Eventually the Panthers would have chapters in New York City, Chicago, Oakland, and Los Angeles as well as other cities.

Black Panther rhetoric was harsh and featured references to police as "pigs" and calls for blacks to arm themselves and begin a revolution. The party claimed to support socialism as a substitute for capitalism. ELDRIDGE CLEAVER, an ex-con with a lengthy criminal record and the author of the inflammatory book *Soul on Ice,* became the Panthers' information minister.

Newton had been working with the Panthers for only a year when he was indicted in the killing of an Oakland police officer, John Frey, in a gun battle that followed a routine traffic stop in 1967. Wounded in the shoot-out, Newton was charged with manslaughter and convicted in 1968. Newton

Huey P. Newton ca. 1968. Newton, a felon with several convictions for assault and burglary, was minister of defense of the Black Panther Party during the late 1960s and early 1970s. *(Courtesy Bancroft Library, University of California, Berkeley, Newton, Huey, POR-1)*

spent two years in California prisons but was released in 1970, when the charges were overturned on appeal. After two further trials in the early 1970s that ended in hung juries, the state of California dropped the charges.

After his release from prison, Newton toned down the Panthers' revolutionary rhetoric. He split with Eldridge Cleaver and then joined with Seale to guide Black Panther activity into the cre-

ation of breakfast programs for poor children and free medical clinics.

In spite of this new image, Newton continued to get into trouble on the street. By this time addicted to cocaine, he also ran drug and prostitution rings to raise money for himself and the Panthers. In 1974, he was indicted for the murder of a prostitute. After jumping bail, Newton made his way to Cuba, where he spent the next three years. When he returned to the United States in 1977, the trial produced two hung juries before a third finally acquitted him of murder charges.

Newton was awarded a Ph.D. from the University of California at Santa Cruz in 1978. By the 1980s, although the Black Panthers still existed, they had become a fringe organization with little influence. Newton was arrested for embezzling funds from several government-funded programs in the mid-1980s. He was killed in a dispute with a drug dealer on August 22, 1989.

In 2001, director Spike Lee released *A Huey Lewis Story*, a film recording Roger Guenveur performing his one-man play of the same name. The film received many awards, including two Obie Awards and three NAACP awards.

Further Reading

Hilliard, David, and Kent Zimmerman: *Huey: Spirit of the Panther*. New York: Basic Books, 2006.

PBS. "A Huey P. Newton Story." Available online. URL: http://www.pbs.org/hueypnewton/index. html. Downloaded July 8, 2009.

Pearson, Hugh. *Shadow of the Panther: Huey Newton and the Price of Black Power in America*. Reading, Mass.: Addison Wesley, 1994.

Owen, Chandler

(1889–1967) *journalist, labor leader, civil rights activist*

A crusading radical journalist and activist for African-American civil rights, Chandler Owen in later life became a writer for hire employed by the Republican Party and large corporations. Owen was born in Warrenton, North Carolina, on April 5, 1889. He entered Virginia Union University in 1909 and graduated with a B.A. in 1913.

After his graduation, Owen moved to New York City, where the recently formed National Urban League had given him a student fellowship. Supported by the Urban League, Owen studied graduate-level political philosophy and social work at the New School of Philanthropy and Columbia University.

While still a student, Owen met ASA PHILIP RANDOLPH, another ambitious young African-American student. The two men discussed the work of radical political thinkers, especially the writings of Karl Marx. By 1916, they both had become activists in the Socialist Party.

In 1917, Owen and Randolph founded the *Messenger,* one of the most important radical periodicals of that era. The *Messenger* mixed observations about the African-American condition in the United States with articles about socialism in the Soviet Union (which Owen at that time

admired) and radical trade unionism at home. When the United States entered World War I in 1917, Owen, through the *Messenger,* opposed the war both because he was a pacifist and because he thought the war was being fought for the interests of big business and against those of working people of all races.

For his militancy, Owen was jailed on charges that he had violated the Espionage Act. Although he was soon released, Owen had to contend with continuing government persecution. The *Messenger* had its second-class mail license revoked by the U.S. Postal Service, making the periodical too expensive to mail to subscribers. The New York City police also raided *Messenger's* offices several times.

After the war, one of the *Messenger's* major campaigns was to encourage the government to deport MARCUS GARVEY. Arrested in 1922 on fraud charges stemming from mismanagement of his financial empire, Garvey was seen as a reactionary threat by both Owen and Randolph. Garvey, a native of Jamaica, was found guilty of fraud in 1923 and eventually deported in 1927.

By 1923, Owen had become disenchanted with socialist ideology and radical politics. That year he moved to Chicago, where he took a job as managing editor of the *Chicago Bee,* one of that city's leading black newspapers. Moving into the African-American mainstream, Owen used his

Chandler Owen ca. 1940. Coeditor of the *Messenger,* an influential radical newspaper, Owen later became a Republican and worked as an executive at a steel plant in Pennsylvania. *(Library of Congress, Prints and Photographs Division, LC-USF344-091190B)*

position at the *Bee* to support the cause of forming a union among African-American Pullman car porters, an effort being led by A. Philip Randolph, who had also edged away from socialism into union organizing.

In the 1930s, Owen moved out of newspaper work and became more of a behind-the-scenes figure as a publicist for various causes. For a number of years in the late 1930s and early 1940s, he worked for the Anti-Defamation League of B'nai B'rith, a Jewish group, to defuse negative feelings among blacks toward Jews.

As early as the mid-1920s, Owen had switched allegiance from the Socialist Party to the Repub-

licans. In 1928, he ran for a congressional seat in Illinois and lost. Just before the start of World War II, he worked as a speechwriter for the Republican presidential candidate, Wendell Willkie.

During the war, though he was no fan of President Roosevelt's policies toward African Americans, Owen worked for the Allied war effort. He took a job with the U.S. Office of Information, a government propaganda bureau, and wrote *Negroes and the War,* a booklet that presented arguments in favor of black support of the war effort.

After the war, Owen picked up where he had left off with Wendell Willkie by working for such Republican politicians as Thomas Dewey and Dwight D. Eisenhower.

Owen was a complicated man with a sharp tongue. His life and personality were probably best summarized by his fellow writer at the *Messenger* George Schuyler, who described Owen as "a facile and acidulous writer, a man of ready wit and agile tongue endowed with the saving grace of cynicism." Owen continued working for the Republicans in Illinois until his death in November 1967.

Further Reading

Black Past. "Owen, Chandler (1889–1967)." Available online. URL: http://www.blackpast.org/?q=aah/ owen-chandler-1889-1967. Downloaded July 8, 2009.

Foner, Philip S. *American Socialism and Black Americans: From the Age of Jackson to World War II.* Westport, Conn.: Greenwood Press, 1977.

Walton, Haynes. *Black Republicans: The Politics of the Black and Tans.* Metuchen, N.J.: Scarecrow Press, 1975.

Wilson, Sondra K., ed. *The Messenger Reader: Stories, Poetry, and Essays from* The Messenger. New York: Modern Library, 2000.

Wintz, Carry D., and Paul Finkelman, eds. *Encyclopedia of the Harlem Renaissance.* New York: Taylor & Francis, 2004.

P

Parks, Rosa
(Rosa Louise McCauley)
(1913–2005) *civil rights activist*

The central figure in the Montgomery bus boycott, one of the most important civil rights campaigns of the 20th century, Rosa Parks was an ordinary woman who became embroiled in an extraordinary struggle for human dignity. Rosa Louise McCauley was born on February 4, 1913, in Tuskegee, Alabama. She lived in Tuskegee and Montgomery, Alabama, with her mother and grandmother. After attending segregated public schools, she enrolled in Alabama State College, a historically black university located in Montgomery, in 1931. In 1932, she married Raymond Parks, a barber.

The range of jobs that Parks could get was severely restricted by racial customs in the South. Eventually, she took work as a seamstress for private customers and department stores in Montgomery. Parks and other African Americans in Alabama and other southern states also faced restrictions in their public life. Jim Crow laws segregated blacks and whites in public places and transportation. Blacks could not stay at most hotels, had to take the worst seats in public theaters, could not eat in many restaurants, and had to sit in the back of public buses and trains.

To combat these kinds of racial discrimination, Parks and her husband joined the National Association for the Advancement of Colored People (NAACP), the nation's leading civil rights organization, in the 1940s. By the early 1950s, she had become very active in the NAACP's Montgomery chapter.

On Thursday, December 1, 1955, after working all day at the Montgomery Fair department store, Parks boarded a bus that would take her home. This was a public bus, operated by the city of Montgomery, and Parks used this bus to take her back and forth to work almost every day. Blacks were supposed to pay the driver at the front entrance, then go to the back entrance to board. Seats from the fifth row to the last row were available for blacks. However, if all seats were taken, blacks were supposed to give up their seats to white passengers. That day, Rosa Parks refused to give up her seat to a white passenger and was arrested for violating Montgomery's racial segregation laws.

That evening the Women's Political Council, a mostly black civil rights group, began printing fliers urging African Americans in Montgomery to protest the segregation laws and the arrest of Parks by refusing to ride the public buses. The next day, Parks, with the help of a white lawyer named Clifford Durr, began a legal battle against the city of Montgomery and its Jim Crow laws. The following

Monday, after Parks was tried and convicted at a municipal court, African Americans again met and formed the Montgomery Improvement Association. A young preacher named MARTIN LUTHER KING, JR., who had only recently arrived to take a pastorate in Montgomery, was chosen to lead this new organization.

Under King's brilliant leadership, and with the steadfast determination of the Montgomery African-American community, the bus boycott held for a year. Instead of riding the buses, blacks walked and organized their own transportation. On December 21, 1956, the U.S. Supreme Court ruled against the city of Montgomery and ordered the city to integrate its buses fully. That day Rosa Parks boarded a bus for the first time in more than a year and rode to work.

To escape harassment that resulted from her courageous stand, Parks moved to Detroit, Michigan, in 1957 and continued to work for civil rights causes during the 1960s and 1970s. In 1980, she received the Martin Luther King, Jr., Nonviolent Peace Prize, and in 1987, she founded the Rosa and Raymond Parks Institute of Self Development.

In 1992, she published her first book, *Rosa Parks: My Story*; in 1994, her second, *Quiet Strength*, was published. Also in 1994, she traveled to Sweden to accept the Rosa Parks Peace Prize. In 1996, Parks was given the Presidential Medal of Freedom. In 1999, she was awarded the Congressional Gold Medal. Troy University in Montgomery, Alabama, opened its Rosa Parks Library and Museum in 2000. The building is

Rosa Parks riding a bus in Montgomery, Alabama, in December 1956 after the U.S. Supreme Court struck down a Montgomery law that reserved certain sections of seats on public transportation for whites only *(Library of Congress, Prints and Photographs Division, LC-USZ62-111235)*

located on the corner where she boarded the bus 45 years earlier.

Rosa Parks died on October 24, 2005. The U.S. Congress allowed her body to lie in state in the rotunda of the U.S. Capitol. She was only the 31st person—and the first woman—to receive this honor. On the day of her funeral, October 30, 2005, all flags in U.S. public areas were flown at half-mast. Congress also authorized a sculpture of Parks to be commissioned and placed in the Capitol's National Statuary Hall. Parks will be the first African-American honoree in the hall.

Further Reading

Academy of Achievement. "Rosa Parks." Available online. URL: http://www.achievement.org/autodoc/page/par0bio-1.Downloaded July 8, 2009.

Brinkley, Douglas. *Rosa Parks.* New York: Viking, 2000.

Carson, Clayborne, Tenisha Armstrong et al., eds. *The Martin Luther King, Jr., Encyclopedia.* Westport, Conn.: Greenwood, 2008.

Dove, Rita. "The Torchbearer: Rosa Parks." Available online. URL: http://www.time.com/time/time100/heroes/profile/parks01.html. Downloaded July 8, 2009.

Parks, Rosa, with Jim Haskins. *Rosa Parks: My Story.* New York: Dial, 1992.

Patterson, Frederick Douglass

(1901–1988) *educator*

A president of the Tuskegee Institute, Frederick Patterson also was the founder of the United Negro College Fund (UNCF). For five decades he was one of the most active leaders in African-American education.

Frederick Douglass Patterson was born on October 10, 1901, in Washington, D.C. A brilliant student, he finished high school at the age of 14 and enrolled in Prairie View State College, a his-torically black university located in Prairie View, Texas, in 1915. In four years at Prairie View, Patterson earned not only a B.A. in science but a master's degree as well.

In 1923, Patterson was hired as director of agriculture at Virginia State College, a position he held until 1928. During this time, he also was working on a doctorate in veterinary science from Iowa State University. He was awarded the doctorate in 1927. In 1928, Patterson enrolled at Cornell University, where he continued his veterinary training, winning a second Ph.D. in veterinary medicine in 1932.

In the late 1920s, Patterson went south to Alabama to work at the famed Tuskegee Institute, founded by BOOKER TALIAFERRO WASHINGTON in 1881. Patterson served as director of the School of Agriculture and founded the only School of Veterinary Medicine at a historically black college in the United States.

In 1935, Patterson was chosen to be the president of Tuskegee. During his 25-year tenure at Tuskegee, Patterson raised the level of academic training at this traditionally vocational school. He was also active in issues beyond the boundaries of the campus. For example, he highlighted the need for providing elementary and secondary students with proper nutrition and won commitment from federal and state agencies for school lunch programs that would give needy students free meals at their schools.

Patterson was a dynamic fund-raiser, both for Tuskegee and for African-American education at large. In 1942, in the pages of the *Pittsburgh Courier*, he called for the creation of a pooled fund that would raise money for all of the nation's historically black colleges and universities. The next year, this initiative resulted in the creation of the United Negro College Fund (UNCF), a fund-raising organization whose goal was to help infuse new capital into black universities and provide scholarships for black students.

Frederick Douglass Patterson ca. 1940. Patterson was president of the Tuskegee Institute and founder of the United Negro College Fund. *(Library of Congress, Prints and Photographs Division, LC-USZ62-114998)*

The UNCF was Patterson's most enduring legacy to African-American education. By 1947, the UNCF was raising more than $2 million a year. Since its founding it has raised more than $1.3 billion. Besides providing money for training programs, the UNCF offers direct scholarships to students. Of these scholarship students 34 percent are members of families with an income of less than $25,000 a year, and 40 percent are the first in their families to attend college.

Patterson retired as president of the Tuskegee Institute in 1960. In 1987, he was selected as a recipient of the Presidential Medal of Freedom, the nation's highest civilian honor. He died in 1988.

Further Reading

Frederick D. Patterson Research Institute. "Frederick Douglass Patterson." Available online. URL: http://www.patterson-uncf.org/bio/fdp_bio.pdf. Downloaded July 8, 2009.

Gasman, Marybeth. *Envisioning Black Colleges: A History of the United Negro College Fund.* Baltimore, Md.: Johns Hopkins University Press, 2007.

Pelham, Robert A.

(1859–1943) *newspaper publisher, community activist*

A shrewd entrepreneur, Robert A. Pelham, through his paper, the *Plaindealer,* was active in the community affairs of Detroit, Michigan, in the 1880s and 1890s. During the latter part of his life, he was involved in politics and publishing in Washington, D.C.

Born near Petersburg, Virginia, in 1859, Pelham was one of five children of Robert and Frances Pelham, free blacks who owned a prosperous farm. Because of tensions arising from the election of Abraham Lincoln and jealousy of whites of the Pelhams' success, the family moved from Virginia to Ohio when young Robert was still an infant. The family moved to Detroit around 1862, there the elder Pelham worked as a carpenter and building contractor.

Robert Pelham attended segregated public schools in Detroit. After his graduation from high school in 1877, he served with the military for three years before returning to Detroit to work in the subscription department of the *Post,* a major white-owned newspaper that generally supported the Republican Party. By 1884, Pelham and his brother founded a company that distributed the *Post.*

The year before he founded his distribution company, Pelham entered the newspaper business with his own paper, the *Plaindealer,* a periodical that was aimed at Detroit's African-American community and had as one of its goals "the dislodgement of prejudice and . . . the encouragement of patriotism."

Besides being one of the owners of the *Plaindealer,* Pelham served as its managing editor. During his eight-year tenure, he lured such famous writers as FREDERICK DOUGLASS and IDA B. WELLS to write for him and built up circulation so that the *Plaindealer* became the most widely read African-American newspaper in the Midwest.

Using the clout he gained as owner and editor of the *Plaindealer,* Pelham became a player in Michigan politics during the 1880s. He was one of the founders in 1884 of the integrated Michigan Club, a political organization, and later that year he was appointed a clerk in the Detroit city revenue office. In 1888, he attended the Republican National Convention as a delegate, and in 1889 Pelham was active in the Afro-American League, an all-black organization that protested growing discrimination against blacks in the United States.

In 1891, Pelham left his job as managing editor of the *Plaindealer* for what seemed to be the greener pastures of Republican Party patronage politics. Because of his political connections, he was appointed an agent of the U.S. Land Office in Detroit in that year, a job that, as a result of the Republican loss of the presidency in 1892, he held for only two years. He married Gabrielle Lewis in 1893; the couple would have four children. By 1897, with the Republicans back in power, Pelham regained his job.

In 1900, Pelham moved to Washington, D.C., where he was appointed to a position in the U.S. Census Bureau. He remained at this government agency for 37 years. During his later life in Washington, the energetic Pelham earned a law degree from Howard University in 1904 and patented several adding machine inventions.

After his retirement from the Census Bureau in 1937, he returned to the news business by founding the *Washington Tribune,* a weekly newspaper, and the Capital News Service, a news agency directed at African Americans. Pelham died on June 12, 1943.

Further Reading

City of Detroit. "Detroit Plaindealer Office." Available online. URL: http://www.ci.detroit.mi.us/historic/districts/plaindealer_office.pdf. Downloaded July 8, 2009.

Lawson, Staci. "Detroit's Plaindealer Newspaper Office." Available online. URL: http://www.livinglibrary.com/freedomtour/Plaindealer.html. Downloaded July 8, 2009.

Pleasant, Mary Ellen

(ca. 1814–1904) *abolitionist, business leader, civil rights activist*

A shrewd and enterprising businesswoman during the California gold rush and afterward, Mary Ellen Pleasant was also involved in the struggle to end slavery and gain full rights for African Americans.

There is much that is either unknown or mysterious about Pleasant's life, beginning with the circumstances surrounding her birth and childhood. The details of her birth and names of her parents are unknown. Some sources claim that she was born on a Georgia cotton plantation and was sent to Boston to be educated; others place her birth in Virginia. It is more likely that she was born free in Philadelphia around 1814. Her father may have been white; her mother was a free woman of color.

When she was young, she was sent to Nantucket Island in Massachusetts to live with a white family. She seems to have received a basic education there. When she was probably in her late teens or early 20s, she moved to Boston. There she met notable abolitionists such as William Lloyd Garrison and married a man named John Pleasant. She may have been active in abolitionist circles.

In 1849, Pleasant and her husband headed west to the California gold fields. When they arrived, they remained in San Francisco rather than striking out for the gold country farther inland. During the 1850s, Pleasant opened a restaurant and established a boardinghouse in San Francisco. She also may have engaged in less conventional business such as running a house for prostitutes and a high-interest loan business. She was financially successful in San Francisco and was respected and well liked in that wide-open town.

Around 1858, Pleasant returned east, probably by way of Canada. She may have met the abolitionist John Brown, who was then plotting his raid on Harpers Ferry. Some sources have speculated that she gave Brown money to support his activities, although this cannot be confirmed. She may also have made forays into Virginia to help slaves escape on the Underground Railroad.

By the early 1860s, Pleasant was back in California. She became a member of the Franchise League, founded by Jeremiah Burke Sanderson, which was formed to fight California laws that denied blacks the right to vote, to serve in the

Mary Ellen Pleasant, an early civil rights leader and businessperson in California *(San Francisco History Center, San Francisco Public Library)*

militia, or to testify in court. Pleasant also organized protests that forced the city of San Francisco to allow African Americans to ride in the city's streetcars.

For much of the later 1800s, Pleasant worked as a housekeeper for a San Francisco banker, Thomas Bell. It seems that she was much more than a domestic servant, although the nature of her relationship with Bell is unclear. After Bell's death, in the 1890s, she remained in his house until 1899. She died on January 11, 1904.

Further Reading

Bibbs, Susheel. "Meet Mary Ellen Pleasant." Available online. URL: http://www.mepleasant.com/. Downloaded July 8, 2009.

City of San Francisco Museum. "Mary Ellen Pleasant." Available online. URL: http://www.sfmuseum.org/hist10/mammy.html. Downloaded July 8, 2009.

Drago, Harry Sinclair. *Notorious Ladies of the Frontier.* New York: Dodd, Mead, 1969.

Hudson, Lynn Maria. *The Making of "Mammy Pleasant": A Black Entrepreneur in Nineteenth-Century San Francisco.* Champaign: University of Illinois Press, 2002.

Prosser, Gabriel
(ca. 1755–1800) *slave revolt leader*

A slave in Virginia, Gabriel Prosser organized what might have been one of the largest slave revolts in American history had it not been betrayed by one of the conspirators. The date of Prosser's birth is uncertain, but he was probably born around 1775 on a tobacco plantation that belonged to Thomas Prosser in Henrico County. Nothing is known about Prosser's parents. Clearly intelligent, Gabriel Prosser was taught to read and write on the orders of Thomas Prosser.

A big man, Prosser was apprenticed as a blacksmith, and he quickly established a reputation as a skilled artisan. When Thomas Prosser died, the estate was passed to his son, John Henry Prosser.

The new master hired out Gabriel as a blacksmith to people in nearby Richmond, where Gabriel had the opportunity to become acquainted with a large number of slaves and whites.

Because he could read, Prosser was keenly aware of the hypocrisy of the rhetoric of the new United States of America. Even though its Declaration of Independence stated that "all men are created equal, that they are endowed by their creator with certain inalienable rights [such as] life and liberty," the U.S. government overlooked the practice of enslavement of the majority of its African-American inhabitants.

Inspired by his reading of the Bible (especially the story of the Jews' flight from Egypt to freedom) and the recent revolt against the French by blacks in Haiti, Prosser began to conceive of a way out of slavery. In his time spent in Richmond, he met a number of white radicals who were opposed to slavery and to the ruling elite of Virginia. These men, such as Charles Quersey and Alexander Beddenhurst, who were French immigrants, increased Prosser's growing political awareness.

After Prosser was branded on the hand as punishment for striking a white man in 1799, he decided to act on his belief that blacks should rise up to revolt against their enslavement. Enlisting his brothers, he slowly began to gather recruits among slaves in the nearby countryside and in other Virginia counties for an insurrection that was planned for August 1800.

Recruiters talked with the Catawba Indian tribe, although it is unclear whether the Catawba agreed to help in the revolt. Also recruited were free blacks living in Richmond and a few whites. Prosser envisioned that all of the recruits would mobilize suddenly, march on Richmond, seize the center of the city, and take Governor James Madison hostage. The goal would be to negotiate the creation of a free black territory in Virginia where former slaves and sympathetic white working families would be allowed to live. Plans were made for slaves to revolt in the towns of Petersburg and Norfolk too.

News of Prosser's rebellion inevitably reached the ears of white planters before the event itself. These reports were relayed to Governor Madison, but not believing the news, Madison did not act. A heavy rain began to fall on August 30 a number of hours before the revolt was to occur, and flooded rivers prevented the mutineers from moving to Richmond. In the meantime, several more slaves informed on Prosser, this time gaining the attention of the governor, who sent out the state militia to hunt down the conspirators.

Hearing that he was being sought, Prosser fled Henrico County. After hiding in the woods for nearly two weeks, he swam to a schooner and was taken aboard by the white captain, Richardson Taylor. Sympathetic to Prosser, Taylor agreed to try to take him to freedom. However, Prosser was captured a few days later, when the ship docked in Norfolk and one of the black sailors told authorities to search the ship.

Prosser was found guilty of insurrection during a one-day trial on October 6, 1800. He was hanged on the city gallows of Richmond on October 10.

Prosser's bold plan badly scared the southern planter class and resulted in new laws that forbade the education of blacks and limited their movement off the plantations where they worked.

In 2007, Virginia governor Timothy Kaine issued an informal pardon to Prosser. Kaine said that he had been motivated by "his devotion to the ideals of the American Revolution" in his attempt to secure liberty.

Further Reading

Egerton, Douglas R. *Gabriel's Rebellion: The Virginia Slave Conspiracies of 1800 and 1802.* Chapel Hill: University of North Carolina Press, 1993.

Henrico County, Virginia. "Gabriel's Rebellion." Available online. URL: http://www.co.henrico.va.us/rec/gabriel.htm. Downloaded November 4, 2001.

PBS. Africans in America, Resource Bank. "Gabriel's Conspiracy 1799–1800." Available online. URL: http://www.pbs.org/wgbh/aia/part3/3p1576.html. Downloaded July 9, 2001.

Rodriguez, Junius P., ed. *Encyclopedia of Slave Resistance and Rebellion.* Westport, Conn.: Greenwood, 2007.

R

Randolph, Asa Philip
(A. Philip Randolph)
(1889–1979) *labor leader, civil rights activist*

A. Philip Randolph was the most important African-American labor leader of the 20th century and arguably one of the most important 20th-century leaders in the struggle for full civil and political rights for African Americans in the United States. Born in Crescent City, Florida, on April 15, 1889, Asa Philip Randolph was the son of James William and Elizabeth Robinson Randolph. His father, a minister in the African Methodist Episcopal (AME) Church, encouraged Randolph and his brother to study and read about contemporary events. When Randolph was still an infant, the family moved to Jacksonville, Florida, where Randolph received his primary and secondary education and graduated from the Cookman Institute high school in 1909.

After his graduation from high school, Randolph, who had little money to pay for college, held menial jobs in Jacksonville for several years. In 1911, he decided to move to Harlem in New York City, which was becoming a Mecca for ambitious young blacks. In New York, Randolph worked at odd jobs while he took classes at the City College of New York. Eugene Debs, a labor leader and political activist who was running for the U.S. presidency for the Socialist Party in 1912,

captivated Randolph. Randolph soon joined the Socialist Party and began working for the ideals of racial justice and fair labor conditions for all Americans.

By this time, Randolph had met CHANDLER OWEN, a black man who, like Randolph, had come to New York City from the South. Owen, a student at Columbia University, was also interested in radical politics and the struggle for racial equality. In 1917, the two men began publishing the *Messenger*, a paper that publicized their socialist philosophy and was aimed at black working men and women. Around this time, Randolph married Lucille Green. They were to remain together until her death in 1961.

Randolph clearly stated the purpose of the *Messenger* in an article he wrote in one of its first issues:

> The history of the labor movement in America proves that the employing classes recognize no race lines. They will exploit a White man as readily as a Black man . . . they will exploit any race or class in order to make profits. The combination of Black and White workers will be a powerful lesson to the capitalists of the solidarity of labor. It will show that labor, Black and White, is conscious of its interests and power. This will prove that unions are not based upon race lines, but

upon class lines. This will serve to convert a class of workers, which has been used by the capitalist class to defeat organized labor, into an ardent, class conscious, intelligent, militant group.

In the pages of the *Messenger,* Randolph also protested lynching of blacks in the South and called on African-American men to avoid the draft, which had been activated when the United States entered World War I in 1917. Randolph was a pacifist and did not believe in fighting wars under any circumstances. He also pointed out that even blacks who were not pacifists should not fight a war for a government that was unwilling to extend the full benefits of democracy to its African-American citizens.

Because of Randolph's outspokenness about the war and racial politics, the U.S. attorney general, Mitchell Palmer, labeled Randolph "the most dangerous Negro in America." In 1918, the federal government arrested Randolph and Owen on charges of treason. Although the charges were soon dropped, the government revoked the *Messenger's* second-class mailing privileges, thus making it too expensive to mail the paper to its subscribers outside the New York City area.

After the war, Randolph reassessed the needs of the African-American community and its relationship with the Socialist Party. Though he would remain a socialist for the rest of his life, Randolph concluded that blacks were not responding to the message and leaders of the party. Accordingly, he quit the party and began to work full time to organize black workers into unions.

In 1925, a group of blacks who worked as porters for the Pullman Company asked Randolph to help them organize into a union. Pullman porters were exclusively black men, and Randolph saw at once that organizing a union of these workers would put into practice many of his beliefs.

Even though the company bitterly resisted Randolph's efforts, Randolph and the porters clung tenaciously to their goal of forcing the com-

A. Philip Randolph ca. 1960. Randolph founded the *Messenger,* a socialist newspaper, and later organized the Brotherhood of Sleeping Car Porters (BSCP), the first successful all-black labor union. *(Library of Congress, Prints and Photographs Division, LC-USZ62-119496)*

pany to recognize them as the porters' official union. Randolph's work was aided by legislation that was passed in Franklin D. Roosevelt's first term in office, legislation that forced companies to negotiate with unions. In 1935, the Pullman Company had to meet with the Brotherhood of Sleeping Car Porters, the porters' union. They finally signed an agreement with the union in 1937, at last granting official recognition.

By the late 1930s, Randolph was venturing again into national African-American civil rights work. In 1937, he became president of the National Negro Congress, a group working for full rights for blacks. However, he quit this group in 1940 when it became clear that it was controlled by the

Communist Party. "The communists," he explained, "are not only undemocratic but antidemocratic, they are opposed to our concept of the dignity of the human personality, . . . and . . . they represent a totalitarian system in which civil liberties cannot thrive."

In 1941, with World War II closing in on the United States, Randolph organized the March on Washington, a movement that demanded that the government hire African Americans in defense plants operating under government contract. After briefly resisting Randolph's demands, President Roosevelt gave in and established the Fair Employment Practices Committee, which enforced the hiring of African Americans in defense factories.

After the war, Randolph again confronted the U.S. government to demand a change in the practice of segregating black soldiers and sailors in racially separate units. Again the president, this time Harry Truman, resisted Randolph's demands. However, after intense pressure from Randolph and his group, the League of Nonviolent Civil Disobedience, Truman signed an executive order integrating the U.S. Armed Forces in 1948.

In the 1950s and 1960s, Randolph continued to press unions to open their doors to black workers. His organizing methods and use of the tactics of nonviolent disobedience were copied by a new generation of civil rights leaders, most notably MARTIN LUTHER KING, JR.

To dramatize his feelings that the task of achieving full racial justice was an unfinished job, Randolph again organized a march on Washington in August 1963. Held on the steps of the Lincoln Memorial, this rally allowed a forum for a full spectrum of labor and civil rights leaders to speak to a crowd of some 200,000 who had assembled on the Mall in Washington and many millions more who viewed the event on television.

This gathering, which was billed by Randolph as the March for Jobs and Freedom, would be a fitting end to Randolph's career as a labor leader and civil rights champion. From it sprang the Civil Rights Act of 1964 and the Voting Rights Act of 1965, two of the most important civil rights bills of the 20th century. For his role as a civil rights and labor leader, Randolph was awarded the Presidential Medal of Freedom by President Lyndon Johnson in 1964.

Although Randolph lived for almost 15 years more, he gradually withdrew from active organizing and died at age 90 in 1979. His left a legacy as a pragmatic and determined opponent of injustice and oppression, a committed believer in democracy, and a champion of common people of all races.

Further Reading

Anderson, Jervis. *A. Philip Randolph: A Biographical Portrait.* Berkeley: University of California Press, 1986.

A. Philip Randolph Institute. "Biographical Notes on A. Philip Randolph." Available online. URL: http://www.apri.org/ht/d/sp/i/225/pid/225. Downloaded November 6, 2001.

A. Philip Randolph Pullman Porter Museum. "Museum History." Available online. URL: http://www.aphiliprandolphmuseum.com/history.html. Downloaded July 15, 2009.

California Newsreel. "A Philip Randolph: For Jobs and Freedom." Available online. URL: http://www.newsreel.org/nav/title.asp?tc=CN0001. Downloaded July 15, 2009.

Davis, Daniel S. *Mr. Black Labor: The Story of A. Philip Randolph, Father of the Civil Rights Movement.* New York: E. P. Dutton, 1972.

Kersten, Andrew Edmund. *A. Philip Randolph: A Life in the Vanguard.* Lanham, Md.: Rowman & Littlefield, 2006.

Pfeffer, Paula F. *A. Philip Randolph, Pioneer of the Civil Rights Movement.* Baton Rouge: Louisiana State University Press, 1990.

Rucker, Walter C., and James N. Upton, eds. *Encyclopedia of American Race Riots.* Westport, Conn.: Greenwood, 2007.

Rayner, John Baptis

(1850–1918) *educator, community activist*

At times a teacher, minister, and administrator, John Rayner is mainly known for his work as an organizer of the Populist Party in Texas and as an advocate of BOOKER TALIAFERRO WASHINGTON's philosophy of self-help and economic advancement for African Americans. Born into slavery in 1850, John Baptis Rayner was the son of Kenneth Rayner, a white plantation owner, and Mary Ricks, a slave. After emancipation and the end of the Civil War, the elder Rayner made sure that his son received an elementary and secondary education in Raleigh. Rayner then attended Shaw University and St. Augustine's Collegiate Institute in North Carolina.

After finishing his college education, Rayner taught school in rural areas of North Carolina for several years. He married Susan Staten in 1874; they would have two children. Soon after his marriage, he was elected deputy sheriff of Tarboro, North Carolina. In the late 1870s, he also became an occasional Baptist preacher.

Rayner and his family moved to Texas in 1881, settling in Robertson County in eastern Texas, where he took a job as a teacher. After his first wife died in the 1880s, he married Clarissa Clark. They would have three children.

In the late 1880s, Rayner became involved in the Farmer's Improvement Society, an organization that emphasized self-help policies for small farmers. He also began to be attracted to the ideas of the Populists, who had become active in Texas and other southern and midwestern states as a result of a crisis in farm economics.

With many farmers going out of business because of unfair rail charges that discriminated against small farmers and federal government economic policies that farmers believed favored wealthy corporations back east, the Populist Party developed to express farmers' interests. Rayner worked as an organizer in the Texas African-American community for the Populist Party and served on the party's executive committee in 1895 and 1896.

After the Populist Party collapsed in the late 1890s, Rayner returned to the Republican Party, although he was not as active in it as he had been with the Populists. In 1902, Rayner helped found the Texas Law and Order League, which tried to get jobs for Texas blacks and ran programs in the African-American community educating poor blacks about the need to follow the law.

Rayner ended his career by serving as a financial administrator at the Farmers Improvement Society School in Ladonia, Texas. He died in Calvert, Texas, on July 15, 1918.

Further Reading

Cantrell, Gregg. *Kenneth and John B. Rayner and the Limits of Southern Dissent.* Urbana: University of Illinois Press, 1993.

Davies, Carole Boyce, ed. *Encyclopedia of the African Diaspora: Origins, Experiences, and Culture.* Santa Barbara, Calif.: ABC-CLIO, 2008.

Handbook of Texas Online. "John Baptis Rayner." Available online. URL: http://www.tsha.utexas.edu/handbook/online/articles/view/RR/fra52.html. Downloaded July 15, 2009.

Logan, Rayford, and Michael Winston. *Dictionary of American Negro Biography.* New York: W. W. Norton, 1982.

Remond, Charles Lenox

(1810–1873) *abolitionist, civil rights activist*

A leading abolitionist of his day, Charles Remond was also a staunch advocate of women's rights, including the right to vote. Believing that all people, regardless of their gender or race, should have the same rights under law, he was a ceaseless advocate for civil rights. Charles Lenox Remond was born free in Salem, Massachusetts, in 1810 to John and Nancy Remond. He grew up in a relatively prosperous family. (His sister was the well-known civil rights activist Sarah Parker Remond.)

His father, a native of the Caribbean island of Curaçao, was an entrepreneur who ran a barbershop, catering business, and general store. Remond received a good education in Salem's public schools but also suffered much abuse and discrimination because of his race.

After the completion of his education, Remond may have worked for a number of years as a barber and caterer. He became increasingly active in the budding movement against slavery, known as abolitionism, that was rising in the North.

One of the most important abolitionist leaders was William Lloyd Garrison, a white man, who helped found the American Anti-Slavery Society (AAS) in 1833. Garrison was also the publisher of the *Emancipator,* an influential periodical that publicized the evils of slavery and worked to create a national mood and political momentum against this practice.

Remond met Garrison soon after the AAS was founded. Impressed with Garrison's message that "moral suasion," rather than armed conflict, was the only way to stop slavery, Remond joined the AAS as a paid lecturer in 1838.

For a period of almost 20 years, from 1838 to 1856, Remond traveled the antislavery circuit, giving talks and speeches before audiences in the towns and cities of New England, the mid-Atlantic states, and the Midwest. Called by one leading abolitionist the most forceful speaker of his day, one whose "power of speech, argument, and eloquence" moved and thrilled his audiences, Remond also spoke before city councils and state legislatures on behalf of the abolition of slavery.

In 1840, when he was 30, Remond was selected by the AAS as one of its delegates to the World Anti-Slavery Convention held in London. When delegates at this convention decided to exclude women as voting members and seat them in a separate section of the hall, Remond and several other American abolitionists sat with the women as a sign of protest and support for women's rights.

Remond stayed in Great Britain for a year and a half, during which he traveled throughout England, Scotland, and Ireland, giving speeches against slavery in the United States. By all reports, he was a great success and helped enlighten the people of the United Kingdom about the deplorable conditions that existed under the slave system in the American South.

Remond returned to the United States in December 1841. Beginning to show the effects of tuberculosis, a disease that would eventually kill him, he had to spend some time recuperating from his journey. By February 1842, he was well enough to give a speech that became well known at that time, "Rights of Colored Persons in Travelling," to a committee of the Massachusetts legislature. This speech protested the racial segregation policy practiced by railroad companies in Massachusetts, which required African Americans to sit in a car separate from whites.

During the late 1840s, Remond married Amy Matilda Williams. After her death in 1856, he married Elizabeth Thayer Magee. Four of Remond and Magee's children would die before their 20th birthday.

In 1856, tired of the perpetual poverty of the lecture circuit, Remond opened a restaurant in Boston. During the middle of the Civil War, he served as a federal army recruiting agent to find African-American enlistees for the 54th Massachusetts Regiment, an all-black unit. After the war, Remond won coveted political patronage jobs, first as a street light inspector in Boston, then as a clerk in the U.S. Customs House in Boston.

During the late 1860s and early 1870s, Remond held steadfast to his belief that all citizens of the United States, regardless of color or gender, should have equal rights. At a meeting of the National Convention of the American Equal Rights Association in 1867, he declared in a speech, "No class of citizens in this country can be deprived of the ballot without injuring every other class." He also fought for the inclusion of blacks on juries in Massachusetts.

Remond died on December 22, 1873, at the age of 63, in Wakefield, Massachusetts.

Further Reading

Beaver County History Online. "Charles Lenox Remond." Available online. URL: http://www. bchistory.org/beavercounty/booklengthdocuments/ AMilobook/21Remond.html. Downloaded July 15, 2009.

Finkelman, Paul, ed. *Encyclopedia of African American History, 1619–1895: From the Colonial Period to the Age of Frederick Douglass.* New York: Oxford University Press, 2006.

Quarles, Benjamin. *Black Abolitionists.* New York: Oxford, 1969.

Woodson, Carter G. *Negro Orators and Their Orations.* Washington, D.C.: Associated Publishers, 1925.

Robeson, Eslanda Cardozo Goode
(1896–1965) *civil rights activist, pan-Africanist*

Wife and manager of the famed actor and singer Paul Robeson, Eslanda Robeson was active in the Civil Rights movement in the United States and the struggle for freedom and self-rule in Africa. She was born Eslanda Cardozo Goode in 1896 in Washington, D.C., the daughter of John and Eslanda Goode. Her father was an official in the U.S. War Department, and her mother was the daughter of an educator. Her father died when she was six, so young Eslanda moved with her mother and two brothers to New York City to be educated in racially integrated public schools.

A good student, she graduated from high school in 1914. She later attended the University of Chicago and Columbia University in New York City. She was awarded a B.S. in chemistry in 1923 and took a job as an analytical chemist at the Columbia Medical Center.

While a student at Columbia University, Eslanda met Paul Robeson, a student at Columbia Law School. They were married in 1921, the same year that Robeson began working in the summers as an actor in Eugene O'Neill's Provincetown Players theatrical troupe. After his graduation from law school, Paul Robeson briefly worked as a lawyer in a New York City firm. He decided to leave law for a theatrical career after experiencing racial discrimination at his law office.

After her husband's career shift, Eslanda Robeson became his theatrical manager. She arranged for his famous performances in plays such as *Emperor Jones* and *Showboat,* and she traveled with him on numerous overseas tours that took them to the big cities of Europe and the Soviet Union.

During the 1930s, both Robesons became active in groups that were affiliated with the Communist Party. They both probably secretly joined the Communist Party at this time. This decision was based on their perception that the Soviet Union and its Communist allies throughout the world were far ahead of other groups in confronting the evils of racial discrimination and European colonial rule in Africa and Asia.

In the late 1930s, after an extended trip through Africa, Robeson began to study anthropology seriously, first at the University of London, then at the Hartford Seminary Foundation. She was awarded a Ph.D. in anthropology from Hartford in 1945. That same year she published *African Journey,* a book that documented observations from her time in Africa.

In 1945, the Council on African Affairs, a private group composed of numerous U.S. Communists, sent Robeson as an observer to the San Francisco Conference, a meeting that would result in the formation of the United Nations (UN). She later testified before the UN's Trusteeship Council about colonial misrule in Africa, and she worked hard during the late 1940s and 1950s for political independence for African colonies.

In the late 1940s, Robeson and her husband became targets of the members of the U.S. Congress for their alleged Communist sympathies. Paul Robeson was forced to testify numerous times before congressional committees. In 1952, his passport was confiscated when he refused to take a loyalty oath.

The Robesons' income dropped dramatically as a result of Paul Robeson's political problems. Nonetheless, in Communist periodicals such as the *Daily Worker*, Eslanda Robeson continued to speak out against racial oppression inside the United States and colonialism abroad.

In 1958, the Robesons moved to the Soviet Union, where they lived until 1963. Battling cancer, Eslanda Robeson returned to New York City with her husband. She died there on December 13, 1965.

Further Reading

DuBois Learning Center. "Paul and Eslanda Robeson." Available online. URL: http://www.duboislc.org/ShadesOfBlack/PaulRobeson.html. Downloaded July 15, 2009.

Federal Bureau of Investigation. Freedom of Information Act. "Paul and Eslanda Robeson." Available online. URL: http://foia.fbi.gov/robeson.htm. Downloaded July 15, 2009.

Smith, Jessie Carney, Millicent Lownes Jackson, and Linda T. Wynn, eds. *Encyclopedia of African American Business*. Westport, Conn.: Greenwood, 2006.

Robinson, Randall

(1941–) *community organizer, pan-African activist*

An activist at home and abroad, Randall Robinson was one of the principal founders of TransAfrica, an African-American advocacy group whose goal is to influence U.S. policy toward countries that have large black populations. Robinson was born in Richmond, Virginia, on July 6, 1941, to Maxie Cleveland and Doris Robinson Griffin. Both parents were teachers, and his father was a well-known local high school history teacher whom Robinson credited with being "a pillar" during his youth.

Robinson attended segregated public schools in Richmond and graduated from high school in 1959. A talented basketball player, he won a scholarship to Norfolk State College. After dropping out of Norfolk State in his junior year, Robinson was drafted into the U.S. Army. After a tour of duty in Georgia, he returned to college at Virginia Union University in Richmond. Receiving a degree in sociology from Virginia Union in 1967, Robinson was admitted to the Harvard Law School. He was awarded a LL.B. from Harvard in 1971.

During college, Robinson became interested in learning about the evolution from colonial rule to self-government that was occurring in the newly independent nations of Africa. To witness this process directly, he traveled to Tanzania on a Ford Foundation grant in 1970 and 1971. On his return home, Robinson took a job as director of a community development organization in the black neighborhood of Roxbury in Boston. In 1975, he moved to Washington to begin working as an aide for Congressman William Clay of Missouri. In 1976, he worked for Congressman Charles Diggs of Michigan. With Diggs, Robinson took his first trip to South Africa to examine the effects of apartheid, the racially discriminatory system in that country.

Believing that there was a need for an organization to lobby the U.S. Congress for policy changes in Africa, Robinson persuaded the Congressional Black Caucus to help create TransAfrica, a political action and education group, in 1977. He was appointed TransAfrica's executive director, a position he held until 1995, when he was named president of the group. In 1981, an offshoot of TransAfrica, known as TransAfrica Forum, was created to educate Americans about conditions in Africa and the Caribbean. Robinson is also president of that organization.

Robinson first reached the attention of the general public in the United States with the protest movement he organized against the white South African regime during the mid-1980s. For more than a year, thousands of people protested in front of the South African embassy in Washington against the South African government's apartheid policies. In 1986, this protest campaign resulted in passage of the Comprehensive Anti-Apartheid Act by the U.S. Congress, a bill that imposed economic sanctions on South Africa until it changed its racially discriminatory policies. During the 1990s,

Randall Robinson, founder of TransAfrica, a lobbying group that represents countries with large black populations. Robinson has also been active in the movement to force the U.S. government to pay reparations to the descendants of slaves. *(© Bettmann/CORBIS)*

Robinson organized protest campaigns against the restrictions placed by the U.S. government on Haitian immigration and against U.S. trade policies toward Caribbean countries.

In the late 1990s, Robinson and TransAfrica became embroiled in a controversial issue—that of reparations by the U.S. government to African Americans for the enslavement of blacks from the 1600s to the Emancipation Proclamation in 1863. Robinson is a principal leader in this movement and is demanding that the government compensate all African Americans for, in the words of TransAfrica's Black Manifesto, the "unjust expropriation of uncompensated labor by enslaved Africans, the subordination and segregation of the descendants of the enslaved, as well as from discrimination against African Americans." Robinson's 2001 book, *The Debt: What America Owes to Blacks,* examined the reparations issue. The sequel, *The Reckoning: What Blacks Owe to Each Other* (2002), discussed ways in which the African-American community can help itself.

This position has attracted numerous black and white critics in the United States, who point out that none of the people who would pay for such compensations through taxes has ever owned slaves and that none of the African Americans receiving payments has ever been enslaved. Critics also note how divisive such proposals would be in a multiethnic society like the United States.

In 2001, Robinson moved out of the United States, choosing to live in St. Kitts, an island in the Caribbean. In *Quitting America: The Departure of a Black Man from His Native Land* (2004), he examines the issues that drove him to leave the country and conveys the agony of making the decision to live in exile. Robinson travels to the United States to give speeches and lectures and to appear on television shows.

Further Reading

Mjagkij, Nina, ed. *Organizing Black America: An Encyclopedia of African American Associations.* New York: Taylor & Francis, 2001.

PBS. Charlie Rose. "A Conversation with Author Randle Robinson." Available online. URL: http://www.charlierose.com/view/interview/8852. Downloaded July 15, 2009.

Robinson, Randall. *Quitting America: The Departure of a Black Man from His Native Land.* New York: Dutton, 2004.

Rock, John Sweat

(1825–1866) *abolitionist, physician, civil rights activist*

Active in abolition groups in the 1850s, John Rock served as a recruiter for black regiments that fought for the North during the Civil War. He also spoke out on behalf of equal rights for African Americans in the northern states. Born in 1825, in Salem, New Jersey, John Sweat Rock was the son of free black parents. Because of his family's relative prosperity, Rock was able to attend public schools in Salem.

After his graduation from high school in 1844, Rock taught school for two years while he studied medicine with two white doctors. When, because of racial discrimination, he was denied admission to a medical school in Philadelphia, Rock studied dentistry instead. He opened a dental practice in Philadelphia in 1850. Later that year, he was admitted to medical school in Philadelphia at the newly opened American Medical College. He was granted a master's degree in medicine from the school in 1852.

Soon after he had attained a medical degree, Rock moved to Boston, where he was admitted into the Massachusetts Medical Society in 1854. He was to live in Boston for the rest of his life.

For the next four years, Rock practiced medicine and dentistry in Boston. He also became active in Boston's Vigilance Committee, composed of black and white members, who aided escaped slaves from the South. Rock treated numerous sick black men and women when they settled in Boston after escaping from bondage.

Rock was not content merely to help slaves who had escaped from the South. He knew first-hand about the prejudice and racial discrimination that existed in the North, too, and he acted to try to change the laws and customs that held blacks back. "Massachusetts has a great name and deserves much credit for what she has done," he declared in a speech

> but the position of the colored people in Massachusetts is far from being an enviable one. While colored men have many rights, they have few privileges here. To be sure, we are seldom insulted by passers-by, we have the right of suffrage, the free schools and colleges are open to our children, and from them have come forth young men capable of filling any post of profit or honor. But there is no field for these young men. . . . You can hardly imagine the humiliation and contempt a colored lad must feel by graduating first in his class and then being rejected everywhere else because of his color.

Rock was a key member of a committee of African Americans who protested racial discrimination in Boston's public schools. In 1855, this group forced the city of Boston to admit blacks to the school system. That same year he traveled with CHARLES LENOX REMOND to a meeting of the Colored National Convention in Philadelphia.

Rock also spoke out against the activities of the American Colonization Society. This group, founded by a northern white minister, advocated sending free blacks from the United States to the colony of Liberia in Africa. Rock protested that blacks who were born and lived in the United States were Americans. America was their home, and instead of sending African Americans to Africa, the federal government and state governments needed to change their laws to allow blacks a full range of rights equal to those of white Americans.

In May 1858, Rock journeyed to France to consult French doctors about a throat condition. Before he could travel, he had to petition the Massachusetts legislature to issue him a state passport because the federal government, declaring that blacks were not American citizens, had refused to issue him an American passport. The Massachusetts legislature complied with his request, and he received his operation in Paris in the fall of 1858.

After his return to the United States in 1859, Rock curtailed his medical practice but began to study law. He was admitted to the Massachusetts bar in 1861 and set up a law practice. In 1863, when the U.S. Congress allowed African Americans to join the U.S. Army in segregated units, Rock worked to recruit black soldiers into several Massachusetts regiments. He was granted the right to argue cases before the U.S. Supreme Court in 1865, but by then he was weakened from tuberculosis. Rock died of the disease in Boston on December 3, 1866.

Further Reading

Contee, C. G. "John Sweat Rock, M.D., Esq., 1825–1866." *Journal of the National Medical Association* 63, no. 3 (May 1976). Available online. URL: http://www.pubmedcentral.nih.gov/articlerender.fcgi?artid=2609666. Downloaded July 15, 2009.

Pease, Jane H., and William H. Pease. *Bound with Them in Chains: A Biographical History of the Antislavery Movement.* Westport, Conn.: Greenwood Press, 1972.

Quarles, Benjamin. *Black Abolitionists.* New York: Oxford, 1969.

Ruggles, David

(1810–1849) *journalist, writer, medical practitioner*

Active in the abolitionist movement in New York City, David Ruggles later became a well-known hydrotherapist, a medical practitioner skilled in the use of water treatments, diet, and rest to cure illness. Born in Norwich, Connecticut, in 1810, Ruggles was one of five children of David and Nancy Ruggles, who were free. Ruggles received an elementary education in a church school in Norwich. At age 17, Ruggles moved to New York City, where he began working as a clerk in the grocery business. By 1829, he owned his own grocery business, which he ran until 1833.

In 1833, Ruggles took a job as an agent for the *Emancipator and Journal of Public Morals,* a weekly antislavery newspaper published in New York City. In this position, he traveled throughout New York and nearby states, giving lectures against slavery and soliciting subscriptions for the paper. He also wrote articles for the *Emancipator* and for his own publishing venture, which he set up in a bookstore in New York City that he founded in 1834. In his articles and in pamphlets such as *Extinguisher, Extinguished . . . ,* Ruggles argued for the immediate freeing of slaves and against the schemes of the American Colonization Society, which wanted to induce African Americans to immigrate to Liberia on the west coast of Africa.

By 1835, Ruggles had become well known for his outspokenness. In September of that year, a white mob burned down his bookstore and put it permanently out of business. In response, Ruggles shifted his efforts from writing to taking direct action to help runaway slaves. He joined the New York Vigilance Committee, one of several organizations in the Underground Railroad. As a member of this group, he helped move fugitive slaves from Philadelphia to New York then on to upstate New York and other places in the North. He also developed a tactic to force New York State to recognize the free status of escaped slaves by going to state court to win legal recognition of a former slave's freedom. One of the most famous runaway slaves helped by Ruggles was Frederick Washington

Bailey, who would change his name to FREDERICK DOUGLASS.

In 1838, Ruggles shifted his efforts back to writing. That year he founded a newspaper, *Mirror of Liberty*, which he published and wrote articles for until 1841. A contentious man, Ruggles not only tangled with supporters of slavery but he also ran afoul of many of his own allies in the abolitionist movement. In the late 1830s, he was frequently involved in lawsuits with colleagues and worked himself hard. This turmoil resulted in a physical collapse in 1842. Almost completely blind, he was also broke and unemployable because of his illness. Taken in by Lydia Maria Child, a white abolitionist from Northampton, Massachusetts, Ruggles recuperated for a year and a half.

During his recovery, Ruggles experimented with the use of baths, diet change, and relaxation as a means of recovery. He also developed intuitive means of healing using touch, a technique he dubbed "cutaneous electricity." In 1846, he bought a building in Northampton where he set up a health clinic devoted to hydrotherapy. There, over the next three years, he gave treatments to patients such as SOJOURNER TRUTH and William Lloyd Garrison, two famous abolitionists. However, true to his nature, Ruggles began to overwork again. His earlier illness flared up, and he died, possibly of a ruptured appendix, on December 26, 1849.

Further Reading

Curry, Richard O., ed. *The Abolitionists*. Hinsdale, Ill.: Dryden Press, 1973.

David Ruggles Center. "David Ruggles: Bookseller, Abolitionist, Hydropathic Doctor." Available online. URL: http://www.davidrugglescenter.org/davidruggles.html. Downloaded July 15, 2009.

Quarles, Benjamin. *Black Abolitionists*. New York: Oxford, 1969.

Smith, Jessie Carney, Millicent Lownes Jackson, and Linda T. Wynn, eds. *Encyclopedia of African American Business*. Westport, Conn.: Greenwood, 2006.

Russwurm, John Brown

(1799–1851) *abolitionist, publisher, colonial official*

Founder and editor of the first black-owned newspaper in the United States, John Russwurm later became an advocate of colonization, the proposal that African Americans should move back to Africa to live. The son of a white father and a black slave woman, John Brown Russwurm was born in 1799 in Port Antonio, Jamaica. Treated as a free person by his father, Russwurm was sent to Quebec, Canada, in 1807 to begin his elementary education. Russwurm remained in Quebec for five years before rejoining his

John Brown Russwurm, founder of *Freedom's Journal*, the first black-owned newspaper in the United States. Russwurm later promoted colonization, the idea that African Americans should return to Africa. *(Moorland-Spingarn Research Center, Howard University)*

father, also known as John Russwurm, in Portland, Maine, which at that time was a part of the state of Massachusetts.

When Russwurm's father remarried, John Russwurm was well received into his new family and treated as a full family member even after his father's death in 1815. In 1819, he was sent to Hebron Academy in Maine to finish his secondary education. After his graduation from Hebron in 1824, he was accepted as a student at Bowdoin College, one of the first African Americans to attend college. Russwurm graduated from Bowdoin with a B.A. in 1826.

After his graduation, Russwurm moved to New York City, the commercial center of the United States and one of most active markets for newspaper publishing. In New York, Russwurm quickly met a group of middle-class free blacks who believed that African Americans in the city needed a paper to express their views on the issues of the day, especially slavery. With SAMUEL ELI CORNISH, a minister, Russwurm in 1827 founded *Freedom's Journal,* the first African-American-owned and -published periodical in the United States.

Russwurm worked as the editor of *Freedom's Journal* for two years. In the first issue of the paper, he published "Walker's Appeal," an impassioned plea by Boston abolitionist DAVID WALKER for blacks to rise up in revolt to end slavery. This and other articles that appeared in the paper over the next several years were an attempt by Russwurm to offer a view different from that presented in most of the white-owned New York newspapers, many of which favored slavery and opposed equal rights for free blacks.

Russwurm, who had earlier opposed the colonization of African Americans in Africa, had by 1829 begun to favor this solution to the problem of racial conflict in the United States. Because he believed that blacks would never be treated as equals in the country of their birth, he began to champion the return of African Americans to Africa, specifically to the newly established colony of Liberia.

Founded in 1821 by agents of the American Colonization Society, Liberia was targeted as the destination point for any African Americans who were willing to leave the United States. Russwurm arrived in Liberia in November 1829 and by 1830 had become the editor of the *Liberia Herald,* one of the major newspapers in the colony. In 1833, he married Sarah McGill. They would have four children.

Russwurm worked as editor of the *Herald* until 1836, when he became governor of the Maryland Settlement in Liberia. He resided at Cape Palmas, the major town of the colony. Russwurm would remain governor of the Maryland Settlement until his death on June 9, 1851.

Further Reading

Aptheker, Herbert. *Abolitionism: A Revolutionary Movement.* Boston: Twayne Publishers, 1989.

Asante, Molefi K. *100 Greatest African Americans: A Biographical Encyclopedia.* Amherst, N.Y.: Prometheus, 2003.

Beyan, Amos. *African American Settlements in West Africa: John Brown Russwurm and the American Civilizing Efforts.* New York: Palgrave, 2005.

Bowdoin College. "John Brown Russwurm Collection." Available online. URL: http://library.bowdoin.edu/arch/mss/jbrg.shtml. Downloaded July 15, 2009.

Sagarin, Mary. *John Brown Russwurm: The Story of Freedom's Journal, Freedom's Journey.* New York: Lothrop, Lee & Shepard, 1970.

Rustin, Bayard
(1912–1987) *civil rights activist*

Bayard Rustin was one of the most important behind-the-scenes strategists in the movement for civil rights that peaked with passage of the Civil Rights Act and Voting Rights Act of 1964 and 1965. Born in West Chester, Pennsylvania, on March 17, 1912, Rustin was the son of Archie Hopkins and Florence Rustin. Florence Rustin

Bayard Rustin ca. 1963. Cofounder of the Congress of Racial Equality (CORE), Rustin was the primary organizer of the 1963 March on Washington. *(Library of Congress, Prints and Photographs Division, LC-U9-10332)*

been accused, on flimsy evidence, of raping a white woman in Alabama during a train trip in 1931. Impressed by the efforts of the American Communist Party in defending the Scottsboro Boys, Rustin joined the party in 1936. He worked for the Young Communist League until 1941, when, on the advice of labor leader ASA PHILIP RANDOLPH, he quit the party.

The same year he quit the Communist Party, Rustin began working with Randolph's Brotherhood of Sleeping Car Porters, a union of African-American railroad workers. Rustin also became involved with the Fellowship of Reconciliation (FOR), a liberal group involved in various social causes. Rustin became FOR's race relations secretary and toured the United States promoting civil rights for minorities. In 1941, Rustin helped Randolph organize what was to be a March on Washington to protest racial discrimination in the U.S. Armed Forces. However, at the last moment, this march was called off when President Franklin Roosevelt issued an executive order that banned racial discrimination in the defense industries and the federal government, an act that benefited numerous African-American workers.

Not content to work solely with FOR or with Randolph, Rustin and two other FOR members, JAMES LEONARD FARMER, JR., and George Houser, founded the Congress of Racial Equality (CORE) in 1942. Rustin was unable to do much work with CORE at that time because he was arrested when he refused to be drafted into the U.S. Army in 1942. A pacifist, he had been taught by his Quaker grandparents that warfare and killing were immoral. He refused induction into the army on religious grounds and spent three years in prison for this decision.

Out of prison by 1947, Rustin immediately plunged into civil rights work. With his CORE comrades, he organized the Journey of Reconciliation, a multistate test of a recent Supreme Court decision that forbade racial discrimination in interstate transportation. Racially integrated teams of protesters boarded buses in North

was 17 and unmarried when she gave birth, and Bayard was raised by his Quaker grandparents, Janifer and Julia Rustin. Rustin did not know that Florence, who he thought was his sister, was his mother until he was 10 years old.

After graduation from high school in 1930, Rustin entered Wilberforce University, a historically black college, in 1932. Rustin left Wilberforce in 1936 before completing his studies. Moving to New York City, he enrolled in the City College of New York but never earned a degree from that or any other college.

Already experienced as a civil rights activist during his youth in West Chester, where he protested with his grandparents against local laws discriminating against blacks, Rustin became involved in the trial of the Scottsboro Boys soon after he moved to New York. The Scottsboro Boys were nine young African-American men who had

Carolina—blacks sitting in the front, which was set aside for whites only, and whites sitting in the back, which was the "black" section of the buses. State and local police arrested Rustin and numerous others. Rustin spent almost a month in jail and was sent out to work on a chain gang.

A homosexual, Rustin experienced discrimination and persecution because of his sexual orientation. After he was arrested on a sex charge in 1953, he was fired from the position he held at FOR. However, because of his skill and courage as an organizer, he soon found work at the War Resisters League and continued to work with A. Philip Randolph.

In 1956, Rustin began a 12-year-long association with MARTIN LUTHER KING, JR. That year Rustin traveled to Montgomery, Alabama, to help King organize the Montgomery bus boycott, one of the opening salvos in what would become a nationwide campaign of protest on behalf on full rights for African Americans. By 1957, King, with Rustin's help, had prevailed in Montgomery and won agreement from city fathers to end racial segregation on the city's buses. Emboldened, King and Rustin founded the Southern Christian Leadership Conference (SCLC), arguably the most important civil rights protest organization of the 1950s and 1960s.

Although not directly employed by SCLC, Rustin worked tirelessly behind the scenes to organize many SCLC protests. In 1963, Rustin organized the March on Washington for Jobs and Freedom, an event that showed the nation the determination of the civil rights crusaders. On August 28, more than a dozen civil rights leaders from a wide range of organizations spoke to 200,000 people gathered at the steps of the Lincoln Memorial. Carried on nationwide television, the highlight of that day was King's "I Have a Dream" speech.

Rustin continued civil rights work into the late 1960s, 1970s, and 1980s. In 1964, he was appointed director of the A. Philip Randolph Institute, a civil rights organization funded by the American Federation of Labor-Congress of Industrial Organizations (AFL-CIO). During the late 1960s, he organized protests against the Vietnam War, and in the late 1970s and early 1980s he worked to help refugees fleeing from Vietnam and Cambodia. By the early 1980s, Rustin had turned his attention to the gay rights movement, declaring, "The barometer of where one is on human rights questions is no longer the black community, it's the gay community. Because it is the community which is most easily mistreated." Bayard Rustin died in New York City on August 24, 1987.

In 2003, directors Nancy Kates and Bennet Singer released their film *Brother Outsider: The Life of Bayard Rustin*. The film chronicles Rustin's lifelong struggle to overcome discrimination. The documentary was shown at the prestigious Sundance Film Festival and won many awards.

Further Reading

Bayard Rustin Fund. "Bayard Rustin." Available online. URL: http://www.rustin.org/?page=id=2. Downloaded July 15, 2009.

D'Emilio, John. *Lost Prophet: The Life and Times of Bayard Rustin*. New York: Simon & Schuster, 2003.

Levine, Daniel. *Bayard Rustin and the Civil Rights Movement*. New Brunswick, N.J.: Rutgers University Press, 2000.

PBS. "Brother Outsider: The Life of Bayard Rustin." Available online. URL: http://www.pbs.org/pov/brotheroutsider/. Downloaded July 15, 2009.

S

Sash, Moses

(1755–unknown) *farmer, community activist*

A farmer in rural western Massachusetts, Moses Sash is noteworthy for the leading role he seems to have taken in Shays's Rebellion, the first major instance of civil unrest that occurred after the United States won its independence from Britain. He was born in Stoughton, Massachusetts, in 1755, to Moses and Sarah Colly Sash. His parents and grandparents were free blacks who farmed around Stoughton, in eastern Massachusetts. There are no records to indicate whether Sash was educated or the extent of his education.

By 1777, Sash seems to have moved to Cummington in Hampshire County in western Massachusetts. In August of that year, he enlisted as a private in a regiment of the American revolutionary army that was fighting the British during the War of Independence. He spent more than three years in this regiment, commanded by Colonel Ruggles Woodbridge.

After the war, Sash returned to farming in western Massachusetts, and it appears that he became a well-known and respected member of the community. It was a difficult time for all farmers in that part of the state. The war had imposed burdens on the state treasury. To collect money to pay this debt, state authorities, the most powerful of whom were located on the coast and in the capital of Boston, imposed harsh taxes on landholders. Furthermore, former soldiers were not paid for their service during the war. These conditions angered western farmers and penalized them doubly—as war veterans and as landowners.

In 1786, Daniel Shays, one of Moses Sash's neighbors, organized an armed uprising among farmers in western Massachusetts to protest the seizure of land by state authorities from farmers who could not pay their state taxes. One of Shays's chief lieutenants was Moses Sash. This revolt lasted into the early part of 1787 but was put down by troops of the Massachusetts state militia.

State records show that Sash was indicted for his part in the insurrection. However, he was never tried because of pardons issued by the new governor, John Hancock, to most participants in the conflict. Sash seems to have remained in Hampshire County for the rest of his life. There is no record of his death.

Further Reading

Calliope Film Resources. "Shays's Rebellion." Available online. URL: http://www.calliope.org/shays/shays4.html. Downloaded July 23, 2009.

Logan, Rayford, and Michael Winston. *Dictionary of American Negro Biography.* New York: W. W. Norton, 1982.

Richards, Leonard L. *Shays's Rebellion: The American Revolution's Final Battle.* Philadelphia: University of Pennsylvania Press, 2003.

Saunders, Prince

(ca. 1784–1839) *educator, colonizationist*

A teacher in the northern United States, Prince Saunders became an enthusiast for the colonization of African Americans in Haiti. He devoted much of his later life to this cause. Born in Lebanon, Connecticut, around 1784, Saunders was the son of Cuff and Phyllis Saunders. His father was born in Africa and almost certainly was enslaved for a period in Connecticut but seems to have been freed by the time of Prince's birth.

When Saunders was still a child, the family moved to Thetford, Vermont, where he received a good basic education. Later he studied at Moor's Charity School at Dartmouth College. He taught at a segregated school for blacks in Colchester, Connecticut, then in 1808 moved to Boston to teach at the African School.

Boston broadened Saunders's world. He became active in the African Masonic Lodge, an organization composed of the most successful blacks in the city. He met the wealthy ship captain PAUL CUFFE, and through Cuffe he became convinced that the best solution for the continuing discrimination faced by African Americans was the emigration of American blacks back to Africa.

In 1815, Saunders traveled to England with a delegation of black Masons who were looking into the possibility of organizing missionary work in Africa. In England, Saunders met William Wilberforce, a prominent opponent of slavery and the slave trade. Wilberforce suggested to Saunders that Haiti rather than Africa would be the best place for emigrating African Americans to go when they left the United States. Haiti had undergone its own revolution against its colonial master, France, and now was an independent nation, the only independent black nation in the Western Hemisphere at that time.

In 1816, Saunders left England and sailed to Haiti to meet King Henri Christophe, the ruler of Haiti. At first, the two men got on well. Saunders set up a school and began teaching Haitians and training other teachers. Later that year, full of enthusiasm about his experiences, he returned to England to recruit other teachers. While in England, he published *Haytian Papers,* a translation of the laws decreed by Henri Christophe for Haiti.

On his return to Haiti in December 1816, Saunders found that his publication of *Haytian Papers* had upset Christophe. Nonetheless, Saunders was allowed to continue his educational work in Haiti. In 1818, Saunders went to Boston to recruit teachers and African Americans willing to immigrate to Haiti. Apparently not finding much interest, he settled in Philadelphia, where he continued his colonization work.

Saunders returned to Haiti in 1820, but shortly thereafter Henri Christophe was overthrown in a revolt of his own army and committed suicide. Without a patron in a position of political power, Saunders's colonization schemes languished. He returned to Philadelphia at least one more time but seems to have recruited few people willing to follow him to the place he once called "the paradise of the New World."

By 1823, Saunders seems to have settled more or less permanently in Haiti. Little is known about the 16 years he spent there before his death. Most likely, he was the principal of a school. He died in Port-au-Prince, Haiti, in 1839.

Further Reading

Duffy, John J., Samuel B. Hand, and Ralph H. Orth. *The Vermont Encyclopedia.* Lebanon, N.H.: University Press of New England, 2003.

Scott, Emmett Jay

(1873–1957) *journalist, business leader, administrator*

A journalist in Texas, Emmett Scott became a trusted aide to BOOKER TALIAFERRO WASHINGTON, the most important African-American leader of the late 19th and early 20th centuries. After Washington's death, Scott pursued a career as a businessman, university administrator, and political operative. Born in Houston, Texas, on February 13, 1873, Emmett Jay Scott was the son of Horace and Emma Scott. After graduating from high school at the age of 14, he enrolled in Wiley College in Marshall, Texas, in 1887. Scott studied for a B.A. at Wiley for three years but dropped out to become a reporter at the white-owned *Houston Post* for three years. At the age of 21, Scott founded his own paper, the *Houston Freeman*, which was marketed to that city's black community. He edited the *Freeman* for three years.

After impressing Booker T. Washington by organizing a well-run appearance by him in Houston, Scott was hired as Washington's personal assistant in 1897. He moved to Tuskegee, Alabama, with his new bride, Eleanora Baker. The couple would have five children.

Very quickly, the efficient Scott made himself indispensable to Washington. He answered correspondence, arranged meetings, handled Washington's schedule, and acted as an adviser on the most sensitive and important topics. Scott was probably the most essential part of what was called the Tuskegee Machine, the network of African-American churches, newspapers, educational institutions, and politicians who owed allegiance to Booke T. Washington and supported his worldview about race relations in the United States.

The basis of Washington's philosophy was a trade with white authorities between the absence of civil rights and economic advancement. A firm believer that blacks could and must pull themselves up by the bootstraps through education, job training, and entrepreneurship, Washington brokered an unwritten agreement with white establishment figures. In exchange for his acceptance of racial segregation and greatly hindered voting rights for blacks, he asked for money to be spent on schools and job training. To prop up this agreement, he relied on sympathetic African-American newspapers and black politicians who would promote this agenda.

Scott was the extremely busy emissary who held all of this together. He was sent on countless secret missions to talk to white and black politicians, newspaper editors, and church leaders. He also orchestrated attacks on African-American editors and civil rights leaders who denounced Washington as too timid about attacking civil rights violations directly.

When Washington died in 1915, Scott remained at Tuskegee for two years before being appointed special assistant to the secretary of war for Negro affairs during World War I. After the war, he was hired as business manager of Howard University in Washington, D.C., a position he held until he retired in 1938.

Scott, true to Washington's self-help philosophy, actively pursued a business career from 1900. Secretary of the Tuskegee-run National Negro Business League, he also was the owner or part-owner of a number of businesses, including the Afro-American Realty Company of Harlem; the *Voice of the Negro* magazine; the Bank of Mound Bayou, Mississippi; and the Standard Life Insurance Company.

Scott was a lifelong Republican and active as a National Convention delegate in the Republican Party during Washington's lifetime. During World War II, Scott was rewarded for his efforts on behalf of the party by being appointed manager of Yard Number Four, an all-black construction unit in the Sun Shipbuilding Company of Chester, Pennsylvania. Sun was owned by John H. Pew, a major contributor to the Republican Party.

After the war Scott retired from politics and hands-on business. He died on December 12, 1957.

Further Reading

Handbook of Texas Online. "Emmett J. Scott." Available online. URL: http://www.tsha.utexas.edu/ handbook/online/articles/view/SS/fsc42.html. Downloaded July 23, 2009.

Wintz, Carry D., and Paul Finkelman, eds. *Encyclopedia of the Harlem Renaissance.* New York: Taylor & Francis, 2004.

Shadd, Mary Ann
(Mary Shadd Cary)
(1823–1893) *abolitionist, publisher, educator*

Although she was a teacher and school principal for many years, Mary Ann Shadd was best known as a writer and editor of the *Provincial Freeman,* a newspaper marketed to fugitive slaves and exiled free blacks in Canada just before the American Civil War. Born on October 9, 1823, in Wilmington, Delaware, Shadd was the daughter of Abraham Doros and Harriet Schad, free blacks living in a slave state. (She used a different spelling of the last name.)

Because there were no schools for African Americans in Delaware, Shadd's parents sent her to a Quaker school in Pennsylvania when she was 10. When Shadd finished her schooling in Pennsylvania at age 16, she returned to Wilmington and organized a private school there. In the 1840s, she continued her teaching career in New York City and Pennsylvania. She also became active in the movement to abolish slavery and was an opponent of the plan to send African Americans to the colony of Liberia on the west coast of Africa.

In 1850, when the U.S. Congress passed the Fugitive Slave Law, which required northern states to arrest and return runaway slaves to their owners in the South, Shadd and her brother, Isaac, decided to immigrate to Canada to live in a community of African-American exiles. They moved to Chatham, a town in Ontario province in an area known as Canada West. The town and surrounding area had already become a magnet for

Mary Ann Shadd, a teacher and principal in Washington, D.C., was editor of the *Provincial Freeman,* the most important voice of exiled African Americans living in Canada before the Civil War. *(Moorland-Spingarn Research Center, Howard University)*

escaped slaves from the United States as well as free blacks such as Shadd who had decided that life in the United States had become too dangerous and oppressive.

As Shadd settled into her new life, she began looking for ways to help her new community. One of the first things she did was write *Notes on Canada West,* a book that gave an account of life among African-American immigrants in Canada and refuted stories about American blacks starving there. In 1853, Shadd began working with Samuel Ringgold Ward to publish the *Provincial Freeman,* a paper aimed at African-American immigrants in Canada and blacks in the United

States who were thinking about moving to Canada. In 1856, she married Thomas Cary. They would have one daughter.

For five years, from 1853 to 1858, when the *Freeman* went out of business, Shadd wrote and edited articles about Canada West, the abolition of slavery, and the place of African Americans in the larger American society. Although a believer in racial pride and self-help, Shadd did not think that African Americans should segregate themselves from the larger white society in Canada or the United States. In articles and speeches, she opposed colonizationists who wanted blacks to go to Africa and black separatists such as HENRY WALTON BIBB who believed that blacks should segregate themselves into all-black communities and have nothing to do with white society.

After the demise of the *Freeman*, Shadd helped write another book, *Voices from Harpers Ferry*, the only account of the Harpers Ferry insurrection from the only survivor of John Brown's raiding party, Osborne Anderson. In 1863, Shadd returned to the United States and was appointed a recruiting officer for the U.S. Army. She helped enlist scores of African-American troops to fight against the South.

After the Civil War, Shadd settled in Washington, D.C., where for many years she worked as a school principal. She also wrote occasional articles for FREDERICK DOUGLASS's newspaper, the *New National Era*. In 1883, at age 60, she was awarded a law degree by Howard University. She also joined the Women's Suffrage Association and campaigned for the right of women to vote. Shadd died on June 5, 1893, in Washington, D.C.

Further Reading

Bearden, Jim. *Shadd: The Life and Times of Mary Shadd Cary.* Toronto: NC Press, 1977.

Davies, Carole Boyce, ed. *Encyclopedia of the African Diaspora: Origins, Experiences, and Culture.* Santa Barbara, Calif.: ABC-CLIO, 2008.

National Park Service. "Mary Ann Shadd Cary House." Available online: URL: http://www.nps.gov/history/ nR/travel/underground/dc2.htm. Downloaded July 23, 2009.

Quarles, Benjamin. *Black Abolitionists.* New York: Oxford, 1969.

Rhodes, Jane. *Mary Ann Shadd Cary: The Black Press and Protest in the Nineteenth Century.* Bloomington: Indiana University Press, 1998.

Sharpton, Al
(Alfred Charles Sharpton, Jr.)
(1954–   ) *civil rights activist*

A controversial and outspoken activist, Alfred ("Al") Charles Sharpton, Jr., has reached beyond his New York City base to attempt to become a national civil rights leader. However, because of his past actions, he is not highly regarded by many whites, and some African Americans doubt his integrity. Sharpton was born in Brooklyn, New York, in 1954, into a middle-class family. He was educated at public schools and was active in his church.

Sharpton began his public speaking career at age four, when he gave a sermon at the Washington Temple Church in Brooklyn. Groomed for a career as a preacher, Sharpton had become junior pastor of the Washington Temple Church by the age of nine. However, in 1964, when Sharpton was 10, his parents separated, and Sharpton moved with his mother into a housing project. Together, mother and son would struggle to survive during Sharpton's adolescent years. During this time, Sharpton continued his preaching career in Pentecostal churches and became known as the "boy wonder." He appeared with such notable gospel singers as Mahalia Jackson.

Sharpton ventured into civil rights activism in 1969 at age 15 when he began working as a youth director for JESSE JACKSON's Operation Breadbasket. In 1971, he founded his own organization, the National Youth Movement, which worked on voter registration drives and job training for African-American young people in New York

City. He would lead the National Youth Movement until 1988.

After graduation from high school in 1972, Sharpton attended Brooklyn College for several years before dropping out. In 1974, he became touring manager for soul singer James Brown. Sharpton entered politics in New York State in 1978 when at age 24 he ran for a seat in the New York State Senate. After losing this race, Sharpton turned to organizing protests around civil rights issues in New York.

During the 1980s and 1990, Sharpton, who previously had been a relatively unknown and obscure figure, became famous for his flamboyant personality, loud and often loose talk, and shameless media posturing. Never deeply concerned with long-term strategy, Sharpton instead developed the tactic of showing up soon after the occurrence of racial incidents to protest the treatment of black citizens. His protests often seemed to many observers to aggravate tense conditions rather than to attempt reconciliation and long-lasting solutions.

The first of the incidents that propelled Sharpton into the media spotlight occurred in Howard Beach, a mainly white community in Brooklyn, where in 1986 a black man named Michael Griffiths was chased through the streets by a mob of white men. Run out onto an expressway, Griffiths was struck by a car and killed. Sharpton and his supporters immediately went to Howard Beach to hold demonstrations demanding an investigation of the incident.

A year later, Sharpton plunged into an incident in Wappingers Falls, New York, that would tar his reputation. After an African-American teenager named Tawana Brawley accused unidentified white men of abducting and raping her, Sharpton descended on Wappingers Falls and began to orchestrate a media campaign on behalf of Brawley against local authorities. He and attorney Alton Maddox accused police officers of having raped Brawley, then further accused the local prosecutor, Stephen Pagones, of covering up the

officers' crimes. However, a local grand jury could find no evidence linking any police officer to Brawley's alleged abduction. Several years later, after Brawley admitted that she had fabricated the story, Pagones successfully sued Sharpton for defamation, and Sharpton was ordered to pay part of a $345,000 settlement. Sharpton has never apologized for his role in the Brawley fiasco, other than to say that he often "gave in to being flippant, to shooting from the hip, to overplaying the theatrics and not the issues."

After a black man, Yusuf Hawkins, was killed by whites in Brooklyn in 1989, Sharpton organized another series of protest marches calling for an investigation of the incident. These demonstrations lasted off and on for two years and ended only when Sharpton was stabbed by a white assailant during a march. By his own account, the stabbing seems to have mellowed Sharpton. "It really came home to me that if you're going to die for something, you ought to make sure that it's more than some slogans and some loud talking—that you really get something done," Sharpton said. "I made up in my mind that I was going to try to make a difference."

Since then, Sharpton has returned to electoral politics. He ran for the Senate from New York in 1992 and 1994, and in 1997 he ran for mayor of New York City, all unsuccessful bids. Sharpton entered the Democratic presidential primary in 2003. He participated in early primaries and debates but withdrew from the race in March 2004. The following year, he agreed to return $100,000 in public campaign funds because his personal spending for the campaign exceeded legal limits. In 2009, the Federal Election Commission levied a $285,000 fine for his campaign's poor record-keeping and other irregularities. That same year, Sharpton arrived at a settlement with the Internal Revenue Service to repay part of the more than $1 million in back taxes allegedly owed by Sharpton and his business.

Sharpton did not give up ad hoc civil rights protests. In 1997, he showed up on the streets to protest the brutal treatment of a Haitian immigrant, Abner Louima, by New York City police. In 2001, he was jailed for 90 days for his protests in Puerto Rico against the continued use of the U.S. Navy bombing range in Vieques, a small island near Puerto Rico. In 2008, Sharpton led a slowdown march to protest the acquittal of three New York City detectives who had been charged in the 2005 death of Sean Bell, an unarmed African-American man shot by police outside a nightclub. Sharpton and more than 200 other protesters were arrested. In 2010, Sharpton delivered the eulogy at the funeral of a five-year-old girl who had been killed during a police raid. Sharpton asserted that the girl's death "should be a wake-up call not only for those in authority, but for those of us in the community who have allowed this violence and recklessness to go on too long."

Further Reading

Domenico, Roy Palmer, and Mark Y. Hanley, eds. *Encyclopedia of Modern Christian Politics*. Westport, Conn.: Greenwood, 2006.

Greenfield-Sanders, Timothy, and Elvis Mitchell. *The Black List*. New York: Atria, 2008.

National Action Network. "Rev. Al Sharpton: President & Founder." Available online. URL: http://www.nationalactionnetwork.net/about_leadership_sharpton.html. Downloaded July 23, 2009.

Sharpton, Al, and Anthony Walton. *Go and Tell the Pharaoh: The Autobiography of Reverend Al Sharpton*. New York: Doubleday, 1996.

Sharpton, Al, and Karen Hunter. *Al on America*. New York: Dafina Books, 2003.

Shuttlesworth, Fred Lee

(1922–   ) *civil rights leader, community activist, minister*

A native of Alabama, Fred Lee Shuttlesworth was a key leader in the movement for civil rights in the South in the late 1950s and early 1960s. Born in Birmingham, Alabama, in 1922, Shuttlesworth received his college education in his home state. He enrolled in Selma State University in 1940, earning a B.A. from that school in 1944; he later earned a degree from Alabama State Teachers College.

By the 1950s, Shuttlesworth had become a preacher at the Bethel Baptist Church in Birmingham, Alabama. A fiery and passionate speaker, he began a campaign to end the practice of racial segregation in Birmingham's schools after the Supreme Court decision to outlaw school desegregation in *Brown v. the Board of Education of Topeka* in 1954.

In 1956, Shuttlesworth founded the Alabama Christian Movement for Human Rights, an organization he used to push for civil rights. In response, white racists firebombed his house. Fortunately none of his family was injured. The next year, Shuttlesworth helped found the Southern Christian Leadership Conference (SCLC), which would soon be headed by MARTIN LUTHER KING, JR.

In 1957, while attempting to enroll his daughter in a segregated public school in Birmingham, Shuttlesworth and his wife were attacked by a white mob. Shuttlesworth was beaten with a chain and his wife was stabbed. Both recovered, and in spite of constant pressure on him from local authorities, Shuttlesworth pressed ahead with the drive to end racial discrimination. According to Shuttlesworth, "Several times they put a vagrancy warrant against me to keep me in jail. But I was a full-time pastor, so after two or three days, they'd charge me with something else.... I was in jail so many times, I quit counting after twenty. But I knew what they were doing, and it wasn't going to stop me."

The efforts to force desegregation in Birmingham reached a climax in 1963. That year, Shuttlesworth began a series of ongoing street demonstrations protesting racial segregation in all of its forms. Shuttlesworth organized local black youth to take the lead in these peaceful, nonviolent demonstrations. Many were beaten, attacked by police dogs, and knocked over by water from fire hoses as the Birmingham police—under the leadership of its director, Eugene "Bull" Connor—tried to break the spirit of the demonstrators. In September of that year, four young African-American girls were killed when a bomb exploded at the 16th Street Baptist Church, one of the centers of the Birmingham protests.

The ugly violence directed against Shuttlesworth and his followers repulsed whites in other parts of the United States and generated sympathy for the Civil Rights movement. This sympathy would ultimately be expressed in the Civil Rights Act of 1964 and the Voting Rights Act of 1965, which put teeth into a federal effort to destroy legalized racial discrimination once and for all.

In the 1960s, Shuttlesworth moved to Cincinnati to take a job as a preacher at churches in that city. In 1988, he founded the Shuttlesworth Housing Foundation, which has raised money to help more than 400 poor families buy homes.

From 2003 to 2004, Shuttlesworth served as interim president of the SCLC. In 2006, he retired and returned to Birmingham. In 2008, the Birmingham Airport Authority honored the veteran civil rights leader by renaming the airport. It is now known as the Birmingham-Shuttlesworth International Airport.

Further Reading

Encyclopedia of Alabama. "Fred Lee Shuttlesworth." Available online. URL: http://www.encyclopediaofalabama.org/face/Article.jsp?id=h-1093. Downloaded July 23, 2009.

Manis, Andrew M. *A Fire You Can't Put Out: The Civil Rights Life of Birmingham's Reverend Fred Shuttlesworth.* Birmingham: University of Alabama Press, 1999.

White, Majorie Longenecker, and Andrew Michael Manis, eds. *Birmingham Revolutionaries: The Reverend Fred Shuttlesworth and the Alabama Christian Movement for Human Rights.* Macon, Ga.: Mercer University Press, 2000.

Simmons, Ruth J.

(1945–) *educator, Brown University president*

A lifelong educator and scholar of African and Caribbean writing, Ruth J. Simmons is a leader in American higher education. Born on July 3, 1945, in the small East Texas town of Grapeland, Simmons moved with her parents to Houston when she was a child. A diligent student, she attended public schools there and, with the support of her parents, excelled in her studies.

After graduating from high school in 1963, Simmons enrolled in Dillard University in New Orleans. She graduated summa cum laude with a B.A. in Romance languages in 1967, then was

Ruth Simmons, a leading American educator, is president of Brown University. *(Courtesy Brown University, photo by Clark Quin)*

accepted in the graduate program at Harvard University. Concentrating her studies on the works of writers such as David Diop and Aimé Césaire, Simmons earned an M.A. in 1971 and a Ph.D. in 1973.

After briefly serving as an interpreter at the U.S. State Department, Simmons began her teaching career at the University of New Orleans as an assistant professor of French. From 1977 to 1979, she was an associate professor at California State University Northridge in Los Angeles, where she also served as acting director of the international studies program. After four years as the associate dean of graduate studies at the University of Southern California, Simmons moved back east to Princeton University in 1983. She would eventually become vice-provost at Princeton. In 1995, she was hired as president of Smith College.

During her career as an education administrator, Simmons has been an unabashed supporter of opening the doors of higher education to women and minorities. At Smith, a women's college, she worked tirelessly to raise $300 million, much of which was used to establish an engineering school. She nearly doubled African-American enrollment at Smith by personally visiting predominantly black neighborhoods in cities around the country to recruit students. An advocate of openly discussing racial problems and trying to resolve racial conflict on campus, Simmons has vetoed racially exclusive dormitories and supported campus organizations that host open and civil discussions of racially divisive issues. "There's no safe ground for anybody in race relations," she says. "But campuses, unlike any other institution in our society, provide the opportunity to cross racial lines. And even if you're hurt, you can't walk away. You have to walk over that line."

In 2000, Brown University hired Simmons as president. She was the first African American to head an Ivy League school. She spearheaded a $1.4 billion fund-raising campaign to improve the university's academic programs. Under Sim-

mons's leadership, the funding goal was reached in 2009.

Further Reading

Brown University. "Office of the President." Available online. URL: http://www.brown.edu/Administration/President/. Downloaded July 20, 2009.

Hine, Darlene Clark, ed. *Black Women in America*. New York: Oxford University Press, 2005.

Morse, Jodie. "Campus Crusader." *Time*. Available online. URL: http://www.time.com/time/magazine/article/0,9171,1000831,00.html. Downloaded July 20, 2009.

Singleton, Benjamin
(Pap Singleton)
(1809–1892) *community activist, Kansas Exoduster*

A community activist in Tennessee, Pap Singleton gained renown as the front man for the promotion of African-American migration out of the South to the plains of Kansas. Benjamin Singleton was born into slavery in 1809 in Nashville, Tennessee. Little is known of his early life or his parents. He apparently was sold a number of times, often to owners in the Deep South. The young Singleton managed to escape from his new owners at least twice and made his way back to Nashville. Sometime before the Civil War, perhaps in the 1830s or 1840s, he escaped from bondage permanently, settling in Detroit, Michigan. There, he worked at odd jobs and ran a boardinghouse.

At the end of the Civil War, Singleton, now almost 60, returned to Nashville. Protected by the federal occupation of the city, he and several colleagues set up a real estate company that tried to purchase high-quality farmlands for sale to newly freed slaves. This project failed when whites refused to sell their land.

In the early 1870s, Singleton became aware of several black families from Nashville who had migrated to Kansas to homestead cheap land that was offered for sale by the federal government. Quickly realizing the potential for profit, he organized a real estate company and began promoting the value of Kansas as a site for African-American settlement.

Between 1877 and 1879, Singleton printed thousands of fliers that were distributed in Tennessee, Mississippi, Louisiana, and Texas promoting land in Cherokee and other counties in Kansas. What began as a slow trickle of migrants turned into a deluge by 1879, when thousands of southern blacks from Mississippi, Louisiana, and Texas made the journey to Kansas. These later migrants were known as the Exodusters, and their trip was fueled by religious fervor as they imagined themselves following in the footsteps of Moses and the Jews who left bondage in Egypt for freedom in Israel.

Benjamin Singleton promoted black immigration from the South to Kansas during the 1870s. The families who went west at this time were known as Exodusters. *(Courtesy the Kansas State Historical Society)*

By 1881, Singleton was living in a part of Topeka, Kansas, that, because of the large number of black Tennessee natives living there, was known as Tennessee Town. For a while, he organized a group called United Colored Links, which sought to promote industrial development in Tennessee Town. Because of lack of funds, this venture lasted less than a year.

Between 1883 and 1887, Singleton promoted several immigration schemes for American blacks. Singleton's Chief League attempted to arrange a colony for blacks in the Mediterranean island of Cyprus. In a later venture called the Trans-Atlantic Society, Singleton tried to take African-Americans to the "Fatherland" of Africa. "The sons and daughters of Ham," a Trans-Atlantic brochure promised, "may return to their God-given inheritance, and Ethiopia regain her ancient renown. . . . We shall not die out. We shall not wear out." Neither of these organizations lasted more than a few years nor transported any immigrants out of the United States.

Singleton died in Saint Louis in 1892 at the age of 83.

Further Reading

Entz, Gary R. "Benjamin 'Pap' Singleton: Father of the Kansas Exodus." In *The Human Tradition in America: 1865 to the Present,* edited by Charles William Calhoun, 13–28. New York: Rowman & Littlefield, 2003.

Kansas State Historical Society. "Benjamin 'Pap' Singleton: A Kansas Portrait." Available online. URL: http://www.kshs.org/portraits/singleton_benjamin.htm. Downloaded July 23, 2009.

Painter, Nell Irvin. *Black Migration to Kansas after Reconstruction.* New York: Knopf, 1977.

PBS. *The West.* "Benjamin 'Pap' Singleton." Available online. URL: http://www.pbs.org/weta/thewest/people/s_z/singleton.htm. Downloaded July 23, 2009.

Yount, Lisa. *Frontier of Freedom: African Americans in the West.* New York: Facts On File, 1997.

Smith, Harry Clay

(1863–1941) *publisher, civil rights activist*

The founder of the *Cleveland Gazette,* Harry Smith was one of the most outspoken advocates of equal rights for African Americans in the late 19th and early 20th centuries. Harry Clay Smith was born on January 28, 1863, in West Virginia but lived for most of his life in Cleveland, Ohio, a city he moved to with his parents when he was a child. After graduating from Cleveland's Central High School in 1881, Smith plunged into the world of newspaper publishing when he founded his own paper, the *Cleveland Gazette,* in 1882. He would remain the owner and editor of the *Gazette* for the rest of his life.

Smith quickly made the *Gazette* the premier African-American newspaper in Ohio. An eight-page weekly, the *Gazette* covered African-American social life, business, and politics in Cleveland as well as other cities in Ohio. Smith used the *Gazette* to promote his views about race relations in Ohio and the United States at large. He was an uncompromising believer in demanding full and complete civil rights for African Americans. Unlike BOOKER TALIAFERRO WASHINGTON, who was arguably the most important black leader at that time, Smith did not think that African Americans should back down from demanding their rights. He favored political pressure, lawsuits, and boycotts of businesses that discriminated against blacks as the best ways to achieve parity with white Americans.

Smith was also active in Republican Party politics in Ohio. As did most blacks of his time, Smith viewed the Republicans, the party of Lincoln, as the friend of African Americans. In 1885, Smith was given a political patronage job, as deputy inspector of oils, as reward for his work in helping a Republican be elected as governor. He ran for the Ohio legislature in 1894 and won. He would serve in that body from 1894 to 1898 and again from 1900 to 1902. His greatest achievement was persuading the legislature to pass an antilynching act, the Anti–Mob Violence Act, in 1896.

Embittered by President Theodore Roosevelt's treatment of African-American soldiers after a racial incident in Brownsville, Texas, in 1906, Smith gradually soured on the Republicans. In 1924, he supported Robert LaFollett, the Progressive Party candidate, in his run for the presidency. Smith ran for governor of Ohio four times during the 1920s. He lost every race.

One of the founders of the Afro-American League in 1890, Smith later was a supporter of W. E. B. DuBois's Niagara Movement, which was founded in 1905. When the Niagara Movement morphed into the National Association for the Advancement of Colored People (NAACP), Smith served on committees of that organization. He died in Cleveland on December 10, 1941.

Further Reading

African-American Experience in Ohio. "The Gazette." Available online. URL: http://dbs.ohiohistory.org/ africanam/nwspaper/gazette.cfm. Downloaded July 23, 2009.

Giffin, William W. *African Americans and the Color Line in Ohio, 1915–1930.* Columbus: Ohio State University Press, 2005.

Murray, Percy E. *Harry Clay Smith: Black Journalist and Legislator.* Oxford, Ohio: Miami University Press, 1997.

Ohio History Central. "Harry C. Smith." Available online. URL: http://www.ohiohistorycentral.org/ entry.php?rec=345. Downloaded July 23, 2009.

Still, William

(1821–1902) *abolitionist, community activist, writer*

The author of *The Underground Railroad,* one of the best books about the system that helped fugitive slaves escape from bondage before the Civil War, William Still was also an important leader in the African-American community in Philadelphia. Still, the youngest of 18 children, was born in 1821 in Burlington County, New Jersey, to Levin and Sidney Still. Still's father was a former slave who had purchased his freedom, and his mother was an escaped slave.

In 1844, when he was 23, Still moved to Philadelphia, where he found work as a handyman and secretary for the Pennsylvania Society for the Abolition of Slavery. He soon made it his job to secure temporary accommodations and food for escaped slaves who would stop in Philadelphia on their journey through the Underground Railroad to upstate New York, Massachusetts, and Canada. He married Letitia George in 1847; they would have four children.

After the passage of the Fugitive Slave Law in 1850, Still was named chairman of the Philadelphia Vigilance Committee, a group that protected free blacks and fugitive slaves from arrest by southern bounty hunters. An astute businessman, Still opened a store that sold heaters at the beginning of the Civil War and founded a successful retail coal business.

After the war, Still wrote about his experiences in the Underground Railroad and told of the many former slaves he had met during his days with the Vigilance Committee in Philadelphia. One of these was his own brother, Peter Still, who had been left behind by his mother when she had fled slavery in the early 1800s. *The Underground Railroad* proved to be a hit, selling out three editions.

During and after the war, Still played an important role as a leader of the Philadelphia African-American community. He led a successful campaign, which culminated in a bill in the Pennsylvania legislature, to ban racial discrimination on rail cars in Pennsylvania. He also organized an early Young Men's Christian Association (YMCA) for African Americans in 1890 and served on the boards of homes for elderly blacks and abandoned African-American children. He died on July 14, 1902.

Further Reading

Darby Historical Commission. "William Still, Darby, and the Desegration of Philadelphia Streetcars." Available online. URL: http://www.darbyhistory.com/. Downloaded July 23, 2009.

Khan, Lurey. *One day, Levin . . . He Be Free; William Still and the Underground Railroad.* New York: E. P. Dutton, 1972.

Quarles, Benjamin. *Black Abolitionists.* New York: Oxford, 1969.

Rodriguez, Junius P., ed. *Slavery in the United States: A Social, Political, and Historical Encyclopedia.* Santa Barbara, Calif.: ABC-CLIO, 2007.

William Still Underground Railroad Foundation. "Still, William." Available online. URL: http://www.undergroundrr.com/stillbiofr.html. Downloaded July 23, 2009.

Straker, David Augustus
(1842–1908) *civil rights activist, lawyer*

A politically active lawyer in South Carolina, David Straker moved to Detroit, Michigan, after the end of Reconstruction and built a successful career as a lawyer, politician, and newspaper publisher. Born in Bridgetown, Barbados, in 1842, David Augustus Straker was the son of John and Margaret Straker. He graduated from Codrington, a college in Barbados, in 1863 and then served several years as principal of a high school.

In 1868, Straker moved to the United States to take a job as a teacher at a school for former slaves in Louisville, Kentucky. After a year there, he enrolled in the law school at Howard University in Washington, D.C., and he earned a law degree from that institution in 1871. That year he also married Annie M. Carey, with whom he would adopt a daughter.

After working several years as a clerk for the U.S. Post Office in Washington, in 1875 Straker moved to South Carolina to join a law firm in Orangeburg, a city in the south-central part of that state. At this time, the Reconstruction era in the South had already peaked, although some federal troops remained in the South to protect black activists and officeholders. Straker was elected to the South Carolina legislature in 1876 but got caught up in a compromise that threw the presidency to Rutherford B. Hayes. In exchange for votes from southern Democrats in the electoral college, Hayes agreed to withdraw federal troops from the South, thus ending an attempt at political and social reform. As a result of this compromise, Straker was denied his legislative seat.

Straker remained active in Republican electoral politics in South Carolina until 1880. That year he accepted a political patronage job as inspector of customs at Charleston. In 1882, he won the position of dean and professor of law at Allen University in Columbia. He also took on private clients and built a reputation as an innovative attorney. He pioneered the use of the temporary insanity defense to exempt a defendant from the guilty penalty in a murder trial.

In 1887, tired of fighting a losing battle against the rising tide of racism in the South, Straker moved to Detroit, where he began a new law practice. Again, he quickly built up a strong reputation as a fine attorney and attracted a racially mixed clientele. He also lectured about the South and wrote *The New South Investigated* (1889), a book about his experiences. In 1889, Straker filed a civil rights lawsuit against a well-known restaurant in Detroit that had refused service in its "white" section to William Ferguson, another African-American man. Although he lost this case in a local court, Straker won it on appeal to the Michigan Supreme Court.

After this court case, Straker won election as a circuit court commissioner in Detroit. He spoke out for full rights for African Americans in Detroit and the nation. He was a founder and first president of the National Federation of Colored Men in 1895. From 1901 to 1908, he expressed his opinions in a newspaper he founded, the *Detroit Advocate*. He died on February 8, 1908, in Detroit.

Further Reading

City of Detroit. "David Augustus Straker Informational Site." Available online. URL: http://www.ci.detroit.mi.us/historic/districts/straker_site.pdf. Downloaded July 23, 2009.

Foner, Eric. *Freedom's Lawmakers: A Dictionary of Black Officeholders during Reconstruction.* New York: Oxford University Press, 1993.

Smith, J. Clay. *Emancipation: The Making of the Black Lawyer, 1844–1944.* Philadelphia: University of Pennsylvania Press, 1999.

T

Terrell, Mary Eliza Church

(1863–1954) *civil rights activist, women's club organizer*

An outspoken advocate for the civil rights of African Americans, Mary Church Terrell was also deeply involved in the struggle for women's suffrage, and she was a notable organizer in the African-American community in Washington, D.C. Born Mary Eliza Church in Memphis, Tennessee, on September 23, 1863, she was the daughter of Robert Reed and Louisa Ayers Church. Her father, a former slave, was a businessman who made a sizable fortune in real estate holdings.

Not wanting to educate his daughter in Memphis's segregated schools, Robert Church sent Mary to primary and secondary schools run by Antioch College in Ohio. After graduating from high school in 1881, she attended Oberlin College, earning a B.A. in 1884 and an M.A. in humanities in 1888.

After teaching French and German at Wilberforce University for several years, Mary Church moved to Washington, D.C., to teach Latin at an African-American high school. In 1891, she married Robert Terrell, a lawyer who would eventually become a judge in Washington.

During the 1890s, Mary Church Terrell became active in the woman's rights and suffrage movement. She helped found the National Association of Colored Women in 1896 and also worked with white women's suffrage advocates

Mary Eliza Church Terrell ca. 1900. Terrell was a leading community activist in Washington, D.C., at the start of the 20th century and later became an advocate of women's suffrage. *(Library of Congress, Prints and Photographs Division, LC-USZ62-54722)*

such as Susan B. Anthony and Jane Addams to agitate for the right to vote for women. She was active in the National American Woman Suffrage Association, and during World War II she picketed the White House, pressing home the demand for the vote.

In 1909, Terrell joined other African-American leaders to form the National Association for the Advancement of Colored People (NAACP). Although she and her husband had been supporters of BOOKER TALIAFERRO WASHINGTON, they believed that Washington's avoidance of confrontation with white authorities was delaying progress in achieving full rights for blacks in the United States.

In her later years, Terrell did not stop her crusade for civil rights. In 1949, she forced the Washington branch of the American Association of University Women, which had never admitted black women, to grant her membership. That same year, she organized pickets to march outside restaurants and department stores that practiced racial segregation. Several of these businesses dropped their segregation policy as a result of Terrell's activities. In 1953, all were forced to integrate as a result of a ruling by the U.S. Supreme Court. Terrell died on July 24, 1954, at the age of 90.

Further Reading

Jones, Beverly Washington. *Quest for Equality: The Life and Writings of Mary Church Terrell*. New York: Carlson, 1900.

Library of Congress. "Mary Church Terrell." Available online. URL: http://memory.loc.gov/ammem/aap/terrell.html. Downloaded July 7, 2009.

Rucker, Walter C., and James N. Upton, eds. *Encyclopedia of American Race Riots*. Westport, Conn.: Greenwood, 2007.

Voices from the Gaps. "Mary Church Terrell." Available online. URL: http://voices.cla.umn.edu/artistpages/terellmary.php. Downloaded August 27, 2010.

Terry, Wallace
(1938–2003) *journalist, author, veterans' rights activist*

The journalist and author Wallace Terry is best known for his eyewitness accounts of the Civil Rights movement and of the experience of black soldiers in the Vietnam War. He was born on April 21, 1938, in New York City. His family later moved to Indianapolis. Terry's love of journalism showed at an early age. He gathered stories from his friends and neighbors and printed a newspaper using a toy printing press. He handed out the newspaper in his neighborhood. When Terry reached high school, he worked on the school paper. The *Shortridge Echo* was one of the few high school newspapers that published daily editions. During summers, he took writing and photography classes at local colleges and attended summer journalism programs. In his senior year, Terry became the first black student at the predominantly white school to be selected as one of the newspaper's editors.

Terry enrolled at Brown University in Providence, Rhode Island. He immediately joined the college newspaper staff. During his freshman year, the Arkansas governor Orval Faubus came to Providence to meet with President Dwight Eisenhower. The president had summoned the governor to meet with him to discuss the crisis arising from efforts to integrate Little Rock's Central High School. The segregationist governor had used his state's National Guard to prevent black students from entering the school. Terry managed to evade Faubus's guards to ask the governor for an interview. Faubus half-heartedly agreed to give an interview the next day and shook Terry's hand. A photograph of the handshake appeared on the front page of the *New York Times*. The *Washington Post* editor Ben Gilbert saw the photograph and contacted Terry, offering him a summer job as copy boy. Terry declined, saying that he was already a reporter. Gilbert then offered him a job as reporter for the summer. Terry accepted and spent the summer reporting in the nation's capital for the *Post*. Returning to Brown, Terry was selected as editor in chief of Brown's *Daily Herald*, becoming the first African American to head the newspaper.

After graduating in 1959, Terry began working full time as a *Washington Post* reporter. During the early 1960s, he covered the Civil Rights movement. As one of the few African-America reporters covering the struggle for equal rights, he gained the confidence of such leaders as MARTIN LUTHER KING, JR., and MEDGAR EVERS. Terry wrote insightful stories about desegregation battles and protests throughout the south. In 1962, he went undercover to provide an insider's account of the Nation of Islam. His story, presented by the *Washington Post* as a weeklong series of articles, introduced white America to the term *black power* and to MALCOLM X, who was almost unknown at the time.

Terry left the *Washington Post* in 1963 to take a job at *Time* magazine. He was the first African American to work as a reporter for a major American newsmagazine. He covered riots in Harlem, Watts, Detroit, and Newark. He interviewed leading black newsmakers, including Martin Luther King, Jr., Lyndon Johnson, Malcolm X, Adam Clayton Powell, and Bobby Seale. In 1967, he arrived in Vietnam as *Time*'s deputy bureau chief. He covered the war for two years. His cover story about black soldiers in Vietnam was hugely successful.

After returning from Vietnam, Terry became a professor of journalism at Howard University. He helped find jobs for his students in major news organizations. He also wrote for *Parade* magazine and *USA Today* and appeared on radio and television shows as a news analyst. The University of Missouri awarded him a medal of honor for distinguished contributions to journalism.

Terry became a tireless advocate for all veterans of the Vietnam War. He served on many national boards and committees that addressed veterans' issues and gave speeches and lectures about the hardships faced by veterans. His book *Bloods: An Oral History of the Vietnam War by Black Veterans* was published in 1984. It received widespread praise and was nominated for a Pulitzer Prize. The book became the basis of a PBS series, *The Bloods of 'Nam,* and a one-man show, "Bloods: An Evening with Wallace Terry," that he performed at colleges around the country. The National Association of Campus Activities named Terry entertainer of the year in 1987. In 2000, he organized a national symposium, Rendezvous with War, that commemorated the 25th anniversary of the end of the Vietnam War.

On May 29, 2003, Terry died at age 65 of a rare disease. His second book, *Missing Pages: Black Journalists of Modern America, An Oral History,* was published in 2007. It presented his interviews with 19 black men and women journalism pioneers. During his career as a reporter and writer, Terry's groundbreaking work enabled many white Americans to look more sympathetically on the lives of blacks. "Bloods achieved what I've always tried to achieve as a journalist," he once said. "[It showed] that the black experience is first and foremost a universal experience."

Further Reading

Maynard Institute. "Wallace Terry." Available online. URL: http://www.mije.org/black_journalists_ movement/wallace_terry. Downloaded June 28, 2009.

Roberts, Gene, and Hank Klibanoff. *The Race Beat: The Press, the Civil Rights Struggle, and the Awakening of a Nation.* New York: Knopf, 2006.

Terry, Wallace. *Missing Pages: Black Journalists of Modern America, An Oral History.* New York: Basic Books, 2007.

Totten, Ashley L.
(1884–1963) *labor organizer*

A Pullman sleeping-car porter, Ashley L. Totten would rise from the ranks of workingmen to become a leader in the struggle to form a union to represent workers against the Pullman Company. Born in 1884 on the island of St. Croix in what was the Danish West Indies (now the U.S. Virgin Islands), Totten was the son of Richard and Camilla Totten. He received a secondary education at a high school in St. Croix.

After his graduation from high school, Totten moved to the United States in 1905. For 10 years he worked at a variety of jobs, but in 1915, then a naturalized citizen, he was hired as a porter by the Pullman Company, an organization that manufactured and operated sleeping cars on most of the railroads in the United States.

The Pullman Company had made it a policy to hire only African Americans as maids and porters in its rail empire. These were relatively well-paid and prestigious jobs, although black porters and maids did not make as much as other rail workers who were white. They also had to work 16-hour days.

By the early 1920s, Totten had begun trying to organize Pullman porters into a union with the goal of attaining better pay and work hours. His efforts were ferociously resisted by the company and condemned even by some African-American newspapers and politicians. After being fired because of his organizing efforts, Totten persuaded ASA PHILIP RANDOLPH, a black radical and labor activist, to head organizing efforts. The Brotherhood of Sleeping Car Porters (BSCP) was formed in 1925 with Randolph as the head and Totten as a key organizer.

Totten and Randolph worked ceaselessly for 12 years to win recognition of the union from the Pullman Company. In the process Totten, who was no longer employed by the company, struggled with poverty and threats from the company. In 1929, he was severely beaten by company thugs during a labor dispute. Although he never fully recovered from this attack, he continued to work for the union. Finally, in 1937, the company cracked under pressure from the Roosevelt administration and recognized the brotherhood, the first time a major American company had recognized an African-American union.

For the next 20 years, Totten served the Brotherhood of Sleeping Car Porters as its secretary-treasurer and vice president. In the late 1950s, he retired to the Virgin Islands, where he died on January 26, 1963.

Further Reading

Kersten, Andrew Edmund. *A. Philip Randolph: A Life in the Vanguard.* Lanham, Md.: Rowman & Littlefield, 2006.

Library of Congress. "Brotherhood of Sleeping Car Porters: A Register of Its Records in the Library of Congress." Available online. URL: http://lcweb2.loc.gov/cgi-bin/query/h?faid/faid:@field(DOCID+ms000016). Downloaded July 1, 2009.

Trévigne, Paul
(1825–1908) *educator, newspaper editor*

A teacher in New Orleans for almost 40 years, Paul Trévigne was best known as the editor of two African-American-owned newspapers published in New Orleans during the 1860s. Trévigne, the son of a veteran of the Battle of New Orleans, was born into a family of free blacks in New Orleans in 1825. He was educated in Catholic schools. From 1845, Trévigne worked as a teacher at the Catholic Indigent Orphan School in New Orleans, a position he would hold until the mid-1880s.

Trévigne was a member of an elite class of African Americans in a city that had always practiced, by American standards, a high degree of tolerance toward racial mixing in daily life and an acceptance of ambition and economic success of blacks. Early in the Civil War, New Orleans was captured by Union forces and held for the duration of the war. Ruled by federal military authorities, New Orleans was an oasis for African Americans, who flocked to Lincoln's Republican Party.

In 1862, Trévigne accepted the position of editor of *L'Union,* a newspaper founded by an African-American businessman, Louis Charles Roudanez. For the next two years, Trévigne in the pages of

L'Union agitated for greater civil rights for the African-American citizens of Louisiana. Much of Trévigne's agenda was accomplished under the Louisiana Constitution of 1864, which abolished slavery and extended voting rights to African Americans who fought for the Union, owned property, or were literate. Full voting rights for all African Americans would not materialize until passage of the Fifteenth Amendment, which was adopted in 1870.

From 1864 to 1869, the high period of Reconstruction in the South, Trévigne edited *La Tribune de la Nouvelle-Orleans,* the successor to *L'Union,* which had folded in 1864. The first page of each edition was printed in French, the language of the Creole African-American elite. The second page was printed in English, the language of the many freed slaves who were being taught to read by instructors from the Freedmen's Bureau.

Trévigne's success at *La Tribune* generated a number of death threats from whites angry at black success in politics during Reconstruction. In spite of these threats, Trévigne continued his aggressive editorializing in favor of black rights until the paper ceased publication in 1869.

In later years, Trévigne wrote the *Centennial History of the Louisiana Negro* (1875–76), a memoir of African-American life in New Orleans. He died in New Orleans in 1908 at the age of 83.

Further Reading

Battle, Karen. "New Orleans' Creoles of Color." Available online. URL: http://www.loyno.edu/history/journal/1991-2/battle.htm. Downloaded July 1, 2009.

Blassingame, John W. *Black New Orleans, 1860–1880.* Chicago: University of Chicago Press, 2007.

Trotter, William Monroe

(1872–1934) *civil rights activist, publisher, business leader*

Perhaps the most militant civil rights leader of the early 20th century, Monroe Trotter was a dogged critic of BOOKER TALIAFERRO WASHINGTON. Through his newspaper, the *Guardian,* Trotter attacked Washington's meek response to the worsening discrimination against African Americans.

Born in 1872 in Chillicothe, Ohio, William Monroe Trotter was the son of James and Virginia Trotter. Trotter's father was an army officer who retired to Hyde Park, a mostly white suburb of Boston, where Trotter grew up. Active and well liked in school, Trotter, who was the only black student in his class, eventually became class president of Hyde Park High School. After graduating with excellent grades, he enrolled in Harvard College in 1891.

Trotter thrived at Harvard, where he seems to have encountered no overt racism. Studying politics and history, he became a member of Phi Beta Kappa in his junior year and graduated in 1895. After graduation, he began work in Boston as a broker of real estate mortgages. He set up his own business in this specialized niche in 1899. That year he married Geraldine Pindell, a white Bostonian.

Trotter came of age at a time when African Americans were being systematically discriminated against in both the North and the South. At the turn of the century, many states adopted new laws that restricted blacks to segregated parts of cities and required them to sit in separate parts of restaurants, theaters, trains, and other public places. Employment in certain industries and jobs was also banned.

Booker T. Washington, the most visible black leader of this era, accepted such discrimination in return for a promise by white leaders to fund schools where African Americans could learn trades. Washington urged blacks to pull themselves up by their bootstraps and advance economically. Only through economic success, Washington argued, could blacks eventually attain equality with whites.

Trotter vigorously disagreed with Washington's outlook. To counter Washington, in 1902, Trotter founded the *Guardian,* aimed at African-

American audiences in Boston and across the nation. The next year, Trotter and a group of his supporters interrupted a speech that Washington was giving in a Boston church by shouting questions at him from the audience. For his impertinence, Trotter was arrested and spent a month in jail.

In 1905, Trotter joined W. E. B. DuBois, then a professor at Atlanta University, in forming the Niagara Movement. The Niagara Manifesto, written by Trotter and DuBois, clearly lays out Trotter's views about tactics to advance African-American civil rights:

> Persistent manly agitation is the way to liberty. . . . We black men have our own duties . . . to respect ourselves, even as we respect others. But in doing so, we shall not cease to remind the white man of his responsibility. We refuse to allow the impression to remain that the Negro-American assents to inferiority, is submissive under oppression and apologetic before insults.

In 1908, Trotter formed his own national civil rights organization, the National Equal Rights League, which aimed for an all-black membership and leadership. Trotter opposed the National Association for the Advancement of Colored People (NAACP), formed by DuBois and a number of white liberals in 1909, on the grounds that African Americans needed to seize hold of their own destiny and did not need white leadership to achieve full rights in the United States.

Trotter, who had been a Republican, drifted from the Republican Party after President Theodore Roosevelt's scapegoating of black soldiers as the cause of a riot in Brownsville, Texas, in 1906. In 1912, he supported Woodrow Wilson, a Democrat, for the presidency. However, Trotter's support evaporated when Wilson declared that he approved of Jim Crow racial segregation laws.

After the death of his wife in the influenza epidemic of 1918. Trotter became increasingly iso-lated from mainstream black leadership. He died, possibly by suicide, in 1934.

Further Reading

Bridgewater State College. "William Monroe Trotter." Available online. URL: http://www.bridgew.edu/hoba/trotter.htm. Downloaded July 1, 2009.

Jackson, Derrick Z. "About William Monroe Trotter." Available online. URL: http://www.trottergroup.com/trotter.htm. Downloaded July 1, 2009.

National Park Service. "William Monroe Trotter House." Available online. URL: http://www.nps.gov/history/nr/travel/civilrights/ma1.htm. Downloaded July 1, 2009.

O'Connor, Thomas H. *Boston A to Z.* Cambridge: Harvard University Press, 2000.

Truth, Sojourner
(Isabella Baumfree)
(ca. 1797–1883) *abolitionist, women's rights activist*

Born into slavery in New York, Sojourner Truth escaped captivity just before slavery was abolished in that state. She became a committed abolitionist and speaker against slavery in the North, and in later years she was an equally committed advocate of full rights for women.

She was born Isabella Baumfree in Hurley, New York, around 1797, to James and Elizabeth Baumfree.

Little is known about Isabella's childhood. Growing up on a farm owned by a New York Dutch couple, she learned Dutch as her first language. She was sold four times, and by 1810 she had landed on the farm of John Dumont, located near New Paltz, New York. She became the common-law wife of another slave named Thomas and with him had five children.

Life in the Dumont household was difficult for Isabella. John Dumont's wife abused her, and one of her children was sold into slavery in Alabama. In 1826, a year before slavery was outlawed in New

York, Isabella ran away from the Dumont household and found refuge with a Quaker couple. One of the first things she did was petition a local court for the release of her son, which she accomplished around 1827.

In 1829, Isabella moved to New York City, where she fell in with a religious commune run by Elijah Pierson. Through Pierson, she joined another commune, known as the Kingdom of Matthias, in Ossining, New York. When this commune fell apart, she moved back to New York City, where around 1843 she underwent an ecstatic religious experience and believed herself to have been commanded by God to change her name to Sojourner Truth. She felt that she had been told to travel throughout the North testify-

Sojourner Truth ca. 1860. A spiritualist and abolitionist, Truth later became a strong supporter of women's rights. *(Library of Congress, Prints and Photographs Division, LC-USZ62-119343)*

ing to the sinfulness in which Americans were living.

In the mid-1840s she settled in Northampton, Massachusetts, at the Association of Education and Industry, a utopian community. There she met abolitionists such as William Lloyd Garrison, Wendell Phillips, and FREDERICK DOUGLASS. For the next five years, Truth traveled and spoke in the North about her experiences with slavery and argued that it should be abolished.

In 1850, Truth met Lucretia Mott, Elizabeth Cady Stanton, and other feminists at a women's rights conference in Massachusetts. With a fervor equal to her dedication to abolitionism, Truth threw herself into agitating for full and equal rights, including the right to vote, for women. Over six feet tall and with intense eyes, she must have been a formidable figure. At a women's rights conference in Akron, Ohio, in 1851, she delivered a famous speech, "Ain't I a Woman." "That man over there says that women need to be helped into carriages and lifted over ditches," she said.

> Nobody ever helps me into carriages, or over mud-puddles, . . . And ain't I a woman? . . . I have ploughed and planted, and gathered into barns, and no man could head me! And ain't I a woman? . . . I have borne thirteen children, and seen most all sold off to slavery, and when I cried out with my mother's grief, none but Jesus heard me! And ain't I a woman?

In the mid-1850s, Truth moved to Battle Creek, Michigan, to live with her three daughters and her grandsons. After the outbreak of the Civil War, she recruited African-American troops and for a while lived in Washington, D.C., where she nursed wounded black soldiers and worked in soup kitchens set up for displaced former slaves.

After the war, she tried to interest senators in the idea of establishing a state in some part of the West for African Americans. This proposal was never adopted, but her ideas may have contributed to the migration of blacks out of the South to Kansas in the late 1870s.

Truth died in Battle Creek on November 26, 1883.

Further Reading

Butler, Mary G. "Sojourner Truth: A Life and Legacy of Faith." Available online. URL: http://www. sojournertruth.org/Library/Archive/LegacyOf Faith.htm. Downloaded July 1, 2009.

Marable, Manning, and Leith Mullings, eds. *Let Nobody Turn Us Around: Voices of Resistance, Reform, and Renewal: An African American Anthology.* Lanham, Md.: Rowman & Littlefield, 2009.

Nyquist, Corrine. "On the Trail of Sojourner Truth in Ulster County, New York." Available online. URL: http://www.newpaltz.edu/sojourner_truth/. Downloaded July 1, 2009.

Quarles, Benjamin. *Black Abolitionists.* New York: Oxford, 1969.

Stetson, Erlene, and Linda David. *Glorying in Tribulation: The Lifework of Sojourner Truth.* East Lansing: Michigan State University Press, 1994.

Truth, Sojourner. *The Book of Life.* London: X Press, 1999.

Women in History. "Sojourner Truth." Available online. URL: http://www.lkwdpl.org/wihohio/trut-soj. htm. Downloaded July 1, 2009.

Tubman, Harriet
(Harriet Ross)
(ca. 1820–1913) *abolitionist, Underground Railroad activist*

Born a slave, Harriet Tubman escaped from captivity in 1849. Operating from Pennsylvania and Canada, Tubman was a leader of the Underground Railroad and made repeated forays into the South to guide slaves to freedom. Born around 1820 in Dorchester County, Maryland, Harriet Ross was the daughter of Benjamin Ross and Harriet Green, slaves on a farm on Maryland's Eastern Shore.

Because she was a slave, Harriet received no formal education. She was forced to marry John Tubman, a free black who lived near the farm on which she worked, in 1844.

After the death of the owner of the farm in 1849, Harriet Tubman feared she would be sold to another owner—perhaps farther south—so she fled slavery. Aided by a white neighbor, who gave her the name of an Underground Railroad activist, she moved from one house to another on a journey that would soon take her to Philadelphia. In that city she met WILLIAM STILL, a black activist who helped escaped slaves. Still found Tubman work and a room to live in. Soon, though, Tubman demanded a role for herself as an Underground Railroad scout.

Between 1850 and 1858, Tubman returned again and again to slave states, mainly to Maryland, to guide slaves to freedom in Pennsylvania, New York, and Canada. It is estimated that she made as many as 19 trips into the South and helped as many as 300 slaves, including her own parents, escape. She was famous for her determination. On several occasions, she brandished a pistol at her charges when they were tired or discouraged and told them, "You'll be free or die."

After passage of the Fugitive Slave Law in 1850, Tubman operated out of West Ontario, Canada, a site chosen as a permanent home by many escaped slaves. From this base, she slipped across the border to the United States to assume various disguises on her trips south. She needed to be disguised because she had become notorious among southerners, who had offered a $40,000 reward for her capture.

During the Civil War, Tubman volunteered as a civilian aide to Union general David Hunter, who was camped in Hilton Head, South Carolina. She served as a cook, nurse, and spy for federal troops and made numerous scouting trips into Confederate territory to gather information for the northern forces.

After the war, Tubman married Nelson Davis, a black war veteran. She moved to Auburn in

Harriet Tubman made as many as 19 trips into the South before the Civil War to lead slaves to freedom in the North. *(© CORBIS)*

upstate New York and dictated her memoirs, *Scenes in the Life of Harriet Tubman,* in 1869. In 1908, she built a house on her property in which she took in and cared for poor elderly African-American men and women. Tubman died on March 10, 1913.

Further Reading

Conrad, Earl. *Harriet Tubman: Negro Soldier and Abolitionist.* New York: International Publishers, 1942.

Harriet Tubman Home. "Life of Harriet Tubman." Available online. URL: http://www.nyhistory.com/harriettubman/life.htm. Downloaded July 1, 2009.

Lowry, Beverly. *Harriet Tubman: Imagining a Life.* New York: Anchor, 2008.

PBS. Africans in America, Resource Bank. "Harriet Tubman." Available online. URL: http://www.pbs.org/wgbh/aia/part4/4p1535.html. Downloaded July 1, 2009.

Quarles, Benjamin. *Black Abolitionists.* New York: Oxford, 1969.

Turner, Henry McNeal
(1834–1915) *colonizationist, educator, minister*

Born into a free family in South Carolina, Henry Turner would become an abolitionist preacher before the Civil War. After the war, he was involved in Reconstruction politics in Georgia and became a college president. At the end of the 19th century, he was known as a passionate advocate of African Americans returning to Africa.

Born in 1834 in Abbeville, South Carolina, Henry McNeal Turner was the son of free blacks, Hardy and Sarah Turner. Taught to read and write by sympathetic whites, Turner worked for a time as a clerk at a law firm. In 1853, he became a minister of the Methodist Episcopal Church, a predominantly white organization with some black congregations. He would marry four times and have a number of children.

Settling in Saint Louis in 1857, Turner switched his affiliation to the African Methodist Episcopal (AME) Church, an all-black group. During his term as a pastor of the Israel Church in Washington, D.C., Turner worked to recruit soldiers for the Union army at the beginning of the Civil War. He was appointed an army chaplain by President Lincoln in 1863 and served until 1865.

After working for a few years as a teacher in the Freedmen's Bureau in Georgia after the war, Turner returned to religion as an administrator and bishop, setting up a string of churches in Georgia. Using these churches as a base, he became a member of the Georgia constitutional convention in 1867. He also held a seat in the Georgia legislature, although, because of the political turmoil between whites and blacks during the mid-1860s, he would serve only one term, from 1868 to 1870. In the 1880s, he was president of Morris Brown College in Atlanta.

Beginning in 1874, when he was elected vice president of the American Colonization Society, Turner became interested in the idea of colonizing American blacks in Africa, especially in Liberia on the coast of West Africa. Believing that African Americans had no future in the United States because of the intensity of white racism, Turner called on the federal government to pay the costs of relocating black Americans to Africa as a form of reparation for slavery. Congress ignored these proposals, and black leaders such as FREDERICK DOUGLASS dismissed them. Nonetheless, Turner made four trips to Liberia during the 1890s and declared of African Americans who opposed colonization, "A man who loves a country that hates him is a human dog and not a man."

Turner died on May 8, 1915 in Windsor, Ontario.

Further Reading

Angell, Stephen Ward. *Bishop Henry McNeal Turner and African-American Religion in the South.* Knoxville: University of Tennessee Press, 1992.

New Georgia Encyclopedia. "Henry McNeal Turner (1834–1915)." Available online. URL: http://www.georgiaencyclopedia.org/nge/Article.jsp?id=h-632. Downloaded July 1, 2009.

University of North Carolina. "Henry McNeal Turner." Available online. URL: http://docsouth.unc.edu/church/turneral/bio.html. Downloaded July 1, 2009.

Turner, Nat

(1800–1831) *slave rebellion leader*

Born into slavery and—except for a brief moment of freedom after an attempted escape—enslaved all his life, Nat Turner was the leader of one of the most violent slave insurrections in American history. Born in Southampton County, Virginia, in 1800, Turner was the son of slaves whose names are not known. His father escaped from bondage when Nat was a child; he may have joined a community of escaped slaves in the Great Dismal Swamp on the Virginia-North Carolina border. Turner's father never returned.

Turner learned to read and write as a child, although it is unclear who taught him because slaves were rarely educated. He worked both as a field hand tending cotton and tobacco and as a blacksmith. He used his learning to acquaint himself with the Bible. By his early 20s, Turner began to preach to other slaves and to a few whites. He baptized at least one white resident of Southampton County, and possibly more. He also developed a common-law marriage with another slave and fathered several children.

The 1820s, the years of Nat Turner's youth, was a time of great turbulence in U.S. race relations and in relations between the North and South. In 1822, a large slave revolt in South Carolina led by DENMARK VESEY had narrowly been averted when word of the revolt leaked out prematurely. In 1829, DAVID WALKER, a free African American living in Boston, published his *Appeal*, which called on all blacks, slave and free, to revolt against white rule. In 1831, growing antislavery sentiment in the North finally found a voice in William Lloyd Garrison's newspaper, the *Liberator*.

It is not clear whether Turner knew of these currents in American life, although it is possible that he knew of David Walker because of the distaste that Walker's tirade had caused among southern planters. He also may have known about Vesey's plot, which raised alarm throughout the South. These events caused a general tightening of control on slaves in the South, which curtailed their freedom of movement in local areas, although these laws were not rigorously followed everywhere.

Turner, who was a Christian mystic, decided to raise a rebellion against the slave masters of Southampton County in February 1831 when he witnessed a solar eclipse. Interpreting the occurrence as a divine sign, he conferred with several other slaves he felt he could trust, and they set a date of July 4, Independence Day, for the uprising. However, Turner fell ill shortly before this date and postponed it to August.

Around 2:00 A.M. on August 23, Turner and six other slaves crept into the house of their masters and killed the entire family of five, including women, men, and children. Turner seized weapons from the plantation and sent runners to raise other slaves in rebellion. Some 60 to 80 answered the call. For almost three days, this band roamed over Southampton County, killing whites and collecting arms from their homesteads. Not all whites the band encountered were killed. Some poor whites and some with religious ties to Turner were spared. In all, about 60 whites were killed.

By August 26, state militia, armed citizens' groups, and federal troops had crushed the revolt. Turner fled to the wilds but never left the county. He was captured at the end of October and tried, found guilty, and sentenced to death on November 5. He was hanged on November 11, 1831.

This incident has produced a famous fictional account of the revolt, William Styron's *The Confessions of Nat Turner* (1966). Styron's book caused considerable controversy among black intellectuals and was answered by a collection of critical essays, *William Styron's Nat Turner: Ten Black Writers Respond* (1968).

Further Reading

Clarke, John Henrik, ed. *William Styron's Nat Turner: Ten Black Writers Respond.* Boston: Beacon Press, 1968.

Greenberg, Kenneth S., ed. *Nat Turner: A Slave Rebellion in History and Memory.* New York: Oxford University Press, 2004.

Oates, Stephen B. *The Fires of Jubilee: Nat Turner's Fierce Rebellion.* New York: Harper & Row, 1975.

PBS. Africans in America, Resource Bank. "Nat Turner's Rebellion." Available online: URL: http://www.pbs.org/wgbh/aia/part3/3p1518.html. Downloaded July 1, 2009.

Rodriguez, Junius P., ed. *Encyclopedia of Slave Resistance and Rebellion.* Westport, Conn.: Greenwood, 2007.

Styron, William. *The Confessions of Nat Turner.* New York: Random House, 1966.

Turner, Nat, with Thomas Gray. "The Confessions of Nat Turner." Available online. URL: http://www.melanet.com/nat/nat.html. Downloaded July 1, 2009.

Tyler, Ralph Waldo

(1859–1921) *journalist*

A journalist who worked for many years in Columbus, Ohio, Ralph Tyler was best known for the dispatches he filed from the battlefield in France during World War I. Born in Columbus, Ohio, in 1859, Ralph Waldo Tyler was the son of James and Maria Tyler.

After his graduation from high school, Tyler worked as a teacher and stenographer in Columbus during most of his 20s. In 1888, when he was 29, he was hired as a stenographer at the *Columbus Dispatch.* He gradually worked his way up at the *Dispatch* and eventually became a reporter covering African-American politics and statehouse maneuverings.

By virtue of his contact with black politicians in Ohio, Tyler became involved in politics as a participant as well as a reporter. He joined the Mark Hanna faction of the Ohio Republican Party, and in 1896 he attended the Republican National Convention as a reporter. He filed his first stories under his own name at that time.

After new management bought out the *Dispatch* in 1905, Tyler won an appointment as an auditor at the Department of the Navy in Washington in 1906. Tyler worked there for seven years, until 1913, when he left to serve as national organizer of Booker Taliaferro Washington's National Negro Business League. At the league, Tyler observed and wrote numerous articles about the great northern migration of southern blacks during that era.

In 1918, Tyler was appointed as the official African-American War Department correspondent to the front in France during the final months of World War I. Attached to General Pershing's headquarters, he filed numerous stories about the valor of black troops, articles that were syndicated in African-American newspapers in the United States.

Tyler returned to the United States in 1919 and took a job as editor of the *Cleveland Advocate,* a leading black newspaper in Ohio. He remained at that position until his death on June 2, 1921.

Further Reading

The African-American Experience in Ohio. "Ralph Waldo Tyler." Available online. URL: http://dbs.ohiohistory.org/africanam/page.cfm?Id=10046. Downloaded July 1, 2009.

Logan, Rayford, and Michael Winston. *Dictionary of American Negro Biography.* New York: W. W. Norton, 1982.

V

Vann, Robert Lee

(1879–1940) *lawyer, publisher, civil rights activist*

Born into a poor family in North Carolina, Robert Vann doggedly pursued an education and moved north when he was in his early 20s. After earning a law degree, he began work for the *Pittsburgh Courier,* a newly founded black newspaper. He would make the *Courier* one of the leading black newspapers of the 1920s and 1930s.

Born on August 27, 1879, in Ahoskie, North Carolina, Robert Lee Vann was the son of Lucy Peoples. The identity of his father is unknown. Vann's mother worked as a cook for a white family, the Vanns, in Ahoskie (from whom he took his surname), and Vann attended segregated schools in nearby Harrellsville.

After graduating from high school in 1892, Vann worked odd jobs for nearly eight years. By 1900, having put together some savings, he returned to school at the Waters Training School in Winston, North Carolina. He then attended the Wayland Academy in Richmond, Virginia, from 1901 to 1903, and from 1903 he was a student at Western University in Pittsburgh, Pennsylvania. At Western, Vann became the first African-American editor in chief of the school newspaper. He graduated with a B.A. in 1906,

attended Western's law school, and graduated with an LL.B. in 1909.

One of Vann's first jobs after passing the bar was as counsel of the *Pittsburgh Courier,* a newspaper founded by a group of black investors in 1910. Within months, Vann had also become the paper's editor and treasurer.

Vann quickly attracted attention to the paper by aggressively attacking the practices of racial segregation and discrimination that were common during that era. Vann shrewdly hired talented writers and columnists, such as Walter White, George Schuyler, and Louis Lautier. He covered such black social events and labor issues as the struggle of the Brotherhood of Sleeping Car Porters (BSCP) to win recognition of their all-black union from the Pullman Company.

Vann was not consistent in his opinion about labor issues. After first supporting ASA PHILIP RANDOLPH, the leader of the BSCP, he later attacked Randolph's socialist beliefs. A strong supporter of the capitalist system, Vann opposed the goals of a 40-hour workweek and higher wages advocated by the American Federation of Labor (AFL).

In spite of these inconsistent and often unpopular stances, Vann increased readership of the *Courier* during the 1930s by focusing adulation on black sports figures, such as the sprinter Jesse Owens and boxer Joe Louis. He also dispatched

Robert Lee Vann was editor and publisher of the *Pittsburgh Courier,* one of the leading African-American newspapers of the 1920s and 1930s. *(Moorland-Spingarn Research Center, Howard University)*

correspondents to cover Italy's invasion of Ethiopia, adventurism that Vann railed against in editorials. By 1938, the *Courier* had hit a circulation of 250,000 copies per issue.

With the approach of World War II, Vann directed his reporters to focus attention on the poor treatment black soldiers received in the U.S. Armed Forces. He urged the federal government to recruit and train more black officers, stop assigning blacks predominantly to jobs as cook and laborers, and form a separate African-American division headed by black officers.

In 1932, Vann took part in the historic shift of black voters away from the Republican Party to the Democrats when he broke with the Republi-

cans to back Franklin D. Roosevelt for president. At his urging, millions of African-American voters followed him in supporting Roosevelt at the polls. In Pennsylvania, Vann was instrumental in persuading the legislature to enact an equal rights law in 1935. Vann returned to the Republicans in 1940 when he backed Wendell Willkie for president against Roosevelt, who had disappointed him with his tepid support for African-American issues. Robert Vann died on October 24, 1940.

Further Reading

Buni, Andrew. *Robert L. Vann of The Pittsburgh Courier: Politics and Black Journalism.* Pittsburgh: University of Pittsburgh Press, 1974.
Hill District: Robert L. Vann. Available online. URL: http://www.clpgh.org/exhibit/neighborhoods/hill/hill_n103.html. Downloaded July 1, 2009.
PBS. "Robert Lee Vann." Available online. URL: http://www.pbs.org/blackpress/news_bios/vann.html. Downloaded July 1, 2009.

Vesey, Denmark
(ca. 1767–1822) *slave revolt leader*

A freed slave living in Charleston, South Carolina, Denmark Vesey led a large slave revolt conspiracy that was betrayed before it began. Vesey was born around 1767; his birthplace and the names of his parents are unknown; he may have been born in Africa or Saint Thomas in the Danish West Indies. He first appears in the historical record in 1781, around his 15th birthday, as one of a cargo of slaves being delivered by Captain Joseph Vesey to the French-held island of Saint-Domingue. A clever youngster, Denmark stuck up a friendship with the ship's captain. Captain Vesey apparently purchased Denmark, who then used his surname, on his next trip to Saint-Domingue and used him as a personal servant on his slave voyages between Africa and the Americas.

In 1783, Captain Vesey retired to Charleston, South Carolina, taking Denmark Vesey with him.

For 16 years, Vesey was held in bondage; during that time he seems to have had several common-law wives and children and learned carpentry. In 1799, Vesey won $1,500 on a lottery ticket, money he used to buy his freedom. He established his own carpentry business and became wealthy.

Both before he was free and afterward, Vesey was deeply concerned with the issue of slavery. The successful 1791 slave revolt in Saint Domingue (later called Haiti after gaining independence in 1804) inspired him to imagine that a similar revolt might be successful in the United States. He read the Bible and was especially interested in passages concerning the liberation of the Jews from slavery in Egypt. He also kept abreast of current events in the United States, becoming familiar with abolitionist pamphlets and debates about slavery in the Congress. After he was freed, Vesey let his feelings be known in sermons he gave at the African Methodist Church in Charleston and in street-corner conversations.

In late 1821 and early 1822, Vesey put together a plan and gathered recruits for what promised to be a massive insurrection in and around Charleston. With four main aides, most of whom were slaves, he built a network of as many as 9,000 slaves who knew of the plot and stood ready to act when word was given that the revolt had started.

Vesey set the date of the rebellion for July 14, 1822, but word of the plot leaked out in bits when some slaves informed their masters about the gossip circulating in the African-American community. To hurry the revolt, Vesey sent word that it would begin on June 16, but even this date was too late as the governor called out the state militia when other rumors of a revolt surfaced.

On the night of June 17, state authorities arrested 10 blacks for their involvement in the plot, and by June 20 the plot had completely unraveled because some of the prisoners began to talk. Dozens of slaves were arrested, and Vesey hid in Charleston. Arrested on June 22, he was tried and found guilty on June 28. He and five other blacks were hanged on July 2, 1822.

Further Reading

Egerton, Douglas R. *He Shall Go Out Free: The Lives of Denmark Vesey.* Madison, Wis.: Madison House, 1999.

Higginson, Thomas Wentworth. "Denmark Vesey." *Atlantic.* Available online. URL: http://www.the-atlantic.com/issues/1861jun/higgin.htm. Downloaded July 1, 2009.

PBS. Africans in America, Resource Bank. "The Vesey Conspiracy." Available online. URL: http://www.pbs.org/wgbh/aia/part3/3p2976.html. Downloaded July 1, 2009.

Robertson, David. *Denmark Vesey.* New York: Vintage, 2000.

Rodriguez, Junius P., ed. *Encyclopedia of Slave Resistance and Rebellion.* Westport, Conn.: Greenwood, 2007.

Walker, David
(1785–1830) *abolitionist, publisher*

A firebrand writer and speaker, David Walker was an original thinker who introduced the ideas of black nationalism, pan-Africanism, and armed revolt into the American scene in the late 1820s. Born free in Wilmington, North Carolina, in 1785, Walker was the son of a free mother and slave father. Under the laws of North Carolina, a child inherited his mother's status; thus Walker was free at birth though his father was a slave.

Little is known about Walker's early life. During his 20s, Walker seems to have worked at odd jobs and done considerable traveling through the South. He made a point of observing the customs of slavery, noting the many forms of cruelty employed by white masters on their slaves.

By the 1820s, when Walker was in his mid- to late 30s, he moved to Boston, then one of the most sympathetic cities for opponents of slavery. He set up a used-clothing business on the docks, buying and selling goods from sailors as well as the general public.

During the 1820s, Walker began to speak out at public meetings against slavery, using his own observations and experiences to illustrate his points. By the late 1820s, he was arguably the leading abolitionist in Boston. He met SAMUEL ELI CORNISH and JOHN BROWN RUSSWURM, the edi-

tors of *Freedom's Journal*, an abolitionist paper based in New York. One of the speeches he gave in Boston, "Address Delivered before the General Colored Association," was printed in *Freedom's Journal* in 1828. That same year he married a woman named Eliza, perhaps a fugitive slave, in Boston. They would have one child.

In 1829, Walker published his own abolitionist tract, *David Walker's Appeal*, which had an immediate and sensational impact on the debate about slavery and race in the United States. In his *Appeal*, Walker defined whites as the "natural enemies" of blacks worldwide. He wrote that the "coloured people of these United States, are the most degraded, wretched, and abject set of beings that ever lived since the world began. . . . I tell you Americans! that unless you speedily alter your course, *you* and your *Country are gone!*"

Walker also extended the idea of black liberation from the United States to all blacks in the world, the first mention of an idea of pan-Africanism. "Your full glory and happiness, . . ." he wrote to African Americans, "shall never fully be consummated, but with the entire emancipation of your enslaved breatheren all over the world."

Using his venue on the Boston docks to maximum advantage, Walker sent his *Appeal* to the South through black sailors and sympathetic white seamen. Many copies were smuggled into the South, where they aroused the ire of white southerners. A group of white Georgians placed a bounty—$1,000 dead, $10,000 alive—on Walker's head. This bounty would never be paid. Walker died in 1830 in Boston, probably of tuberculosis.

Walker left an uncompromising legacy for African Americans who believed that real progress would result only from black organizations with black leaders, not white goodwill. *David Walker's Appeal* would inspire many of the next generation of African-American leaders, notably HENRY HIGHLAND GARNET.

Further Reading

Aptheker, Herbert. *Abolitionism: A Revolutionary Movement*. Boston: Twayne, 1989.

Documenting the South. "David Walker, 1785–1830." Available online. URL: http://docsouth.unc.edu/nc/walker/bio.html. Downloaded July 1, 2009.

Hinks, Peter R. *To Awaken My Afflicted Brethren: David Walker and the Problem of Antebellum Slave Resistance*. University Park: Pennsylvania State University Press, 1997.

PBS. Africans in America, Resource Bank. David Walker." Available online. URL: http://www.pbs.org/wgbh/aia/part4/4p2930.html. Downloaded July 1, 2009.

———. Africans in America, Resource Bank. "David Walker's Appeal." Available online. URL: http://cgi.pbs.org/wgbh/aia/part4/4h2931t.html. Downloaded July 1, 2009.

Walker, Flora

(1939–) *union official, labor activist*

As a labor union organizer and leader, Flora Walker is a tireless advocate for working families. She was born in Corinth, Mississippi. Her parents worked hard as sharecroppers and struggled to make a decent living. To find jobs and build a better life, her parents moved to Memphis and then to Detroit. A good student, Flora was admitted to Detroit's High School of Commerce. She was one of only six African Americans in the school, which had 600 students. Her parents wanted Flora to attend college, but she accepted a job offer from Michigan Bell, the region's telephone company.

While working full time as a 411 operator, Walker took classes at Wayne State University. She graduated with a degree in labor studies. Her father, Willie, was a committed union man. He worked days as a painter at an auto factory, where he was a member of the United Auto Workers union. At nights, he worked at a dairy, where he had joined the International Brotherhood of Teamsters union. Mr. Walker had taught his daughter the value of unions in helping workers. Unions bargained for higher wages, provided health care and other benefits, and mediated disputes between workers and management.

Walker worked at Michigan Bell for 10 years. Although she had been promoted to executive assistant, she still earned low wages. To make more money, she decided to accept a typist job at the City of Detroit's building and safety engineering department. Because the position required a three-month probationary period, in which she could be fired without cause, she kept working at Michigan Bell. For three months, she maintained a grueling schedule. She worked at Michigan Bell from 11 P.M. to

In 2005, Flora Walker won the Dream Keepers Award given by Reverend Al Sharpton and his National Action Network to individuals who have carried on the spirit of Dr. Martin Luther King, Jr., with their work. (*© Axel Koester/CORBIS*)

7 A.M. and then rushed to her new job, working from 8 A.M. to 4 P.M. At the end of three-month period, she quit her job at Michigan Bell.

Walker grew to dislike her job because of a tense relationship with her supervisor. Listening to her coworkers complaining about their jobs, she suggested that they should organize a union. Walker pointed out that some other city employees, including traffic court workers and garbage collectors, had already unionized. Risking her job—workers are often fired for trying to unionize—Walker approached the local chapter of the American Federation of State, County, and Municipal Employees (AFSCME). Working with the union's staff, she convinced her coworkers to form a union.

Walker's organizing skills impressed AFSCME officials, who offered her a job as a union organizer in 1968. Her first assignment was to organize nurses at Detroit Memorial Hospital. Walker bought a nurse's uniform and walked around the hospital, discussing with nurses how the union could help them. More than 600 nurses signed up for union representation. She also helped organize the city's department of corrections and other departments.

In 1971, Walker was promoted to staff member of the AFSCME's Detroit office. She was the office's first female staffer. In 1982, she was promoted to supervisor, overseeing the work of AFSCME staff in three counties. The president of the AFSCME's Michigan labor council hired her as vice president. When he retired in 1992, she decided to run for the elective office. Union members voted her in as council president. She now represented 65,000 workers in 300 local unions throughout Michigan. Under her leadership, the council simplified the union's grievance and arbitration processes, increased its staff, and created new educational programs for members.

Walker was reelected in 1997 but decided to resign two years later. She wanted to devote more time to her family. She moved to Nevada to care for her ailing father. After his death, Walker returned to work in 2003. AFSCME offered her a position supervising AFSCME unions in 17 western states, where she continues to make a difference in the lives of workers.

When Walker stepped down as council president in 1999, Congressman David Bonier recognized her service to Michigan workers on the floor of the U.S. House of Representatives. He proclaimed, "Flora is a woman who dedicated her life to securing the dignity and respect of all people. She has been a champion of civil rights and civil liberties, and has helped create a stronger, more united community. . . . Few people have given to their community with the vision and commitment that Flora Walker has given to hers."

Further Reading

Gavilovich, Peter, and Bill McGraw, eds. *The Detroit Almanac: 300 Years of Life in the Motor City.* Detroit: Detroit Free Press, 2000.

San Diego Union Tribune. "Union Leader Who's Ready for a Challenge." Available online. URL: http://www.signonsandiego.com/uniontrib/2005 0802/news_1b2walker.html. Downloaded July 7, 2009.

Washington, Booker Taliaferro
(1856–1915) *educator, national activist*

The preeminent African-American leader of his era, Booker T. Washington began his career as an educator and ended it as arguably the single most influential black man in the United States. Born into slavery in Franklin County, Virginia, in 1856, Washington was the son of Jane, a slave, and an unknown white man. Jane named him Booker Taliaferro; he would later add the surname Washington. With his mother, half-brother, and half-sister, Washington lived on the farm of James Burroughs, a white man. When Washington was still a child, his mother would marry Washington Ferguson, who became his proxy father.

After the Civil War, Washington's family moved to Malden, West Virginia, where by the age of nine Washington had begun work in salt and coal mines. He learned to read and write by attending school in Malden part time and through his own efforts. When he was 15, he began working as a houseboy for a mine owner, and the next year, with the encouragement of the owner's wife, he enrolled in the Hampton Institute in Virginia, a school for African Americans run by the American Missionary Society. He famously walked from West Virginia to the Hampton Institute, arriving hungry, exhausted, and dirty. He was put to work as a janitor to pay for his room and board.

At Hampton, Washington, who had already shown considerable industry and initiative, learned to revere these traits. He favorably impressed Samuel Chappman Armstrong, the white school principal, and became an even stronger believer in the value of cleanliness, personal character, and morality. Washington graduated from Hampton with honors in 1875 and returned to Malden to teach. By 1879, he was back at Hampton as a teacher.

In 1881, Samuel Armstrong recommended Washington as principal of a new school that had been created by the Alabama legislature for the education of black students in Tuskegee, a small town in central Alabama. When Washington arrived in Tuskegee, he found that the legislature had not allocated any money for land or buildings for the school.

Operating from a shack that had been donated by a local black Baptist church, Washington began working with characteristic determination to build a campus. Beginning a lifetime of fundraising, he borrowed money to buy a derelict plantation on the edge of town. He then set his first students to work constructing a brick kiln, which they used to make bricks for the construction of the first campus buildings.

By 1888, the school had a campus of 540 acres and more than 400 students. Washington would never stop raising money, and he was especially adept at getting money from sympathetic northern white industrialists and financiers such as

Booker Taliaferro Washington, first president of Tuskegee Institute in Alabama. Washington would become the most influential black leader of the late 19th and early 20th centuries. (© Oscar White/CORBIS)

Andrew Carnegie, John Wanamaker, and Collis P. Huntington. By 1915, the school's endowment had grown to almost $2 million, which supported a staff of 200.

In his philosophy about the education of African-American students, Washington emphasized practical skills such as the study of agriculture and teaching and training in carpentry, printing, and shoemaking. He strongly believed that the only way African Americans would progress was through economic development. He accepted the status quo in the United States of his time—that is, the rigid system of racial segregation that separated blacks and whites in schools, jobs, and public facilities. Washington believed that blacks should develop separately from whites, that they had to pull themselves up by the bootstraps, and he never publicly challenged the Jim

Crow system that kept the races separate and unequal under the law.

Washington gave the most famous rendering of his philosophy in his address before the Cotton States and International Exposition in Atlanta, Georgia, in 1895. In that speech, he spoke of whites and blacks as races that "could work together as one hand while socially remaining as separate as the fingers. . . . The wisest among my race understand that the agitation of questions of social equality is the extremest folly."

By the turn of the century, Washington had become a wildly popular black leader, respected by moderate whites, admired by the emerging black middle class, and appreciated by open-minded white southern leaders. His autobiography, *Up from Slavery*, published in 1901, became a bestseller, and he had a famous lunch with President Theodore Roosevelt in the White House soon thereafter. He became a powerful behind-the-scenes adviser about black issues to Roosevelt and William Taft. It was difficult for an African American to get a federal appointment at that time without Washington's blessings.

Washington's acceptance of segregation and second-class status for blacks was not universally admired among African Americans, especially among African-American intellectuals. He was savagely attacked by WILLIAM MONROE TROTTER in the *Guardian* of Boston and harshly criticized by W. E. B. DuBois, a professor of sociology and economics at Atlanta University. DuBois, who had once been a Washington ally, founded the Niagara Movement in 1905. This organization morphed into the interracial National Association for the Advancement of Colored People (NAACP) in 1910. The NAACP would soon shove Washington and his ideas aside and become the most important black organization in the country.

Washington died at the age of 59 on November 14, 1915. The Tuskegee Institute would remain his greatest legacy.

Further Reading

Harlan, Louis R. *Booker T. Washington.* 2 vols. New York: Oxford University Press, 1972.

Library of Congress. "African-American Odyssey: The Booker T. Washington Era." Available online. URL: http://memory.loc.gov/ammem/aaohtml/exhibit/aopart6.html. Downloaded July 1, 2009.

Moore, Jacqueline M. *Booker T. Washington, W. E. B. DuBois, and the Struggle for Racial Uplift.* Lanham, Md.: Rowman & Littlefield, 2003.

PBS. *Frontline.* "The Two Nations of Black America." Available online. URL: http://www.pbs.org/wgbh/pages/frontline/shows/race/etc/road.html. Downloaded July 1, 2009.

Spencer, Samuel R. *Booker T. Washington and the Negro's Place in American Life.* Boston: Little, Brown, 1955.

Washington, George
(1817–1905) *explorer, founder of Centralia, Washington*

An enterprising explorer and businessperson, George Washington moved west with his adoptive parents, homesteaded a farm, and eventually turned it into the town of Centerville (later named Centralia). Born on August 15, 1817, in Frederick County, Virginia, Washington was the son of an enslaved black man and a white woman. Shortly after George's birth, his father was sold and his mother gave him up for adoption to James and Anna Cochran, a white couple living in Frederick County.

Although he received no formal schooling, Washington taught himself to read and write. In the 1820s, when Washington was a child, he traveled with the Cochrans to Ohio, Illinois, and Missouri. Time and again, Washington faced discrimination because of his race. After leaving Illinois because the state had enacted a "behavioral tax" on all blacks who resided there, he left for Oregon Territory, hoping "to find a place in the world, if there was any, where a Negro would be treated like a man."

The Cochrans and Washington moved to Oregon Territory in 1850. By 1851, they reached Oregon City, where they settled and where Washington took work as a lumberjack. The next year Washington moved farther north into Oregon Territory and staked a claim for himself at the confluence of the Skookumchuck and Chehalis Rivers.

When Washington Territory was carved out of Oregon Territory in 1853, George Washington found his property threatened by new territorial laws that prohibited black ownership of property in the territory. To safeguard his claim, he had the Cochrans deed the land in their name. When this law was repealed in 1857, they sold the land back to him. He then set up a ferry across the Chehalis River and began to make improvements on his land. He married Mary Cornie during this time. After her death in 1889, he would marry Charity Brown. He had one child with his second wife.

Fortune landed at Washington's feet when the Northern Pacific Railroad built a main line of track through his farm in 1872. After the arrival of the railroad, Washington decided to plat his land and establish a town, which he named Centerville because it was roughly halfway between the towns of Kalama and Tacoma.

Centerville boomed during the 1880s as Washington sold lots and built houses, a town square, and a Baptist church. By 1889, the town had nearly 1,000 residents, and Washington had sold 2,000 lots for $10 each.

The town was caught in a nationwide economic downturn that began in 1893. After an ironworks and sawmill failed, many residents were forced to move elsewhere. Washington offered relief in the form of clothes and food for residents who stayed in the town. By the late 1890s, the town had stopped losing population and businesses, and had begun a modest recovery. George Washington died on August 26, 1905.

Further Reading

HistoryLink. "George and Mary Jane Washington Found the Town of Centerville (now Centralia) on January 8, 1875." Available online. URL: http://www.washington.historylink.org/index. cfm?DisplayPage=output.cfm&File_Id=5276. Downloaded July 1, 2009.

Katz, William Loren. *The Black West: A Documentary and Pictorial History of the African American Role in the Westward Expansion of the United States.* New York: Random House, 2005.

Wattleton, Alyce Faye

(1943–) *foundation administrator, women's rights activist*

As a nurse and foundation administrator, Faye Wattleton has fought to ensure reproductive and other rights for women. She was born in St. Louis, Missouri, on July 8, 1943. Her father, George, worked in a factory, and her mother, Ozie, was a seamstress and minister. Faye excelled at her studies, graduating from high school at age 16. She enrolled in Ohio State University, where she earned a nursing degree. She taught nursing courses for a year in Dayton, Ohio. When she received a scholarship to pursue an advanced degree at Columbia University, she moved to New York City. While studying at Columbia, she trained to be a midwife at a Harlem hospital. There, she witnessed the consequences of illegal abortions.

At the time, many states outlawed abortions. Having no access to doctors or hospitals, women desperate to end their pregnancies either sought out people willing to perform the illegal medical procedure or tried to end their pregnancies themselves. Women had suffered injuries at the hands of poorly trained people or from the effects of sharp objects or chemicals that they had used themselves. Seeing the injuries suffered by women from botched abortions motivated Wattleton to pursue a career that would advance women's rights to reproductive freedom.

After earning her master of science degree in maternal and infant care in 1967, Wattleton returned to Dayton and began working as a nurse at the county health department. As a public health nurse, she managed pregnancy and prenatal care programs. In 1970, she became executive director of the local Planned Parenthood chapter. The Planned Parenthood Federation of America is the oldest and largest family planning service provider in the United States. Wattleton's successes in developing family planning programs and in fund-raising gained the attention of Planned Parenthood's national office. In 1978, the organization named her as president. Wattleton was the youngest person, and first African American, to serve in that role.

As head of Planned Parenthood, Wattleton helped develop policies and programs to assist women in family planning. Under her leadership, the organization worked to maintain women's right to abortion and to improve reproductive health of women with low incomes. Through its health services programs, Planned Parenthood provides birth control, gynecological exams, and prenatal care. Because it also operates family planning clinics that perform abortions, the organization remains at the forefront of the tense national debate over abortion rights.

With its decision in *Roe v. Wade* (1973), the U.S. Supreme Court had guaranteed women the right to choose an abortion. Federal and state governments, however, soon began chipping away at the controversial decision. During the 1980s, the Reagan administration reduced federal funding for family planning clinics. In *Webster v. Reproductive Health Services* (1989), the U.S. Supreme Court ruled that state legislatures could regulate abortion. *Webster* led to many new state laws that restricted access to abortions. Abortion rights supporters challenged many of these laws, which they viewed as unconstitutionally infringing on the right of women to make their own health and family planning decisions.

As the abortion issue raged during the 1980s, Wattleton became a high-profile public advocate for reproductive freedom. Because of her position as head of Planned Parenthood and her strong pro-choice positions, Wattleton received death threats. During her tenure, anti-choice groups picketed Planned Parenthood clinics. Bombs exploded at several clinics.

In 1992, Wattleton resigned from Planned Parenthood. She left to become host of a syndicated talk show in Chicago. Three years later, she cofounded the center for Gender Equality. She now serves as president of the organization, which has been renamed the Center for the Advancement of Women. To ensure and advance the rights of women, the center conducts public-opinion research focused on American women. Wattleton also serves on Columbia University's board of trustees.

Wattleton has received many honors, including the Fries Prize for service to improving public health and the American Public Health Association's award of excellence. *Business Week* magazine named her as one of the best managers of nonprofit organizations, and *Ebony* magazine selected her as one of the 100 most fascinating black women of the 20th century. Wattleton was inducted into the National Women's Hall of Fame in 1993.

Further Reading

Greenfield-Sanders, Timothy, and Elvis Mitchell. *The Black List*. New York: Atria, 2008.

Solinger, Rickie. *Wake Up Little Susie: Single Pregnancy and Race before* Roe v. Wade. New York: Routledge, 2000.

Wattleton, Faye. *Life on the Line*. New York: Ballantine, 1996.

Women's Hall of Fame. Women of the Hall. "Faye Wattleton." Available online. URL: http://www.greatwomen.org/women.php?action=viewone&id=165. Downloaded July 8, 2009.

Wells, Ida B.
(Ida Bell Wells-Barnett)
(1862–1931) *journalist, civil rights activist*

One of the most outspoken journalists of her day, Ida B. Wells was editor of *Free Speech*, a Memphis weekly. She later campaigned for women's right to vote. Ida Bell Wells was born on July 6, 1862, in Holly Springs, Mississippi, to Jim and Elizabeth Wells. Both of her parents were slaves at the time of her birth. Her father worked as a carpenter on the plantation where he lived, and her mother was a cook. After emancipation, Wells and her family remained in Holly Springs, a small town near Memphis, where she received a primary and secondary education at Shaw University.

In 1878, when she was 16, Wells began to work as a schoolteacher in Holly Springs after the death of both of her parents during a yellow fever epidemic. She moved to Memphis with several of her siblings the following year and obtained a job as a schoolteacher in a town outside Memphis.

In 1884, while riding a train from Memphis to work, Wells refused to move from a car reserved for white passengers to another car that the railroad designated for black passengers. Arrested and removed from the train, Wells was determined to resist this form of racial segregation and discrimination. She sued the company and eventually won $500 in a state court. This judgment was reversed by a Tennessee Supreme Court decision that ruled in favor of the rail company in 1887.

In 1891, Wells was fired from a teaching job in the Memphis public schools after she wrote an article criticizing the school board for spending more money on white schools than on black ones. The following year, she became editor of the *Free Speech*, a recently founded local newspaper aimed at Memphis's African-American community.

Soon after becoming editor, Wells was confronted with the murder of three African-American grocery store owners by a mob of whites. The three men, who were being held in jail after an attack on their store by off-duty white police officers, were removed from their jail cell by the mob and lynched. Wells wrote scathing articles in the *Free Speech* about the incident. Outraged by her boldness, another white mob attacked the *Free Press*'s offices and burned down the building in

Ida B. Wells, a fiery journalist, wrote numerous articles and books about racism in the South and exposed the horror of lynching. *(© Bettman/CORBIS)*

which it was housed. Fortunately, Wells was not in the building at the time and was unharmed.

After the destruction of her paper, Wells moved north, first to New York City, then to Chicago. She worked for the *New York Age* and other black papers, writing a series of articles about lynching in the South. In 1895, she published *A Red Record*, a book about southern lynchings that documented the increase in lynching that had occurred in the 1890s. That year, Wells married Ferdinand Barnett, a lawyer and politician in Chicago. The couple would have four children.

In 1896, Wells helped organize the National Association of Colored Women. Throughout the late 1890s and early 1900s, she continued to speak out against racial segregation, taking on segregated housing laws in Chicago and writing about attacks against blacks by whites that occurred in

East Saint Louis in 1917 and Chicago in 1919. She served on the executive committee of the new National Association for the Advancement of Colored People (NAACP) in 1910.

Wells also worked to get women the right to vote. In 1913, she formed the Alpha Suffrage Club to push for voting rights for women in Illinois. With other women's suffrage advocates, she picketed the White House in 1918. Ida Wells-Barnett died in Chicago on March 25, 1931.

Further Reading

Library of Congress. "Progress of a People: Ida B. Wells-Barnett." Available online. URL: http://memory. loc.gov/ammem/aap/idawells.html. Downloaded July 1, 2009.

McMurry, Linda O. *To Keep the Waters Troubled: The Life of Ida B. Wells.* New York: Oxford University Press, 1998.

Schechter, Patricia A. "Biography of Ida B. Wells." Available online. URL: http://dig.lib.niu.edu/ gildedage/idabwells/biography.html. Downloaded July 1, 2009.

———. *Ida B. Wells-Barnett and American Reform, 1880–1930.* Chapel Hill: University of North Carolina Press, 2001.

Toyster, Jacqueline Jones, ed. *Southern Horrors and Other Writings: The Anti-Lynching Campaign of Ida B. Wells, 1892–1900.* Boston: Bedford, 1997.

Wesley, Carter Walker

(1892–1969) *lawyer, publisher, civil rights activist*

A crusading lawyer for the rights of African Americans, Carter Wesley was also the publisher and editor of the *Houston Informer,* the most important black newspaper in the largest city in Texas. Born on April 19, 1892, Carter Walker Wesley was the son of Mabel and Harry Wesley. After the separation of his parents when he was still a child, Wesley lived with his mother. He attended public schools in Houston.

In 1913, Wesley enrolled in Fisk University in Nashville, Tennessee. He received a bachelor's degree cum laude from Fisk in 1917. A few months after his graduation and the declaration of war on Germany by the United States, Wesley volunteered for the officer-training program of the U.S. Army. He served as a lieutenant in the army in France until 1918.

After the war, Wesley studied law at Northwestern University; he was awarded a law degree in 1922. He moved to Muskogee, Oklahoma, that year 1922 and set up practice with Alston Atkins, a friend from his days at Fisk University. During his five years in Muskogee, Wesley specialized in trying cases for blacks who had been embezzled out of land they were owed under an agreement between Indian tribes and the state government. These blacks, former slaves of members of the Indian tribes, were entitled to 160 acres of land. Many had been cheated out of their land by unscrupulous whites. Wesley won 11 of 13 cases he brought to Oklahoma's Supreme Court.

After the death of his first wife in 1925, Wesley returned to Houston in 1927 to set up a law practice with his partner Atkins. In the late 1920s, Wesley invested in the *Houston Informer,* an African-American-owned newspaper. When his other business interests soured with the Great Depression, Wesley turned to the *Informer,* which he steadily expanded into other cities in Texas. By 1946, the paper had a circulation of 66,000 copies per issue.

In a weekly column, "Ram's Horn," Wesley spoke out against policies of racial segregation and discrimination in Texas. He pushed for and won more money for black schools in Houston and challenged the all-white primary of the Texas Democratic Party. Wesley helped Thurgood Marshall, chief legal strategist of the National Association for the Advancement of Colored People (NAACP), defeat the Texas Democratic Party system of racially segregated primaries in *Smith v. Allwright,* a 1944 U.S. Supreme Court case. In 1950, Wesley gave financial and legal aid to Herman Sweatt, the circulation manager of the *Informer,* when Sweatt tried to enroll in the law school of the University of Texas at Austin. Sweatt was admitted to the law school in 1950 only after the U.S. Supreme Court ruled that the state of Texas could not exclude him because of his race.

Wesley died on November 10, 1969, in Houston.

Further Reading

Bessent, Nancy Eckols. "The Publisher: A Biography of Carter W. Wesley." M.A. thesis, University of Texas at Austin, 1981.

Handbook of Texas Online. "Carter Walker Wesley." Available online: URL: http://www.tsha.utexas. edu/handbook/online/articles/view/WW/fwe28. html. Downloaded July 1, 2009.

West, Cornel

(1953–) *educator*

A prominent African-American intellectual, Cornel West is a writer and educator who has spoken and written extensively about race in the United States in the late 20th and early 21st centuries. Born on June 2, 1953, in Tulsa, Oklahoma, West studied at Harvard University, where he earned a B.A. in 1974. He pursued graduate degrees at Princeton University, where he earned an M.A. and a Ph.D. in the late 1970s. West taught religion and directed the Afro-American Studies Department at Princeton before joining the Harvard faculty in 1994. Following a dispute with Harvard's president, West, formerly a member of Harvard's Faculty of Divinity and the W. E. B. DuBois Institute of Afro-American Research, left the university in 2000 and currently teaches Afro-American studies and philosophy of religion at Princeton University. A self-professed Christian Marxist, West has explored the place of African Americans in American society. He is also deeply inter-

ested in the ideas of liberation theology in recent Christian thought and their usefulness as a tool to achieve a more equitable and humane social order in the United States.

Known as a racial healer and reconciler, West has expressed his ideas in a number of books, including *Prophesy Deliverance! An Afro-American Revolutionary Christianity* (1982), *Beyond Ethnocentrism and Multiculturalism* (1993), and *Race Matters* (1993). He is not universally admired as a scholar, and his works have been criticized as being "humorless, pedantic and self-endeared." He has also been criticized for the soft treatment he has given such racially polarizing figures as LOUIS FARRAKHAN and AL SHARPTON.

Further Reading

Cowan, Rosemary. *Cornel West: The Politics of Redemption.* New York: Wiley-Blackwell, 2003.

PBS. *This Far by Faith.* "Cornel West." Available online. URL: http://www.pbs.org/thisfarbyfaith/ witnesses/cornel_west.html. Downloaded July 1, 2009.

Wood, Mark David. *Cornel West and the Politics of Prophetic Pragmatism.* Urbana: University of Illinois Press, 2000.

Whipper, Ionia Rollin

(1872–1953) *physician, community activist*

A practicing obstetrician, Ionia Whipper helped poor women in the African-American community in Washington, D.C. Born in 1872 in Beaufort, South Carolina, Ionia Rollin Whipper was the daughter of William and Frances Whipper. The Whippers were prominent and relatively well-to-do members of the black community in South Carolina. Mr. Whipper served for a time as a municipal judge, and Ionia's grandfather, WILLIAM WHIPPER, had been a well-known abolitionist in Pennsylvania.

During her childhood, Whipper moved with her family to Washington, D.C. She attended segregated public schools in that city and later studied at Howard University. In 1903, at the age of 31, Whipper earned a degree from the Howard University medical school. After graduation, she worked as a physician for several years at the Tuskegee Institute in Alabama. She then returned to Washington, where she taught school for about six years so she could pay off debts she had accumulated for medical school.

By 1911, Whipper had established an obstetrics practice in Washington. Although she served the whole range of Washington's African-American community, she was especially concerned with the poor black women she encountered during the delivery of babies at Washington's Freeman Hospital. Many of these women were homeless and unmarried, and Whipper began taking some of them into her own home to help them before and after their pregnancies.

To help these destitute black women, Whipper in 1931 established Lend-A-Hand, a charitable organization whose purpose was to raise money for the care of such women. She also founded the Tuesday Evening Club, a group that counseled unwed mothers and helped them find employment. By 1941, Lend-A-Hand had raised enough money to buy a building to house the women Whipper was helping. Known as the Ionia Whipper Home for Unwed Mothers, it was a Washington institution until it was folded into other organizations after desegregation of public services in Washington in the 1960s.

Whipper retired to live in New York City in the mid-1940s. She died in New York on April 23, 1953.

Further Reading

Abram, Ruth J. *Send Us a Lady Physician: Women Doctors in America, 1835–1920*. New York: Norton, 1986.

Logan, Rayford, and Michael Winston. *Dictionary of American Negro Biography*. New York: W. W. Norton, 1982.

Whipper, William
(ca. 1804–1876) *abolitionist, business leader, community activist*

A leading participant in free-black groups from the 1830s to the 1850s, William Whipper was instrumental in establishing the American Moral Reform Society in 1835. He later was a financial backer and participant in the Underground Railroad, which helped escaped slaves from the South resettle in the North and Canada. Whipper was born around 1804 in Little Britain, Pennsylvania. There are no records of his early life. The names of his parents are unknown and the extent of the education he received is uncertain.

Whipper first appears in public records in Philadelphia in 1828. For a time he worked at a steam scouring shop that cleaned clothes. He opened a grocery store in Philadelphia in 1834. In 1835, Whipper moved to Columbia, Pennsylvania, where he married Harriet Smith. They would have one son. His granddaughter was the physician and social activist, IONIA ROLLIN WHIPPER. In Columbia, Whipper formed a partnership with another black entrepreneur in the lumber business. He seems to have done well in the lumber trade and to have sold lumber to the large Philadelphia market.

Whipper attended five conventions of American free-born blacks in Pennsylvania and New York State during the 1830s, 1840s, and 1850s. In 1835, along with JAMES FORTEN, another leader in the Philadelphia African-American community, Whipper founded the American Moral Reform Society. Although open to people of all races, the society sought out black members with its message of abstinence from alcohol, educational advancement, thriftiness, and emancipation of slaves.

Whipper left a record of his thinking in the 1830s through printed copies of speeches he delivered at various meetings. One of these, "Nonresistance to Offensive Aggression," was printed in the *Colored American*, an African-American-owned newspaper, in 1837.

From the late 1840s to the 1860s, Whipper was an active participant in the Underground Railroad, the organized shadowy group of white and black men and women who led fugitive slaves out of the South and harbored them in the North. He is said to have spent $1,000 a year during the 1850s helping escaped slaves.

Whipper died in Philadelphia on March 9, 1876.

Further Reading

Palmer, Colin A., ed. *Encyclopedia of African-American Culture and History: The Black Experience in the Americas.* New York: Macmillan, 2006.

Quarles, Benjamin. *Black Abolitionists.* New York: Oxford, 1969.

Zimmerman, David. "William Whipper in the Black Abolitionist Tradition." Available online. URL: http://muweb.millersville.edu/~ugrr/resources/columbia/whipper.html. Downloaded July 1, 2009.

White, Walter Francis

(1893–1955) *civil rights activist*

A superb organizer and public relations front man, Walter White served as executive director of the National Association for the Advancement of Colored People (NAACP) for more than 25 years. He helped transform the NAACP from a relatively obscure group to the most important civil rights organization in the United States. Born in 1893 in Atlanta, Georgia, Walter Francis White was the son of George and Madeline White. He was educated in the segregated school system in his home city.

Of extremely light complexion, White could easily have passed as Caucasian. When he was 13 he learned firsthand about the viciousness of racism during the 1906 Atlanta riot, a five-day orgy of looting, murder, and arson by white mobs against several black neighborhoods, including the one where White lived. During this riot 25 blacks were killed and 1,000 homes were burned.

Walter Francis White ca. 1940. For more than 25 years, White headed the National Association for the Advancement of Colored People (NAACP). *(Library of Congress, Prints and Photographs Division, LC-USZ62-110593)*

In spite of the violence, the White family stayed in Atlanta, and White earned a B.A. from Atlanta University, a historically African-American college, in 1916. After his graduation, White led a campaign against the white Atlanta school board, which wanted to end all schooling for blacks after the sixth grade. Forming an Atlanta chapter of the recently created NAACP, White managed to stop this plan.

JAMES WELDON JOHNSON, the executive director of the NAACP, noticed White's flair with the press and organizational ability. In 1918, he asked White to move to New York City to be his assistant at the NAACP's national headquarters. White soon distinguished himself as a tireless organizer of NAACP chapters in cities across the nation. He also became one of the chief negotiators for the NAACP when it engaged with government officials. During this time, he married Gladys Powell. They would have two children.

By 1929, Johnson was exhausted from work and took a leave of absence as director. White was appointed to fill this position, which became his permanent office with Johnson's resignation in 1930. During his first year in office, White organized opposition to President Herbert Hoover's nomination of Judge John Parker to a seat on the U.S. Supreme Court. Parker, who had publicly stated that he thought blacks should not have the right to vote, was defeated in a Senate vote after a vigorous letter-writing campaign by the NAACP organized by White and White's skillful behind-the-scenes negotiations with senators.

During the Great Depression of the 1930s, White held the NAACP organization together by slashing its budget and focusing its priorities on a systematic legal campaign against the laws that upheld the Jim Crow system of racial segregation then common in many parts of the United States. White had a confrontation with the legendary NAACP founder W. E. B. DuBois in 1934 that resulted from White's cutting of funds for the NAACP magazine, the *Crisis*, which was edited by DuBois. After seeing his budget cut, DuBois resigned from the NAACP. White replaced DuBois as editor of the *Crisis* with ROY OTTAWAY WILKINS, who would eventually succeed White as executive director in the mid-1950s.

White hired CHARLES HAMILTON HOUSTON and Houston's law partner, WILLIAM HENRY HASTIE, JR., to head the newly created NAACP legal department in 1935. These two brilliant lawyers, aided by THURGOOD MARSHALL, would begin an attack on laws that mandated racial segregation in schools, transportation, and public facilities. This campaign would end in the important 1954 Supreme Court case *Brown v. the Board of Education of Topeka*, which would effectively end segregation in primary and secondary education throughout the United States.

White was also a writer of note. He penned two novels in the 1920s and a number of nonfiction articles for magazines such as *Harper's*, the *Nation*, *American Mercury*, and the *New Republic*. In his memoir, *A Man Called White* (1948), he vividly recalled the Atlanta riot of 1906 and charted its influence on his life.

After his divorce of his first wife and marriage in 1950 to Poppy Cannon, a white woman, White lost much of his influence inside the NAACP. Although he continued to hold the position of executive director until his death in 1955, the NAACP board assigned most of his duties to Roy Wilkins in 1951.

Further Reading

Eleanor Roosevelt National Historic Site. "Walter White (1893–1955)." Available online. URL: http://www.nps.gov/archive/elro/glossary/white-walter.htm. Downloaded July 1, 2009.

White, Walter. "Defending Home and Hearth." Available online. URL: http://historymatters.gmu.edu/d/104/. Downloaded July 1, 2009.

———. *A Man Called White*. 1948. Reprint, New York: Arno Press, 1969.

Whitfield, James Monroe

(1822–1871) *colonizationist, poet, fraternal leader*

An accomplished poet, James Whitfield was also a vigorous supporter of the idea that African Americans should have a colony where they could conduct their own lives free of white interference. James Monroe Whitfield was born in New Hampshire on April 10, 1822. Little is known about his childhood and youth. His later writings show that he must have received a good basic education.

Whitfield attracted public attention at the age of 16 in 1838 as a result of a paper, advocating the immigration of free blacks to California, that he wrote for a convention of free black men in Cleveland. The next year Whitfield moved from New

Hampshire to Buffalo, New York, then a hotbed of abolitionist activity. In Buffalo, to support himself, he began working as a barber, a trade he would rely on for the rest of his life.

Although Whitfield's occupation was as a barber, his avocation was writing, especially poetry and articles about colonization. Between 1839 and 1859, he published numerous poems in FREDERICK DOUGLASS's paper, *North Star,* and he wrote a handful of insightful articles about the advantages for blacks of establishing a separate state and society. Over the next decade, he would work with MARTIN ROBISON DELANY to promote the idea of colonization to the black community. Whitfield's poetry was full of protest about the discriminatory conditions imposed on African Americans by whites and reflected bitterness about a black man's chances in a white-dominated world.

In 1854 and 1856, Whitfield helped organize two National Emigration Conventions, both held in Cleveland. He also spoke out in favor of the idea of establishing a black colony in Central America. In 1859, Whitfield traveled to Central America to determine its worthiness as a possible colony for African Americans. As no report was ever issued about this trip, it is likely that Whitfield was disappointed by what he found.

After traveling to Central America, Whitfield took a sailing ship up the Pacific coast to San Francisco in 1861. He would spend the next 10 years—the rest of his life—in the West, living in California, Oregon, Idaho, and Nevada. He was active in Republican Party politics in Nevada and founded all-black PRINCE HALL Masonic lodges in San Francisco and Virginia City, Nevada.

James Whitfield died in San Francisco on April 23, 1871.

Further Reading

Amistad at Mystic Seaport. "James Monroe Whitfield's 'To Cinque.'" Available online. URL: http:// amistad.mysticseaport.org/library/misc/whitfield. to.cinque.html. Downloaded July 1, 2009.

National Humanities Center. "James Monroe Whitfield: 'How Long?'" Available online. URL: http:// nationalhumanitiescenter.org/pds/maai/identity/ text6/poetwhitfield.pdf. Downloaded July 1, 2009.

Williams, Patricia Ann. *Poets of Freedom: The English Romantics and Early Nineteenth-Century Black Poets.* Urbana: University of Illinois Press, 1974.

Wilkins, Roy Ottaway
(1901–1981) *civil rights activist*

Roy Wilkins was executive secretary of the National Association for the Advancement of Colored People (NAACP) for 22 years and led that organization through the turbulent and ultimately successful Civil Rights movement of the 1950s and 1960s. Born in St. Louis, Missouri, on August 30, 1901, Roy Ottaway Wilkins was raised by an aunt and uncle in St. Paul, Minnesota, after his mother's death when he was four years old. After completing his secondary education in the St. Paul public schools, Wilkins entered the University of Minnesota and graduated with a B.A. in 1923.

The year of his graduation from college, Wilkins moved to Kansas City, Missouri, to become editor of the *Kansas City Call.* Already active in the St. Paul NAACP, he then became active in the NAACP chapter in Kansas City. In his position as editor of the *Call,* Wilkins publicized the NAACP's efforts to combat lynchings in the South and racially discriminatory laws throughout the nation. He was especially active in whipping up opposition to Herbert Hoover's nomination of John Parker as a U.S. Supreme Court judge in 1930, a nomination that was eventually rejected by the Senate.

Partially as a result of his work against Parker, in 1931 the NAACP director, WALTER FRANCIS WHITE, hired Wilkins as the NAACP's assistant national secretary. Wilkins moved to New York City and began working to coordinate efforts of the various local chapters of that organization.

Roy Ottaway Wilkins ca. 1960. Wilkins was head of the National Association for the Advancement of Colored People (NAACP) during the turbulent years of the Civil Rights movement of the 1950s and 1960s. *(Library of Congress, Prints and Photographs Division, LC-U9-9522)*

When W. E. B. DuBois resigned under protest as editor of the NAACP's magazine, the *Crisis*, in 1934, White appointed Wilkins as the new editor. Unlike DuBois, who favored voluntary racial separation by blacks from white society, Wilkins strongly believed in the mainstream NAACP credo: full integration of African Americans into U.S. society and full rights for minorities under U.S. laws.

When White came under fire for divorcing his black wife to marry a white woman in 1950, Wilkins was appointed NAACP administrator; he became full-time executive director of the NAACP when White died in 1955. A pragmatist and soft-spoken man, Wilkins believed in working behind the scenes with business leaders and politicians to enact laws that would put teeth into the federal government's ability to enforce civil rights laws. He also gave financial and legal support to more outspoken black leaders such as Dr. MARTIN LUTHER KING, JR.

The high point of Wilkins's tenure as head of the NAACP was the mid-1960s, with passage of three landmark pieces of civil rights legislation: the Civil Rights Act of 1964, the Voting Rights Act of 1965, and the Fair Housing Act of 1968. These three federal laws would effectively destroy the tradition of overt racial discrimination that had existed in the United States since the nation's founding.

Wilkins continued to serve as executive secretary until 1977, weathering cries by black separatists that he was a tool of the "white establishment" and protests by white conservatives against his unrelenting push for racial equality that he had helped create in his country. Wilkins died in New York City in September 1981.

Further Reading

Finch, Minnie. *The NAACP: Its Fight for Justice.* Metuchen, N.J.: Scarecrow Press, 1981.

Hughes, Langston. *Fight for Freedom: The Story of the NAACP.* New York: Norton, 1962.

Marable, Manning, and Leith Mullings, eds. *Let Nobody Turn Us Around: Voices of Resistance, Reform, and Renewal: An African American Anthology.* Lanham, Md.: Rowman & Littlefield, 2009.

Roy Wilkins Center for Human Relations and Social Justice. "About the Center." Available online. URL: http://www.hhh.umn.edu/centers/wilkins/history_future.html. Downloaded July 1, 2009.

Williams, Fannie Barrier

(1855–1944) *community activist, women's club organizer, intellectual*

A highly educated woman at a time when most women did not pursue college education, Fannie Williams was a popular writer and public speaker in the late 19th and early 20th centuries. She was born Fannie Barrier on February 12, 1855, in Brockport, New York, the daughter of Anthony and Harriet Barrier. A child of middle-class parents, she received her secondary education at Brockport's State Normal School and graduated in 1870. She later attended the New England Conservatory of Music in Boston and the School of Fine Arts in Washington, D.C.

To support herself during her 20s, Barrier taught school, mainly in Washington, D.C. In 1887, she married Laing Williams, a lawyer. By 1890, Fannie Williams had moved to Chicago, where her husband began to practice law. The couple would have no children.

Williams soon became active in social work in Chicago. In 1891, she helped found Provident Hospital, which was run by a racially integrated staff and offered a nursing training program for white and African-American women. Williams soon became friendly with MARY ELIZA CHURCH TERRELL, and the two women founded the National League of Colored Women in 1893. That same year Williams gained notice for a speech she gave before the World's Congress of Representative Women at the Columbian Exposition in Chicago. In this speech, Williams laid out her vision of a just United States with emphasis on equality for African-Americans and whites under the law. However, she also claimed that African-Americans had no desire to be "social equals" with whites, a position that was popular with BOOKER TALIAFERRO WASHINGTON and his supporters.

In the early years of the 20th century, Williams remained a supporter of Washington, primarily to help her husband win a federal appointment with Washington's influence. With Washington's backing, her husband eventually was appointed federal attorney in Chicago. However, when her husband lost his job in 1912 after the election of the Democratic president Woodrow Wilson, Williams turned her support to the more confrontational National Associa-

tion for the Advancement of Colored People (NAACP).

Williams seems to have retired from politics and the women's club movement in the 1920s. She died in Chicago on March 4, 1944.

Further Reading

Page, Yolanda Williams, ed. *Encyclopedia of African American Women Writers*. Westport, Conn.: Greenwood, 2007.

Unitarian Universalist Association. "Fannie Barrier Williams." Available online. URL: http://www25. uua.org/uuhs/duub/articles/fanniebarrierwilliams. html. Downloaded July 1, 2009.

Williams, Hosea

(1926–2000) *civil rights activist, chemist*

Trained as a chemist, Hosea Williams became the chief lieutenant of MARTIN LUTHER KING, JR., and helped King on many of his protest demonstrations in the South during the 1960s. Born on January 5, 1926, in Attapulgus, Georgia, Williams was the son of poor blind parents. Orphaned after his mother's death during his childhood, he was raised by grandparents. In 1940, at the age of 14, he was nearly lynched after rumors spread that he was romantically attached to a white girl. Dropping out of school, Williams left home to work as a laborer in Florida.

In 1942, Williams was drafted into the U.S. Army and was eventually sent to France. Attached to a combat unit, he was severely wounded by a German artillery shell and spent more than a year recovering from his wounds in a hospital. Left with a permanent limp, Williams returned to Georgia, where he was severely beaten by whites when he refused to drink water from the "colored" fountain at a bus station.

Funded by the GI Bill, Williams finished his secondary education in 1947 and enrolled in Morris Brown College and Atlanta University, where he earned a B.S. in chemistry. After his graduation in the early 1950s, he was hired as a research chemist by the U.S. Department of Agriculture.

Swept up in the dramatic demonstrations for civil rights that erupted in the South during the late 1950s and early 1960s, Williams quit his government job to work for King's Southern Christian Leadership Conference (SCLC) in 1962. He soon became King's main lieutenant and worked as the advance organizer on some of SCLC's most important campaigns.

Williams served as an organizer in Mississippi during the Freedom Summer voter registration drives of 1963, and by 1965 he had become chief field organizer for King. In March 1965, Williams ran day-to-day operations for King on the Selma-to-Montgomery Freedom March. During this march, Williams and numerous other marchers were wounded when mounted Alabama state police attacked them with dogs and batons. This shocking event, seen around the world via television, probably helped ensure passage of the important Voting Rights Act later that year. Williams was also by King's side when a white racist assassinated King in Memphis, Tennessee, in April 1968.

In later years, Williams ventured into politics in Georgia. Becoming a Republican in 1970, he lost a race for the Georgia House of Representatives. After a switch back to the Democratic Party, he won a seat in the legislature and served as a state senator from 1974 to 1985. He organized annual holiday dinners for the poor in Atlanta, serving thousands of people at a time. Williams died in Atlanta on November 16, 2000.

Further Reading

Carson, Clayborne, Tenisha Armstrong et al., eds. *The Martin Luther King, Jr., Encyclopedia.* Westport, Conn.: Greenwood, 2008.

New Georgia Encyclopedia. "Hosea Williams (1926–2000)." Available online. URL: http://www.georgiaencyclopedia.org/nge/Article.jsp?id=h-2721. Downloaded July 1, 2009.

Wilson, James Finley
(1881–1952) *fraternal club leader*

The best-known and most powerful African-American fraternal club leader in the early 20th century, James Wilson built the Benevolent Protective Order of the Elks of the World (BPOEW) into the largest black fraternal group of its time. Born in Dickson, Tennessee, a small town near Nashville, in 1881, James Finley Wilson was the son of James and Nancy Wilson. His father was a preacher.

An adventurous young man, Wilson had a wild youth. When he was 13, he left home and headed west. In Denver, he joined up with a group of unemployed workers who had been inspired by Coxey's army, a band of disgruntled workers from Ohio who were marching on Washington to demand that the government invest in more public works projects to hire victims of the severe economic recession of 1893. An aunt in Denver soon snatched him up from this jaunt and returned him to Tennessee. He remained in Tennessee long enough to graduate from Pearl High School. However, when he was 17, he headed out west again; this time he spent three years in Alaska and Utah.

Around 1902, Wilson again returned to Nashville, where he studied for a time at Fisk University. By the teens, he had become involved with the BPOEW, one of several black benevolent orders of the day. The Elks and other groups had advantages for ambitious black men. They presented a forum for such men to network with each other and establish business contacts. These fraternal orders also provided fellowship and emotional support and offered a form of group insurance to members. If a man fell ill or became unemployed, the Elks and other groups would help him make it through a crisis until he could get back on his feet again.

Wilson became president of the Elks in 1922 and held this position until his death in 1952. During his tenure, Wilson boosted membership from 30,000 nationwide to more than 500,000.

He promoted the Elks with lavish annual parades and balls. Through this organization, he also became notable as a power broker in national politics. He was one of the main backers, for instance, of ASA PHILIP RANDOLPH's call for a 1941 March on Washington, protesting discriminatory hiring in the defense industry.

Wilson died in Washington, D.C., in February 1952.

Further Reading

"Elks & Equality" *Time,* 12 August 1935. Available online. URL: http://205.188.238.109/time/magazine/article/0,9171,771774,00.html. Downloaded July 1, 2009.

Logan, Rayford, and Michael Winston. *Dictionary of American Negro Biography.* New York: W. W. Norton, 1982.

Wilson, William Julius

(1935–) *educator, intellectual*

A leading scholar of the causes of urban poverty, William Julius Wilson has also served as a political adviser to Democratic politicians such as President Bill Clinton. Born in 1935 in Pittsburgh, Pennsylvania, Wilson was the son of a coal miner. After graduation from public schools in Pittsburgh in the mid-1950s, Wilson enrolled in Wilberforce University, a historically black university in Ohio, where he earned a B.A. He later earned an M.A. in sociology from Bowling Green State University and a Ph.D. from Washington State University in anthropology and sociology in 1966.

Wilson began his professional academic career at the University of Massachusetts, and in 1972 he was hired as a professor of sociology at the University of Chicago. He made a name for himself with his 1978 book *The Declining Significance of Race,* which argued that economic class, rather than race, was becoming the most important factor in the lives of poor African Americans. Wilson's

1987 book *The Truly Disadvantaged* continued the examination of the causes of poverty in the United States. In 1990, Wilson was appointed director of the University of Chicago's Center for the Study of Urban Inequality.

Wilson's central message is that although racism has historically held back African Americans in the United States, race is increasingly becoming less important as a way to explain poverty as racial barriers have fallen in the wake of such legislation as the 1964 Civil Rights Act. In 21st-century America, Wilson argues, poverty and lack of education do more to hinder a person's ability to advance economically than race. Wilson believes that the government has a role to play in breaking cycles of poverty. It can, for instance, create and fund

William Julius Wilson, a leading black intellectual, has written about race and social class and explored the relationship between poverty and racial discrimination. *(Courtesy Harvard News Office, photo by Jan Chase)*

public-service jobs to provide work to the unemployed, thus beginning a cycle to lift people out of poverty. The government can also fund more education and job-training programs to prepare people for work that is in demand in the new information-based economy. In 2009, he published *More Than Just Race: Being Black and Poor in the Inner City*.

In recognition of the importance of his work, Wilson was awarded a MacArthur Prize in 1987. He is a fellow of the National Academy of Arts and Sciences and the American Philosophical Society. In 1998, he received the National Medal of Science, the nation's highest award for scientific investigation. Wilson received the Talcott Parsons Prize in Social Sciences in 2003. Currently, he is a professor at Harvard University.

Further Reading

PBS. The Two Nations of Black America. "Interview William Julius Wilson." Available online. URL: http://www.pbs.org/wgbh/pages/frontline/shows/race/interviews/wilson.html. Downloaded July 1, 2009.

Wilson, William Julius. *The Declining Significance of Race: Blacks and Changing American Institutions.* Chicago: University of Chicago Press, 1978.

———. *When Work Disappears: The World of the New Urban Poor.* New York: Knopf, 1996.

X, Y

X, Malcolm See MALCOLM X

Young, Plummer Bernard
(P. B. Young)
(1884–1962) *journalist, newspaper publisher*

Known as "dean of the Negro press," P. B. Young was the publisher and editor of the *Norfolk Journal and Guide,* one of the most respected and successful African-American newspapers of its day. Born in Littleton, North Carolina, in 1884, Plummer Bernard Young was the son of Winfield and Sally Young. Because his father was the publisher of a small newspaper, *True Reformer,* Young got a taste for the newspaper business at an early age. After his graduation from high school in Littleton in 1902, Young enrolled in Saint Augustine's College in Raleigh, he received a B.A. in 1905.

In 1910, Young moved to Norfolk, Virginia, when he bought out the newspaper of a small fraternal organization known as the Knights of Gideon. Young changed the paper's name from the *Lodge Journal and Guide* to the *Norfolk Journal and Guide,* and he expanded the number of pages from four to 32 while sticking with a weekly edition.

By nature a courteous and self-contained man, Young kept a tight rein on the editorial tone of the *Journal and Guide.* Unlike some northern black newspapers, the *Journal* did not indulge in yellow journalism. Its stories were serious and factually accurate, and the paper let the facts presented in its articles carry arguments. In the pages of the *Journal and Guide,* Young tried to convince African Americans not to leave the South and head north during the Great Exodus of the late 1910s through 1920s. Although Young preferred to stick to concrete issues such as seeking more money for better housing and roads in black neighborhoods, he also spoke out against lynching of blacks in the South and called for racial integration of the defense industry and the armed forces during World War II.

From the 1920s, Young expanded the range of the *Journal and Guide,* gradually producing editions in Richmond, Virginia; Washington, D.C.; and Baltimore, Maryland. Young also published a national edition of the paper. By the late 1940s, the *Journal and Guide* was in terms of circulation the fourth largest African-American newspaper in the nation.

Over the years, Young served on numerous college and university boards. He was a member of the federal Fair Employment Practices Commission in 1943. Under his stewardship, the *Journal and Guide* won three Wendell Willkie Awards for outstanding journalism. Young died on October 9, 1962.

Further Reading

PBS. "Plummer Bernard Young." Available online. URL: http://www.pbs.org/blackpress/news_bios/newbios/nwsppr/Biogrphs/pbyoung/young.html. Downloaded July 1, 2009.

Suggs, Henry Lewis. *P. B. Young: Newspaperman: Race, Politics, and Journalism in the New South 1910–1962.* Charlottesville: University Press of Virginia, 1988.

Young, Whitney M., Jr.
(1921–1971) *civil rights leader*

A pragmatic civil rights leader during a time of intense racial strife and social change, Whitney M. Young, Jr., is best known for his efforts to enlist the aid of American corporations in the Civil Rights movement. Born on July 31, 1921, in Lincoln Ridge, Kentucky, Young experienced racial segregation firsthand as a child. He attended all-black Kentucky State College, where he studied courses that would prepare him for medical school.

In 1941, at the outbreak of World War II, Young hoped to become a physician and joined an army specialist-training program. To fill its manpower needs, the army transferred him to the Massachusetts Institute of Technology to study engineering and then to an army antiaircraft unit staffed by black soldiers and commanded by white officers. Young's career as a negotiator began during his tour of duty. Resentful of poor treatment by their white officers, the company's enlisted men stopped working. Young stepped in to arrange a deal in which both sides saved face, thereby avoiding conflict and getting the company back into the war effort.

Shortly before the end of the war, Young married Margaret Bruckner. At the war's end he enrolled in the University of Minnesota. He wrote his thesis on the Urban League of Minnesota's capital city, Saint Paul, and earned a master's degree in social work in 1947. After

Whitney M. Young ca. 1960. Young headed the Urban League during the turbulent decade of the 1960s and made it a major player in job training and education for black youth. *(Library of Congress, Prints and Photographs Division, LC-USZ62-121755)*

completion of his degree, Young took a job with the Saint Paul Urban League. He moved to Omaha, Nebraska, in 1950 to work for the Urban League in that city, and in 1954 he was appointed dean of the School of Social Work at Atlanta University in Georgia.

In 1960, the National Urban League reached out to Young, when the board of directors requested that he become the league's national executive director. The league, which was founded in 1910 by white and black social workers, had acquired a reputation among many African-American activists as a conservative organization. In its early years, the league's main goal had been to get jobs for southern blacks who had migrated to northern cities. However, by the time Young took over, the league was seen as an organization whose efforts were directed mainly toward middle-class blacks.

Young agreed to take the helm of the organization but only on the condition that the board let him expand the Urban League's size and reach. His first goal was to persuade major corporations to partner with the league by underwriting self-help programs for jobs, housing, education, and family rehabilitation. He approached hundreds of top corporations in the United States to gain support for these league programs, which targeted poor inner-city blacks.

Preferring negotiation to confrontation, Young won the support of corporate America. Under his tenure, the Urban League's budget rose from $300,000 a year in 1960 to $35 million a year in 1971. He established a National Skills Bank in 1961, and by 1966 the league, under his direction, was placing African Americans in 40,000 jobs a year. Young's call in 1963 for a Marshall Plan for the United States served as the inspiration for President Lyndon Johnson's Great Society, the largest effort to eliminate poverty in the United States since the New Deal in the 1930s.

Young's success and his close ties with white business leaders alienated younger, more militant black activists, many of whom accused him of being a pawn of wealthy white-controlled foundations and companies. Young responded that he was the true warrior for equal rights and social justice, saying,

> Black is beautiful when it is a slum kid studying to enter college, when it is a man learning new skills for a new job. . . . I know you can't fight a tank with a beer can or destroy a regiment with a switch. White racists are not afraid of our fire-power, but they are afraid of our brains, our political and our economic power.

A persistent supporter of racial integration, Young in the late 1960s became an opponent of U.S. involvement in the Vietnam War, which he believed drained money away from domestic programs that helped the poor.

During his tenure as director of the Urban League, Young wrote two books, *To Be Equal* (1964) and *Beyond Racism* (1969). His prestige as a healer of racial division won him respect in Washington, D.C., and he served on a number of federal commissions that investigated race in America. In 1969, President Lyndon Johnson awarded Young the nation's highest civilian honor, the Medal of Freedom, for his efforts to aid the African-American community and promote racial harmony.

Whitney Young drowned in a swimming accident in Lagos, Nigeria, on March 11, 1971, while he was attending an international conference to promote dialogue between Africans and Americans. His legacy is best expressed in his own words: "I am not anxious to be the loudest voice or the most popular. But I would like to think that at a crucial moment, I was an effective voice of the voiceless, an effective hope of the hopeless."

Further Reading

Dickerson, Dennis C. *Militant Mediator: Whitney M. Young, Jr.* Lexington: University of Kentucky Press, 1998.

Lee, Mary Elizabeth. "Whitney M. Young and His Open-Housing Policy." Master's thesis, University of Louisville, 1977.

National Parks Service. "Whitney M. Young, Jr., Birthplace." Available online. URL: http://www.nps.gov/history/nr/travel/civilrights/ky2.htm. Downloaded July 1, 2009.

Weiss, Nancy J. *Whitney M. Young and the Struggle for Civil Rights.* Princeton, N.J.: Princeton University Press, 1989.

BIBLIOGRAPHY AND RECOMMENDED SOURCES

Appiah, Kwame Anthony, and Henry Louis Gates, Jr. *Africana: The Encyclopedia of the African and African-American Experience.* New York: Oxford University Press, 2005.

Arnesen, Eric. *Brotherhoods of Color: Black Railroad Workers and the Struggle for Equality.* Cambridge: Harvard University Press, 2002.

Asante, Molefi K. *100 Greatest African Americans: A Biographical Encyclopedia.* Amherst, N.Y.: Prometheus, 2003.

Asante, Molefi K., and Ama Mazama, eds. *Encyclopedia of Black Studies.* Thousand Oaks, Calif.: SAGE, 2005.

Branch, Taylor. *America in the King Years.* New York: Simon & Schuster, 1988.

Brown, Nikki. *Private Politics and Public Voices: Black Women's Activism from World War I to the New Deal.* Bloomington: Indiana University Press, 2007.

Bullock, Penelope. *The Afro-American Periodical Press: 1837–1909.* Baton Rouge: Louisiana State University Press, 1981.

Carson, Clayborne, Tenisha Armstrong et al., eds. *The Martin Luther King, Jr., Encyclopedia.* Westport, Conn.: Greenwood, 2008.

Connerly, Ward. *Creating Equal: My Fight against Race Preferences.* San Francisco: Encounter, 2000.

Conti, Joseph G., and Brad Stetson. *Challenging the Civil Rights Establishment: Profiles of a New Black Vanguard.* Westport, Conn.: Praeger, 1993.

Curtis, Edward E. *Black Muslim Religion in the Nation of Islam, 1960–1975.* Chapel Hill: University of North Carolina Press, 2006.

Davies, Carole Boyce, ed. *Encyclopedia of the African Diaspora: Origins, Experiences, and Culture.* Santa Barbara, Calif.: ABC-CLIO, 2008.

Domenico, Roy Palmer, and Mark Y. Hanley, eds. *Encyclopedia of Modern Christian Politics.* Westport, Conn.: Greenwood, 2006.

Finkelman, Paul, ed. *Encyclopedia of African American History, 1619–1895: From the Colonial Period to the Age of Frederick Douglass.* New York: Oxford University Press, 2006.

Fleming, G. James, and Christian E. Burckel. *Who's Who in Colored America.* Yonkers, N.Y.: Christian E. Burckel, 1950.

Foner, Eric. *America's Black Past: A Reader in Afro-American History.* New York: Harper & Row, 1970.

Foner, Eric, and Ronald L. Lewis, eds. *The Black Worker: A Documentary History from Colonial Times to the Present.* Philadelphia: Temple University Press, 1978.

Franklin, Jimmy Lewis. *Blacks in Oklahoma.* Norman: University of Oklahoma Press, 1980.

Gasman, Marybeth. *Envisioning Black Colleges: A History of the United Negro College Fund.* Baltimore, Md.: Johns Hopkins University Press, 2007.

Gates, Henry Louis, Jr., and Cornel West. *The African-American Century: How Black Americans Have*

Shaped Our Country. New York: Simon & Schuster, 2002.

Greenberg, Jack. *Crusaders in the Courts: How a Dedicated Band of Lawyers Fought for the Civil Rights Revolution.* New York: Basic Books, 1994.

Greenfield-Sanders, Timothy, and Elvis Mitchell. *The Black List.* New York: Atria, 2008.

Halpern, Monica. *Great Migration: African-Americans Move to the North.* Washington, D.C.: National Geographic Press, 2002.

Hine, Darlene Clark, ed. *Black Women in America.* New York: Oxford University Press, 2005.

Hogan, Wesley C. *Many Minds, One Heart: SNCC's Dream for a New America.* Chapel Hill: University of North Carolina Press, 2007.

Horne, Gerald, and Mary Young, eds. *W. E. B. DuBois: An Encyclopedia.* Westport, Conn.: Greenwood, 2001.

Horton, Lois E. *Slavery and the Making of America.* New York: Oxford University Press, 2004.

Koslow, Philip, ed. *The New York Public Library African-American Desk Reference.* New York: Wiley, 1999.

Lincoln, C. Eric. *Black Muslims in America.* Westport, Conn.: Greenwood, 1973.

Logan, Rayford, and Michael Winston. *Dictionary of American Negro Biography.* New York: W. W. Norton, 1982.

Lowery, Charles, and John Marszalek. *Encyclopedia of African-American Civil Rights.* Westport, Conn.: Greenwood, 1992.

Marable, Manning, and Leith Mullings, eds. *Let Nobody Turn Us Around: Voices of Resistance, Reform, and Renewal.* Lanham, Md.: Rowman & Littlefield, 2003.

Miller, Floyd J. *The Search for a Black Nationality: Black Colonization and Emigration, 1787–1863.* Urbana: University of Illinois Press, 1975.

Mjagkij, Nina, ed. *Organizing Black America: An Encyclopedia of African American Associations.* New York: Taylor & Francis, 2001.

———. *Portraits of African American Life since 1865.* New York: Rowman & Littlefield, 2003.

Moore, Jacqueline M. *Booker T. Washington, W. E. B. DuBois, and the Struggle for Racial Uplift.* Lanham, Md.: Rowman & Littlefield, 2003.

Nieman, Donald G. *The Freedmen's Bureau and Black Freedom.* New York: Garland, 1994.

———. *The Politics of Freedom: African-Americans and the Political Process during Reconstruction.* New York: Garland, 1994.

Nudelman, Franny. *John Brown's Body: Slavery, Violence, & the Culture of War.* Chapel Hill: University of North Carolina Press, 2004.

Page, Yolanda Williams, ed. *Encyclopedia of African American Women Writers.* Westport, Conn.: Greenwood, 2007.

Painter, Nell Irvin. *Black Migration to Kansas after Reconstruction.* New York: Knopf, 1977.

Palmer, Colin A., ed. *Encyclopedia of African-American Culture and History: The Black Experience in the Americas.* New York: Macmillan, 2006.

Parris, Guichard, and Lester Brooks. *Blacks in the City: A History of the National Urban League.* Boston: Little, Brown, 1971.

Pease, Jane H., and William H. Pease. *Bound with Them in Chains: A Biographical History of the Antislavery Movement.* Westport, Conn.: Greenwood, 1972.

Quarles, Benjamin. *Black Abolitionists.* New York: Oxford, 1969.

Record, Wilson. *The Negro and the Communist Party.* 1951. Reprint, New York: Atheneum, 1971.

Reynolds, Barbara A. *And Still We Rise: 50 Black Role Models.* Washington, D.C.: USA Today Books, 1988.

Robertson, Nancy Marie. *Christian Sisterhood, Race Relations, and the YWCA, 1906–46.* Champaign: University of Illinois Press, 2007.

Rodriguez, Junius P., ed. *Encyclopedia of Slave Resistance and Rebellion.* Westport, Conn.: Greenwood, 2007.

———, ed. *Slavery in the United States: A Social, Political, and Historical Encyclopedia.* Santa Barbara, Calif.: ABC-CLIO, 2007.

Rucker, Walter C., and James N. Upton, eds. *Encyclopedia of American Race Riots.* Westport, Conn.: Greenwood, 2007.

Salzman, Jack, David Smith, and Cornel West, eds. *Encyclopedia of African-American Culture and History.* New York: Macmillan, 1996.

Smith, J. Clay. *Emancipation: The Making of the Black Lawyer, 1844–1944.* Philadelphia: University of Pennsylvania Press, 1999.

Smith, Jessie Carney, Millicent Lownes Jackson, and Linda T. Wynn, eds. *Encyclopedia of African American Business.* Westport, Conn.: Greenwood, 2006.

Wilson, William Julius. *The Declining Significance of Race.* Chicago: University of Chicago Press, 1978.

Wintz, Cary D., and Paul Finkelman, eds. *Encyclopedia of the Harlem Renaissance.* New York: Taylor & Francis, 2004.

Woodson, Carter G. *Negro Orators and Their Orations.* Washington, D.C.: Associated Publishers, 1925.

ENTRIES BY AREA OF ACTIVITY

Butts, Calvin Otis, III
Dancy, John Campbell, Jr.
Desdunes, Rodolphe Lucien
Eagleson, William Lewis
Edelman, Marian Wright
Garnet, Sarah
Haynes, George Edmund
Hill, Thomas Arnold
Hilyer, Amanda Victoria Gray
Hunton, Addie D. Waites
Hunton, William Alphaeus
Jones, Eugene Kinckle
McCabe, Edwin
Rayner, John Baptis
Sash, Moses
Singleton, Benjamin
Still, William
Washington, George
Whipper, Ionia Rollin
Whipper, William

EDUCATION
Bethune, Mary McLeod
Brown, Hallie Quinn
Carson, Benjamin S.
Carver, George Washington
Chester, Thomas Morris
Clement, Rufus Early
Corbin, Joseph Carter
Davis, Angela
Day, William Howard
Derricotte, Juliette Aline
Garnet, Sarah
Gates, Henry Louis, Jr.
Greener, Richard Theodore
Hrabowski, Freeman A., III
Johnson, Charles Spurgeon
Johnson, James Weldon
Maynard, Nancy Hicks
Mays, Benjamin Elijah
Moses, Robert Parris
Patterson, Frederick Douglass
Rayner, John Baptis
Simmons, Ruth J.

Terry, Wallace
Washington, Booker Taliaferro
West, Cornel
Wilson, William Julius

GAY RIGHTS
Boykin, Keith O.

FRATERNAL ORGANIZATIONS
Davis, Harry E.
Hall, Prince
Whitfield, James Monroe
Wilson, James Finley

HEALTH CARE
Brock, Rosyln McCallister
Wattleton, Alyce Faye

JOURNALISM
Barber, Jesse Max
Benjamin, Robert Charles
    O'Hara
Boykin, Keith O.
Chester, Thomas Morris
Day, William Howard
Desdunes, Rodolphe Lucien
DuBois, W. E. B.
Dunjee, Roscoe
Eagleson, William Lewis
Gates, Henry Louis, Jr.
Matthews, Victoria Earle
Maynard, Nancy Hicks
Mitchell, John R., Jr.
Owen, Chandler
Shadd, Mary Ann
Still, William
Terry, Wallace
Turner, Henry McNeal
Tyler, Ralph Waldo
Walker, David
Wells-Barnett, Ida B.

LABOR ORGANIZATION
Crosswaith, Frank Rudolph

Lemus, Rienzi Brock
Myers, Isaac
Randolph, Asa Philip
Totten, Ashley L.
Walker, Flora

LEGAL SERVICES
Bolin, Jane Matilda
Chambers, Julius Levonne
Chester, Thomas Morris
Cobb, James Adlai
Guinier, Lani
Hart, William Henry
Hastie, William Henry, Jr.
Higginbotham, Aloysius
    Leon, Jr.
Houston, Charles Hamilton
Jones, Nathaniel R., Jr.
Jones, Scipio Africanus
Marshall, Thurgood
McGhee, Frederick Lamar
Morgan, Clement Garnett
Morial, Marc Haydel
Morris, Robert, Sr.
Motley, Constance Baker

NATIONALISM/SEPARATISM
Carmichael, Stokely
Cleaver, Eldridge
Cuffe, Paul
Delany, Martin Robison
Fard, Wallace D.
Farrakhan, Louis
Garvey, Marcus
Karenga, Ron
Malcolm X
Muhammad, Elijah
Muhammad, Khalid Abdul
Newton, Huey P.
Saunders, Prince

NEWSPAPER PUBLISHING
Chase, William Calvin
Cornish, Samuel Eli

Delany, Martin Robison
Douglass, Frederick
Forbes, George Washington
Forten, James
Fortune, Timothy Thomas
Maynard, Nancy Hicks
Murphy, Carl
Murphy, John Henry, Sr.
Pelham, Robert A.
Ruggles, David
Russwurm, John Brown
Smith, Harry Clay
Trévigne, Paul
Trotter, William Monroe

Vann, Robert Lee
Wesley, Carter Walker
Young, Plummer Bernard

POLITICS
Jackson, Jesse
Morial, Marc Haydel
Sharpton, Al

SLAVE REVOLTS
Cinque, Joseph
Copeland, John Anthony
Green, Shields
Prosser, Gabriel

Turner, Nat
Vesey, Denmark

WOMEN'S RIGHTS
Bowles, Eva Del Vakia
Burroughs, Nannie Helen
Derricotte, Juliette Aline
Forten, James
Garnet, Sarah
Height, Dorothy
Terrell, Mary Eliza Church
Truth, Sojourner
Wattleton, Alyce Faye
Williams, Fannie Barrier

ENTRIES BY YEAR OF BIRTH

1740–1769
Allen, Richard
Cuffe, Paul
Forten, James
Freeman, Elizabeth
Hall, Prince
Sash, Moses
Vesey, Denmark

1770–1799
Cornish, Samuel Eli
Prosser, Gabriel
Russwurm, John Brown
Saunders, Prince
Truth, Sojourner
Walker, David

1800–1809
Singleton, Benjamin
Turner, Nat
Whipper, William

1810–1819
Bibb, Henry Walton
Brown, William Wells
Cinque, Joseph
De Baptiste, George
Delany, Martin Robison
Douglass, Frederick
Garnet, Henry Highland

Pleasant, Mary Ellen
Remond, Charles Lenox
Ruggles, David
Washington, George

1820–1829
Day, William Howard
Ford, Barney Launcelot
Green, Shields
Morris, Robert, Sr.
Rock, John Sweat
Shadd, Mary Ann
Still, William
Trévigne, Paul
Tubman, Harriet
Whitfield, James Monroe

1830–1839
Chester, Thomas Morris
Copeland, John Anthony
Corbin, Joseph Carter
Eagleson, William Lewis
Garnet, Sarah
Leary, Lewis Sheridan
Myers, Isaac
Turner, Henry McNeal

1840–1849
Allensworth, Allen
Brown, Hallie Quinn

Desdunes, Rodolphe Lucien
Greener, Richard Theodore
Murphy, John Henry, Sr.
Straker, David Augustus

1850–1859
Benjamin, Robert Charles
    O'Hara
Chase, William Calvin
Fortune, Timothy Thomas
Hart, William Henry
Hilyer, Andrew Franklin
McCabe, Edwin
Morgan, Clement Garnett
Pelham, Robert A.
Rayner, John Baptis
Tyler, Ralph Waldo
Washington, Booker Taliaferro
Williams, Fannie Barrier

1860–1869
Carver, George Washington
DuBois, W. E. B.
Forbes, George Washington
Hunton, William Alphaeus
Jones, Scipio Africanus
Matthews, Victoria Earle
McGhee, Frederick Lamar
Mitchell, John R., Jr.
Smith, Harry Clay

Terrell, Mary Eliza Church
Wells, Ida B.

1870–1879
Barber, Jesse Max
Bethune, Mary McLeod
Bowles, Eva Del Vakia
Cobb, James Adlai
Hilyer, Amanda Gray
Hunton, Addie D. Waites
Johnson, James Weldon
Scott, Emmett Jay
Trotter, William Monroe
Vann, Robert Lee
Whipper, Ionia Rollin

1880–1889
Burroughs, Nannie Helen
Dancy, John Campbell, Jr.
Dunjee, Roscoe
Fard, Wallace D.
Garvey, Marcus
Haynes, George Edmund
Hill, Thomas Arnold
Jones, Eugene Kinckle
Lemus, Rienzi Brock
Murphy, Carl
Owen, Chandler
Totten, Ashley L.
Wilson, James Finley
Young, Plummer Bernard

1890–1899
Crosswaith, Frank Rudolph
Derricotte, Juliette Aline
Houston, Charles Hamilton
Johnson, Charles Spurgeon
Mays, Benjamin

Muhammad, Elijah
Randolph, Asa Philip
Robeson, Eslanda Cardozo
   Goode
Wesley, Carter Walker
White, Walter Francis

1900–1909
Bolin, Jane Matilda
Clement, Rufus Early
Davis, Benjamin Jefferson, Jr.
Hastie, William Henry, Jr.
Marshall, Thurgood
Patterson, Frederick Douglass
Wilkins, Roy Ottaway

1910–1919
Bates, Daisy Lee Gatson
Hamer, Fannie Lou
Height, Dorothy
Parks, Rosa
Rustin, Bayard

1920–1929
Evers, Medgar Wiley
Farmer, James Leonard
Forman, James
Henry, Aaron
Higginbotham, Aloysius
   Leon, Jr.
Jones, Nathaniel R., Jr.
King, Martin Luther, Jr.
Malcolm X
McKissick, Floyd
Motley, Constance Baker
Shuttlesworth, Fred Lee
Williams, Hosea
Young, Whitney M.

1930–1939
Chambers, Julius Levonne
Cleaver, Eldridge
Connerly, Ward
Edelman, Marian Wright
Farrakhan, Louis
Jordan, Vernon Eulion, Jr.
Moses, Robert Parris
Terry, Wallace
Walker, Flora
Wilson, William Julius

1940–1949
Butts, Calvin Otis, III
Carmichael, Stokely
Davis, Angela
Jackson, Jesse
Karenga, Ron
Maynard, Nancy Hick
Muhammad, Khalid Abdul
Newton, Huey P.
Robinson, Randall
Simmons, Ruth J.
Wattleton, Alyce Faye

1950–1959
Carson, Benjamin S.
Gates, Henry Louis, Jr.
Guinier, Lani
Hrabowski, Freeman A., III
Morial, Marc Haydel
Sharpton, Al
West, Cornel

1960–1979
Boykin, Keith O.
Brock, Rosyln McCallister
Jealous, Benjamin Todd

INDEX

Boldface locators indicate main entries. *Italic* locators indicate photographs. For a full list of references, see the main entry for the individual concerned.